Struts Recipes

Struts Recipes

GEORGE FRANCISCUS
DANILO GUROVICH

MANNING
Greenwich
(74° w. long.)

For online information and ordering of this and other Manning books, please go to
www.manning.com. The publisher offers discounts on this book when ordered in quantity.
For more information, please contact:

    Special Sales Department
    Manning Publications Co.
    209 Bruce Park Avenue   Fax: (203) 661-9018
    Greenwich, CT 06830   email: orders@manning.com

Manning Publications Co.   Copyeditor: Mark Goodin
209 Bruce Park Avenue   Typesetter: Denis Dalinnik
Greenwich, CT 06830   Cover designer: Leslie Haimes

ISBN 1932394249

Printed in the United States of America
2 3 4 5 6 7 8 9 10 – VHG – 08 07 06 05

brief contents

1 ▪ Basic recipes 1

2 ▪ Forms and form elements 42

3 ▪ Struts tag libraries 96

4 ▪ The Struts-Layout tag library 170

5 ▪ Validation within the Struts framework 242

6 ▪ Internationalization 294

7 ▪ Logging in, security, and guarding 317

8 ▪ Advanced recipes 348

9 ▪ Testing 424

contents

preface *xix*
acknowledgments *xx*
about this book *xxii*

1 Basic recipes 1

But what is Struts? 2 ▪ *What Struts isn't 3* ▪ *A note about our*
favorite Ant 3 ▪ *The developer's environment 4*
Chapter 1, in brief 5

1.1 Use Ant to automatically build a Struts project *6*

1.2 Default your application to an ActionForward *14*

1.3 What is "jsessionid" and why do I need it? *16*

1.4 Using modules for large projects *19*

1.5 Specifying a resource property file
in a configuration *25*

1.6 Multiple message-resources in an application *27*

1.7 Using the bundle attribute in Struts' custom tags *28*

1.8 Manage constants throughout your application *32*

1.9 Use <html:base/> for solid page references *35*

1.10   Associating Cascading Style Sheets
       with Struts JSP pages   37

1.11   Implementing DynaActionForms   38

2   Forms and form elements   42

2.1   Display errors and messages   44

2.2   Display errors next to a field   50

2.3   Create a custom message queue   53

2.4   Display errors and messages in groups   57

2.5   Dynamically insert data inside a message   62

2.6   Use message-resources property file
       from inside an Action   69

2.7   Create a wizard   73

2.8   Alternate row colors   80

2.9   Upload a file   89

3   Struts tag libraries   96

Using Struts tag libraries to promote good MVC practice 97
What is a tag library? 99 ▪ What tags do we discuss in
this chapter? 102

3.1   Using <html:link/> to increase your application's
       maintainability   105

3.2   Rendering images mapped from a properties file
       using <html:img/>   109

3.3   Encoding information with a <bean:write/> tag   113

3.4   Using <bean:define/> to expose information
       to your pages   116

3.5   Use <bean:include/> for the simple
       server-side includes   122

3.6   Using <logic:present/> tags to determine
       page content   126

3.7   Debugging your GUI with the <logic:present/> tag   *130*

3.8   Using the <logic:equal/> tag for view decisions   *134*

3.9   Using <bean:resource/> to expose
     the struts.config.xml to your view   *138*

3.10   Using <html:rewrite/> to resolve URLs   *147*

3.11   Cleaning up session-scope attributes   *153*

3.12   Creating a basic Struts Tiles page   *158*

3.13   Using Tiles with XML Definitions   *164*

4   *The Struts-Layout tag library*   **170**

Le Roi du Pot-au-feu 171
    Pot-au-feu 171 ▪ *What do layout tags do? 172*

4.1   Configuring your application
    to use Struts-Layout tags   *175*

4.2   Creating a simple table with Struts-Layout tags   *178*

4.3   Creating a multicolumn dynamic table
    with Struts-Layout tags   *182*

4.4   Using Struts-Layout panels   *187*

4.5   Adding skins to your project with Struts-Layout   *193*

4.6   Creating a table with selectable rows
    using Struts-Layout   *201*

4.7   Creating a tree navigation scheme
    with Struts-Layout   *206*

4.8   Creating "bread crumb trails" with Struts-Layout   *217*

4.9   Creating tabbed panes with Struts-Layout   *224*

4.10   Implementing a "pager" with Struts-Layout   *233*

5   *Validation within the Struts framework*   **242**

5.1   Use an ActionForm to validate   *244*

5.2   Struts Validator files explained (server-side)   *247*

5.3 Struts Validator files explained (client-side) *252*

5.4 Use declarative exception handling *256*

5.5 Aggregate exceptions *261*

5.6 Tailor a form for a DispatchAction *268*

5.7 Use Validator constants *276*

5.8 Validation in a wizard *282*

5.9 Create a pluggable validator for cross-form validation *287*

6 **Internationalization 294**

The "national language" of the United States 295

6.1 Set locale dynamically *296*

6.2 Internationalize your text *298*

6.3 Internationalize your images *302*

6.4 Create a locale-sensitive ActionForward *305*

6.5 Internationalize your tiles *309*

6.6 Internationalize validation *312*

7 **Logging in, security, and guarding 317**

7.1 Tomcat domain authentication and Struts *320*

7.2 Handling log out *326*

7.3 Switch to SSL and back again *329*

7.4 Secure an action mapping using the container *336*

7.5 Customized action mapping security *338*

7.6 Protect areas on a page *343*

7.7 Protect fields *346*

8 **Advanced recipes 348**

Case study—a modern luxury hotel 349

Let's revisit our B2C web application 351

8.1 Caching using a Struts plug-in *352*

8.2 Use the Tiles controller *358*

8.3 Generate a response with XSL *365*

8.4 Generate a PDF *371*

8.5 Hibernate and Struts *377*

8.6 Layering applications *392*

8.7 Enforce navigation *406*

8.8 Use a database to store your
message-resources properties *417*

9 **Testing** *424*

9.1 Testing outside the container with StrutsTestCase *426*

9.2 In-container testing with StrutsTestCase
and Cactus *437*

9.3 Testing DynaActionForm with StrutsTestCase *444*

9.4 Testing modules *449*

9.5 Performance testing Struts applications *454*

9.6 Testing coverage *462*

references *469*

index *473*

best practices

Automate the build process *13*

Heavily parameterize Ant build scripts *13*

Identify interfaces when creating modules *20*

Use multiple resource files *21*

Validate your XML *21*

Do not use wild cards in Ant scripts *28*

*Set <message-resources/> null attribute to true
in production, and false in development* *31*

Prefer classes over interfaces to store constants . *35*

*Avoid using the <html:messages> header
and footer attributes* *49*

Prefer <html:messages> to <html:errors> . . . *50*

*Use consistent naming when relating
message properties to field names* *53*

*Choose unique queue names when creating
custom queues* *56*

Limit upload file sizes *95*

*Prefer Struts tags over any
HTML counterpart* 109

*Keep to a single image directory
in most circumstances* 111

*Beware of sending unfiltered information
to the browser* 115

*Set the type and scope attribute when
using <bean:define/>* 119

*Logic tags do not implement
"try, catch, finally"* 129

Beware of null values 138

*Be careful when using JavaScript
and <html:rewrite/>* 152

*Use Separate directories for file types
when implementing Tiles* 162

When to use Tiles 163

*Don't waste time—start with XML-based Tiles
as soon as possible* 169

*Choose a navigation strategy that is scalable
for your application* 207

Implement crumbs in the proper places 224

Keep tabs on your Tabs! 225

Keep your Actions as short as possible 236

*Don't trust JavaScript as your only
means of validation!* 255

*Always create a global exception tag
  to catch java.lang.Exception* *261*

Apply high cohesion to DispatchAction *276*

*Use Validator constants to increase
  maintainability* *281*

Prefer keyed tag properties *304*

Use SSL judiciously *335*

Use the container to protect resources *338*

Consolidate resource references *357*

*Create solutions independent of
  View implementation* *377*

Enforce navigation where required *417*

*Use Design by Contract
  to design module tests* *454*

Create a performance test plan *461*

Employ continuous coverage testing *468*

preface

A journeyman or apprentice developer may find it difficult to learn the "secret handshake" that more advanced developers seem to know all along. Some of these junior developers will with time become advanced engineers with an excellent knowledge of web application development, but they may find that they still lack experience in implementing a few specific solutions.

This book is written for both the apprentice developer and the advanced engineer. "Theory" books can give you an excellent background on a subject (such as Manning's *Struts in Action*), but often they don't go deep enough into real-world problems. We're a pair of seasoned developers who have seen the good, the bad, and the ugly in the course of our work. We took those experiences, turned them into recipes, and successfully put them to use every day. This is a "hands-on" book. We believe the solutions presented in the recipes will make your life easier and your code better.

Our book is intended for intermediate or advanced developers who live and work "where the rubber meets the road"—in the real world. Complex web applications employ technologies besides Java and JSP to meet their functional requirements. We've attempted to explore these, as well as offer new and fresh solutions for creating GUIs and show many of the core Struts packages used in ways that reflect real-world solutions. Often we poked around mailing lists and found questions that we felt hadn't been answered the way we would have; other times, we show solutions that we discovered in our daily work. Well designed solutions are the goal of every developer—and of this book.

acknowledgments

The opportunity to write for Manning provides a unique platform for authors to nurture high-quality work. The culture to grow good books is largely due to the encouragement, support, and expectations of our publisher Marjan Bace. Getting a book off the ground is no small feat. Clay Andres, senior acquisitions editor, played a critical role in the early stages of this project, helping to shape it and keep it on track.

Only the authors get to put their names on the front cover of a book. While the content is attributed to the authors, there is a dedicated army of others working in the background and as the authors of this book, we owe a debt of gratitude to those individuals who helped us understand you, our readers, and who ensured that we did what we needed to do in order to present content clearly and concisely. In particular, we recognize the efforts of our development editor, Jackie Carter, who helped us time and time again. Once the raw manuscript was written, the Manning production team came to the rescue and polished it up. A special thanks to our technical editor Steve Raeburn, copyeditor Mark Goodin, proofreader Sharon Mullins, typesetter Denis Dalinnik, design editor Dottie Marsico, cover designer Leslie Haimes, publicist Helen Trimes, and project editor Mary Piergies.

As developers yourselves, you understand that quality requires review. David Roberson, review editor, has an uncanny ability to seek out and obtain the commitment from a talented, and demanding, set of reviewers. The review efforts of Vivek Awasthi, Joe Germuska, Jerome Josephraj, Steve Raeburn, Jing Zhou, Martin Cooper, Hemesh Surana, John Yu, Patrick Peak, Brian Gebbie, and Maxim Loukianov were instrumental in helping us craft this book.

In addition to the reviewers listed above, we recruited our own special reviewers. As friends, these reviewers don't mince words. They tell it like it is. We wish to thank Sheng Huang and Hoan Luong for their demanding and brutally honest (sometimes *too* honest) attention to the material in this book. Many developers who use Struts every day injected a dose of reality into several chapters, including those covering Struts tags and Struts-Layout tags. They also proved to themselves and us that these recipes were valid and useful. In particular, we wish to thank Oscar Montoya, Marcos Oliva, Suresh Sharma, Paul Barros, Troung Vo, Stephen Dai, Brian Dilley, and Ara Juljulian.

At times we called upon "the experts" to review our material. Acknowledged Tiles expert Cedric Dumoulin generously donated his time to review the Tiles recipes. Mike Clark, creator of JUnitPerf, reviewed our performance-testing recipe. Peter Morgan, jCoverage expert, made sure our recipe was true to the product. Steve Ditlinger, creator of the SSL extension library, kept a watchful eye on the SSL recipe. Erik Hatcher made sure our automated build recipe was on the up and up. Jean-Noel Ribette helped us ensure layout tags were properly illustrated. Brian Dilley crafted the original code for our recipe to tie message-resources to a database. The labors of our sage reviewers are a wonderful asset to this book. We thank all of them for finding the time to review our work.

Those of you participating in news groups and open source projects understand the power of knowledge sharing. All participants, regardless of their level of expertise, are contributing to a greater and more powerful knowledge base among us all. The information we have garnered from those public domain contributors have influenced the information in this book. To all of those people, we say thank-you.

It goes without saying that the team of Struts developers and committers require a special mention. After all, without them we would have nothing to write about! We wish to thank Ted Husted for his insight and support in the early stages of the book.

A pie can only be split so many ways. The time we spent on this book was sometimes at the expense of those to whom we owe the most—our families. We appreciate the gift of time our spouses and children have afforded us as we spent countless hours pounding at the keyboard.

about this book

How the book is organized

In this book we have done our very best to bring you useful and interesting recipes to meet the challenges of Struts developers. As is the case with most well-garnished dinner tables, these recipes include a little of something for everyone. There are plenty of "meat and potatoes" recipes to guide you through some of the common, everyday things you need to do. To satisfy those with a big appetite we have included recipes to secure and internationalize your applications. An entire chapter has been devoted to making sure you have the tools you need to validate input. If you enjoy a nice dessert, but don't like to spend a lot of time in the kitchen, you are invited to check out an entire chapter devoted to the Struts-Layout library. There is nothing better than a gourmet meal that's ready to serve! For those with exotic tastes we have devoted another chapter to advanced Struts recipes. To make sure your application works as expected, we have included a chapter showing how to apply several facets of testing. The book has a diverse set of recipes in several key areas of interest.

Chapter 1 Basics

This chapter contains some of the simpler and more common recipes in the book. It contains a mixture of everyday recipes you will find yourself using time and time again. Among other things, you will see different ways to work with resource bundles, learn how to default your application to an `ActionForward`, learn to create an automated build, and be introduced to an effective technique to manage constants. The recipe that shows you how to perform an automated build using Ant will take the drudgery out of the implementation process. Almost every application draws something from these recipes.

Chapter 2 Forms

Forms are the heart and soul of most web applications. In this chapter we cover a number of recipes designed to allow you to work with forms. Several recipes are dedicated to using `ActionErrors` and `ActionMessages`. In addition we show you a new way to alternate row colors. We also show how to create a single-form wizard.

Chapter 3 Tags

The Struts tag library plays a critical role to deliver the "view" portion of applications. In this chapter we cover the most significant and useful Struts tags.

Chapter 4 Layout

The Struts-Layout tag library is an exceedingly popular and useful third-party library available to Struts developers. In this chapter we delve into this library by showing you how to create tabs, skins, trees, and much more.

Chapter 5 Validation

No application is complete without validation. In this chapter we show you how to use one of the newest and most useful Struts features—declarative exception handling. We show you how to aggregate your exceptions and present an interesting recipe to bring synergy between the `DispatchAction` and validation. We present recipes showing how to use the Validator to create both server-side and client-side validation. We roll up our sleeves and discuss how to create your own pluggable validator to perform cross-form validation. In addition, this chapter contains a recipe describing one of the most undervalued features in the Validator framework—Validator constants. Finally, we cover applying validation to wizard applications.

Chapter 6 Internationalization

Internationalizing applications is essential in the global marketplace. In this chapter we delve into making the best use of Struts' inherent capability to internationalize applications. We show you how to internationalize both text and images. In addition, we cover how to use the `RequestProcessor` to make your `ActionForward` locale sensitive. We also dig into the built-in internationalization feature bundled inside the Validator and Tiles.

Chapter 7 Security

No application is complete without addressing security. In this chapter we present recipes on signing in and signing out. We present a series of recipes yielding techniques to protect your applications at various levels of granularity, including action mapping, areas, and fields. In addition, we include a recipe showing you how to make good use of the Struts SSL extension for HTTP/HTTPS switching to turn SSL on and off declaratively.

Chapter 8 Advanced

This chapter contains several advanced Struts recipes. In this chapter we show you how to create a PDF and how to generate HTML from XML using XSL. You will find a recipe to create a well-structured layered application using several best practices and patterns. This chapter covers how to cache resources by creating your own custom Struts plug-in. You will find a recipe on how to use the Tiles controller to manipulate data. We also reveal how to use the popular Hibernate project within a Struts application. We are sure you will find many interesting and useful recipes in this chapter.

Chapter 9 Testing

Experienced developers value a diligent testing effort. In this chapter we explore Struts testing by providing several recipes designed to ensure your application is robust and scalable. This chapter gives you step-by-step instructions on how to perform outside-the-container testing with `StrutsTestCase`. Another recipe shows how to combine `StrutsTestCase` and Cactus to test your application in one or more containers. We present an interesting technique to test `DynaActionForms` and a strategy to approach module testing. To make sure your application is performing as expected, we demonstrate how to combine `StrutsTestCase` and JUnit-Perf. Finally, we have included a recipe regarding the use of jCoverage to ensure your application has been tested thoroughly.

The material in this book is wide ranging. There is a little bit of something for everyone, but it's difficult to cover it all. We were undecided about the need for a Struts-EL recipe. One minute it was in, the next it was out. A better approach to this topic would be to discuss the advantages and disadvantages of JSTL and Struts-EL, but, alas, this is out of the scope of a cookbook. For that reason we decided to exclude it from this book.

Recipe structure

Each recipe is divided into six sections:

- *Problem*—A problem statement
- *Background*—Material required to understand the recipe
- *Recipe*—The solution to the problem
- *Discussion*—Describes the recipe in more detail; highlights issues, pros, cons and "gotchas"
- *Related*—Related recipes
- *References*—Material related to the recipe; the material in this section can be used to understand background material or issues in more detail.

Best practices

This book lists several best practices designed to help you avoid common pitfalls and benefit from the experiences of others. The art of creating software involves making choices. Reflecting on past choices allows us to separate the good choices from the bad. Sharing best practices is one of the ways we can leverage each other's knowledge. Although the best practices listed in this book are appropriate for the majority of situations, you are encouraged to evaluate and share best practices to ensure the best practice addresses your particular circumstance.

For your convenience, we have included a table of contents listing all of the best practices in the book on page xv.

Who should read this book

Struts Recipes is for Struts developers of all levels who are interested in building flexible, maintainable, secure, robust, and scalable applications. Junior developers will gain an immediate advantage on the learning curve by leveraging the experiences of others presented in this book. Advanced developers will not only find new techniques for solving problems already encountered on their journey, but they will also find solutions to problems that are only now on their horizon. All developers will walk away with a clearer understanding of the challenges involved in working with Struts, as well as the ability to quickly tackle those challenges. More importantly, developers will be able to use the rationale discussed throughout this book to solve problems hiding just around the corner.

How to use this book

This book has the spirit of a cookbook. If you need to cook something up because you have company coming over, or you have a deadline looming, then this book is designed to let you look up what you need in the table of contents and get to work. For that reason, the best place to start *is* the table of contents. You can use the table of contents as your compass to navigate the book. Although each recipe stands on its own, this doesn't preclude you from reading the book cover to cover. The book is roughly organized in the manner in which you might develop an application. If you want to skip a recipe along the way, then go right ahead. We'll be sure to tell you if we think another recipe is recommended reading.

We have made the best use of the newest features in Struts 1.1. Therefore, we suggest you download Struts 1.1 or later before you set foot in the kitchen.

Source code

This book contains an extensive set of code listings. Different readers have different preferences when it comes to code listings. Some readers want abbreviated code listings, others want all the gory details. We decided to go with the lowest common denominator by providing code listings as complete as possible wherever it made sense. Every effort has been made to assure the correctness of the code listings. However, people are not perfect, including authors. We are very interested in learning about any errors in the code or text. If you discover any, please contact us through the Author Online forum at www.manning.com/franciscus so we can make the necessary corrections as soon as possible.

Typographical conventions

The following conventions are used throughout the book:

- Courier typeface is used in all code listings.
- *Italics* are used to introduce new terms.
- **Courier Bold** is sometimes used to draw your attention to a section of code.
- Code annotations are used when directing your attention to a particular line of code. Annotations are marked with bullets, such as ❶.
- Courier typeface is used in text for the following: Struts classes (Action-Forward, etc.), HTML/XML tags, attributes, events, commands, methods—in general, most code words.

Other conventions

The ramification of good naming conventions is that it's tricky to distinguish between nouns representing different things. One such situation occurs with the word "validator." When referring to the Apache Validator product, we capitalized the letter "V". When referring to an object performing validation logic within the Validator, we use a small case "v". The same convention was used to describe Tiles. When referring to the Apache Tiles project, now integrated into Struts, we capitalize the letter "T". When referring to tile as a software artifact, we use a lowercase "t".

Often concrete implementation of `ActionForm` classes are nicknamed "form beans." This nickname is likely attributed to the `<form-bean>` tag found in the struts-config.xml file. Throughout the book we have used the term "form bean" in this context.

References

Bibliographic references are indicated with square brackets in the body of the text. The contents within the square brackets represents a handle to the reference. The References section of each chapter contains short descriptions of the handles, and the References area at the rear of the book contains full publication details. The Related section of each recipe lists other recipes in the book that relate to the recipe being discussed.

Author Online

Purchase of *Struts Recipes* includes free access to an Author Online forum, a private web discussion board run by Manning Publications. You are encouraged to use this forum to make comments about the book, ask technical questions, and receive help from the authors and other readers. Use your browser to navigate to www.manning.com/franciscus to take advantage of this free service. The forum's welcome page gives you all the information you need to sign up and get going.

The Author Online forum is one of the ways Manning remains committed to readers. The authors' participation in the forum is voluntary and without a specified level of commitment. The forum is a great way to share ideas and learn from each other. The Author Online forum will remain accessible from the publisher's web site as long as the book is in print.

Soapbox

As software developers we are very interested in well-designed solutions. Wherever possible we applied best practices in our code samples. In some circumstances we might have broken our own rules to make the code clearer and less confusing. You might notice that we have placed a good deal of emphasis on the Model-View-Controller design pattern. MVC is the cornerstone of good design for all significant applications. Anyone choosing to work with Struts is a firm believer (or soon will be) in MVC. It is our intention that the recipes in this book show you how to stay true to MVC principles.

Experienced developers understand that no solution is perfect, and not every shoe fits every foot. Usually an advantage leads to some other compromise. The goal is to understand the advantages, and then balance them against the compromises to make the best judgment call for the situation at hand. The Discussion sections address these issues to ensure that you are armed with the correct information to make your own decisions.

Each recipe is written from the vantage point of experience, often the only quality that counts. In writing each recipe we strive to point the way towards a more flexible, maintainable, secure, robust, scalable, and easy-to-use application that is encapsulated and orthogonal. You should do your best to keep these goals in mind as you read each recipe. As you cook up your own recipes, we hope that you draw upon these principles. We encourage you to share your ideas and thoughts as a means to create higher-quality applications for all of us to use.

About the authors

GEORGE FRANCISCUS is a consultant at Nexcel.ca, providing technical and management consulting services. George has almost 20 years of experience in a diverse range of technologies, including Java, J2EE, Domino, relational databases, and mainframe technologies. George is the coauthor of Manning Publications' *Struts In Action*. He holds a BSc in Computer Science from the University of Toronto. George lives in Toronto, Ontario, with his wife and three children.

DANILO GUROVICH is Manager of Web Development at LowerMyBills.com in Santa Monica, California. His experiences include designing and implementing Struts-based applications in high-traffic commerce, enterprise application integration monitoring and controlling, and business process management software. His non-Java experience extends into GUI design, human factors, and graphics. He graduated from Claremont McKenna College a long time ago, when FORTRAN was big, disk space was small, and nobody had heard of a PC. Danilo lives in Northridge, California, with his wife and daughter and spends what little free time he has pursuing old-school fine photography and restoring Citroens.

About the cover illustration

The figure on the cover of *Struts Recipes* is a "Griaega de Atenas," a Greek woman of Athens. Judging by her fancy dress and jewelry, she is clearly well-to-do, the wife of a successful merchant or tradesman perhaps. The illustration is taken from a Spanish compendium of regional dress customs first published in Madrid in 1799. The book's title page states:

> *Coleccion general de los Trages que usan actualmente todas las Nacionas del Mundo desubierto, dibujados y grabados con la mayor exactitud por R.M.V.A.R. Obra muy util y en especial para los que tienen la del viajero universal*

which we translate, as literally as possible, thus:

> *General collection of costumes currently used in the nations of the known world, designed and printed with great exactitude by R.M.V.A.R. This work is very useful especially for those who hold themselves to be universal travelers*

Although nothing is known of the designers, engravers, and workers who colored this illustration by hand, the "exactitude" of their execution is evident in this drawing. The "Griaega de Atenas" is just one of many figures in this colorful collection. Their diversity speaks vividly of the uniqueness and individuality of the world's towns and regions just 200 years ago. This was a time when the dress codes of two regions separated by a few dozen miles identified people uniquely as belonging to one or the other. The collection brings to life a sense of isolation and distance of that period—and of every other historic period except our own hyperkinetic present.

Dress codes have changed since then and the diversity by region, so rich at the time, has faded away. It is now often hard to tell the inhabitant of one continent from another. Perhaps, trying to view it optimistically, we have traded a cultural and visual diversity for a more varied personal life. Or a more varied and interesting intellectual and technical life.

We at Manning celebrate the inventiveness, the initiative, and, yes, the fun of the computer business with book covers based on the rich diversity of regional life of two centuries ago, brought back to life by the pictures from this collection.

Basic recipes

1

Take your thumb and third finger and make a "C." See that gap? That's the way most people do their jobs. They get eighty-five or ninety percent of the way there, and call it a day. Success is finishing it up.

—Jerry Cheuvront, friend and mentor

1

There are many ways to create web applications. You've chosen the Java route, so you know that this widely distributed language offers many means to the same end; your choices have a lot to do with philosophy, best practices, and finally what you and your development team knows well enough to put into practice.

So, what framework should you use? Is Java/JSP the answer? What standards should you follow? The answers to these questions may be simple at first glance. Then again, as you get to thinking about them, they kind of grow legs and run away with your thoughts.

Should we use servlets? How about just straight JSP with scripting? There's always the Java Standard Tag Library! What about applets? Maybe Cocoon? How about something custom?

Any or all of these may be great choices for you. Struts, however, is about narrowing choices and creating a focus on best practices, good design, scalability, ease of maintenance, and steady development. To use Struts is to step into the world of Model-View-Controller, Object-Oriented Design, and good collaboration practices with front, middle and back-end developers.

In case you haven't read Manning's other Struts title, *Struts in Action*, or are not familiar with just what Struts is all about, we'll start with a brief description. Struts was conceived and originally developed by Craig McClanahan in 2000, and then adopted by the Apache Software Foundation for open source development. This open source movement encourages collaboration, consensus, and the creation of a standards-based and thought-elevating environment. The Jakarta Project and all of its modules, including Struts, are available to all under their open source license.

But what is Struts?

Struts is a server-side implementation of the Model-View-Controller framework for web applications. It's the framework or "skeleton" to which you as a developer or team member will add "muscles, tendons, and skin," and create and flesh out web applications that allow for:

- Scalability
- Easier maintenance
- Separation of business logic from your JSP pages
- A familiar and consistent library of code that can be reused
- A standard validation framework
- A standard internationalization framework

- The benefits of Java implementation and J2EE compatibility
- Widespread acceptance by small companies and large enterprises
- Full MVC separation

Struts gives you all that and more. It allows you to assign team members to various complex applications according to their specialties (Model, View, and Controller). Struts supports the software development lifecycle and Extreme Programming, as well as other development methods. Struts is accepted and implemented by major enterprise software engineering companies and their customers around the world. Struts is available literally everywhere that Java meets the web!

Finally, as Struts is open source, it's *free*! Not only is it free, there are developers all over the world developing, debugging, enhancing, and scaling Struts into an ever more powerful and solid system. As you become more familiar and excited about Struts, you too may want to add to the ever-growing code base of this application framework.

Struts allows an astute team to create safe development and integration environments, solid tools for developers from front to back, and packages and libraries that make many of the problematic and overlooked areas of development faster to develop and easier to maintain.

What Struts isn't

Struts is not software in the sense that it actually "does something," any more than a stack of car parts and pieces can drive you down the road. Struts is a means to an end. It takes the raw materials of Java, HTML, and JavaScript, combines them with accepted software design philosophies, and then refines them into pieces that make the assembly of web applications easier. Going back to the automobile parts analogy, it delivers all the parts you need, along with the basic instructions. What you build and what it does is completely dependent upon your requirements and imagination.

A note about our favorite Ant

Another tool from the Apache Software Foundation we talk about in this book is Ant. Ant is a "build tool" that we use to create our deployable WAR (web application resource) files to deploy in a Servlet container (such as Tomcat, Orion, Jetty, Resin, and application servers such as JBoss, Websphere, Weblogic, and so on). Ant is rapidly becoming *the* build tool for complex Java/J2EE projects, and we encourage you to learn more about this tool, as we only get into the peripheries here. Manning's *Java Development with Ant* by Eric Hatcher and Steve Loughran is an excellent resource for more information.

Why do we need to go to all the trouble of using Ant to create WAR files? Because as your applications grow larger and more complex, you'll find that they must be managed outside of their server environment and then redeployed. This allows not only for separation from your deployment, it allows for your applications to be distributed across multiple platforms that may handle the expansion of WAR files differently or expand them into different directories. You're much better off in the long run to step into this type of development environment if you haven't already done so. Ant is a wonderful way to do this and we cannot recommend it enough.

The developer's environment

In smaller applications and development environments, creating a separate build and development environment is often unnecessary and overly complicated. It is easy enough to write the JSP/HTML files, and place them in a container, and recompile the Java classes for deployment in the class path of the application on which you're working. This type of basic environment has a short life span, and in many ways it can make projects overly complicated as they grow. If your project is anything more than the most basic type, you should never begin work using this tightly coupled and limited technique. A wise developer almost always creates separate build and deployment environments early on for any application that is more than just "throw-away" code. Even the simplest of projects can benefit from this, as more often than not it can grow "legs" and become complex.

Developers can work either alone or in team environments, and these experiences, although radically different, often benefit from the same practices—but this may not manifest itself on the surface. The main problem in team environments exists in the various levels of skills, different coding styles, practices, and different areas of expertise, For instance, "basic" ideas in a team environment might become complex to those who have never been exposed to them or do not use them frequently.

As a software engineer, you may have developed your skills in isolated situations and never had to work within a group where many different projects are evolving in a parallel setting. If you are assigned to a group environment, you might be unaware that you can break monolithic Struts applications into modules with multiple struts-config.xml files, multiple message-resource property files, and so forth. You also might never have used the `bundle` attribute in a `<bean:message/>` tag before, simply because you've never needed it.

Others may have worked in groups for their entire careers, and in doing so, specialized in specific tasks within the Struts framework, never working in an environment where they've had to do it all—from managing configurations, writing esoteric JavaScript functions, to managing pop-ups. This chapter will give the reader insight as well as basic and valuable information directly aimed at creating a strong and scalable setting to develop complex and challenging web applications, whether you are working within a huge enterprise or are a force of one.

Struts, as a framework, changes almost daily. There are many recent changes to Struts as it has migrated from 1.0 to 1.1+ that allow for greater encapsulation, scalability and object-oriented architecture, and many of the recipes below are specific to 1.1's release (which we recommend). As Struts matures, it is becoming one of a few de facto Java frameworks for many enterprise-level organizations, and as such it has grown to support team and parallel development paradigms surprisingly well. Many of the recipes in this book are geared toward applications created in this environment, but in many ways these recipes are also valuable to the lone developer working long hours at home with a very large coffee pot percolating only a few feet away.

Chapter 1, in brief

We're not going to begin at the beginning, because this book is for those whose appetites have been whetted already and are eager to progress beyond the basics and find answers to such questions as "Specifically, how do you do that FOO thing, anyway?" in as many ways as possible. That said, we have to begin somewhere, and chapter 1 has a few basic recipes that the more seasoned developer may not care to implement or need to review:

- Use Ant to automate the build process for a Struts project.
- A short discussion about the jsessionid.
- Use multiple configuration (i.e., struts-config.xml) files for large projects. These allow encapsulation and portability between directories and groups, clear up difficulties concerning namespaces, and create pointers to many different avenues of configuration and control.
- Use multiple resource bundles to control messages and internationalization issues (Internationalization is covered in detail in chapter 6).
- Use constants within an application to manage session namespaces, and page-level variables and their mappings to Action classes and form beans.

- Create solid references to other pages, manage pointers to CSS, and Java-Script files. While ubiquitous in their use, these references are often over-looked, and using simple HTML references may sometimes cause unexpected results. Our recipes show how to solidify these references within the Struts framework and make your applications truly portable and flexible.

- Use `DynaActionForms`. Their use makes a developer's life much easier and gets rid of quite a bit of busy work, yet to use `DynaActionForms` the first time can seem difficult. Our recipe clarifies this subject for anyone that has never used these forms before.

1.1   Use Ant to automatically build a Struts project

◆ Problem

You want to use Ant to automatically compile source code and generate a WAR file for a Struts project.

◆ Background

An automated build is a well-recognized best practice for any software project. A "build" is defined as the process of assembling all application deployable arti-facts in preparation for deployment to an application server. In this recipe we show you how to create a WAR file for a Struts project. A web archive resource (WAR) file is a convenient way of packaging servlets, JSPs, other associated files, and JARs into a single file suffixed with the .war extension and in zip format. Upon startup, the application server unzips all WAR files found in the webapps directory into the expected directory structure.

If the source files are already compiled, and the deployable files are already in the structure expected by the application server, you can create a WAR file manually [WAR]. While creating WAR files manually works, it has a number of disadvantages:

- The development directory structure must match the deployable directory structure expected by the application server. Alternatively, you can manu-ally copy files from the development structure to the deployable structure.

- The source files must be compiled before you assemble the WAR file.

- Manually creating WAR files requires more effort.

- Manual processes are error prone.

Automating the creating of the WAR file allows you to expand the scope of the build process to include:

- Compiling source code
- Running functional unit tests
- Running coverage tests
- Emailing notification
- Copying the WAR file to a target location

Ant is "Another Neat Tool" that allows all this to happen and more. Not only can you compile all your Java files, you can check for dependencies, create WAR and JAR files, and even precompile all your JSP files if you wish. Ant is the de facto tool to automate builds; it is both simple and powerful at the same time—a rare combination. Sufficient coverage of Ant and all of its features warrants an entire book of its own. We encourage you to review the references to prepare yourself with sufficient knowledge before starting with Ant. If you have some basic Ant knowledge, then you are ready to proceed.

In this recipe we show you how to create an Ant script that compiles your source code, builds a WAR file, and emails a notification of a successful build. The highly parameterized nature of this Ant script allows you to use this same Ant script for all your Struts projects. Each project customizes the build by tweaking the associated properties file. A single Ant file for all projects empowers your organization with the ability to rollout new build enhancements with a single point of maintenance.

◆ Recipe

Your first task is to download and install Ant. Everything you need to do to get started using Ant is found at the Ant home page at http://ant.apache.org/.

Once you have Ant downloaded and installed, you are ready to get started. In listing 1.1 we present a four-target Ant script to clean the development code (and deployment directories) of earlier builds, compile the source code and build a WAR file. The last target sends out an email to interested parties.

Listing 1.1   build.xml

```
<project name="build recipe" default="notify">        ❶
    <property file="build.properties"/>        ❷
    <property file="${user.home}/build.properties"/>        ❸
```

```
<path id="classpath.base">
   <pathelement location="${servlet.dir}/${servlet.jar}"/>
   <pathelement location="${struts.dir}/${struts.jar}"/>
   <pathelement location="${log4j.dir}/{log4j.jar}"/>
   <pathelement
     location="${commons-logging.dir}/${commons-logging.jar}"/>
   <pathelement
     location="${commons-beanutils.dir}/${commons-beanutils.jar}"/>
   <pathelement
     location="${commons-digester.dir}/${commons-digester.jar}"/>
   <pathelement
     location="${commons-collections.dir}/${commons-collections.jar}"/>
 </path>
```

❹

```
<target name="clean">
<delete dir="${build.src.dir}"/>
<delete dir="${dist.dir}"/>
   <mkdir dir="${build.src.dir}"/>
   <mkdir dir="${dist.dir}"/>
   <echo message="${ant.version}"/>
   <echo message="Java version ${ant.java.version}"/>
 </target>
```

❺

```
<target name="compile-domain"
       description="compile domain"
       depends="clean">
   <javac srcdir="${src.dir}"
       destdir="${build.src.dir}"
       debug="${javac.debug}"
       classpathref="classpath.base"/>
 </target>
```

❻

```
<target name="build-war"
       description="build war file"
       depends="compile-domain">
   <war warfile="${dist.dir}/${warfile.war}"
       webxml="${webapp.dir}/WEB-INF/web.xml"
       manifest="${webapp.dir}/META-INF/MANIFEST.MF">
       <classes dir="${build.src.dir}"/>
       <fileset dir="${webapp.dir}">
          <exclude name="WEB-INF/web.xml"/>
       </fileset>
       <lib dir="${lib.dir}"/>
   </war>
 </target>
```

❼

❽

❾

```
<target name="notify"
       description="email notification"
       depends="build-war">
   <mail
          mailhost="${smtphost}"
```

❿

```
            mailport="${smtpport}"
            subject="${mailsubject}"
            tolist="${toaddress}"
            files="${files}">
        <from address="${fromaddress}"/>
        <message>${mailbody}</message>
      </mail>
   </target>
</project>
```

To kick off the build process you open a console and navigate to the directory containing the build.xml file, then type "ant" at the prompt. By default Ant looks for a build.xml file. In our case we want Ant to create a log file. Later, we show you how to email the log file to interested parties. The following command executes the build

```
ant -l build.log
```

This command invokes Ant and instructs it to store the build output in a file called build.log. Let's walk through listing 1.1 to see how this all works.

The root tag for the build script is the `<project>` tag. The default attribute tells Ant which target to process. We tell Ant the end target, not the starting target. Ant looks at the `<target>` tag's `depends` attribute to execute dependent targets before the current target is executed. Most Ant scripts are comprised of a chained list of targets. If a target specifies multiple dependencies, the dependent targets are executed from left to right. At ❶ we specify `notify` as the default target. In this script, the targets are executed in the following order:

```
1. clean
2. compile-domain
3. build-war
4. notify
```

Notice that this script is peppered with parameters. The parameters are identified by a dollar sign and curly braces, as in: `${myparameter}`. In this script the parameters are defined in the build.properties file. We will delve into the properties file shortly. For the time being we take it on faith that the parameters will be substituted with real values. At ❷ we specify the name of the properties file.

You may want to use a set of standard project properties, but allow users to override them for their own personal environment. ❸ instructs Ant to look in the user's home directory for a build.properties file. If competing properties files exist, the user's properties file ❸ overrides the one specified at ❷. This technique allows you to provide a standard set of properties, but still allow the user to tailor their environment.

At ❹ we declare all the JARs required to compile the source code.

clean target

❺ This segement purges and creates any directories required by the script. First, we prepare the directory holding the compile source from the previous build. Then we prepare the directory holding the previous build's WAR file. We invoke two echo tasks to display the Ant and Java versions used in the build. This may be helpful when builds fail for unexpected reasons.

compile-domain target

❻ These lines declare the target to compile source code. Notice it depends on the clean target. The <javac> tag is an Ant tag used to compile Java source code. The srcdir attribute declares the location of the source code. The destdir specifies where we want the compiled code to be placed. We have parameterized the debug attribute to allow us to turn on debugging declaratively. Finally, we specify the class path used by the compile-domain target by setting the classpath attribute. Notice we use the class path reference declared at ❹.

build-war target

❼ Here the code declares a target to build a WAR file using the compile source code created at ❻. Notice this target depends on the compile-domain target. Creating a WAR file with Ant is very easy. All we need to do is specify all the necessary parameters. The warfile attribute is used to declare the location and name of the WAR file. We specify the location and name of the web.xml file using the webxml attribute. Similarly, the manifest file is specified using the manifest attribute. In order to build a war file we'll need the class files. We use the classes tag to declare the location of the classes required by the WAR file.

At ❽ we indicate the location of the TLDs, JSP, HTML files, and any other files required by the application. Notice we need to exclude the web.xml file because we took care of that at ❼.

We declare the location of the directory holding any JAR files required for deployment at ❾.

notify target

At ❿ we declare a target to send an email to notify interested parties about the build. Notice this target depends on the build-war target. Ant provides a <mail> tag to send emails. The <mail> tag attributes are fairly straightforward. The mailhost attribute specifies the SMTP host used to send emails and the mail port specifies the port used by the SMTP host. As you might expect, the subject attribute provides the content for the email's subject line. The tolist attribute contains the email distribution list. You can even attach files! The files attribute lists the file attachments to be sent along with the email. Later we show you how to attach the build log. The <from> tag specifies the name of the from address. Lastly, the <message> tag provides the body of the email message. The heavy parameterization of the notification target means you can change the message by making a properties file change.

Listing 1.2 presents a sample build.properties file.

Listing 1.2   build.properties

```
#names
appname=myexample      ❶
warfile.war=${appname}.war      ❷

#directories
src.dir=./src/share
build.src.dir=./build/share
webapp.dir=./${appname}
lib.dir=${webapp.dir}/WEB-INF/lib
dist.dir=./dist
app.build.dir=./${appname}/WEB-INF

#compile
javac.debug=true

#mail paramters
buildname=build results
smtpport=25
smtphost=smtp.mycompany.com
mailsubject=${buildname} build results
mailbody=The ${buildname} nightly build has completed
logfile=build.log
#files=${logfile},${dist.dir}/${warfile.war}      ❸
files=${logfile}      ❹
fromaddress=build@mycompany.com
toaddress=user@mycompany.com, buildmanager@mycompany.com

#jars
servlet.dir=./lib
servlet.jar=servlet.jar
struts.dir=./lib
struts.jar=struts.jar
log4j.dir=./lib
log4j.jar=log4j-1.2.7.jar      ❺
```

```
commons-logging.dir=./lib
commons-logging.jar=commons-logging.jar
commons-beanutils.dir=./lib
commons-beanutils.jar=commons-beanutils.jar
commons-digester.dir=./lib
commons-digester.jar=commons-digester.jar
commons-collections.dir=./lib
commons-collections.jar=commons-collections.jar
```

The values used in listing 1.2 will be specific to your project and environment. Notice that you can use substitution parameters within your build.properties file. Using parameters in this way allows you to maintain consistent naming, minimize maintenance, and reduce errors. For example, the application name declared at ❶ is used in the WAR name at ❷. Using this technique automatically changes the WAR file name whenever the application name changes.

At ❹ we specified the name of the build log to be attached to the email. Attaching the log allows everyone on the distribution list to see the results of the build. You can attach the WAR file to the email by commenting out line ❹ and uncommenting line ❸.

Because JAR files often embed the version number within the file name, parameterizing the JAR's file name allows you to swap in new versions without changing the Ant script. At ❺ we used this technique for the log4j JAR file.

Listing 1.3 presents the output created by the Ant script. This output is found in the build.log file.

Listing 1.3 build.log

```
clean:
    [echo] Apache Ant version 1.5.1 compiled on October 2 2002
    [echo] Java version 1.4

compile-domain:

build-war:

notify:
    [mail] Sending email: build results build results
    [mail] Sent email with 1 attachment

BUILD SUCCESSFUL
Total time: 2 seconds
```

The application's WAR file is created and sitting in your distribution directory.

◆ *Discussion*

As you become more comfortable with Ant and the build process, the power of using Ant becomes more obvious and indispensable. Although this may seem less significant on small applications, the dividends yielded by an automated build process increase dramatically for larger ones. Getting started with an automated build process on smaller projects positions you with the knowledge to be ready as your organization grows. Larger organizations will receive immediate payback from this kind of preparation.

> **BEST PRACTICE**   *Automate the build process*—Use an Ant-based automated build process to ensure your application can be built quickly and reliably upon demand. Consider adding testing to the build process to guarantee the integrity of your application at build time.

The build script presented in this recipe is a simple basic build process, but there is plenty of room to grow it. For example, you can extend the build process to build your application from CVS. In the testing chapter we show you how to add automated functional testing, coverage testing, and performance testing to the build process. A fully integrated and rich build process gives you the confidence that you have a working application at a point in time—a goal very difficult to achieve with large teams. As evidence, Ant is used on a daily basis to create builds for Apache projects, including Struts itself!

> **BEST PRACTICE**   *Heavily parameterize Ant build scripts*—Ant build scripts should be reusable across several projects. Customization of runtime parameters should be abstracted into a properties file. You should consider providing a user-specific properties file to allow users to override selected standard build properties.

◆ *References*

- [ANT] Apache Ant, http://ant.apache.org/
- [ANTMAN] *Apache Ant Manual*, http://ant.apache.org/manual/
- [CONTINT] Fowler, Martin, "Continuous Integration"
- [JDANT] Hatcher, Eric, and Steven Loughram, *Java Development with Ant*
- [WAR] Hosanee, Matthew, "Manually creating a simple war file"

1.2 *Default your application to an ActionForward*

◆ **Problem**

You want your application to default to a Struts `ActionForward`.

◆ **Background**

The URL has become the calling card of the future. Businesses spend considerable effort choosing an easy-to-remember domain name. With a domain name under mental lock and key, prospective clients can visit a vendor's web site to obtain all the information they need to make intelligent purchasing decisions. Rarely do people walk around with pens and notepads poised to record important web sites. Consequently, it's important for organizations to acquire easy-to-remember domain names. Because it is a challenge for most people to remember domain names, it's very unlikely you can expect them to remember the URL to your application's start page. We need to make it easy for people to find our application. In this recipe we show you how to default your application to a Struts `ActionForward`. You will be pleasantly surprised how easy this is!

◆ **Recipe**

Whenever a web server receives a request, it inspects the URL to determine the application. It then dissects the URL a bit further to discover the request page. For example, http://127.0.0.1/myapp/welcome.jsp instructs the web server to respond with welcome.jsp in the myapp application. As most J2EE application servers posses web server capabilities, we will refer to application servers instead of web servers throughout this recipe.

A nicer solution condenses the URL to http://127.0.0.1/myapp and has the application automatically default to welcome.jsp. Let's take things a step further. As good MVC students we want the application to default to an `ActionForward` rather than a JSP. This allows us to keep the physical file names encapsulated in the struts-config.xml file.

Let's see how this is done.

Listing 1.4   web.xml welcome-file-list tag

```
<welcome-file-list>
    <welcome-file>index.jsp</welcome-file>
</welcome-file-list>
```

In listing 1.4 we added the `<welcome-file-list>` node to our application's web.xml file, inserting it after the `<servlet-mapping>` closing tag and before the opening `<taglib>`. This tells our application server to respond with index.jsp whenever a page is not specified (listing 1.5).

Listing 1.5   index.jsp with sample forward

```
<%@ taglib uri="/tags/struts-logic" prefix="logic" %>
  <logic:redirect forward="welcome"/>
```

The next step is to transfer the user from index.jsp to an `ActionForward`. The `<logic:redirect>` tag is employed to redirect the response to the welcome global `ActionForward`. So, what's a redirect? In a nutshell, a redirect occurs when the server instructs the client to request a response from a different URL. All this happens behind the scenes without the user's knowledge.

Alternatively, you could use the `<logic:forward name="welcome"/>` tag instead of the `<logic:redirect forward="welcome"/>` tag to achieve the same result. The `<logic:redirect>` tag is only capable of redirecting the client to another URL. The `<logic:forward>` tag only redirects when the `<forward>` tag's redirect attribute is set to true; otherwise, it transfers control to the forward using the controller.

You may be asking yourself why we didn't direct the response to the `ActionForward` from the `<welcome-file>` tag in the web.xml file. The reason is that web.xml does not support the ability to direct to an `ActionForward`. It must specify a file name. Therefore `<welcome-file>` must direct the user to a JSP or HTML file, in this case index.jsp. The index.jsp is capable of redirecting the client to an `ActionForward`.

◆ *Discussion*

This recipe presents a technique to default an application to an `ActionForward`. The technique employs a two-part process. First, we modify the application's web.xml file `<welcome-file>` tag to default to index.jsp whenever a path is not specified. Second, we place a redirect in the index.jsp to redirect the client to the "welcome" global `ActionForward`.

A redirect is a mandated by the HTTP specification [HTTP]. When the client requests a page from the web server, the response is normally HTTP content. However, a redirect engineers the response to return instructions to the client requesting a page from a different location. The browser automatically requests a page using the URL provided in the response. Fortunately, Struts makes redirecting easier by providing a `<logic:redirect>` tag. Behind the scenes this tag is executing `HttpServletResponse.sendRedirect`.

To complete our knowledge we should cover the `<welcome-file>` tag in a little more depth [SERVSPEC]. Notice that `<welcome-file>` is wrapped in a `<welcome-file-list>` tag. Whenever multiple `<welcome-file>` tags are specified, the application server loops over the list of `<welcome-file>` tags from top to bottom looking for a match. The first one it finds is the one returned to the client. It is also important to note that these tags can be defined in both the server config/web.xml file and the application web.xml file. In the absence of this information from the application web.xml file, the server web.xml file presides.

Besides saving the user some typing and easing the burden on his or her memory a little, the real payback is in maintenance. We have kept the physical file name of the final page inside the struts-config.xml file. This allows us to ensure we have one point of maintenance for all physical file names for our application.

◆ **References**

- [HTTP] HTTP specification, redirect
- [SERVSPEC] Java Servlet Specification

1.3 What is "jsessionid" and why do I need it?

◆ **Problem**

You want to know why `jsessionid=` is appended to the link in the address bar.

◆ **Background**

To understand this behavior, we need to explore some of the basics of HTTP. HTTP is a "request-response" mechanism and has no "binding" features to track the session of the user. This must be done by using either cookies or URL rewriting. `jsessionid` is how the servlet container implements URL rewriting.

The original purpose of the Internet was to exchange information, mostly documents and encoded material. Shopping carts, web-based applications, and other more stateful programs for the thin client didn't exist and were far off on the horizon. As the Internet became public and people started dreaming about applications (especially those that generated an income stream!), it became obvious that there was a need to track the state of a connection to a specific user. With the Web being so wonderfully anonymous, tracking through the IP address is useless as there are so many proxy servers and most HTTP requests and responses go through these.

So jsessionid is born. When deemed necessary by the developer, a session is created between a specific user and the server. This session represents a series of contiguous requests and responses between them, and is passed through URL rewriting and/or cookies. While just browsing through pages or traversing across unprotected or public areas of an application may have no need for session tracking, it becomes vital whenever you must keep tabs on such variables as where the user has been, what you want them to do next, and so forth. Whenever you, as a developer, decide who the user is, what they are doing in your application, and what they've *done* in your application are important, it's time to establish a session.

The first time that a user enters an application there is no way for the servlet container to know whether or not a browser accepts cookies until the browser sends back a message. This first callout must be handled through URL rewriting. If a browser accepts session cookies then the servlet container automatically drops this URL rewriting method and the session is managed in cookies.

◆ *Recipe*

It is important to establish this pseudo-handshake between the browser and the server very early in the client's session. The struts-blank.war file gives us a clue in its implementation, but doesn't reveal all the details, so let's explore this now.

> **NOTE**   It's important to understand that a session is only one of four context "scopes" available in Struts—application, session, request, or page. It's also important to understand that session tracking is a "one-to-many" relationship between the server and the user(s); however, there may be *only one session per user* at a time.

If you point your browser to the struts-blank address (http://localhost:8080/struts-blank/), your servlet container immediately loads the index.jsp page, shown in listing 1.6, into the browser. This page is nothing more than an automatic forward to a welcome page, defined by the <global-forward> in your struts-config.xml file, automatically loading your session by generating a request to key, as shown in figure 1.1.

http://localhost:8080/struts-blank/Welcome.do;jsessionid=AAE3C934sSCF7FF893

Figure 1.1 Address bar for a typical first request from the Struts-blank application

Listing 1.6   index.jsp from "struts-blank" WAR file.

```
<%@ taglib uri="/tags/struts-logic" prefix="logic" %>
<logic:redirect forward="signin"/>

<%--

Redirect default requests to Welcome global ActionForward.
By using a redirect, the user-agent will change address to match the path of
   our Welcome ActionForward.

--%>
```

By the time that the actual welcome page is loaded, the server and browser are now "aware" of each other's ability to track the session, because the server and client have now created a handshake as described above.

◆ **Discussion**

Again, it is important to establish this relationship quickly if you wish to take advantage of the session when a user enters your Struts application. This ensures that issues involving URL rewriting, session tracking, and links are resolved.

The Struts tag library also takes advantage of URL rewriting. It takes care of all your URL rewriting and should be implemented in your JSP pages. Often new users make mistakes by using the `<a href>` HTML tag and then wonder why nothing can be retrieved from session. Then they might append the `<%=response.EncodeURL("myFooLink.jsp")%>` tag to their HTML links to correct this. Why bother? Struts provides many tags to facilitate this, such as `<html:link/>`, `<html:include/>`, and `<html:rewrite/>`.

Issues can arise from the user's standpoint if the page with the `jsessionid` appendage is bookmarked, as this key is unique and it changes every time a user goes to this page. To prevent this in Struts, the separation of the index page and welcome page is a good solution. An example of this is a simple HTML page that loads with no request to the server, but still fails under certain circumstances, especially if your application is in a protected domain and the first page that comes up is a login page. You must then make sure that any bookmarking is done around this page by creating nonprotected pages and public areas in your domain.

If you as a developer are expecting that bookmarking may occur, it is important to develop a strategy to work through this, handling the handshake at appropriate times and in ways that suit your application's needs. This can only be discovered through carefully walking through the expected path that the user may take through your particular application and establishing this handshake at the time and place of your choosing.

◆ **Related**

■ 7.1—Tomcat domain authentication and Struts

1.4 *Using modules for large projects*

◆ **Problem**

You want to use multiple Struts configuration files to manage many modules that are being coded in parallel.

◆ **Background**

There are times when a job is not a one-person job, and there are times when a job isn't a one-*team* job. Often large projects have many developers working in parallel and integrating their pieces into a large application. Problems can crop up when integrating files, especially if it is difficult just managing who's doing what, when, and where! Anyone who has merged from a source control system such as CVS and had conflicts has had the experience of nearly yanking all their hair out when confronted with a single file or application full of code that won't compile, run, or even worse, make any sense whatsoever.

The struts-config.xml file is a classic example of this. Before Struts 1.1 only one struts-config file was allowed per deployed WAR file or application. This created significant problems on large projects because teams would "fight over turf" as the project expanded and demand for access to the struts-config file increased. Different members of a large team working in different parts of an application would concurrently try to gain access to the configuration file. Figure 1.2 shows the relationship between the default struts-config.xml file and the module configurations.

During the early development stages, there might be times when the default struts-config.xml file gets passed around too fast and the whole thing gets out of sync, creating issues with namespaces, disappearing code during merges, and large chunks of time lost during development cycles.

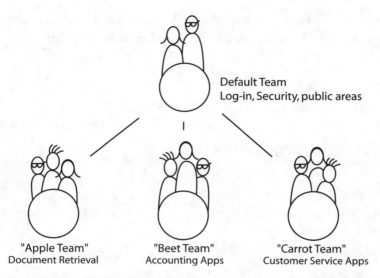

Figure 1.2 A scenario showing the relationship between "default" Struts configuration files and modules in a team environment

BEST PRACTICE	*Identify interfaces when creating modules*—It's important to think through a project and be clear on your design with the team or teams involved. Things are going to change, and when they do, it's going to be vital to have good communication between team members. Often projects may start out with multiple directories and modules with different prefixes, but as the application congeals, you may want to roll them into one root directory and drop the prefix altogether. Then again, the opposite frequently occurs as well! Having good divisions between teams is important—but having good places to shake hands is just as important as making sure applications are isolated and loosely coupled.

Wouldn't it be nice if we could "break these pieces up" into separate, more manageable components? Well, *yes!* Multiple struts-config.xml files allow the development group to create independently of each other, without the worry of stepping on one another's toes. With the maturing and extending of Struts, this issue is effectively put to rest by the introduction of support for multiple struts-config.xml, files for the creation of development modules. Now teams can update their own modules and manage changes in an effective manner.

In listing 1.7 the Default team owns the master configuration file, handling login and security to the entire application, along with any pages that may have public access. In addition, this team is responsible for any global variables, forwards, parameters, actions, and so on. The three subordinate teams concentrate on their specific applications, with the complete ability to create their own directories, actions, JSPs, and so on, with only scant regard as to what the other subordinate teams are doing. (It is important to make sure that package names and directories are clearly delineated across teams. You may or may not wish to share resources, models, or information across modules.)

To create modules, all you have to do is identify the subdirectories you wish to segregate, create configuration files that reference them, and alter your web.xml file. There are a few rules that must be followed after this happens, and we'll go through them below.

BEST PRACTICE   *Use multiple resource files*—Using multiple struts-config files also allow the opportunity for using multiple application resource files (you may also use multiple resource files without multiple modules), tiles definition files, validations, and so on. This further separates your projects if you wish to use them, but they are not required, and often add too many layers of indirection. This can affect maintainability of a site in the future. We will discuss multiple resource files later in this chapter.

◆ *Recipe*

Suppose you are creating an application similar to the one below with three subdirectories: apple, beet, and carrot (figure 1.3). We'll postulate that these three subdirectories are all complete projects in their own right, and consequently it is useful to segregate them into different modules by creating their own configuration files and managing them separately. Because there is a project root directory, these files may need to have

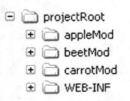

Figure 1.3 An application directory with three modules

some global configurations (also accessible to the modules we are creating). To satisfy this we will have a master, or default, struts-config.xml file.

We must first register the configuration files we intend to use, along with their directories, in the web.xml file in our /WEB-INF/ directory. Let's start by creating the configurations for our modules in this WEB-INF folder. For purposes of clarity, we'll name these struts-config-appleMod.xml, struts-config-beetMod.xml, and struts-config-carrotMod.xml (or whatever you may have named your directories). Save these XML files in the folder and close them.

BEST PRACTICE   *Validate your XML*—It really helps to have a program that validates your XML against its definitions, as well as one that keeps your code formatted. In the long run this helps you create an application in which you can find the information you want to edit or understand with greater ease. There are many commercial and shareware applications available, such as XMLSpy, oXygen, or Peter's XML Editor, to name a few. These tools prevent you from having to track down any small syntactical or ordering errors that can take hours to find otherwise.

Open the web.xml file and find the Struts `ActionServlet` configuration. Add your configuration files' descriptions in the manner of the code snippet in listing 1.7.

Listing 1.7 `web.xml`

```xml
<!-- Standard Action Servlet Configuration (with debugging) -->
<servlet>
<servlet-name>action</servlet-name>
    <servlet-class>org.apache.struts.action.ActionServlet</servlet-class>
<!--default configuration -->
    <init-param>
        <param-name>config</param-name>
        <param-value>/WEB-INF/struts-config.xml</param-value>
    </init-param>
<!--appleMod configuration -->
    <init-param>
        <param-name>config/appleMod</param-name>
        <param-value>/WEB-INF/struts-config-appleMod.xml</param-value>
    </init-param>
<!--beetMod configuration -->
    <init-param>
        <param-name>config/beetMod</param-name>
        <param-value>/WEB-INF/struts-config-beetMod.xml</param-value>
    </init-param>
<!--carrotMod configuration -->
    <init-param>
        <param-name>config/carrotMod</param-name>
        <param-value>/WEB-INF/struts-config-carrotMod.xml</param-value>
    </init-param>
    <init-param>
        <param-name>debug</param-name>
        <param-value>2</param-value>
    </init-param>
    <init-param>
        <param-name>detail</param-name>
        <param-value>2</param-value>
    </init-param>
        <load-on-startup>2</load-on-startup>
 </servlet>
```

The above configuration allows the developer or development team to separate their code into manageable structures and encapsulate applications where appropriate. Upon loading, Struts looks for the default configuration first, then any others with the parameter name of config/{*module name*} in the init file. It then is directed to the proper file in the <param-value/> node of the web.xml file. This structure follows itself through into the actual code to switch between applications and implementations, as is discussed next.

◆ *Discussion*

Once you've registered your new files in the web.xml of your application you may start referring to these struts-config-{*module prefix name*}.xml files. Once you are working inside a particular file and in the corresponding directory, you can treat them as if they are in their own root. Switching between these files and referring back up to the global configuration is easy. Here are some guidelines you need to follow:

- When referring to modules outside of their specific configurations (i.e., outside of *their* module context), it is important to note that their module prefix names are required.

- Under the module's root, you may refer to your actions as /foo.do, bar.do, and so on.

Outside of the module, you must refer to your actions as /appleMod/foo.do, /carrotMod/bar.do, and so on.

- If you change the names of your modules you must also change the prefixes.

To invoke Actions in other modules, the SwitchAction must be substituted for the ForwardAction, or you can refer to the new modules in <global-forwards> with /appleMod/foo.do as your URI and the contextRelative attribute set to true. You may also navigate to another module with the <forward> mapping in an Action, again with the /appleMod/foo.do module reference and the true setting for the "contextRelative" attribute. Here are some examples of SwitchAction, global-forward, and action-mapping switches.

SwitchAction module switch

```
<action-mappings>
...
<action path="
/MoveToApple" type="org.apache.struts.actions.SwitchAction"/>
...
  </action-mappings>
```

The JSP reference looks like:

```
<html:link page ="/MoveToApple.do?prefix=appleMod&page=foo.do"/>
```

Global-forward module switch

```
<struts-config>
...
<global-forwards>
<forward name="moveToApple" path="/appleMod/foo.do"
        contextRelative="true" />
</global-forwards>
...
</struts-config>
```

Action-mapping module switch

```
<action path="/MoveToApple" type="com.foo.bar.BlahBlahAction" ...>
    <forward name="success" path="/appleMod/foo.do"
  contextRelative="true"/>
</action>
...
```

All requests must pass through the Struts controller. Failures can occur when you link directly to resources in other modules or use hard-coded links.

It is also important that all your developers that "touch" the configuration files have a certain understanding of what is happening. Mistakes in the areas of Actions, Forms, controllers, and plug-ins can be common if everyone doesn't know what is going on. To prevent this, it is important to make sure that developers know which module they are working with, and if possible, restrict access to these files and enforce good check-in procedures.

Support and documentation for modules with third-party Struts tools may or may not be available or well documented so it is wise to make sure that the tools you plan to use and implement can be enabled within modules, or you may have to work with these products in the main struts-config.xml file only.

◆ **Related**

- 1.1—Use Ant to automatically build a Struts project
- 1.6—Multiple message-resources in an application
- 3.13—Using Tiles with XML definitions
- 9.4—Testing Modules

1.5 Specifying a resource property file in a configuration

◆ **Problem**

You want to use multiple message files to manage `Strings` and references in your application.

◆ **Background**

Large projects with multiple sub-applications and separate development groups create modules within the overall Struts application to segregate development into parallel paths. Best practices dictate that text `Strings`, messages, and formatting should be moved off the viewed page and referenced dynamically to allow for maintenance and internationalization without making changes to code. An appliance for storing these `Strings` is provided by Struts through `Property-MessageResources` and an `application.properties` file (similar to a Java `Resource-Bundle`). The default location of this property file is in the WEB-INF/classes/resources folder. In the first Struts releases, the pointer to this folder was located in the web.xml file, but with the release of Struts 1.1+, this mapping is now located in the `<message-resources>` tag in the struts-config.xml file. Another benefit of this move is the ability to name multiple resource files (explained in the next recipe).

◆ **Recipe**

Suppose we have a message file, bottledMessages.properties, that we want to use as the file to contain our messages. This file is located in the resources folder, identical to the original application.properties file that came with the struts-blank.war file. The default struts-config.xml file included in this WAR file includes this code in listing 1.8:

> **Listing 1.8   struts-config.xml for a default message-resources listing**

```
...
<!-- Message Resources Definitions -->
<message-resources parameter="resources.application"/>
```

This node is located between the `<controller>` and `<plug-in>` nodes. You will notice that the value of the parameter attribute is `resources.application`. It points to a properties file, application.properties—located in the resources folder.

You may change the name of the resources folder as you wish, dot-delimiting it to the name of the properties file, named concurrently. If you wish to name a new directory structure for your resource bundles as `/props/bundles/text/` and a new properties file in this directory `bottledMessages.properties`, the following configuration results:

```
...
<!-- Message Resources Definitions -->
<message-resources parameter="props.bundles.text.bottledMessages"/>
```

The message files should always be suffixed with "properties."

◆ *Discussion*

With multiple struts-config.xml files (modules) you may use as many resource files as you wish, and to internationalize these files all you need to do is add the proper internationalization and localization suffixes to the name of the file (explained further in Chapter 8).

There is a caveat when implementing modules. Except for a default bundle, you need to specify the directory of your module's root folder in the `key` attribute of your `<message-resources/>` tag in the pertinent module XML configuration file, as shown in listing 1.9. Even though a default resource bundle may be used with no "key" attribute, you may want to name a default bundle with a key for future reference depending upon your development needs.

Listing 1.9   struts-config-modFoo.xml

```
...
<message-resources parameter="resources.modFoo" key="FOO"/>
```

Used on the JSP page in a `<bean:message/>` tag in the modFoo module directory as:

```
...
<bean:message key="this.whatev.string" bundle="FOO/modFoo"/>
```

◆ *Related*

- 1.4—Using modules for large projects
- 1.6—Multiple message-resources in an application
- 9.4—Testing modules

1.6 *Multiple message-resources in an application*

◆ *Problem*

You want to control and implement multiple message resources files in an application or module.

◆ *Background*

Large projects often have several modules and sub-applications that can in their own right be quite extensive. When scaling these projects it may become necessary to create and maintain multiple message-resource properties files configured by the same struts-config.xml file. This is easily accomplished by modifying and extending this module's `<message-resources>` node with the new file name(s) you wish to implement and assigning a `key` attribute to them so they can be picked up with the `<bean:message/>` JSP tag's `bundle` attribute. If no key is named then Struts ignores all but the last named resource file in the list.

◆ *Recipe*

We'll be creating three message-resource property file bundles in the WEB-INF/classes/resources directory, naming them globals.properties, buttons.properties, and data-info.properties. These three files respectively handle global strings, button labels, and database messages. To implement these three files in your application, open the struts-config.xml file and locate the `<message-resources>` tag (if no node exists, place your tags just after the `<controller>` node, or see the struts-blank.war default configurations for reference).

Modifications made to the file follow:

Listing 1.10   struts-config.xml

```
...
</action>
<controller processorClass="org.apache.struts.tiles.TilesRe…../>
<!-- configuring for multiple resource files -->
<!-- default resource -->
<message-resources parameter="resources.globals"/>
<!-- button labels -->
<message-resources parameter="resources.buttons" key="buttons"/>
<!--database messages-->
<message-resources parameter="resources.data-info" key="info"/>

<!-- plug-ins -->
...
```

To use the special messages on the JSP page, the `<bean:message/>` tag should look like this for the default resource:

```
<bean:message key="normal.message.key"/>
```

For specific or secondary resource files:

```
<bean:message key="submit.label.key" bundle="buttons"/>
```

This second message prints the string from the buttons.properties file equal to the `submit.label.key` attribute name. All of the property files reside in your WEB-INF/classes/resources/ directory, unless you specify a different class path in the `<message-resources/>` tag of the XML configuration file, explained further in the previous recipe.

◆ **Discussion**

This is pretty straightforward. The only pitfalls to watch out for are the directory name, the bundle names, and making sure that the files are built correctly if you're using Ant (you can often forget to add them to the Ant build.xml file).

> **BEST PRACTICE** *Do not use wild cards in Ant scripts* —When building with Ant, it is important to specify individual files whenever practical. Including unexpected files may cost you many hours in debugging. Though this may seem laborious and tedious, it pays dividends in maintainability.

It is also important to make sure that you have placed the `<message-resources>` tag in the correct order with respect to the other XML nodes in the struts-config.xml file. The previous recipe "Multiple message resources in an application," explains this in detail.

◆ **Related**

- 1.4—Using modules for large projects
- 1.5—Specifying a resource property file in a configuration
- 9.4—Testing modules

1.7 *Using the bundle attribute in Struts' custom tags*

◆ **Problem**

You have a problem connecting multiple bundles and multiple modules in your application.

◆ *Background*

The first few times you migrate to multiple application resource files, and/or into Struts modules with multiple struts-config.xml *and* multiple application resource files, problems reading the various resource bundles may occur. It is important to make sure that these files point to the right place. This is a common problem when you're new to Struts and are beginning to explore some of the finer points and expand your programming horizons with the framework.

Struts provides many tags that render `Strings` from these property files in specified attributes or in their bodies proper. If you need to internationalize these elements and manage them away from your code (and prevent small mistakes from becoming huge page errors, or provide a single location to manage `Strings`), you are most likely going to use Struts' features for this. As your applications increase in size and scope, it will become apparent that one resource file isn't going to be a scalable solution, and you may want to "split up the duties" of your resources into very logical, multiple parts. When this occurs, as you test your pages, you'll find that some throw errors and others may be rendered with odd information such as:

    ???some.foo.propertyString???

This error translates into our pages not being able to find the proper resource bundle. If you have more than one configuration file and/or more than one properties resource bundle, then the likely culprit is the `key` attribute in the configuration to which the JSP page is registered.

◆ *Recipe*

In a simple application, you may have specified custom or multiple resource bundles in your struts-config.xml:

Listing 1.11 struts-config. xml showing multiple message-resources entries

```
<?xml version="1.0" encoding="ISO-8859-1"?>
<!DOCTYPE …
<struts-config>
  <form-beans>
    ...
  </form-beans>

  <global-forwards>
    ...
  </global-forwards>
  <action-mappings>
```

```
    ...
    </action-mappings>
<plug-in>
    <controller …/>
    <!-- Message Resources Definitions -->
    <!-- default resource -->
    <message-resources parameter="resources.globals"/>
    <!-- button labels -->
    <message-resources parameter="resources.buttons" key="buttons"/>
    <!--image keys-->
    <message-resources parameter="resources.images" key="images"/>
</plug-in>

</struts-config>
```

You've now defined three separate resource files to handle different items; a default file to handle most of the message and key properties, a button file to handle button labels (you've been a good developer and added comments), and finally an image file to handle your image paths. There are many Struts tags that can utilize these resource bundles by using srcKey and bundle attributes:

```
<bean:message/>
<bean:write/>
<html:img/>
<html:image/>
<html:messages/>
<html:option/>
<html:errors/>
```

In this simple case, the bundle attribute is used as follows. If you want to use the simple default resource, try this:

```
<html:messages key="some.foo.key"/>
```

If, on the other hand, you want to use the buttons resource bundle, you must set the bundle attribute:

```
<bean:message key="some.foo.key" bundle="buttons"/>
```

Finally, we can add a srcKey to a Struts image tag:

```
<html:img srcKey="some.image.foo" altKey="alt.foo.name" bundle="images"/>
```

Any string that refers to a key attribute in a property file must now refer to the particular file specified by the corresponding bundle attribute in the JSP page, matching the key attribute in your Struts XML configuration file.

◆ *Discussion*

This is a very simple recipe, yet many times this simple step is overlooked or left out until it's too late. It is important to note that when you are using Struts modules, it is a best practice to make a slight modification to your `<message-resources>` tag in the corresponding configuration, and mandatory to access this property file by appending the module directory name in the `bundle` attribute of your JSPs.

Let's take, for example, a Struts module named `Accounting`, with a configuration file named struts-accounting-config.xml (for more information on modules consult the specific recipe). In the config file we have specified a resource file:

```
<message-resources parameter="resources.accounting" key="ACCOUNTING"/>
```

Notice we have set the key to all caps. Let's also say that the module directories' name is "accts," located as a child of the root. When accessing the messages through a Struts' JSP tag, you must use the following code:

```
<bean:message key="some.accounting.resource.key" bundle="ACCOUNTING/accts"/>
```

Note that the key *and* the module name must be used to access the proper bundle. The reason for this best practice is clear at this point. It is often confusing as to "which is which;" the bundle name and the directory can often get switched around causing delays and wasting development time. By capitalizing the value of the `key` attribute, you can easily delineate what goes where, and can also look at this code months later and remember everything you need to know about this specific string reference.

BEST PRACTICE   *Set `<message-resources/>` null attribute to `true` in production, and `false` in development*—The message-resources node in the struts-config.xml file has a null parameter that may be used for development purposes. When set to true (the default setting), a JspException is thrown if a referenced property key isn't found. When set to false, the page is still rendered, but where the unknown key is displayed you have:

???some.foo.propertyString???

Set the `null` property to `false` during development and to `true` for production, with a user friendly error page to deal with the exception.

◆ *Related*

- 1.4—Using modules for large projects
- 1.5—Specifying a resource property file in a configuration
- 1.6—Multiple message-resources in an application

1.8 *Manage constants throughout your application*

◆ *Problem*

You want to use constants correctly to make your application maintainable.

◆ *Background*

Imagine that you've just walked into a legacy application where your predecessors have used session-level variables to manage information across the forms and pages of the application that you must now maintain and scale. You discover in the Java code that whenever a variable was inserted into the session, the coder just wrote:

```
session.setAttribute("aString", "thisVariableName");
```

And now you have to find out *what* this variable does, *who* uses it, and *where* it is picked up within the rest of the application. Without some kind of registry you have to go through lines and lines of Java and JSP code to make heads or tails of what is going on. Even if documentation exists, there is very little you can do if you need to manage these variables and, heaven forbid, actually modify them!

◆ *Recipe*

Enter the Constants.java file. This file is a simple "registry" or holder of variables, be they session, parameter, or whatever. Let's take a basic Constants.java file and modify it and show the code that accesses it from the rest of the application. A simple Constants.java file with a single constant to manage it would look like listing 1.12:

Listing 1.12   Constants.java

```
package com.foobiedoo.thisapplication;

/** Manifest constants for an example application. */
public final class Constants {
/**
* The session scope attribute,User object, for the currently logged in user.
/
public static final String USER_KEY = "user";
/**
* The session scope attribute, Role object. for the currently logged in user.
*/
public static final String ROLE_KEY = "role";
}
```

The preceding code has two variables, user and role, that are now controlled by the application and can be managed effectively. Let's say that these parameters are to be controlled by the session, and we need to manipulate these from either the Java code or the JSP page. We'll do the Java code first.

In an Action class or within a bean that has access to the HttpRequest, import the Constants file if it is not within the current package so that you may access its name/value pairs.

To set Strings into Session use the same format as listing 1.13:

Listing 1.13   FooAction.java

```java
package com.foobiedoo.thisapplication;
import ...

public final class FooAction extends Action {

    public ActionForward execute (ActionMapping mapping, ActionForm form,
                                  HttpServletRequest request,
                                  HttpServletResponse response)
        throws IOException, ServletException, Exception {

//HttpRequest request is available in the
HttpSession session = request.getSession();
...

// -- to get User info from session. Any string stored under //
   Constants.USER_KEY or Constants.ROLE_KEY will be retrieved.

String aUser;
aUser = (String)session.getAttribute(Constants.USER_KEY);

//"aUser" now has the value of (Constants.USER_KEY);

aUserRole = (String)session.getAttribute(Constants."ROLE_KEY);

//"aUserRole" now has the value of (Constants.ROLE_KEY);

...

//To set user information into session we would use:

...
aUser = "The New Guy";
session.setAttribute(Constants.USER_KEY,aUser);
...
```

That's pretty much it for the Java side of things. Now let's take a look at the JSP. To access the user variable in the JSP write:

```
<bean:write id="user" scope="session/>
```

The scope attribute is optional; Struts searches through the various levels of scope to find user and returns it as soon as it is found. To set the user variable, use the <bean:define> tag:

```
<bean:define id="userOnPage" name="user" value="The New Guy" scope=
   "session"/>
```

It is crucial that every member of your coding team adhere to the use of a Constants file to keep your application scalable and maintainable over the long haul. All strings crossing from the controller to the JSP layer should be defined as static finals. The JSPs should use these strings defined in a Constants.java (or name of your choosing, of course) file, and the Java code should refer to your constants directly from this class. There is no real performance penalty for doing this, and when your application reaches a serious level of complication, you'll appreciate the groundwork laid out in the beginning.

◆ *Discussion*

We are treading on thin ice here, possibly violating some encapsulation and Model-View-Controller architectural boundaries, especially when it comes to the JSP side of things. The Constants class is by far the best way for a team to manage variables across an application, but rules need to be created for their use and agreed to by all those involved, as values that are not registered in the Constants file that may pop up unexpectedly can wreak havoc when this application needs long-term maintenance, as many developers could possibly spend hours digging through code trying to find a connection between a JSP's mapped value and its connection with the controller and model layers.

You have two means at your disposal to declare constants. You can either declare them in an Interface, or you can declare them in a Class. Using an Interface to store constants has a few disadvantages. First, Interfaces define types. Interfaces are used to mask an implementation. Constants are storing a value, not masking an implementation. Secondly, any subclass of a class implementing an Interface automatically inherits the Interface's constant variables. This may not be your intention. The visibility of your constants should be restricted to only those classes that need them [BLOCH].

BEST PRACTICE *Prefer classes over interfaces to store constants*—Classes are preferable to interfaces when declaring constants. When used in this way, interfaces are often incorrectly identified as a type. Moreover, you may unknowingly expose constants to subclasses of any class implementing a "constant interface." Interfaces are a "contract" between the developer and the future. If your constants are defined in Interfaces, you may face serious problems with scalability and version compatibility. Inadvertent exposure of information compromises your application orthogonally.

Even with our constants being registered across the application, it is important for the team to know when and how these variables are populated and used. If these variables can be populated from both the JSP and Java Code, then the Java and JSP coders need to know intimately about what each group is doing, which violates MVC2 rules. Perhaps a best practice is to enforce certain rules and naming conventions at the very least. At most, only a "back-to-front" scheme for variables can be used, whereby variables are only created and named in the Action classes in the Struts code.

With all the variables "controlled" in the same regions, it is possible to continue developing and extending a site almost indefinitely.

◆ *Related*

■ 1.1—Use Ant to automatically build a Struts project

1.9 Use *<html:base/>* for solid page references

◆ *Problem*

You need to create relative references that your browser can resolve.

◆ *Background*

When building complex, multipage web sites in HTML, it is common to use the `<base>` tag in each page to facilitate the construction of a tight directory structure. This `<base>` tag maintains the integrity of an application by specifically defining the common portion of every resource's URL. Struts also provides this tag with the needed enhancements to work within its framework:

```
<html:base/>
```

When this tag is implemented, it resolves all relative URLs on the page to the absolute path of the loaded document.

◆ *Recipe*

When using `<html:base/>`, at runtime, this tag inserts an HTML `<base>` element nested inside the `<head>` element with an `href` attribute pointing to the absolute location of the enclosing JSP page. This allows the developer to safely use relative references in all links, images, style sheets, JavaScript references, and so on.

This tag has no attributes, and must be inserted between the `<head></head>` elements on the page. Let's look at an example. If your JSP page's absolute location is http://localhost:8080/struts-test/myPage.jsp, and you add the `<html:base/>` tag into the document, it is rendered thusly:

```
<base href="http://localhost:8080/struts-test/myPage.jsp">
```

Any links you create on the page are appended and resolved to this URL. For instance, if you create a link to an image with the reference:

```
/struts-test/images/myImage.jpg
```

By appending the directory of the image, it matches your base directory. A browser resolves this to:

```
http://localhost:8080/struts-test/images/myImage.jpg
```

This locates the image and renders it on the page, provided that all the necessary "homework" has been done and the tags, locations, and implementations are correct.

◆ *Discussion*

So what? Why should I go to all this trouble if I already know where everything is and where I put it? Well, there are lots of reasons. First, it's a best-practice. The reason that it is a best practice is simple: you may not be the only person to ever work on this application; it may end up moving to a different server, URL, or, heaven forbid, another contractor!

Small sites may really not need the `<html:base/>` tag, but these small applications have a habit of getting bigger, and when they do, real trouble can result by not putting the tag in the right spot to begin with and using it correctly. `<html:base/>` also "plays well" with all the other Struts tags that need to resolve links and encode them. This tag specifically helps you to create the best, most solid, and portable link references available to a Struts developer.

Portability and scalability are watchwords for application developers. Hopefully you will be called upon to create complex applications where code that you've previously developed may be adapted. By having proper URL references and configurations, making this code fit into the grand scheme of things is a snap.

Think if you had a shopping cart application where all your URL references needed to be changed simply because your directory was appended to another's root, or the directory name had changed. It would take hours of testing and checking just to make sure that every reference is correct, when spending time carefully planning in advance means making changes to your XML configuration file alone! Now *that* is time well spent!

♦ *Related*

  ■ 1.10—Associating Cascading Style Sheets with Struts JSP pages
  ■ 3.1—Using <html:link/> to increase your application's maintainability
  ■ 3.2—Rendering images mapped from a properties file using "<html:img/>"
  ■ Chapter 4—Using Struts-Layout tags in your applications

1.10 Associating Cascading Style Sheets with Struts JSP pages

♦ *Problem*

You want a solid and portable method of associating style sheets with Struts JSP pages.

♦ *Background*

While designing an application it is very likely that you will end up with JSP and other application-related pages in different directories, and often the relative path associations can be obtuse and confusing to any CSS style sheets you may wish to associate with them. Fortunately, Struts has a method of linking your style sheets to the pages using the <global forward/> and <html:rewrite/> tags.

♦ *Recipe*

Let's first put our CSS style sheet somewhere. mystyle.css is located logically in a CSS directory under the root. At this point we need to globalize the link to the style sheet so that any page you wish to associate the file with can find it without having to resort to long path names and trying to figure out the relationship between the files.

In the struts-config.xml file, create a simple <global forward/> :

```
<forward name="myStyle" path="/myroot/css/mystyle.css"/>
```

On any JSP page you wish to associate this file with, use `<html:rewrite>`:

```
<link rel="stylesheet" type="text/css" href="<html:rewrite
   forward='myStyle'/>" />
```

The CSS page is now globally attached to your JSP page.

◆ Discussion

This is a very subtle but powerful tool. At this point you may wish to attach logic tags to this function to change the style sheet based upon the content of the page. To make this application portable and solid it is necessary to use the `<html:base/>` tag to guarantee relative references. You may also attach JavaScript pages with the same method, with the possibility of creating some very interesting and quite complex variations!

Another area where this recipe comes in handy is during the migration of existing applications to Struts. You can immediately achieve quite a bit of progress when you attach all your JavaScript and CSS references to global forwards, then bring them to your JSP pages using the above implementation. At a later time you may wish to skin your application using more complex systems such as those available in Struts-Layout (chapter 4), but often all you need is right here.

◆ Related

- 3.10—Using <html:rewrite/> to resolve URLs
- 4.5—Adding skins to your project with Struts-Layout

1.11 Implementing DynaActionForms

◆ Problem

You want to use `DynaActionForms` in your application.

◆ Background

`DynaActionForm` and `DynaValidatorForm` are two wonderful additions to the Struts 1.1+ developer's toolbox. They allow you to eliminate `ActionForms` and create simple XML form beans inside the struts-config.xml file. This addition allows your team to create and maintain nearly all their form beans in one place, reducing the chance for errors and easing the stress of changes, additions, and deletions at a later date. Further, with these form beans in a single location, it

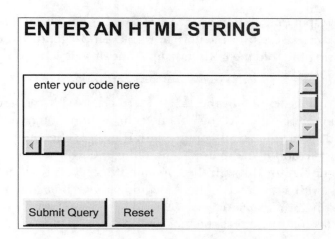

**Figure 1.4
Browser view of
form to convert
HTML Strings**

becomes easier to track the variables that are being used throughout your application. This recipe will show the creation of a very simple DynaActionForm and its associated Action class and the JSP used within the page.

◆ *Recipe*

We'll create a form, shown in figure 1.4, that takes the value of a string inserted into a text area and renders it in HTML with the HTML string pictured below it. It has one field, htmlString.

Let's start with the struts-config.xml file. This is the real "meat and potatoes" of the DynaActionForm, and defines the form properties used by the Struts controller servlet. In this DynaActionForm, we'll create a form with one text area that accepts a String. The DynaActionForm is named within the form beans node of the struts-config file (listing 1.14):

Listing 1.14   struts-config.xml

```xml
<form-beans>
    <!--DynaActionForm for testForm, variable name is "htmlString" -->
    <form-bean name="testForm" type="org.apache.struts.action.DynaActionForm">
        <form-property name="htmlString" type="java.lang.String"/>
    </form-bean>
    <!--more Form Beans added here…… -->
</form-beans>
```

Take a look at the corresponding Action class. A few changes have been made to accommodate the DynaActionForm over the normal form-bean. To get the variables into the Action class using the "old method," a sample line of code looks like:

```
String htmlStringOut = ((TestFooForm)form.getHtmlString();
```

with getHtmlString() being defined in the TestFooForm class. With DynaAction-Forms, this method cannot be called as such or the code will not compile. A few things must be added. First, the struts-config file must be in the compilation class path, which is easy to add if you're using Ant. Otherwise you need to add it to the class path of your IDE or through the command line. Next we'll need to modify the Action class with a different "getter" method, and we'll need to invoke this method by importing org.apache.commons.beanutils.PropertyUtils (which also must be in your class path). Here is the modified code:

Listing 1.15   TestFooAction.java

```
package com.strutsrecipes;

import org.apache.struts.action.*;
import org.apache.struts.action.DynaActionForm;
import org.apache.commons.beanutils.PropertyUtils;
import java.util.Locale;
import javax.servlet.ServletException;
import javax.servlet.http.HttpServletRequest;
import javax.servlet.http.HttpServletResponse;
import javax.servlet.http.HttpSession;

/**
 * Gets a string from a DynaActionForm and adds it to session
 */
public final class TestFooAction
        extends Action {

    public ActionForward execute(ActionMapping mapping, ActionForm form,
                            HttpServletRequest request,
                            HttpServletResponse response)
            throws ServletException,Exception {

...
    // This is where the work gets done,
      // extracting the info from the DynaActionForm!!!

    String htmlStringOut =
    (String)PropertyUtils.getSimpleProperty(form,"htmlString");

...
```

Finally the code within the JSP form:

```
<html:form action="/FormAction">
  <bean:message key="testForm.textareaLabel"/>
  <br/>
  <html:textarea property="htmlString" cols="50" rows="20"
                 titleKey="testForm.textareaTitle"/>
  <br/>
  <html:submit/><html:reset/>
/html:form>
```

◆ *Discussion*

It's very easy to migrate to DynaActionForms, although there can be a few pitfalls that must be addressed. Your Action classes must be changed to reflect the DynaActionForm, and the <html:form> tags must be checked and run to make sure that they do not throw any unexpected results. The DynaActionForms may be extended to populate forms and/or include Boolean, collections, and other non-String objects for more complex actions (these are explained in other recipes). DynaValidatorForms also allow for Validation to be scaled into your DynaAction-Forms (these too, will be discussed in Chapter 5).

If you have your application already developed and wish to move them to DynaActionForms, they cover almost all your needs and work with all Struts Actions except for the notable exception of the FileUpload (this *must* use a traditionally compiled Java FormBean Class).

◆ *Related*

- 2.9—Upload a file
- 5.3—Client-side validation with DynaValidatorForms
- 5.2—Server-side validation with DynaValidatorForms
- 7.1—Tomcat domain authentication and Struts

Forms and form elements

2

Although I can accept talking scarecrows, lions and great wizards of emerald cities, I find it hard to believe there is no paperwork involved when your house lands on a witch.

—Dave James

The Internet, web-based applications, and the paperless office are pretty much a de facto standard. While this environment is the one that we live in, the paper-work continues. Forms are a part of the life of anyone that visits the Internet. This "new" paperwork is a metamorphosis of the paper "forms" that you and your forebears filled out, often having to stuff your address inside a 2-inch line, filling in your first name in the "last name" blank, and then your neighbor ends up getting junk mail at his address with your name on it. The electronic age ful-fills the promise that this junk mail will now be addressed correctly, and of course, it probably won't be in your mail box but your email inbox—but they will have your name right!

The Internet user has become savvy. Those prechecked check boxes are immediately seen as potential junk-mail seeds growing a forest of empty offers of lower mortgage rates, cheaper pharmaceuticals, charitable pleas, and much worse. Forms often become long and unmanageable, just like their paper-based ancestors, but with the instantaneous nature of the Internet, a poorly designed form can result in a lost sale costing a company thousands of dollars.

This chapter is dedicated to the developer creating forms and attempting to make them easier to fill out. Its contents include:

- *Controlling messages*—From propagating a simple message to a page, to managing queues of messages and sending a form's error messages to spe-cific input fields

- *Creating a wizard*—Often a user needs to navigate through a multipage form. Such navigation back and forth needs to be controlled. Messages need to be created and persisted depending upon how the user goes through the form, and finally the information that you are collecting must be persisted and sent properly to the server. Each piece of the puzzle in its own right is a simple, basic task in Struts, but put them all together and the recipe can become quite complex.

- *Create alternating-colored rows in a dynamic table*—Large forms can have multi-ple inputs that are easier to read and disseminate when they have alternating colors. This recipe shows how to do this extending the `<logic:iterate/>` tag.

- *Managing uploads*—Uploads are a different beast, with the data transfer not the same as a normal form. This recipe details how to manage the upload-ing of different files and data using the Struts framework.

Validation is only briefly talked about in this chapter, and many of the recipes found here have direct correlations with those found in the chapters on tags,

Struts-layout tags, validation, internationalization, and advanced recipes. These recipes will definitely whet your appetite for more, but they can definitely stand on their own.

2.1 *Display errors and messages*

◆ *Problem*

You want to display error or text messages on your page.

◆ *Background*

Virtually every application needs to present dynamic messages on the page. The most common type of messages are error messages. Error messages report data entry errors to the user. However, errors are not the only type of messages presented to the user. You might want to provide a list of informational text messages. When you get right down to it, an error message is really nothing more than a specialized text message.

Displaying errors and text messages is one of the repetitive, mundane tasks the Struts framework can take off your plate. Without Struts' support, `Action` classes would need to make error messages available to JSPs by storing them in request attributes. Many developers have built successful applications using this tried-and-true technique, but there are drawbacks. Placing text into a request attribute makes internationalization a little more challenging. In addition, you would need to pepper your JSPs with little scriptlets. A better solution is to use the built-in Struts messaging feature designed to address this need.

In this recipe we present the `<html:errors>` and `<html:messages>` tags. We compare them, reveal their warts, and discuss when it makes sense to use them.

◆ *Recipe*

This recipe shows you three ways to use the Struts messaging feature. The first method delves into the use of the `<html:errors>` tag; our coverage of the second method shows you how to use the `<html:messages>` tag to achieve the same effect. Lastly, we show you how to use the `<html:messages>` tag for purposes other than errors.

The `<html:errors>` tag is the simplest way to present error messages. Only three steps are required to handle errors using the `<html:errors>` tag. First, you need to create and aggregate `ActionErrors` in your `Action`. Second, you need to create key-value pairs in one of the resource bundles loaded during startup.

Finally, you need to generate the text messages for your errors by placing an <html:errors/> tag on your JSP. Let's move through the process step by step.

Listing 2.1 Create `ActionErrors` in `Action`

```
ActionErrors errors = new ActionErrors();      ❷
errors.add(
      ActionErrors.GLOBAL_ERROR,
      new ActionError ("error.name.required"));      ❶

errors.add(
      ActionErrors.GLOBAL_ERROR,
      new ActionError("error.address.required"));

errors.add(
      ActionErrors.GLOBAL_ERROR,
      new ActionError ("error.phone.numeric"));

saveErrors(request, errors);      ❸
```

Each error is encapsulated in an `ActionError` ❶. The `ActionError` constructor takes a key ❶ defined to a resource bundle loaded during startup. The `Action-Errors` are aggregated into the `ActionErrors` collection ❷. The `ActionErrors` collection features the ability to segregate the errors by "property." You can think of "property" as a `Map` nested inside the `ActionErrors` collection. In listing 2.1, we use the `ActionErrors.GLOBAL_ERROR` global queue. We explore in more depth the use of queues and property in recipe 2.2, "Display errors next to a field" and recipe 2.4, "Display errors and messages in groups." For the purpose of this recipe we restrict our interest to the global queue. The logic to store the messages in the request under the `Globals.ERROR_KEY` is inherited from the `Action` class in the `saveErrors` method ❸.

Listing 2.2 Resource bundle properties file for `<html:errors>` tag

```
errors.header=You must correct the following error(s):<ul>
error.name.required=<li>Username is required</li>
error.phone.numeric=<li>Phone number must be numeric</li>
error.address.required=<li>Address is required</li>
errors.footer=</ul><hr>
```

In listing 2.2 we create a key-value pair for each `ActionError` created in listing 2.1.

Finally, place the `<html:errors/>` tag anywhere on the page you want the list of errors to be presented. The `<html:errors/>` tag iterates over the errors, in the order they were added to `ActionErrors`, writing the unescaped contents to the page. This means you need to add HTML to your properties file to achieve the look you want. Notice the `errors.header` and `errors.footer` keys. The `<html:errors>` tag automatically searches for these keys. If found, the list of errors is wrapped with the `errors.header` and `errors.footer` values.

The above approach is very simple to implement, but probably raises a few eyebrows. Many MVC purists object to mixing[1] HTML with data in properties files. The `<html:messages>` tag was added to Struts version 1.1 to subdue the voices of MVC purists. The `<message>` tag allows you to keep HTML where it belongs—in the JSP. Let's step through the same scenario, this time using the `<message>` tag.

First we create `ActionError` in the exact same manner as listing 2.1.

Listing 2.3   Resource bundle properties file for `<message>` tag to display errors

```
errors.header=You must correct the following error(s):
error.name.required=Username is required
error.phone.numeric=Phone number must be numeric
error.address.required=Address is required
```

Second, we create key-value pairs in a resource bundle loaded at startup. Listing 2.3 is identical to listing 2.2 except the HTML is removed from the value. Notice we removed the `errors.footer` tag since it did not contain text. The `errors.footer` is available should you have the need to present a footer.

Listing 2.4   JSP using `<html:messages>` to display errors

```
<logic:messagesPresent>           ❶
  <bean:message key="errors.header"/>    ❷
    <ul>    ❸
      <html:messages id="error">    ❹
        <li><bean:write name="error"/></li>    ❺
      </html:messages>
    </ul>    ❻
</logic:messagesPresent>
```

In listing 2.4 we show you how to use the `<bean:message>` tag.

---

[1] Mixing of data and HTML can be mitigated by using `errors.prefix` and `errors.suffix`.

❶ Verify the existence of error messages. By default, the `<logic:messagesPresent>` tag looks for error messages stored in the `Globals. ERROR_KEY` in the request.

❷ Use the `<bean:message>` tag to write the header. Alternatively, we could have placed the text directly into the JSP, but the `<bean:message>` tag allows us to easily internationalize the text.

❸ Open the unordered list. In contrast to the `<html:errors>` tag technique, we have removed the `<ul>` tag from the properties file and placed it into the JSP.

❹ Use the `<html:messages>` tag to iterate over the list of errors. By default, the `<html:messages>` tags looks for error messages stored in the `Globals.ERROR_KEY` in the request. The `id` attribute defines the name of the scripting variable used to expose the error message text.

❺ Use a `<bean:write>` to write the content of the bean created at **❹**.

❻ Close the unordered list. Once again, HTML has been removed from the properties file and placed in the JSP.

Let's step back and review what took place in listing 2.4. We use the `<logic: messagesPresent>` tag to verify the existence of messages. If there are no messages, then we shouldn't be generating a header. If messages exist, then we leverage the `<bean:message>` tag to generate the header text. The messages tag iterates over the collection of messages placed in the request by the `Action`. During each iteration, the messages tag exposes the message text to the JSP by creating a bean identified as `error`. The `<bean:write>` tag accesses the `error` bean to generate the content. In the background, the `Action saveErrors` method stores the collection of errors in request scope under `Action.ERROR_KEY`. By default the messages tag is hardwired to look for the errors collection in the request under that key.

So far, we have explored errors and messages in terms of errors. The `<bean:message>` tag can be used to present a list of messages outside the context of errors. In fact, you can use the `<bean:message>` tag to present both text messages and errors in the same response. In listing 2.5 we step through an example of text messages.

Listing 2.5 Create `ActionMessages` in `Action`

```
ActionMessages messages = new ActionMessages();
messages.add(
    ActionMessages.GLOBAL_MESSAGE,
    new ActionMessage("message.news.0"));
messages.add(
    ActionMessages.GLOBAL_MESSAGE,
    new ActionMessage("message.news.1"));
```

```
messages.add(
    ActionMessages.GLOBAL_MESSAGE,
    new ActionMessage("message.news.2"));

saveMessages(request, messages);
```

As illustrated in listing 2.5, creating `ActionMessages` closely resembles creating `ActionErrors` with a couple of notable differences. Instead of using an `Action-Error`, you use `ActionMessage`. Similarly, you use `ActionMessages` to aggregate messages instead of `ActionErrors`. Lastly, `saveMessages` is used instead of `saveErrors`.

Listing 2.6 Resource bundle properties file for `<message>` tag to display text messages

```
messages.header=Here are today's news items:
message.news.0=The doors will be closed at 6pm
message.news.1=Production will be down at 10pm
message.news.2=Development will be down at 8pm
```

Create key-value pairs in a resource bundle loaded at startup.

Listing 2.7 JSP using `<html:messages>` to display text messages

```
<logic:messagesPresent message="true">
  <bean:message key="messages.header"/>
    <ul>
      <html:messages message="true" id="msg">
        <li><bean:write name="msg"/></li>
      </html:messages>
    </ul>
</logic:messagesPresent>
```

Rendering messages on your JSP is identical to listing 2.4 except the messages tag uses the message attribute to indicate the messages should be retrieved from the `Action.MESSAGES_KEY` request attribute instead of the `Globals.ERROR_KEY` request attribute. In listing 2.7 we chose to use `msg` as the value for the message tag `id` attribute, but there is no special significance to that value.

◆ *Discussion*

The `<html:errors>` tag is the easiest way to deliver error messages to the user. Because of its early introduction into the Struts framework, it is the most well-known means to present error messages. Over the course of time, some Struts application developers have become disenchanted with the need to embed HTML inside of the text. Placing format instructions inside of the data values raises heated discussions among MVC purists. Dogmatic purity aside, it is clear that maintainability is reduced by this kind of practice.

Struts 1.1 introduced the `<html:messages>` tag to enable Struts developers to keep HTML on the JSP. Struts developers no longer need to maintain HTML in the properties files. It became apparent that errors were nothing more than a special kind of message. Under Struts 1.1 the errors were generalized as a generic messaging mechanism, leading to the introduction of the `<html:messages>` and `<logic:messagesPresent>` tags. This allows you to use `<html:messages>` for both errors and text messages. The inherent use of keys and properties files makes internationalization a snap.

In the recipe section we showed you how to use the `<bean:message>` tag to generate headers, and opened the door to using the same technique to generate footers. However, we purposely avoided discussing the use of the message tag `header` and `footer` attributes until this section. These attributes have a small wart. The header attribute triggers functionality within the messages tag to automatically generate text before iterating over the list. If you refer to listing 2.4 and listing 2.7 you notice the header is generated after the `<ul>` tag. To make everything look nice, you need the header to be before the `<ul>` tag. The same type of issue occurs with the footer attribute. One workaround is to place the `<ul>` tag in the header and the `</ul>` in the footer, but now you are back to mixing HTML with your data—one of the very issues the `<html:messages>` tag was designed to solve. It is best not to use the header and footer attributes on the messages tag.

BEST PRACTICE   *Avoid using the `<html:messages>` header and footer attributes*—The header and footer attributes place their text contents at the `<message>` tag prior to iterating over the list of messages. This precludes the opportunity to insert open list tags until after the header text has been rendered. Similarly, footer text is rendered prior to closing the list tag. Generating content in this way places compromises on the quality of the presentation.

Mixing order tags with the header and footer contents solves this problem, but at the expense of maintainability and portability.

So when do you use `<html:messages>` and when do you use `<html:errors>`? Here are a few guidelines. Use the `<error>` tag if you feel there is little chance you need to modify the format of the errors list. In addition, if you feel your application might use another HTML variant, such as WML, you should avoid using the `<html:errors>` tag. You could consider using `<html:errors>` for a small throwaway application or perhaps a proof of concept. Then again, it is not much more work to use `<html:messages>` instead of `<html:errors>`. `<html:messages>` tags should be used in all other circumstances.

BEST PRACTICE *Prefer `<html:messages>` to `<html:errors>`*—`<html:errors>` forces you to mix HTML with your text message. This reduces maintainability and portability to other XML-based presentation technologies.

◆ *Related*

- 2.2—Display errors next to a field
- 2.4—Display errors and messages in groups

2.2 *Display errors next to a field*

◆ *Problem*

You want to display errors next to a field.

◆ *Background*

An intuitive, easy-to-use user interface is the hallmark of a well-designed application. We recognize superior applications, but are sometime unable to express which characteristics make them that way. Just under the conscious level, our minds are processing the information on our computer screens. Poorly organized user interfaces cause us to work harder and make us less productive. A well-crafted user interface allows us to focus our mental energy upon the business task at hand. Using the application should be as effortless as possible. An intuitive user interface increases productivity by reducing the "hidden workload."

Placing error messages next to the field is one of the small ways we can reduce cognitive workload. Placing error messages in a list at the bottom of the page forces the user to interpret the error message, identify the associated input field, and locate the field on the page. Placing the error message next to the associated field eliminates these steps and contributes to the subjective feeling of a "good application."

In this recipe we show you how to use Struts message properties to place your error messages next to the associated input field.

MESSAGE QUEUES AND PROPERTIES Struts 1.0 offered just one predefined queue—the error queue. The error queue provided a means of collecting `ActionErrors` from the `Action`. The collection of errors are displayed on the JSP using an `<html:`

errors/> tag. In Struts 1.1 the concept of errors were generalized into messages, as errors are just one type of message. As you might expect, `ActionErrors` and `ActionMessages` are aggregated into either `Action-Errors` or `ActionMessages`. In addition to `ActionMessages`, Struts 1.1 offers an additional queue—the message queue. Although these two queues satisfy most needs, you are free to create your own queue.

Within a queue you can subdivide your errors and messages by associating them with a property. You can think of a "property" as a queue within a queue.

For more information on creating `ActionErrors` and `ActionMessages` see recipe 2.1, "Display errors and messages."

◆ *Recipe*

Struts offers two means of presenting property associated messages to the screen: `<html:errors>` and `<html:messages>`. For a refresher on these two features see recipe 2.1 "Display errors and messages."

Let's start by demonstrating how to place an `ActionError` on the name property.

Listing 2.8   Create `ActionErrors` in `Action`

```
ActionErrors errors = new ActionErrors();
errors.add("name", new ActionError ("error.name.required"));

saveErrors(request, errors);
```

In our `Action` we create, add, and store `ActionErrors` in the usual way. The only difference is that you specify the name property as the first argument to the `ActionErrors` add method (listing 2.8).

Listing 2.9   Resource bundle properties file for `<html:errors>` tag

```
error.name.required=Username is required
```

The resource bundle contains key-value pairings used to translate the error, header, and footer keys (listing 2.9).

Listing 2.10   JSP using `<html:errors>` to display errors on name property

```
name:<html:text property="name"/>
<html:errors property="name"/>
```

The `<html:errors>` tag is placed next to the `<html:text>` tag, as shown in listing 2.10. By convention, the `<html:text>` tag's `property` attribute value is the same as the `<html:text>` tag's `property` value—in this case `name`. The `<html:errors>` tag `property` attribute specifies the property name. It is a good practice to use the same values for both a tag's property attribute and queue name to highlight the relationship between the queue name and the field. The `<html:errors>` tag displays the resource bundle value mapping for all `ActionErrors` placed on the `name` property.

Listing 2.11   JSP using `<html:messages>` to display errors on `name` property

```
name:<html:text property="name"/>

<logic:messagesPresent>
      <ul>
        <html:messages id="error" property="name">
          <li><bean:write name="error"/></li>
        </html:messages>
      </ul>
</logic:messagesPresent>
```

The `<html:messages>` tag behaves in an analogous manner to the `<html:errors>` tag. Again, the only difference is that the `<html:messages>` tag `property` attribute specifies the property `name` (listing 2.11).

Next we show you how to associate `ActionMessages` with `property` and relate them to a field name.

Listing 2.12   Create `ActionMessages` in `Action`

```
ActionMessages messages = new ActionMessages();
messages.add("name", new ActionMessage ("error.name.required"));
saveMessages(request, messages);
```

In our `Action` we create, add, and store `ActionMessages` in the standard manner. The only difference is that you specify the property name as the first argument to the `ActionMessages` add method (listing 2.12).

Listing 2.13   Resource bundle properties file for `<html:errors>` tag

```
error.name.required=Username is required
```

In listing 2.13 we create key-value pairing for the message keys.

Listing 2.14 JSP using `<html:messages>` to display errors on `name` property

```
<logic:messagesPresent message="true">>
    <ul>
      <html:messages id="message" property="name" message="true">
        <li><bean:write name="message"/></li>
      </html:messages>
    </ul>
</logic:messagesPresent>
```

As shown in listing 2.14, `ActionMessages` are rendered in the normal way, with one small notable difference. The property `name` is specified in the `<html:message>` `property` attribute.

◆ *Discussion*

In this recipe we show you how to create and use message `property` to aggregate `ActionErrors` and `ActionMessages`. Placing your errors and messages next to field names is a simple and effective technique to enhance application usability.

> **BEST PRACTICE** *Use consistent naming when relating message properties to field names*—When relating properties to fields, the properties' names should be identical to the corresponding fields. This allows you to easily relate the two and ease the maintenance effort down the road.

◆ *Related*

- 2.1—Display errors and messages

2.3 *Create a custom message queue*

◆ *Problem*

You want to create a custom message queue to supplement the error and message queues.

◆ *Background*

Queues provide a means of logically grouping messages. Messages can be further subdivided within a queue by using a property. Most times the message queue, and its specialized cousin the error queue, are sufficient to meet your application needs. However, there are times when you might need the increased flexibility of additional queues. We invite you to consult the Related section at the end of this recipe for additional information on errors, messages queues, and message properties.

In this recipe we show you how to create a custom queue.

◆ *Recipe*

We start by showing you how to create a message and place it on the myqueue queue. With the message firmly placed on the custom queue, we show you how to display them using a JSP.

Listing 2.15   Create Messages on myqueue queue using GLOBAL_MESSAGE property in Action

```
ActionMessages messages = new ActionMessages();
messages.add(ActionMessages.GLOBAL_MESSAGE,
            new  ActionMessage ("message.update"));
saveMessages(request, messages, "myqueue");
```

In listing 2.15 we add a newly minted ActionMessage to the ActionMessages collection. In this example we use the ActionMessages.GLOBAL_MESSAGE property, but we could have decided to use any property. Notice we have overloaded the saveMessages message to take a third argument. The additional argument allows us to specify the name of our custom queue.

Listing 2.16   Save message on myqueue queue using the saveMessage method in Action

```
protected void saveMessages(
        HttpServletRequest request,
        ActionMessages messages,
        String queueName) {

        if ((messages == null) || messages.isEmpty()) {       ❶
            request.removeAttribute(queueName);
            return;
        }

        request.setAttribute(queueName, messages);            ❷
    }
```

In listing 2.16 we present the overloaded `saveMessage` method created in the `Action` and used in listing 2.15. The third argument allows us to specify a queue name of our own choosing.

❶ Delete the queue when the message reference is null or contains an empty list of messages. There is little reason to maintain a request attribute to a null or empty list of messages.

❷ Set an attribute in the request using the queue name as the attribute name.

Listing 2.17   Display message from the myqueue queue on the JSP

```
<logic:messagesPresent name="myqueue">     ❶
    <ul>
      <html:messages id="message" name="myqueue">      ❷
        <li><bean:write name="message"/></li>
      </html:messages>
    </ul>
</logic:messagesPresent>
```

In listing 2.17 we present an excerpt from a JSP showing how to present messages from a custom queue.

❶ Use a `<logic:messagesPresent>` tag specifying the name of the custom queue in the `name` attribute.

❷ Iterate over messages in the `myqueue` queue. Each message is exposed as the "message" scripting variable and written to the page using the `<brean:write>` tag.

◆ Discussion

The recipe section presented a straightforward way to place messages on a custom queue. We create an `ActionMessage` in the usual way, but overload the `saveMessages` method to save our messages to a custom queue. The queue is implemented by saving the collection of messages to a request attribute.

This recipe works and will serve you well, but there is always room for improvement. If you plan to frequently use custom queues you should consider creating a base `Action` class to hold the `saveMessages` logic. In addition, you might want greater control over message queue creation. This can be done by changing the third argument of `saveMessages` to a typesafe enumeration to enumerate custom message queue names. This allows you to restrict the creation of message queues to the enumeration and enforce compliance at compile time.

NOTE   *Typesafe Enumeration*—A typesafe enumeration is a design pattern in which a single class represents a single element of an enumerated type.

Typically, the class provides public static final types of itself to represent each element. Typesafe enumerations guarantee that a method argument belongs to a finite set by declaring the argument as a typesafe enumeration type [BLOCH].

For example:

```
public class Color {
    private final String name;
    private Color(String name) {
            this.name = name;
    }

    public getName() {
            return name;
    }

    public static final Color RED = new Color("red");
    public static final Color BLUE = new Color("blue");
    public static final Color GREEN = new Color("green");
}
```

A call to the `setColor(Color color)` method guarantees that the argument must be one of the three Color enumerations; `Color.RED`, `Color.BLUE` or `Color.GREEN`.

There is a "gotcha" to keep an eye on here. You need to be very careful when choosing a queue name. Because the queue name is used to create the request attribute, there is the chance you could choose the name of an existing request attribute. This would wipe out the previously set attribute, replacing it with a list of messages. Conversely, you may trump your message queue with a request attribute somewhere downstream. There are at least three possible mitigations to that risk. First, you can take special care to choose unique queue names. A good convention is to use a package name. Second, you can add logic in the `saveMessages` method to prefix the queue name with a unique name. Third, you can store all your custom message queues in a JavaBean dedicated to that purpose. The JavaBean would be placed in request context under a unique name. All three of these solutions require you to adjust the queue name on the `<logic:messagesPresent>` and `<html:messages>` tags to suit the unique queue name.

BEST PRACTICE *Choose unique queue names when creating custom queues*—Because the queue name is used to create the request attribute, there is the chance you might choose the name of an existing request attribute. This would overwrite the existing request attribute. Conversely, you might destroy your message queue by setting a request attribute while processing the request downstream. To minimize these problem you should take special care to choose unique queue names.

◆ **Related**

- 2.1—Display errors and messages
- 2.2—Display errors next to a field

◆ **Reference**

- [BLOCH] *Effective Java Programming Language Guide*; Item 21: Replace enum constructs with classes

2.4 Display errors and messages in groups

◆ **Problem**

You want to display errors and messages in groups.

◆ **Background**

Some pages present a generous supply of error messages to the user. This is often the case in a wizard application where the last page is responsible for cross-page validation. The user must inspect each and every message to plot a course to resolve them. Generally, many messages are related and should be dealt with together. However, a page presenting a large unorganized list of error messages burdens the user with the unpleasant challenge of sorting and collating errors. That's a job best left to computers!

In this recipe we show you how to use message property to categorize your errors and messages. Leveraging message "property," we present a technique to present your errors and message in logical groups on the page.

We suggest you read recipe 2.2, "Display errors next to a field" for background material on creating and using message "property."

◆ **Recipe**

We take the following steps to place messages and errors in groups:

1 Place errors or messages in message "property" to segregate them into logical groupings.

2 Add key-value pairs for errors or messages to a resource bundle loaded upon startup.

3 Iterate over the list of "property." At each iteration, all errors or messages associated with a "property" are output together as a group. Each iteration generates a header to clearly delineate the groups.

Let's try out this technique with errors.

Listing 2.18 Create `ActionErrors` in `Action` to group errors by "property"

```
ActionErrors errors = new ActionErrors();
errors.add("error.account",
  new ActionError("error.account.required"));
errors.add("error.account",
  new ActionError("error.account.pininvalid"));          ❶

errors.add("error.order",
  new ActionError("error.order.pastdue"));
errors.add("error.order",
  new ActionError("error.order.unauthorized"));          ❷

errors.add("error.delivery",
  new ActionError("error.delivery.surcharge"));
errors.add("error.delivery",
  new ActionError("error.delivery.modeunavailable"));    ❸
saveErrors(request, errors);
```

In listing 2.18 we create `ActionErrors` and add them to an `ActionErrors` collection. In listing 2.20 we add two errors to the `error.account` property ❶, another two errors to the `error.order` property ❷, and yet another two errors to the `error.delivery` property ❸. In listing 2.18 we fictitiously create errors without conditional business logic. In your application you would create errors based on your business rules.

Listing 2.19 Resource bundle properties file for `<html:errors>` tag

```
error.account=The following "account" errors have been found:
error.account.required=Account number must be entered
error.account.pininvalid=PIN number is invalid

error.order=The following "order" errors have been found:
error.order.pastdue=The order is past due
error.order.unauthorized=You are not authorized to order

error.delivery=The following "delivery" errors have been found:
error.delivery.surcharge=A surcharge must be applied
error.delivery.modeunavailable=Mode is not available
```

In listing 2.19 we create key-value pairs to map the error keys to text values. "error.account," "error.order," and "error.delivery" represent "property" names. Normally, key-value pairs are not required for "property" names, but we are going to use the "property" names to look up and output header text for all errors for a "property."

Listing 2.20   JSP technique to display groups of errors using `<html:errors>` tag

```
<bean:define id="errors"          ❶
   name="<%=org.apache.struts.Globals.ERROR_KEY%>"    ❷
   type="org.apache.struts.action.ActionErrors"/>    ←┐
                                                       ❸
 <logic:iterate id="property_name"
              collection="<%=errors.properties()%>">    ❹
  <p>
  <bean:message
    key="<%= (String) pageContext.getAttribute("property_name") %>"/>    ❺
  <html:errors
   property="<%= (String) pageContext.getAttribute("property_name") %>" />  ❻
 </logic:iterate>
```

In listing 2.20 we present a technique for outputting errors in groups. The technique is a 3-step process. First, we obtain the list of errors stored in context. Second, we obtain a list of "property" used in the list of errors. Third, for each "property" we output a header and a list of errors associated with the "property."

Let's step through listing 2.20 in detail to see exactly how this is done.

❶ Expose the collection of `ActionErrors` as a the `errors` scripting variable. The collection is stored as an `ActionErrors` type.

❷ Specify the key name used to locate the bean containing `ActionErrors` set by the `Action` class `saveErrors` method. The `saveErrors` method uses this constant to save the errors in scope.

❸ Specify the class type of the object retrieved at ❷.

❹ Iterate over a list of "property" names. The "property" names are obtained by invoking the `ActionErrors` properties method of the bean retrieved at ❶. The properties method returns an `Iterator`. Each element in the `Iterator` represents the "property" name and each "property" name is exposed as the "`property_name`" scripting variable.

❺ Use the "`property_name`" scripting variable as the key to look up the associated value in the resource bundle. The key's value acts as header text for the group of errors associated with the "property".

❻ Use the `<html:error>` tag to output all the errors for the "property" name.

```
<logic:iterate id="property_name"
            collection="<%=errors.properties()%>">          ❶
    <p>
  <bean:message
  key="<%= (String) pageContext.getAttribute("property_name") %>"/>   ❷
  <ul>
    <html:messages
         id="error_text"
  property="<%= (String) pageContext.getAttribute("property_name") %>">   ❸

      <li><bean:write name="error_text"/></li>   ❹
      </html:messages>
  </ul>
</logic:iterate>
```

Next, let's look at an equivalent technique for the <html:messages> tag. The same
3-step process demonstrated in listing 2.20 is applied in listing 2.21.

❶ Assume the list of errors have been exposed as the errors scripting variable and
obtain a list of "property" names in the same way demonstrated in listing 2.20.

❷ Use the "property" name to output header text for the messages associated with
the "property."

❸ Use <html:messages> to expose a list of errors for a "property." The errors were
saved in context by the Action saveErrors method. The text value of the error
key is exposed as the "error_text" scripting variable.

❹ Output the text message exposed at ❸.

Let's see how to do the same thing for ActionMessages.

```
ActionMessages messages = new ActionMessages();
messages.add("message.account", new
  ActionMessage("message.account.required"));
messages.add("message.account", new
  ActionMessage("message.account.pininvalid"));

messages.add("message.order", new ActionMessage("message.order.pastdue"));
messages.add("message.order", new
  ActionMessage("message.order.unauthorized"));

messages.add("message.delivery", new
  ActionMessage("message.delivery.surcharge"));
```

```
messages.add("message.delivery",
        new ActionMessage("message.delivery.modeunavailable"));

saveMessages(request, messages);
```

In listing 2.22 we create, aggregate, and store `ActionMessages` in the usual manner. In listing 2.22 we use three properties to segregate our messages; "`message.account`," "`message.order`," and "`message.delivery`."

Listing 2.23   Resource bundle properties file for `<html:message>` tag

```
message.account=The following "account" errors have been found:
message.account.required=Account number must be entered
message.account.pininvalid=PIN number is invalid

message.order=The following "order" errors have been found:
message.order.pastdue=The order is past due
message.order.unauthorized=You are not authorized to order

message.delivery=The following "delivery" errors have been found:
message.delivery.surcharge=A surcharge must be applied
message.delivery.modeunavailable=Mode is not available
```

In listing 2.23 we populate our resource bundle in the same manner as listing 2.19, except we changed the "property" names to match listing 2.22.

Listing 2.24   JSP technique to display groups of messages using `<html:messages>` tag

```
<bean:define id="messages"
            name="<%=org.apache.struts.Globals.MESSAGE_KEY%>"
            type="org.apache.struts.action.ActionMessages"/>

 <logic:iterate id="property_name"
               collection="<%=messages.properties()%>">
   <p><bean:message
      key="<%= (String) pageContext.getAttribute("property_name") %>"/>
   <ul>
     <html:messages id="message_text"
    property="<%= (String) pageContext.getAttribute("property_name") %>"
         message="true">
       <li><bean:write name="message_text"/></li>
     </html:messages>
   </ul>
 </logic:iterate>
```

In listing 2.24 we present the same 3-step process used in listing 2.20 and listing 2.21. In fact, listing 2.24 is functionality equivalent to listing 2.21. The only difference is that listing 2.21 obtains a list of errors found using the `org.apache.struts.Globals.ERROR_KEY` key, whereas listing 2.24 obtains a list of messages using `org.apache.struts.Globals.MESSAGE_KEY`. The `<html:messages>` tag message attribute value of `true` directs the tag to look for messages in context using the `org.apache.struts.Globals.MESSAGE_KEY` key instead of `org.apache.struts.Globals.ERROR_`.

◆ *Discussion*

In this recipe we show you how to use message "property" to organize messages. Struts message "property" features exist to pigeonhole messages. How you fill each hole is your business, but Struts provides the facility. Spending a little time planning your message classification strategy will lead to well-organized groups of messages.

Organizing messages is one way to make the application easy to use. Anything you can do to make an application more intuitive leads to greater user productivity and results in wider acceptance by your audience.

◆ *Related*

- 2.1—Display errors and messages
- 2.2—Display errors next to a field

2.5 *Dynamically insert data inside a message*

◆ *Problem*

You want to dynamically insert data inside a message.

◆ *Background*

Messages presenting static information serve a useful purpose, but applications often demand more. On occasion message content sometimes needs to contain information only available at runtime. For example, airline reservation transactions often provide a confirmation number only available after the transaction has been processed.

Experienced Java programmers recognize Java's inherent message-formatting capability as a solution to this problem. In fact, Struts leverages the `java.text.`

`MessageFormat` class to integrate parameter replacement and message formatting into the Struts messaging feature.

Before getting started, let's discuss replacement markers. Replacement markers are specially formatted text embedded in static text. At runtime the replacement markers are replaced with data. As there can be multiple replacement markers embedded in the text, the markers denote their ordinality. Let's look at an example of a message containing replacement markers.

> "Your reservation was recorded at the {0} location. Your confirmation number is {1}"

In this message we have two replacement markers. Each replacement marker is indicated with curly bracket pairs enclosing a number. The number represents the ordinality. An array of replacement parameters is used to replace the replacement markers. The array's order corresponds to the number enclosed between the curly brackets. The first element in the array replaces {0}, the second replaces {1}, and so on. This means you can rearrange the text without impacting the array of replacement parameters. The message example above may be changed without impacting the array of replacement parameters. Note that you can repeat the same replacement parameter in multiple places in the text.

> "Your confirmation number is {1}. Your reservation was recorded at the {0} location"

In this recipe we show you how to replace parameter markers. In addition, we show you how to format the replacement data to present neatly formatted dates, numbers, time, or custom formats. We present two techniques, contrast their strengths, and point out their weaknesses.

◆ Recipe

Struts provides two ways to replace parameter markers; the `<bean:message>` tag on the JSP, or the `ActionMessage` and `ActionError` classes in the `Action`.

Let's start with the `<bean:message>` tag.

Listing 2.25   Resource bundle containing message text

```
message.update.short=Your reservation was recorded at the {0} location.
Your confirmation number is {1}.
```

Listing 2.25 shows an entry in a resource bundle loaded at startup. Notice the message contains two replacement markers.

Listing 2.26 Use `<bean:message>` tag to output replacement parameters

```
<bean:define id="infobean"
      name="info"
      type="com.strutsrecipes.replacementparms.beans.InfoBean"/>        ❶

<bean:message key="message.update.short"        ❷
      arg0="<%=infobean.getLocation()%>"                ❸
      arg1="<%=infobean.getConfirmationNumber()%>"/>
```

In listing 2.26 we show you how to replace the replacement markers with data.

❶ The "info" JavaBean has been placed in scope and has been exposed as the "infobean" scripting variable.

❷ Declare the key used to look up the message text in the resource bundle.

❸ Use scriptlets to access bean properties to populate the message tag `arg0` and `arg1` attributes.

The page displays the following text

> "Your reservation was recorded at the **Downtown** location.
> Your confirmation number is **1234567**."

Let's take a look at using the `ActionMessage` technique to do the same job. Using this technique, the resource bundle entry remains the same, but an `Action-Message` object is used to store the message key and replacement parameters. The message is output to the page using the `<html:message>` tag in the usual way. Let's see how it is done.

Listing 2.27 `ActionMessage` with replacement parameters

```
ActionMessages messages = new ActionMessages();
ActionMessage am = new ActionMessage("message.update.short",
            bean.getLocation(),
            bean.getConfirmationNumber());
  messages.add(ActionMessages.GLOBAL_MESSAGE, am);
saveMessages(request, messages);
```

We illustrate this technique with `ActionMessage`, but the exact same technique can be applied to the `ActionError`. Listing 2.27 shows you how to create an `ActionMessage` using replacement parameters. An `ActionMessage` is placed on the global message queue in the usual way, with only one exception. The `Action-Message` constructor takes in two additional arguments. The trailing two arguments represent the replacement parameters. The order of replacement parameter arguments dictate the ordinality.

Listing 2.28 Use `<html:message>` tag to output message with replacement parameters

```
<logic:messagesPresent message="true">
    <ul>
      <html:messages id="message" message="true">
        <li><bean:write name="message"/></li>
      </html:messages>
    </ul>
</logic:messagesPresent>
```

In listing 2.28 messages are presented in the usual way. The JSP has no knowledge that replacement markers are being replaced.

The `ActionMessage` technique offers formatting not available to the `<bean:message>` technique. Let's explore how we can use this technique to format replacement parameters.

Listing 2.29 Resource bundle message using formatted replacement markers

```
message.update.long=Your reservation was recorded on {0, date, long} at the
{1} location. Total cost is {2, number, currency}. Your confirmation number
is {3}.
```

In listing 2.29 we added a few additional replacement parameters. The replacement parameters we have seen so far have been `String`. The new replacement parameters in listing 2.29 are objects. Specifically, {0} is a `Date` object and {2} is a `Float` object. The changed replacement parameters now have three arguments instead of one. The second argument defines the format type. The format type describes the type of object to be formatted. It must be one of the following: number, date, time, and choice. Each format type can optionally have a corresponding format style. The style represent a formatting pattern for the type. If the style is omitted, the date and time formats are defaulted to medium. Table 2.1 lists the valid format type and format style combinations.

Table 2.1 Replacement markers format type and style combinations. See java.text.ChoiceFormat javadoc for custom formats.

Format Type	Format Style	Example	Output
Number	integer	{0,number,integer}	12
	currency	{0,number,currency}	$12.34
	percent	{0,number,percent}	1,234%
	default	{0,number }	12.34
Date	short	{0,date,short}	9/24/03
	medium	{0,date,medium}	Sep 23, 2003
	long	{0,date,long}	September 23, 2003
	full	{0,date,full}	Tuesday, September 23, 2003
	default	{0,date }	Sep 23, 2003
Time	short	{0,time,short}	10:09 PM
	medium	{0,time,medium}	10:09:34 PM
	long	{0,time,long}	10:09:34 PM EDT
	full	{0,time,full}	10:09:34 PM EDT
	default	{0,time}	10:09:34 PM
Choice	Choice of sections of text which might contain replacement markers	See below	See below

Listing 2.30   Create an `ActionMessage` using object replacement parameters

```
//assume "ib" has been created
ActionMessages messages = new ActionMessages();
Date date = new Date(System.currentTimeMillis());
Float amount = new Float(50.23);
ActionMessage am = new ActionMessage("message.update.long",
                                     date,
                                     ib.getLocation(),
                                     amount,
                                     ib.getConfirmationNumber());
messages.add(ActionMessages.GLOBAL_MESSAGE, am);
saveMessages(request, messages);
```

In listing 2.30 we show you how to add `Object` replacement parameters to the `ActionMessage`. Notice we have added `Date` and `Float` object replacement parameters. The replacement data is added to the `ActionMessage`, but the formatting of the replacement parameters is delegated to the replacement markers. Let's look back at listing 2.29 to see how the replacement markers were used to generate the following output:

> "Your reservation was recorded on **September 23, 2003** at the **Downtown** location. Total cost is **$50.23**. Your confirmation number is **1234567**"

You can see from the output that the {0, date, long} replacement marker uses the Date object to render "September 23, 2003." By specifying a format type and style you have made short work of formatting a Date object and inserting it into message text. Similarly, {2, number, currency} formats a Float object as "$50.23." The hidden gem is that formatting is locale sensitive. This means that you can employ the Struts internationalization feature to automatically format replacement parameters to meet the needs of your locale without making a single code change to this recipe.

Let's complete our introduction to message formatting by looking at choice formats. Choice formats provide the ability to choose a section of text from a range of possible choices.

Listing 2.31   Resource bundle message using choice format replacement markers

```
message.status={0,choice,0#No purchase has|0<{0, number} purchases have}
been processed
```

Listing 2.31 presents a technique to modify the output based on the value of a replacement parameter. The replacement marker has three arguments, but the third argument looks much different than the ones we saw previously. The third argument can be broken down into multiple segments and each segment is delineated from the other by a pipe character (|). The portion of the segment preceding the # or < character is the "limit." If the "limit" is true, then the characters in the segment after the # or < character are produced as output.

In listing 2.31 we have two segments:

1 0#No purchase has

2 0<{0, number} purchases have}

The following logic statement serves to describe the evaluation process for choice formats. This statement has been rephrased from a similar statement found in the java.text.ChoiceFormat javadoc.

A parameter value matches a segment if and only if the limit of the segment is less than or equal to the parameter value, and the parameter value is less than the limit of the next segment. Often, the < is used in the last segment to denote that the parameter value must be greater than the limit of that segment.

Let's have a look at the replacement parameters stored in the `ActionMessage`.

Listing 2.32   `ActionMessages` used to demonstrate choice format

```
Integer count = new Integer(0);
am = new ActionMessage("message.status",count);
messages.add(ActionMessages.GLOBAL_MESSAGE, am);

count = new Integer(3);
am = new ActionMessage("message.status",count);
messages.add(ActionMessages.GLOBAL_MESSAGE, am);

saveMessages(request, messages);
```

In listing 2.32 we create messages using replacement parameters in the same fashion as listing 2.30. In listing 2.32 we create three messages to demonstrate the conditions required to display both segments.

Listing 2.33   JSP code used to output choice format

```
<logic:messagesPresent message="true">
   <ul>
     <html:messages id="message" message="true">
       <li><bean:write name="message"/></li>
     </html:messages>
   </ul>
</logic:messagesPresent>
```

In listing 2.33 we render our messages in the usual way. The results are as follows

1   No purchase has been processed
2   3 purchases have been processed

◆ *Discussion*

In this recipe we presented two techniques to replace parameters in message text. The first technique employs the <bean:message> tag by populating arg attributes from a JavaBean. This technique is appropriate when you need to consistently place a message on the page and you are prepared to place a JavaBean in context. Under these circumstances this technique can be useful, but there are drawbacks. First, unless you are willing to implement a scriptlet, the message key is static in the JSP. Second, you must be prepared to accept the maintenance effort to add additional `arg` attributes to the `<bean:message>` tag when new replacement parameters are required. Finally, you must take responsibility for your own formatting because the `arg` attribute can only accept `String`. That's a piece of coding we could do without!

The `ActionMessage` technique provides a richer alternative. Using `Action-Message` you can determine your message key at runtime. Additional replacement parameters can be introduced without a change to the JSP. Probably the greatest benefit to the `ActionMessage` technique is the integration of message formatting into the message feature.

In this recipe we give you a taste of formatting capabilities. Under the covers Struts is using the `java.text.MessageFormat` class. An explanation of formatting possibilities can be found in the `java.text.MessageFormat` javadoc. Using message formats and styles you can easily take advantage of several built-in localized formats for number, date, and time. We also took at a peek at choice formats. Choice formats allow you to use rudimentary Boolean logic to choose among a range of text segments. However, be careful of the "gotcha." The results are unpredictable when the replacement parameter array values are not in ascending order. Regardless, choice formats are a popular solution to handling plurals. This solution can easily be adapted to handle more complex plural situations such as the gender specific plurals of the French language.

◆ Related

- 2.1—Display errors and messages

◆ Reference

- [CFJD] ChoiceFormat javadoc
- [MFJD] MessageFormat javadoc

2.6 Use message-resources property file from inside an Action

◆ Problem

You want to use message resources inside an `Action` class.

◆ *Background*

Message resources are commonly used to look up key values within JSPs, but there are other uses. When you get right down to it, message resources hold runtime properties. How you use those properties is up to you. In this recipe we present a simple technique using message resources within an `Action` class to access runtime configuration parameters.

◆ *Recipe*

To demonstrate some relevance, the `Action` class in this recipe communicates with the business layer by sending a JMS message. The JMS queue name is obtained from a message resource. This recipe has a three-step process; (1) create a properties file, (2) define a message resource, and (3) access the message resource from the `Action` class.

Listing 2.34 `messagingparms.properties`

```
queuename=queue/testQueue
```

In listing 2.34 we create a properties file. The properties file defines a key to the JMS message queue name. You can place the properties file anywhere on the class path.

Listing 2.35 `<message-resources>` tag in struts-config.xml file

```
<message-resources key="jms" parameter="messagingparms"/>
```

A message resource is created in the usual way. Simply nest the `<message-resources>` tag under `<struts-config>`. In listing 2.35 we create a message resource labeled `jms` and associate it with the properties file. The message resource in listing 2.35 is linked to the `jms` key, but we could have used the `default` message resource instead. In practice, using message resources to store runtime parameters warrants specifying a key attribute. This reduces the chances of the property values being misused in the JSP.

Listing 2.36 Action using message resource

```
package com.strutsrecipes.actionmsgresources.actions;

import java.util.Locale;
import javax.servlet.http.HttpServletRequest;
```

```
import javax.servlet.http.HttpServletResponse;

import org.apache.commons.beanutils.BeanUtils;
import org.apache.struts.Globals;
import org.apache.struts.action.Action;
import org.apache.struts.action.ActionForm;
import org.apache.struts.action.ActionForward;
import org.apache.struts.action.ActionMapping;
import org.apache.struts.util.MessageResources;

import com.strutsrecipes.actionmsgresources.beans.ProductBean;
import com.strutsrecipes.actionmsgresources.forms.ProductForm;
import com.strutsrecipes.actionmsgresources.utils.MessageUtils;

public class OrderProductAction extends Action {

    public ActionForward execute(
        ActionMapping mapping,
        ActionForm form,
        HttpServletRequest request,
        HttpServletResponse response)
        throws Exception {

        ProductForm productForm = (ProductForm) form;
        ProductBean productBean = new ProductBean();
        BeanUtils.copyProperties(productForm, productBean);

        MessageResources mr = getResources(request, "jms");      ❶
        Locale locale =
            (Locale) request.getAttribute(Globals.LOCALE_KEY);   ❷
        String queueName = mr.getMessage(locale, "queuename");
                                                                 ❸
        if (!MessageUtils.sendProduct(productBean, queueName)) {
            return mapping.findForward("failure");
        }                                                        ❹

        return mapping.findForward("success");
    }
}
```

The last step is to access the message resource from the Action class. Struts has made this very easy for us because the base org.apache.struts.action.Action class has methods [SAC] to do the work for us.

Let's step through listing 2.36 to see how it is done.

❶ Obtain a reference to MessageResource by calling getResource(..) on the parent Action class. Notice we specify the key defined in listing 2.35. MessageResource represents the properties file in listing 2.34.

❷ Message resources are locale sensitive. Unless we are willing to let `Message-Resources` default to the default locale, we are obligated to provide a locale object. The `Locale` argument allows you to vary runtime parameters by locale. In this case we have just one properties file for all locales. Because we have not created localized properties files, all locales default to `messagingparms.properties`. Here we access the Struts known locale key.

❸ Obtain the JMS queue name from the `jms` message resource by specifying the properties file key.

Although it is not relevant to the technique at hand, at ❹ we show you how the queue name is passed to a utility class responsible for placing the product object on the JMS queue. The `Action` forwards accordingly.

◆ *Discussion*

Normally, using a properties file involves loading it from a `FileInputStream` or using the class loader to load it off the class path. In either of those cases you need to specify the physical file name. If the file name changes, then so does your code. Struts built-in message resource capabilities allows you to assign a logical name to a properties file. File name changes are maintained by changing the `<message-resources>` parameter attribute. No code changes are required! Moreover, Struts caches the properties file to give your application a performance boost.

Message resource locale sensitivity can come in handy. In this example, you can choose a queue name based on language and country code—all without writing a single line of logic. Other message resource features may also come into play. For example, you can leverage the replacement parameter feature to dynamically use a customer-specific JMS queue. All you need to do is create JMS queues with the customer name embedded in the queue name. At runtime replace the substitution parameter with the runtime value to yield the customer's queue name.

◆ *Related*

   ■ 2.5—Dynamically insert data inside a message
   ■ 6.2— Internationalize your text

◆ *Reference*

   ■ [JMS] Sun's Java Message Service Tutorial
   ■ [SAC] Struts Action `Class`

2.7 Create a wizard

◆ Problem

You want to create a wizard.

◆ Background

Wizards are a great way to lead a user through a series of screens. Each screen contains a logical grouping of data, but together the screens formulate a transaction to the business layer. There are a couple of ways to go about this. One option is to persist each page to a database as the user navigates from one screen to the next. The final screen is responsible for marking the data complete or purging it all together. This technique is sometimes called a *multiform* wizard. Another option available to Struts developers uses a single `ActionForm` as a buffer for all screens. The data is buffered by telling Struts to store the `ActionForm` bean in the session context. Each `ActionMapping` in the wizard refers to the same `ActionForm` bean, but the JSP for that action mapping exposes the `ActionForm` bean properties pertinent to that page. You can think of the JSPs as masks sitting in front of the `ActionForm` bean. This design pattern is sometimes called *single-form wizard*. In this recipe we present a single-form wizard.

◆ Recipe

Let's get a bird's eye view of things by looking at the struts-config.xml file of a wizard application.

Listing 2.37   struts-config.xml file

```
<?xml version="1.0" encoding="ISO-8859-1"?>
<!DOCTYPE struts-config PUBLIC "-//Apache Software Foundation//DTD Struts
   Configuration 1.1//EN"
           "http://jakarta.apache.org/struts/dtds/struts-config_1_1.dtd">

<struts-config>

    <form-beans>
        <form-bean name="sampleForm"
                type="com.strutsrecipes.wizard.forms.SampleForm"/>
    </form-beans>

    <global-forwards>
        <forward name="sample" path="/clearForm.do"/>
    </global-forwards>

    <action-mappings>
```

❶

```
<action
    path="/clearForm"
    type="com.strutsrecipes.wizard.actions.ClearForm"
    name="sampleForm"
    scope="session">
    <forward name="next" path="/pages/page1.jsp"/>
</action>

<action
    path="/SampleAction1"
    name="sampleForm"          ❷
    scope="session"           ❸
    forward="/pages/page2.jsp"/>        ❹

<action
    path="/SampleAction2"
    name="sampleForm"
    scope="session"
    forward="/pages/page3.jsp"/>        ❺

<action
    path="/SampleAction3"
    type="com.strutsrecipes.wizard.actions.Submit"        ❻
    name="sampleForm"          ❼
    scope="session">          ❽
    <forward name="next" path="/clearForm.do"/>
</action>
</action-mappings>

<message-resources parameter="resources.application"/>

</struts-config>
```

Let's look over listing 2.37 to understand the navigational flow. In this application the index.jsp (not shown) forwards the user to the global sample forward. The sample forward directs the request to clearForm.do to clear Form properties and presents page1.jsp. Submitting page1 to SampleAction1.do forwards the user to page2. Similarly, submitting page2 to SampleAction2.do forwards the user to page3. Finally, submitting page3 to SampleAction3.do uses the Submit Action to process the data and forwards the user back to clearForm.do. The user flows from page to page gathering data until the last Action processes the business transaction.

Now that we have some understanding of the wizard, let's use the struts-config.xml to walk through the flow once more. This time we stop along the way to describe how it works and to look at some of the pieces in detail. You should use the struts-config.xml file as a roadmap through the wizard.

Listing 2.38 `ClearForm` clears the form's properties

```
package com.strutsrecipes.wizard.actions;

import javax.servlet.http.HttpServletRequest;
import javax.servlet.http.HttpServletResponse;

import org.apache.struts.action.Action;
import org.apache.struts.action.ActionForm;
import org.apache.struts.action.ActionForward;
import org.apache.struts.action.ActionMapping;

import com.strutsrecipes.wizard.forms.SampleForm;

public class ClearForm extends Action {

    public ActionForward execute(
        ActionMapping mapping,
        ActionForm form,
        HttpServletRequest request,
        HttpServletResponse response)
        throws Exception {

        SampleForm sampleForm = (SampleForm) form;
        sampleForm.clear();
        return mapping.findForward("next");
    }
}
```

To enter the wizard the user is directed to the `clearForm` action mapping to clear out the Form's properties and direct the response to page1.jsp. This ensures the Form properties are cleared out before data inputting begins. See listing 2.38 for details. Note we purposely didn't use the `reset` method. Struts is hardwired to call the `reset` method before the Form bean is populated with the input controls. If the `reset` method clears all the fields, then all input would be cleared each time the page is submitted.

Listing 2.39 page1.jsp

```
<%@ taglib uri="/tags/struts-bean" prefix="bean" %>
<%@ taglib uri="/tags/struts-html" prefix="html" %>

<html:html>
```

```
<head>
<title>wizard - page 1</title>
<html:base/>
</head>
  <h1>wizard - page 1</h1>

  <html:form action="/SampleAction1 ">         ❶
    first name<html:text property="firstName"/>
    <br>
    last name<html:text property="lastName"/>
    <p>

  <html:submit value="next"/>
  </html:form>

</body>

</html:html>
```

Listing 2.40 ActionForm

```
package com.strutsrecipes.wizard.forms;

import org.apache.struts.action.ActionForm;
public class SampleForm extends ActionForm {
    private String firstName;
    private String lastName;
    private String productNumber;
    private String quantity;
    private String comment;

    public String getComment() {
        return comment;
    }

    public void setComment(String comment) {
        this.comment = comment;
    }

    public String getFirstName() {
        return firstName;
    }

    public void setFirstName(String firstName) {
        this.firstName = firstName;
    }

    public String getLastName() {
        return lastName;
    }
```

```java
    public void setLastName(String lastName) {
        this.lastName = lastName;
    }

    public String getProductNumber() {
        return productNumber;
    }

    public void setProductNumber(String productNumber) {
        this.productNumber = productNumber;
    }


    public String getQuantity() {
        return quantity;
    }

    public void setQuantity(String quantity) {
        this.quantity = quantity;
    }

    public void clear() {
        setComment("");
        setFirstName("");
        setLastName("");
        setProductNumber("");
        setQuantity("");
    }
}
```

The first thing the user sees is the page1.jsp (listing 2.39). Notice page1 submits to SampleAction1.do (listing 2.39 ❶) and the input controls map to the Form bean (listing 2.40). The user enters data into the input controls and submits the page to SampleAction1.do. Struts finds the SampleAction1.do action mapping and creates the sampleForm (listing 2.37 ❶❷) bean. The SampleAction1.do action mapping scope attribute (listing 2.37 ❸) instructs Struts to place the form bean in the session context. The Form bean is automatically populated with the input controls and the action mapping forwards the request to page2.jsp (listing 2.37 ❹). We have chosen to forward directly to the next page because we are not processing the Form bean, but we could have used a custom Action instead.

The process is repeated when page2 is submitted. The only difference is that the Form bean created in the previous request is taken from the session context and the page is submitted to SampleAction2.do. The Form bean has properties for input controls for all pages in the wizard. When the page is submitted to

`SubmitAction2.do`, Struts populates only the Form bean properties mapping to the input controls on page2.jsp (not shown)—the others are left untouched. The action mapping forwards to page3.jsp (listing 2.37 ❺). You can see that the wizard is slowly populating pieces of the Form bean as the user progresses through the wizard. The Form bean is acting as a cache for user input between requests.

Listing 2.41 Last Action in wizard

```
package com.strutsrecipes.wizard.actions;

import javax.servlet.http.HttpServletRequest;
import javax.servlet.http.HttpServletResponse;

import org.apache.commons.beanutils.BeanUtils;

import org.apache.struts.action.Action;
import org.apache.struts.action.ActionForm;
import org.apache.struts.action.ActionForward;
import org.apache.struts.action.ActionMapping;

import com.strutsrecipes.wizard.business.BusinessFacade;
import com.strutsrecipes.wizard.business.TransactionBean;
import com.strutsrecipes.wizard.forms.SampleForm;

public class Submit extends Action {

    public ActionForward execute(
            ActionMapping mapping,
            ActionForm form,
            HttpServletRequest request,
            HttpServletResponse response)
            throws Exception {

        SampleForm sampleForm = (SampleForm) form;          ❶

        TransactionBean transactionBean = new TransactionBean();   ❷
        BeanUtils.copyProperties(transactionBean, sampleForm);     ❸

        BusinessFacade businessFacade = new BusinessFacade();      ❹
        businessFacade.save(transactionBean);     ❺

        sampleForm.clear();     ❻

        return mapping.findForward("next");     ❼
    }
}
```

The next step is the last step, and is a little different from the previous two. Page3. jsp (not shown) submits the page to `SampleAction3.do`. As was the case in the previous steps, Struts harvests page3 input controls into the Form bean cached in the session context (listing 2.37 **❼❽**). However, this time `com.strutsrecipes.wizard.actions.Submit` is used to process the request (listing 2.37 **❻**).

Let's step through the `Submit Action` in listing 2.41.

❶ Cast the form to `SampleForm`.

❷ Instantiate a `TransactionBean` to act as a Data Transfer Object [PEAA] to the business layer.

❸ Populate the `TransactionBean` from the Form bean using `BeanUtils.copyProperties(..)`.`BeanUtils` is a good choice here because both beans share the same property names.

❹ Obtain a façade to the business layer.

❺ Request the business layer to save the `TransactionBean`.

❻ Since this is the last page in the wizard, we clear the Form bean properties. This step is optional if you send the user back to `clearForm.do`.

❼ Forward the request to the `next` forward. The struts-config.xml file directs the request back to `clearForm.do` to start the process all over again. We have chosen to send the user back to the start of the wizard, but you are free to do whichever is appropriate for your use case. If you want to save the user some typing, you can omit clearing the Form properties and send the user to page1.jsp.

◆ *Discussion*

Working with a large amount of information can be overwhelming. Wizards are an effective ergonomic technique that allows users to focus their attention on logical groupings of information. Some of the more popular wizard page designs are tabs, menus, or simply page numbers.

Wizards are made easy by leveraging Struts' built-in ability to cache Form beans in session context. This is a great way to cache data in the presentation layer and minimize chattiness with the business layer. Caching all user input in a single form allows you to move data between wizard pages by moving input controls from one JSP to another. Although this popular technique is very effective, there is one "gotcha" out there. Struts does not persist Form beans. The Form bean is an in-memory object which disappears whenever the servlet container is shut down. If you can live with this limitation, this technique allows you to develop wizards quickly and easily.

◆ *Reference*

■ [PEAA] Patterns of Enterprise Application Architecture

2.8 Alternate row colors

◆ *Problem*

You want to alternate row colors in an HTML table.

◆ *Background*

Providing visual cues is an important factor to consider when creating user friendly applications. Easy-to-use applications have a better chance of becoming successful. Most people find HTML tables are the best way to represent tabular data. Although tables provide a means to organize and locate information readily, the user must visually track a row of data from one side of the page to the other. Table borders help track a row full of data, but sometimes that is not enough. A popular technique is to color code each row. The row color allows the user to track information across the row without smudging the screen with fingerprints.

In this recipe we show you how to alternate colors by extending the Struts iterate tag. The Struts iterate tag is commonly used to create HTML tables, but does not support alternating colors. We customize the iterate tag to make it alternate the color as it iterates. Quite often alternating between two colors is sufficient, but other times you might need the lines to alternate between more colors than that. Our custom iterate tag is not bounded by a predetermined set of colors. Moreover, our tag exposes the color by using a scripting variable declared in the JSP.

◆ *Recipe*

The strategy of extending the Struts iterate tag functionality is straightforward. We create a custom JSP tag in the usual way, but extend the Struts iterate tag instead of creating one from scratch. In the JSP we create a namespace for our new tag, and use it instead of the Struts iterate tag.

Before jumping into the Java code, let's have a look at listing 2.42 to see how the new iterate tag is used.

Listing 2.42   JSP

```
<%@ taglib uri="/tags/cookbook-logic" prefix="cblogic" %>   ❶
<%@ taglib uri="/tags/struts-html" prefix="html" %>
```

```
<%@ taglib uri="/tags/struts-bean" prefix="bean" %>

<html:html>
<head>
<html:base/>
</head>

<table border="1">
   <cblogic:iterate id="row" name="items"       ❷
     indexId="i"    ❸
     colorId="c"    ❹
     colors="#00FF00 #FF0000 #0000FF"> <!-- green, red, blue -->    ❺

       <tr bgcolor="<bean:write name="c"/>">    ❻
           <td><bean:write name="row"/></td>
           <td><bean:write name="i"/></td>    ❼

       </tr>
   </cblogic:iterate>
</table>

</body>
</html:html>
```

Listing 2.42 presents a JSP that uses the iterate tag we want to create in this recipe. Let's review the JSP, taking time to describe the new features we have added and review some of the features already packaged with the existing Struts iterate tag.

❶ Declare the taglib containing our extended iterate tag. Notice, our iterate tag is in the cblogic namespace. Separating the Struts iterate tag from our own allows us to use them both in the same page by qualifying them with the desired namespace.

❷ Generate rows within an HTML table by iterating over the items collection. The Struts iterate tag uses the id attribute to expose an element of the items collection as a scripting variable. In this case, the scripting variable is row. The name attribute declares the name of the collection found in context.

❸ Use the Struts iterate tag's indexId attribute to declare the name of the scripting variable holding the iteration index number. The iteration index number starts at one and continues until the end of the collection is reached.

❹ So far we have revisited existing Struts iterate tag features. Here we see one of the two new attributes we have introduced. colorId is the name of the scripting variable holding the color code used on a particular iteration. In this case, we have chosen c as the name of the scripting variable. The contents of c is used to set the color of a row.

❺ Here we list the colors. Each color is separated by a space. The first row uses the first color, the second row uses the second color, and the third row uses the third color. The fourth color wraps around to the first color again. The process continues until all the iterations have been executed. The color is made available through the scripting variable declared at **❹**—in this case c. The tag can handle any number of colors.

❻ Use the <bean:write> tag to write out the value of the c scripting variable. The color code is written inside the bgcolor attribute of the <tr> tag.

❼ Write out the iteration index number using the scripting variable declared at **❸**.

Let's jump into the Java code to see how this is done. We need to write two Java classes to implement this tag. We need a BodyTagSupport and a TagExtraInfo class. The BodyTagSupport is the workhorse. It traps tag-processing events. The TagExtraInfo class is used to provide information on scripting variables created by the tag at runtime. In listing 2.43 we look at the IterateRowTag class.

Listing 2.43 `IterateRowTag.java`

```
package com.strutsrecipes.altrows.taglib.logic;

import java.util.StringTokenizer;
import javax.servlet.jsp.JspException;
import org.apache.struts.taglib.logic.IterateTag;

public class IterateRowTag extends IterateTag {            ❶

    protected String colorId = null;

    public String getColorId() {
            return (this.colorId);
    }                                                       ❷

    public void setColorId(String colorId) {
            this.colorId = colorId;
    }

    protected String colorInput = null;

    public String getColors() {                             ❸
            return colorInput;
    }

    protected String[] colors = null;
        public void setColors(String colorInput) {          ❹
            this.colorInput = colorInput;
```

```
            if (null == colorInput) {
                  return;                          ❺
            }

            StringTokenizer st = new StringTokenizer(colorInput);
            colors = new String[st.countTokens()];

            int count = 0;                                              ❻
            while (st.hasMoreTokens()) {
                  colors[count++] = st.nextToken();
            }
      }

      public int doStartTag() throws JspException {
            int i = super.doStartTag();
            determineColor();                      ❼
            return i;
      }

      public int doAfterBody() throws JspException {
            int i = super.doAfterBody();
            determineColor();                      ❽
            return i;
      }

      protected void determineColor() {
            if (null != colorId) {                                      ❾
                  if (null != colors && 0 != colors.length) {
                  pageContext.setAttribute(colorId,             ❿
                        colors[getIndex() % colors.length]);
                  }
            }
      }

      public void release() {
            super.release();
            colors = null;
      }
}
```

Let's step through listing 2.43.

❶ Extend org.apache.struts.taglib.logic.IterateTag. This allows us to continue to provide all of the existing Struts iterate tag features.

❷ Create a getter and setter for the colorId attribute. Recall, this attribute represents the name of the scripting variable used to expose the color for a particular iteration.

❸ Create a getter for the colors attribute.

④⑤⑥ Create a setter for the colors attribute. Line **④** sets the `colorInput` instance variable. If the user has not set any colors, then we exit **⑤**. Use `StringTokenizer` **⑥** to split `colorInput` on spaces. Each color is placed in an element of the colors array.

Let's continue looking at the `IterateRowTag` (listing 2.43) by examining how the color is set.

⑦ This override the `doStartTag`. The `doStartTag` is called when the start of the tag is encountered. To us it represents our first iteration through the collection. The parent `doStartTag` calculates the iteration index number. We need the iteration index number to determine the color. The parent's `doStart` method return value determines whether or not the body should be processed. We save this value in the `i` variable until we can determine the color. We use the `determineColor` method to figure out what the color should be. More on the `determineColor` method later.

⑧ Override the `doAfterBody` method to determine the color on all subsequent iterations over the collection. The `doAfterBody` method is called after the body is processed. We apply the same approach as **⑦**.

⑨ ⑩ Determine the color.

If either the `colorId` or `colors` attributes were not specified, we abandon determining the color at **⑨**. Otherwise, we calculate the color at **⑩**. The color is retrieved from the color array created at **⑥**. The array element is chosen by using the parent's `getIndex` method to obtain the current iteration index number and applying the mathematical mod operation against the total number of colors declared. The resulting color code is placed in page context using the name of the scripting variable provided at **②**.

In listing 2.43 we determine the appropriate color for a particular iteration and place the value in page context. In listing 2.44 we extend the iterate tag's `IterateTei`, which in turn extends the `TagExtraInfo` class, to make the color available as a scripting variable.

Listing 2.44 `IterateRowTei.java`

```java
package com.strutsrecipes.altrows.taglib.logic;

import java.util.ArrayList;

import javax.servlet.jsp.tagext.TagData;
import javax.servlet.jsp.tagext.VariableInfo;

import org.apache.struts.taglib.logic.IterateTei;
```

```
public class IterateRowTei extends IterateTei {   ❶

    public VariableInfo[] getVariableInfo(TagData data) {
        ArrayList list = new ArrayList();   ❷

        VariableInfo[] superVariableInfo =
                super.getVariableInfo(data);   ❸
        for (int i = 0; i < superVariableInfo.length; i++) {
            list.add(superVariableInfo[i]);                    ❹
        }

        String colorId = data.getAttributeString("colorId");   ❺

        if (null != colorId) {
            list.add(
                new VariableInfo(
                    colorId,
                    "java.lang.String",              ❻
                    true,
                    VariableInfo.NESTED));
        }

        return (VariableInfo[]) list.toArray(new VariableInfo[0]);   ❼
    }
}
```

The TagExtraInfo class getVariableInfo method returns an array of Variable-Info objects. Each object in the array declares a scripting variable. In listing 2.44 you can see that the IterateRowTei class extends the iterate tag's IterateTei class. Since the iterate tag has scripting variables, we need to merge the parent's getVariableInfo method return value with the colorId scripting variable, but only when colorId is declared. Let's step through listing 2.44 to see how that's done.

❶ Extend org.apache.struts.taglib.logic.IterateTei.

❷ Create a List. We will use this list to aggregate VariableInfo objects.

❸ Call the super's method to obtain the parent's array of VariableInfo objects. The super's VariableInfo array is stored in superVariableInfo.

❹ Copy over the array into the list created at ❷.

❺ Obtain the value of colorId.

❻ Check the value returned from ❺. This value is null when colorId is not declared. If colorId is declared, we add its VariableInfo object to the list.

❼ Convert the list to a VariableInfo array and return it to the caller.

Now that we have created the tag and `TagExtraInfo` class classes, we need to register them in a tag library descriptor (TLD), as shown in listing 2.45.

Listing 2.45   recipes-logic.tld

```xml
<?xml version="1.0" encoding="UTF-8"?>
<!DOCTYPE taglib PUBLIC "-//Sun Microsystems, Inc.//DTD JSP Tag Library 1.1/
    /EN" "http://java.sun.com/j2ee/dtds/web-jsptaglibrary_1_1.dtd">

<taglib>
    <tlibversion>1.0</tlibversion>
    <jspversion>1.1</jspversion>
    <shortname>logic</shortname>
    <uri>http://www.strutscookbook.com/struts/tags-logic</uri>

    <tag>
        <name>iterate</name>

        <tagclass>
                com.strutsrecipes.altrows.taglib.logic.IterateRowTag      ❶
        </tagclass>

        <teiclass>
                com.strutsrecipes.altrows.taglib.logic.IterateRowTei      ❷
        </teiclass>

        <bodycontent>JSP</bodycontent>

        <attribute>
            <name>colors</name>
            <required>false</required>
            <rtexprvalue>true</rtexprvalue>                               ❸
        </attribute>

        <attribute>
            <name>colorId</name>
            <required>false</required>                                    ❹
            <rtexprvalue>true</rtexprvalue>
        </attribute>

    . . .   the Struts iterate tag's attributes found in struts-logic.tld    ❺

    </tag>
</taglib>
```

Let's review the TLD in listing 2.45.

❶ Declare the tag class created in listing 2.43.

② Declare the `TagExtraInfo` class created in listing 2.44.

③ Declare the `colors` attribute as optional.

④ Declare the `colorId` attribute as optional. Note that `colorId` is mandatory when colors are specified. Unfortunately, there is no way to represent that dependency in a TLD.

⑤ Copy over all the other attributes used by the Struts iterate tag.

Lastly, we register the TLD in web.xml, as shown in listing 2.46.

Listing 2.46   register recipes-logic.tld taglib in web.xml

```
<taglib>
    <taglib-uri>/tags/cookbook-logic</taglib-uri>
    <taglib-location>/WEB-INF/recipes-logic.tld</taglib-location>
</taglib>
```

Listing 2.46 presents the snippet that must be placed in the web.xml alongside the Struts tag libs. Note that `<taglib-location>` specifies the location of the TLD file created in listing 2.45.

◆ *Discussion*

Everything we can do to make an application easier to use will serve users well. Visual cues lead to intuitive applications. Alternating row colors allow the user to easily track information from one side of the page to the other. There are a number of techniques available to achieve this effect including third-party packages, scriptlets, and JSTL. Unfortunately, most third-party JAR files are limited to two colors, and scriptlets and JSTL are verbose. In this recipe we showed you how to extend the Struts iterate tag to incorporate alternating colors into the existing iterate functionality. This means you can alternate over any number of colors any place you are using the Struts iterate tag. As you extend the Struts iterate tag, you automatically incorporate any new iterate tag features coming down the pipe.

An important point to take away from this recipe is that Struts tags are meant to be extended. If you find yourself wishing a Struts tag did more, then you should consider extending the tag to meet your needs. This recipe lays out the steps to do that.

Before ending this recipe, let's consider a simple technique to make this recipe more maintainable. At **⑤** in listing 2.42 we specified a list of colors in the iterate tag's `colors` attribute. If we wanted to use the same list of colors in several pages, then the technique presented in listing 2.42 would result in multiple points of maintenance. We can reduce our points of maintenance to just one by placing the list of colors in a resource bundle, as shown in listing 2.47.

Listing 2.47 Application.properties

```
colorlist=#00FF00 #FF0000 #0000FF
```

In listing 2.48, we show you how to access the `colorlist` key and place it in context.

Listing 2.48 JSP

```
<%@ taglib uri="/tags/cookbook-logic" prefix="cblogic" %>
<%@ taglib uri="/tags/struts-html" prefix="html" %>
<%@ taglib uri="/tags/struts-bean" prefix="bean" %>

<html:html>
<head>
<html:base/>
</head>

<bean:define id="beanColors">
  <bean:message key="colorlist"/>                    ❶
</bean:define>

<table border>
   <cblogic:iterate id="row" name="items"
     indexId="i"
     colorId="c"
     colors="<%=beanColors%>">                ❷
        <tr bgcolor="<bean:write name="c"/>">
            <td ><bean:write name="row"/></td>
            <td><bean:write name="i"/></td>
        </tr>
   </cblogic:iterate>
</table>

</body>
</html:html>
```

Listing 2.48 is identical to listing 2.42 except for two small changes. Let's look at the changes to listing 2.48.

❶ Use the `<bean:message>` tag to access the default application resource. The `<bean:define>` tag is used to place the return value of the `<bean:message>` tag in context under the `beanColors` key.

❷ Use a very small scriptlet to populate the iterate tag's `colors` attribute.

This recipe showed you how to implement alternating colors by extending the Struts iterate tag. Although Struts tags are feature rich, you might find yourself wishing they did more. If you find yourself in that kind of situation, you can use this recipe to guide you through the process of extending an existing Struts tag to do the things you need them to do.

◆ *Related*

■ 6.2—Internationalize your text

◆ *Reference*

■ [LAYOUT] Struts Layout

2.9 *Upload a file*

◆ *Problem*

You want to upload a file to the server.

◆ *Background*

Data is transferred between the browser and the server in a transparent way. Browser users, and many developers, take this transmission for granted, but there is a little more going on than we realize. Encoding is used as an added measure to ensure the data arrives as intended. Under normal circumstances, the browser automatically encodes the transmitted data using the Internet Media Type "application/x-www-form-urlencoded" encoding format. The form's fields are sent in name/value pairs. If there are multiple fields, then the fields are separated with an ampersand. All the fields are strung together into one long URL.

Listing 2.49 presents a typical "application/x-www-form-urlencoded" form.

Listing 2.49 `application/x-www-form-urlencoded` **encoded request**

```
firstname=george&lastname=franciscus
```

This encoding scheme converts spaces to plus signs and nonalphanumeric characters into a percent sign followed by two hexadecimal ASCII codes for that character. It can be hard to read, but that's generally the browser's problem, not ours.

Transmitting a file requires a different encoding scheme. To transmit a file the request must be encoded as "multipart/form-data." This encoding scheme is easier to read, but more verbose. The request is broken down into multiple parts—hence the term "multipart." Each field is in its own part. Each part is delineated with a random number preceded by thirty dashes. The last demarcation tacks on an extra two dashes.

The file content is treated just like field text. Listing 2.50 presents a form encoding three fields—"firstname," "lastname," and "afile." Notice the Content-Disposition has a field called "fieldname" to record the file name.

Listing 2.50 `multipart/form-data` encoded request

```
----------------------------2838492192303834
Content-Disposition: form-data; name="firstname"

george
----------------------------2838492192303834
Content-Disposition: form-data; name="lastname"

franciscus
----------------------------2838492192303834
Content-Disposition: form-data; name="afile"; filename="myfile.txt"
Content-Type: text/plain

This is text at the start of the file
    Blah, blah
    This is text at the end of the file
----------------------------2838492192303834--
```

Now that we have covered the theory, let's jump into the code.

◆ *Recipe*

To upload a file we'll need a JSP, a matching `ActionForm`, and an `Action` to do the heavy lifting. Let's start with the JSP, shown in listing 2.51.

Listing 2.51 JSP

```
<%@ page language="java" %>
<%@ taglib uri="/WEB-INF/struts-html.tld" prefix="html" %>

<html:html>
<html:form action="upload.do" enctype="multipart/form-data">    ❶
    Select file:<html:file property="file" /><br/>    ◁┐
    <html:submit />                                       ❷
</html:form>
</html:html>
```

The JSP in listing 2.51 is typical of many JSPs, except for two things. At ❶ we specify an encoding type of "multipart/form-data." At ❷ we use an <html:file> tag to generate the file selection control.

In listing 2.52 we look at the JSP's associated `ActionForm`.

Listing 2.52 `ActionForm`

```
package com.strutsrecipes.loadfile.forms;

import org.apache.struts.upload.FormFile;
import org.apache.struts.action.ActionForm;

public class UploadForm extends ActionForm {
    private FormFile file;

    public FormFile getFile() {
        return file;
    }

    public void setFile(FormFile file) {
        this.file = file;
    }
}
```

In listing 2.52 we see the `UploadForm` has a single property. Notice the property data type is `org.apache.struts.upload.FormFile`. You must use this class to receive the file and it must have a matching <html:file> tag on the JSP.

In listing 2.53 we see how the `Action` extracts the file's contents from the Form's `FormFile` field and persists it to the file system.

Listing 2.53 `Action package com.strutsrecipes.loadfile.actions;`

```
import java.io.File;
import java.io.FileNotFoundException;
import java.io.FileOutputStream;
import java.io.IOException;
import java.io.InputStream;

import javax.servlet.http.HttpServletRequest;
import javax.servlet.http.HttpServletResponse;

import org.apache.commons.lang.NumberUtils;
import org.apache.struts.action.Action;
import org.apache.struts.action.ActionError;
import org.apache.struts.action.ActionErrors;
import org.apache.struts.action.ActionForm;
import org.apache.struts.action.ActionForward;
```

```
import org.apache.struts.action.ActionMapping;
import org.apache.struts.upload.FormFile;
import org.apache.struts.util.MessageResources;

import com.strutsrecipes.loadfile.forms.UploadForm;

public class UploadAction extends Action {

    public ActionForward execute(ActionMapping mapping,
                                    ActionForm form,
                                    HttpServletRequest request,
                                    HttpServletResponse response)
        throws Exception {

        UploadForm uploadForm = (UploadForm) form;

        FormFile inputFile = uploadForm.getFile();           ❶
        String fileName = inputFile.getFileName();           ❷

        try {
            MessageResources mr =
                getResources(request, "upload");             ❸

            String location = mr.getMessage("location");     ❹
            int max_size =
                NumberUtils.stringToInt(mr.getMessage("size"));  ❺

            if (inputFile.getFileSize() > max_size) {
              ActionErrors errors = new ActionErrors();
              errors.add(ActionErrors.GLOBAL_ERROR,
                    new ActionError ("error.maxsize"));       ❻
              saveErrors(request, errors);
              return mapping.findForward("failure");
            }


            InputStream inputStream =
                    inputFile.getInputStream();              ❼

            byte[] fileContents =
                    new byte[inputFile.getFileSize()];       ❽
            inputStream.read(fileContents);                  ❾
            File outputFile =
                    new File(location + fileName);           ❿
            FileOutputStream fos =
                    new FileOutputStream(outputFile);        ⓫
            fos.write(fileContents);                         ⓬
            fos.close();                                     ⓭

        } catch (FileNotFoundException e) {
            e.printStackTrace();
```

```
        ActionErrors errors = new ActionErrors();
        errors.add(ActionErrors.GLOBAL_ERROR,
            new ActionError ("error.io"));
        saveErrors(request, errors);
        return mapping.findForward("failure");

    catch (IOException e) {
        e.printStackTrace();
        ActionErrors errors = new ActionErrors();
        errors.add(ActionErrors.GLOBAL_ERROR,
            new ActionError ("error.io"));
        saveErrors(request, errors);
        return mapping.findForward("failure");
    }

    return mapping.findForward("success");
    }
}
```

Let's walk through the code line by line.

❶ Extract the `FormFile` from the file.

❷ Get the file's name so we know how to name it on the file system.

❸ Obtain a `MessageResource` containing runtime parameters

❹ Extract the `location` parameter from the `MessageResource`. This parameter contains the file system target directory.

❺ Extract the `size` parameter from the `MessageResource`. This parameter contains the maximum permissible size, in bytes, of the upload file.

❻ Verify that the file size is less than the maximum file size obtained at ❺. If the file is too large, the request is directed to the failure `Forward`.

❼ Obtain an `InputStream` from the `FormFile`.

❽ Use the `FormFile`'s length to build a byte array of the appropriate size.

❾ Read the contents of the file into the byte array created at ❽.

❿ Create a file on the file system using the file name we obtained at ❷.

⓫ Create a `FileOutputStream` as preparation for writing to the file.

⓬ Write the contents of the byte array containing the uploaded file's contents to the file on the file system.

⓭ Close up the `FileOutputStream`.

Thanks to Struts, the whole job is rather uneventful. That's exactly what a good framework is supposed to be.

◆ *Discussion*

Struts makes short work of what might seem to be a tough task. If you were to view the HTML source generated by the JSP you would see that the JSP translates the Struts tag `<html:form action="upload.do" enctype="multipart/form-data">` to `<form name="uploadForm" method="POST" action="/upload/load.do" enctype="multipart/form-data">`. Notice, the `enctype` attribute is populated with the required encoding type necessary to transmit a file. Similarly, the JSP translates the Struts tag :`<html:file property="file" />` on the JSP page to `<input type="file" name="file" value="">`. Notice that the input's tag property is `file`. The input tag presents a button allowing users to navigate through their local file system to select the file they want to send to the server. The user submits the page in the usual way.

The `ActionForm` must have a property of type `FormFile` to receive the file. This special Struts class means that there is very little for you to do to extract the file contents. The `Action` does the real work, but once you see how it's done, it's rather anticlimactic. Using the standard Java IO package, we simply read data from the `FormFile` as an `InputStream` and write it to the file system in the usual way. Although we have declined to do so here, you may decide to use some of the other features in the Java IO library to process the files more efficiently.

There is one "gotcha" to watch out for. At ❻ in listing 2.53 we checked to make sure the file was less than an application's specific maximum size. This is an important part of the recipe. Failing to enforce some kind of "sanity" check leaves the door open to a denial-of-service attack. A clever hacker could upload very large files in an attempt to gobble up disk space and memory.

Struts provides built-in support to manage the resources required to upload files. The `<controller>` tag in the struts-config.xml file has four attributes to manage file uploads for all uploads within an application, as listed in table 2.2.

Table 2.2   `<controller>` tag attributes governing file uploads

Attribute name	Description	Default
bufferSize	The size of the input buffer used when processing file uploads.	4096
maxFileSize	The maximum size (in bytes) of a file to be accepted as a file upload; can be expressed as a number followed by a K, M, or G, which are interpreted to mean kilobytes, megabytes, or gigabytes, respectively.	250 M

Table 2.2   <controller> tag attributes governing file uploads *(continued)*

Attribute name	Description	Default
memFileSize	The maximum size (in bytes) of a file whose contents will be retained in memory after uploading. Files larger than this threshold are written to some alternative storage medium, typically a hard disk. Can be expressed as a number followed by a K, M, or G, which are interpreted to mean kilobytes, megabytes, or gigabytes, respectively.	256 K
multipartClass	The fully qualified Java class name of the multi-part request handler class to be used with this module	org.apache.struts.upload.CommonsMultipartRequestHandler

If you are not happy with the default values, you can create a <controller> tag in the struts-config.xml file specifying the appropriate values for your application. These configuration parameters apply to all file uploads in your application. If you would like to restrict file upload sizes on specific pages, you can use the technique shown at ❻ in listing 2.53 to further restrict the value specified in the max-FileSize attribute. However, keep in mind the controller settings are applied before the Action is invoked. Therefore, any limitation in the Action must be more restrictive than the one specified in the controller tag.

BEST PRACTICE   *Limit upload file sizes*—Applications providing file upload capabilities should enforce a maximum file size to protect against denial-of-service attacks. Large uploads can consume large amounts of disk space and memory. Review the <controller> tag default setting to ensure they are suitable.

◆ *Reference*

- [HTML401] HTML 4.0.1 Specification www.w3.org/TR/html401/
- [RFC1738] RFC 1738 www.ietf.org/rfc/rfc1738.txt

Struts tag libraries 3

Men have become the tools of their tools.

—Henry David Thoreau

Struts tag libraries stand out as indispensable tools available to web application developers. You can actually create Struts applications without them if you try hard enough, but you soon realize that it is a waste of time and energy to develop an application of any size or usefulness in such a manner. JSP tags in general, and Struts tags specifically, make it easier for you and your team to create solid, scalable, and maintainable applications. They give you more layers of separation and encapsulation on your JSP pages, further separating the Model, View, and Controller parts of your applications. When used judiciously, you can also create a "pseudo," or "mini," Model, View, and Controller framework inside your JSPs, effectively segregating your logic and text/graphics further.

Using Struts tag libraries to promote good MVC practice

The Struts tag libraries allow developers to make smart decisions about MVC separation, but can also be a trap if they are not used properly and with thoughtful consideration. One should constantly ask, "Does this logic belong on the page in the View layer, or am I better off leaving this on the server-side?" Logic almost always belongs in the Model and Controller layer. The JSP page should be treated as a View layer, and only logic that allows the data to render into the desired view belongs here. If the data is being changed or mutated, it's time to rethink what you're doing and move it back to the server.

MVC2 DESIGN PATTERNS — Model-View-Controller was born in the early 1980s with Smalltalk-80. MVC is a well accepted architectural pattern used as a basis for all Struts applications. The Model represents Data Objects, which could be a persistence layer, JavaBeans, EJBs, and so on. The View component is the user interface, in this case, the JSP pages. Finally the Controller is the "referee" in your application. It handles the flow of information through your work, routes information in the proper direction, and tells the GUI what to do based upon the information the Model sends it.

JSP without Struts (or *any* controller servlet) creates a condition where the View and Controller are amalgamated. Although this is a workable solution, you can find yourself in trouble maintaining it. What if requirements change? You would probably have to rewrite most or all of the application. Whenever any part of the code changes, it could break in unforeseen places and need major refactoring. While JSPs represent the View in the Model, View, and Controller framework, rendering and logic can still occur in the other layers, altering this view, depending upon what changes a particular `Action` class invokes upon the Business Object with which you're working.

There are times when a page might need different views depending upon a tab being clicked, or a button being pressed. The debate centers around whether *all* control should be handled by a middle tier (Actions), or *almost all* of the control. It is important to stay as close to this ideal (a.k.a. MVC2) as possible; but as in life, there are exceptions. The "right" or "wrong" path to take can become ambiguous, or you might have to make compromises based upon many factors, as illustrated by the following hypothetical situation.

Say you need to create an application with five tabs corresponding to five different views. You might decide to use a frame that has five tabs across the top, linked to five different pages in a frame below it (option 1). The tabs can be viewed as "up" or "in the background," depending upon which corresponding page is being viewed. Instead of using such frames, you could decide to create numerous pages that each have all the tabs in them with the "up" and "back" position depending upon the content of a particular page (option 2). Another option is to create many tiles and make definitions for each clicked page (option 3). Finally, you could create only one page that uses conditionals such as struts-logic tags to alter the style of each tab, depending upon its clicked state (option 4).

The above scenario is interesting in that the JSP must "know" something about what it expects; definitely not an ideal situation. Ideally, pages should receive information and create themselves using parameters that are as normalized and generic as possible. It's as if a page linked to another is saying, "I'm handing control over to you. Here are some parameters, I have no idea what you're going to do with them." While this is an ideal situation, borderline conditions arise when time, skills, managers, and customers get involved in the mix. Great code is easy to write when things are simple—great coders write great code when compromises must be made.

All four of the above development paths are viable choices. While each one of the paths are workable solutions, to some degree they *all* violate encapsulation, MVC architecture, code reuse, maintainability, and scalability objectives. The final answer comes down to a compromise between what will work in the long run versus what works best in the current situation with the currently available information.

Option 1, using frames, is risky. Frames themselves can be difficult to manage and add their own complexity, and you might need to concoct exotic methods of handling stateful information between the different sets.

Option 2 creates many pages that handle each situation completely and are independent of each other. Although you might reject this out of hand as a complete waste and a horrible maintenance nightmare with repeated code everywhere, let's take a look at it from a different angle. Is it MVC? Yes, it is—every `Action` has a corresponding View, and the logic is encapsulated beautifully within the `Action` classes! The view only shows what it is given and has no responsibility at all for who is viewing it or any conditions upon its creation. The only drawback is the tons of graphics, text, and images that are cut and pasted "all over the place" which are probably a maintenance nightmare to the front-end coders. But there are conditions where much of this might be handled with CSS and `includes`. Still, in our tabs case, any changes, additions, or deletions of tabs or code would have to be normalized across five different pages and this solution would be messy in the long run.

Option 3 is to use Struts Tiles. This templating system is also a tag library and we will discuss it at length. The tabs problem above is probably best solved by using a template and XML-based Tiles definitions. We'll show you how to create templates and a single XML file that can potentially hold your entire application. This solution to your tabs problem is clean and *much* more encapsulated. The only real drawback is its sophistication. Once it's implemented, everyone on your team needs to understand it thoroughly, and it must be strictly maintained—not so easy in a team environment with compressed deadlines, various abilities, and no time for a good training regime.

Option 4, the route with struts-logic tags, violates some MVC architecture patterns, as you are using logic to alter the view *inside* the view component. This may well be the biggest transgression. Even though it might seem like bad design externally, the benefits we receive implementing it might be more important over the long run. We get a single point of entry and a page that can do many things. We end up with a page that has little indirection—we don't have to maintain code in separate places with multiple dependencies. This is especially important in a team environment where skill sets vary wildly and there are a lot of "hands in the dough."

Struts' tag libraries offer lots of choices, some excellent, some less than excellent. It's up to you as a developer to make critical decisions early on in the process to ensure the long-term viability of your project. A complete knowledge of the tools available and the different ways of putting them to use goes a long way when planning to create any software. This chapter attempts to give solid answers to many questions, and present valid, real-world examples of Struts tags in proper use.

What is a tag library?

If you're reading this book, you probably know what a JSP tag is. Taking a second to review, the first custom tags emerged as JSP became prevalent. Before JSP, back in the bad old days (before the end of 1998), dynamic content was rendered through the Common Gateway Interface (CGI), server-side JavaScript, and later, Java Servlets. These technologies brought a lot to the table, but they were often hard to maintain, develop, and had some performance issues (CGI requires one process per request!). When JSP came about, we began mixing and matching Java scriptlets and HTML, making dynamic development much simpler and easier to maintain, but still, business logic was all over the page, and a misplaced %> or semicolon could ruin your day. Something was needed to "take the business logic off the page" and make things easier for the GUI designers, but also keep them from breaking the logic!

BUSINESS LOGIC AND TAG LIBRARIES Business logic is "program-centric" code; it is that part of your application that "does" something. It might monitor a process, deliver a document, load and store products in a shopping cart, charge your credit card, or almost anything. The development time for these business processes is often more detailed and time consuming than the graphics, formatting, and view deliverables. It is crucial to find straightforward ways to expose this data to the page. These strategies must be isolated and decoupled from the page. This encapsulation allows for testing, debugging, and maintenance of the Logic and View separately. JSP tag libraries are a means to this end and more. Many tag libraries specifically "pipeline" data to the page—others allow this data to be formatted "automatically" so a developer working on the View component of a project has less code to write and more latitude in doing his or her job without worrying about making a mess of the back-end or business logic.

How do tags work?

JSP tags are interpreted on the server using Java, and might or might not return an expression or perform some logic. They are commonly used to transfer data to the JSP page from the various scopes available to it, manipulate and format data, and even hide or block sections of a page depending upon the value of some item. Tags are like a superset of reusable and highly generic code, and are often treated like a "black box"—set some parameters in the tag and get the data you want out of it. You don't really care what happens under the covers.

But, because you asked, what happens under the covers looks similar to figure 3.1.

The first time[1] a page is accessed, the container compiles JSP tags and their attributes into a Servlet. Tags operate as a black box to the developer, meaning

---

[1] Unless precompiled.

if he or she abides by the tag's rules, then he or she will get predictable, consistent results.

There are many different flavors and varieties of JSP tag libraries. Struts works well not only with its own specific tags, but also with the most accepted and popular tag libraries, as well as with many custom tag libraries. Deeper explanations and specifics of tag libraries are out of the scope of this book, although Manning Publications offers an excellent book, *JSP Tag Libraries*, by Shawn Bayern.

How do tags work?

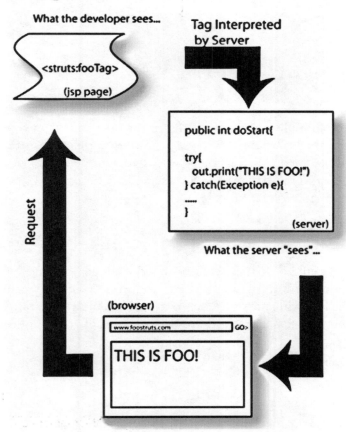

Figure 3.1 The JSP tag life cycle from Request to Response

What tags do we discuss in this chapter?

The tags that we discuss in this chapter are of two main types. They include tags with less complexity that emulate HTML tags in many respects but that incorporate Struts' ability to expose data and integrate it seamlessly into JSPs. The other type of tags have greater complexity, allowing you to create rich, complex web applications with greater ease, scalability, and maintainability.

The first type of tags discussed are those that emulate HTML tags or supplant JSP scripting. They are:

- `<html:rewrite/>`
- `<html:link/>`
- `<html:img/>`
- `<bean:write/>`
- `<bean:define/>`
- `<bean:include/>`

Use of these tags initially gives a big bang for the buck, but soon you are wanting more. Although they can help you create complex applications, there are times when you need to create richer pages with dynamic dependencies and states, and you need to add more tags from Struts' tag libraries:

- `<logic:present/>`
- `<logic:equal/>`
- `<bean:resource/>`

Using these tags allows for showing and hiding parts of pages or resources, depending upon the information passed around by your application. You can incorporate the following tags to create solid and reliable applications that cleanly encapsulate the Model, View, and Controller sections of your applications:

- `<tiles:insert/>`
- `<tiles:getAsString/>`
- `<tiles:put/>`
- `<tiles:definition/>`
- `<tiles:add/>`
- `<tiles:putList/>`

These tags represent the Struts Tiles tag library. Tiles allow you to create pages that use templates and break them into specific components. There are two parts to a Tiles-enabled application—the "definition" and the "tile." The definition pages (or the tiles-definitions.xml file, explained in recipe 3.13, "Using tiles with XML definitions") defines the templates that your pages use, assembling their respective components or "tiles" into the View component. Tiles can take parameters that allow you to build rich, dynamic content. There are two recipes involving Struts Tiles and their associated tags and methods:

3.12—Creating a basic Struts Tiles page
3.13—Using Tiles with XML definitions

Between logic tags and tiles, a battle in the development world rages. What does logic have to do with presentation? Are we violating MVC2 architecture by putting *any* logic on a JSP page? What is the theory versus the reality in development environments? These questions are addressed in different recipes within this chapter. It is important early in the design process to decide where and how your Model, View, and Controller components fit in. Do they represent Business Objects in your application? Do they tell these objects what to do? Or, do they display and format objects so they are acted upon by a user? Your code remains scalable, extendable, and relevant for years if you make sure that design and implementation are separated far in advance.

What did we leave out?

We left out tags that might not be used very often in the development process, or tags that, although useful, are more associated with forms (covered later in chapter 2), layout (we cover that in chapter 4), and other third-party libraries.

We also haven't covered the Java Standard Tag Library here, because Manning Publications has an excellent book, *JSTL in Action*, by Shawn Bayern. It covers JSTL in great detail and is recommended for those using Struts with the Java Standard Tag Library. These tags allow for the removal of a tremendous amount of Java source code from your JSP pages, but as with any tools, care must be taken to use them properly to ensure business logic is kept from the View layer whenever possible. More information is available at Sun's Java site, and Shawn's book is complete if you decide to pursue this subject further.

Struts also has a release of its product using JSTL tags, known as Struts-EL. Struts-EL's libraries incorporate the JSTL wherever the traditional Struts tags' functionality overlaps. The following detailed definition of Struts-EL comes from the Jakarta Struts web site.

**THE STRUTS-
EL TAG
LIBRARY**

"The Struts-EL tag library is a contributed library in the Struts distribution. It represents an integration of the Struts' tag library with the JavaServer Pages Standard Tag Library, or at least the "expression evaluation" engine that is used by the JSTL.

The base Struts' tag library contains tags which rely on the evaluation of `Java-Server` (runtime scriptlet expressions) to evaluate dynamic attribute values. For instance, to print a message from a properties file based on a resource key, you would use the `bean:write` tag, perhaps like this:

```
<bean:message key='<%= stringvar %>'/>
```

This assumes that `stringvar` exists as a JSP scripting variable. If you're using the Struts-EL library, the reference looks similar, but slightly different, like this:

```
<bean-el:message key="${stringvar}"/>
```

If you want to know how to properly use the Struts-EL tag library, there are two important things you need to know:

- The Struts' tag library
- The JavaServer Pages Standard Tag Library

Once you understand how to use these two, consider Struts' tag attribute values being evaluated the same way the JSTL tag attribute values are. Past that, there is little else you need to know to effectively use the Struts-EL tag library.

Although the Struts-EL tag library is a direct "port" of the tags from the Struts' tag library, not all of the tags in the Struts' tag library were implemented in the Struts-EL tag library. This was the case if it was clear that the functionality of a particular Struts tag could be entirely fulfilled by a tag in the JSTL. It is assumed that developers will want to use the Struts-EL tag library along with the JSTL, so it is reasonable to assume that they will use tags from the JSTL if they fill their needs."

Source: http://jakarta.apache.org/struts/userGuide/building_view.html#struts-el

There is a debate about the future of the Struts' tag libraries versus JSTL in general. Which library will prevail? What direction should you take for long-term success? As of this writing, all Struts tag libraries are fully supported, and whatever path you choose, it is imperative to know how to work with both tag libraries if you do decide to implement more JSTL-centric solutions. It will be easy to make any needed changes if your requirements evolve and the direction of Struts' development moves towards unification of the JSTL and existing Struts tags.

3.1 Using <html:link/> to increase your application's maintainability

◆ **Problem**

You want to use <html:link/> and its associated attributes to create more maintainable applications.

◆ **Background**

Let's look specifically at the Struts version of the <a/> tag: <html:link/>. The <html:link/> tag provides additional functionality over its HTML counterpart by incorporating the following features into it:

- Automatic URL encoding, so you do not need <%=response.EncodeURL ("myURL")%> to manage your session state
- Complete context path resolving—no need to add <%=request.getContext-Path()%> in your code
- Access to global-forwards in the struts-config.xml file through the forward attribute
- You can request pages through the page attribute, as in <html:link/> which, along with the href and action attributes (the "destination resource"), provides access to the paramId, paramName, and name attributes (the "request parameters").
- You can "roll your own" URL using the href attribute, which gives you client-side access to JavaScript variables that can be added to your URL as a request string.
- You can attach Maps with name-value pairs to append request strings.

If you choose not to use <html:link/> in your Struts application, moving from page to page becomes difficult. All directory paths and your session state would have to be carefully coded, because Struts doesn't "go from page to page" like a simple static HTML application. The <html:link/> tag specifically addresses these issues and works within the Struts framework. This allows you to create code that is much easier to maintain, extend, and deploy.

Once rendered by the browser, the <html:link/> transforms into a typical HTML "anchor" element with the URL properly rewritten, based upon the specific tag attribute you choose. Session state is maintained, and all URLs are rewritten with the proper context path where applicable.

There are four ways to create URLs for hyperlinks:

1 By using the `forward` attribute, you map the URL to a predefined `<global-forward/>` in the struts-config.xml file.

2 By using the `page` attribute, you map the URL directly to an application- or module-relative page *or* `action` defined in the Struts configuration.

3 By using the `action` attribute, you map a URL to a specifically named `Action` in your configuration.

4 By using the `href` attribute, the URL string is completely unchanged. creating a link with the value output as a `String` literal.

You can pass a parameter into the URLs using the `paramId` attribute, or pass multiple parameters as a key-value collection using the `name` attribute.

Consider listing 3.1 and the huge URL string that must be managed.

Listing 3.1 Messy URL strings without the `<html:link/>` tag

```
<%
  String cPath = request.getContextPath();
  String myUrl = "/this/huge/url?manageability=horrible&length=tooLong"
      + "&readability=ridiculous&
      + "numberOfVariables=impossible
      + "&etc=etc"
%>
<%-- must use response.encodeURL() to maintain session without cookies --%>
<a href="<%=response. encodeURL(cPath+myUrl);%>"/>my url </a>
```

This coding strategy is messy, hard to scale, and leaves way too much room for human error (which you'll discover when you try to track down a misspelled request parameter). It's easy enough for the wheels to fall off a project, so it's worth starting off on the right foot. This recipe shows you how to use `<html:link/>` to cut the messy code from the page and make your applications easier to maintain and scale.

◆ *Recipe*

`<html:link/>`, like all Struts tags, is well thought out and integrated into the overall framework to manage its specific task, meaning `<html:link/>` integrates Struts' functionality into JSPs with encapsulated code that is easy to learn and maintain. `<html:link/>` can connect global-forwards, mappings, and simple URLs, and automatically append strings and beans (`java.util.Map`) into request parameters.

There are also attributes that map directly to their HTML counterparts to deliver preexisting features. We'll explain how these most commonly used attributes are implemented by comparing the HTML anchor tag and the <html:link/> tag. In the first example, standard HTML tags used with JSP scripting and the <bean: message/> tag combine to create a usable URL link (*not recommended*).

```
<%
String cPath = request.getContextPath();
%>
<a href="<%=response.
            encodeURL(cPath+"/thisThing.do?firstVariable=one")%>    ❶
    title="<bean:message key="thisThing.title"/>"    ❸
    accessKey="<bean:message key="thisThing.mnemonic"/>"    ❷
    class="linkClass"
    tabindex="2" >
  <bean:message key="thisThing.linkName"/>    ❹
</a>
```

Indeed, the above link coded in this style *does* work; it renders and calls the Action class ❶ and passes the single parameter (firstVariable), the accessKey ❷, and toolTip ❸, and then the link name is rendered properly with the correct resource bundle ❹. But would you want to open this program up in two years and try to understand what was going on? It's a nightmare just to track the opening and closing tags, not to mention the nested tags or all the quotation marks!

The <html:link/> tag in this next snippet is more maintainable and easier to read. Notice the lack of nesting between the rendered and compiled code. Each tag has a specific job and works harmoniously with the rest of the code on the page, with no JSP scripting:

```
<html:link action="/thisThing"
      paramId=firstVariable" paramName="one" titleKey="thisThing.title"
      accesskey="thisThing.mnemonic" styleClass="linkClass"
      tabindex="2"><bean:message key="thisThing.linkName"/></html:link>
```

The second version would be a nice gift to the future, as it is completely encapsulated in the Struts framework and can be managed in a straightforward manner. Many of the attributes affecting accessibility and usability are set. The text is completely encapsulated and ready for internationalization, and the Action is encoded and referred to in the correct context. Finally, the code is linear and easy to read and maintain.

Let's extend the above ideas and look at how the <html:link/> tag can embed multiple request parameters in the URI using a java.util.Map. The following code snippet shows a HashMap placed in pageContext(), and then added to the <html:link/> tag using the name attribute:

```
<%
java.util.HashMap params = new java.util.HashMap();
params.put("p1", "FirstParam");
params.put("p2", "SecondParam");
params.put("p3", "ThirdParam");
pageContext.setAttribute("linkParams", params);
%>

<html:link action="thisThing" name="linkParams">a link</html:link>
```

The URL string rendered in the browser automatically appends the ?, &, and = characters in the proper places to create:

```
<a href="/myapp/thisThing.do?p1=FirstParam&p2=SecondParam&p3=ThirdParam">
      a link</a>
```

There will be many times when you find this method indispensible. And you can retrieve this kind of information from objects in any scope, not just from the page scope.

The above code addresses most of the attributes needed for nearly all <html:link/> tags you will ever use. For specific cases where you might need the other attributes, you should consult the excellent documentation available at the Jakarta Struts web site.

◆ *Discussion*

There are two other tags with many identical attributes to <html:link/>. It is possible to take most of the above recipe and apply it to these tags:

■ <html:rewrite/>—Renders a request URI string without creating the <a> hyperlink. This tag is used to generate a URL string constant for use by a JavaScript procedure, CSS link, or URL information in a standard HTML tag.

■ <html:frame/>—Renders an HTML <frame> element with the src attribute generated in an identical manner to the <html:link> or <html:rewrite/> tag for the href attribute.

Once you understand the functionality of one tag and are comfortable with its use, you can use the others in this family to good effect. It is wise to pay a short visit to the documentation to be clear on implementation-specific behaviors and attributes for each tag. Most tags in the Struts framework with URL attributes as references or sources have similar functionality. They can even use many of the same attributes (for example, <html:img/>) to implement their specific graphic or logical tasks, as explained in many corresponding recipes throughout this chapter.

Your application needs to be scalable and maintainable. Your code and its long-term success depends heavily upon making good decisions early and often. Using tags that normalize your paths, cleanly integrate with Struts, and implement well-known and documented tag libraries can create an environment that will remain valid over many subsequent releases. The Struts HTML tag library, with its ability to resolve and encode paths, represents some of the best tools available.

BEST PRACTICE   *Prefer Struts tags over any HTML counterpart*—Do not use HTML tags when a simpler Struts tag rewards you with the same result. "Mixing and matching" HTML code, JSP scriptlets, and Struts tags is possible and some-times even necessary under certain conditions, but designers should use this style sparingly and only after exhausting other avenues.

The best way to reduce the amount of time you spend maintaining code is to reduce the number of lines of it. Struts tags represent a great deal of code in only a few lines. It is much easier to maintain HashMaps with name-value pairs for parameter-rich URLs than it is to use up a good pair of eyes keeping track of long request strings. Using Struts tags dramatically reduces duplication, which is the single largest problem faced by an organization when maintaining a large code base.

The above recipe shows how <html:link/> can help you increase your appli-cation's maintainability. On the average, every Struts tag used replaces at least five lines of HTML or JSP scripting code. As you populate your pages with tags for beans, images, links, logic, strings, and messages, you can easily note signifi-cant decreases in the time you spend keeping programs running smoothly.

◆ *Related*

- 3.2—Rendering images mapped from a properties file using <html:img/>
- 3.10—Using <html:rewrite/>to resolve URLs

3.2 *Rendering images mapped from a properties file using <html:img/>*

◆ *Problem*

You want to use <html:img/> tag to get image references mapped in a properties file.

◆ *Background*

<html:img/> is processed by the servlet engine into an HTML <img/> tag. The image path for this tag is resolved depending upon which attribute you set when

creating it. You *must* use one of the four following attributes: src, page, action, or srcKey.src. The most common attribute, src, applies URL rewriting to the specific path of the image that you specify. page provides a URL that is a module-relative path of the image to be displayed. action appends to a named Action, beginning with a (/) that renders the image requested. Finally, srcKey.src references the image URL from a resource bundle named by the bundle attribute (if no bundle is specified, the default is used). Here are the most common, but not all, of the attributes implemented by the ubiquitous HTML <img/> tag:

- align—The alignment of the image
- alt—The text to display before the image is rendered or if the image cannot be rendered by the client
- height—The height of the image
- width—The width of the image
- border—The border of the image to be displayed in pixels
- src—The location of the image to be displayed

Not only does the Struts <html:img/> tag support and implement all of the above attributes for images (just like its HTML counterpart), it also supports Struts' linking and URL manipulation mechanisms. In this recipe, we'll show you how to use the tag's srcKey attribute to point to a URL reference in a Struts message-resource properties file, effectively storing all image references in a single property file. This is *especially* helpful when you have many images in your application, or when you have special URL links for high-speed caching purposes at remote servers, such as Akamai, and so on. Once your image references are stored within a message-resource properties file, the possibility of duplicate entries is drastically reduced, making management of your images and their associated directories less time intensive.

◆ *Recipe*

Incorporating images into your web application is necessary. They add flavor, impart mood, and extend the printed information on your pages. Look and feel are important to the user's experience, but management and control of these images are more important to *you*, the developer, before and after the application is deployed.

Image location and retrieval are the big concerns for the developer, but other considerations can come into play as well. Are these images localized? Would someone from France need a different image? What about links from them? The

Struts <html:img/> tag offers excellent answers to these questions through its rich attribute set. By setting a few attributes in this tag, we'll show you how it is possible to implement functionality that only a few years ago required many lines of code.

BEST PRACTICE   *Keep to a single image directory in most circumstances.*—A single image directory should be used in most circumstances. This directory is best located at a level equal to your pages directory. Unrelated, nested, or multiple directories to handle images can be cumbersome and extremely confusing as your application grows. It is important to remember that these images will eventually need to be accessed from more than just pages (i.e., tiles, layout-templates, scripts, and CSS directories).

Let's look at a typical image on a Struts JSP page, dissect it, and gain an understanding of image incorporation using property files within the Struts framework. The code snippet below shows an entry in the struts-config.xml file specifying an image resource bundle (for more information on resource bundles, see recipe 1.5, "Specifying a resource property file in a configuration").

```
<message-resources parameter="resources.images" key="images"/>
```

The JSP page in listing 3.2 contains an introduction message and an image reference to the above-named resource bundle.

Listing 3.2   JSP page with Struts `<html:img/>` tag

```
<html:html locale="true">
<head>
<html:base/>
<title><bean:message key="imagePage.title"/></title>
</head>
<body>
   <bean:message key="imagePage.IntroductionMessage"/><br/>
<html:img pageKey="images.foo.reallyBigImageWithLink.jpg"      ❶
      bundle="images" height="175" width="300" styleClass="bigimages"/>      ❷
</body>
</html:html>
```

We've referred to the image using the pageKey attribute ❶; this in turn refers to a reference in the image resource bundle corresponding to its specific key-value pair. This image reference contains the proper context with respect to the page—the <html:img/> tag appends and rewrites the context path when it is compiled by the servlet engine. You will also notice that the height and width attributes ❷ are included to give an example of the "carryover" HTML attributes included in this tag's functionality. Finally, the `styleClass` ❷ attribute refers to the CSS class in your style sheet—in this case `bigimages` in the CSS.

There are distinct advantages to this. Your images' links are referenced through a `key` resource bundle, which can be internationalized and maintained far away from the JSP code and business logic. In this instance, a link or path to an image is mapped to a properties file specified in a message-resources entry in the struts-config.xml. When the page is rendered, the `pageKey` attribute reads the properties file, renders the context-relative URL of the image, and attaches the CSS class of `bigimages` via the `styleClass` attribute.

◆ *Discussion*

There are few perfect solutions, and the `<html:img/>` tag is no exception. Large high-traffic sites often require images to have `width` and `height` attributes to speed up loading on browsers. Adding width and height attributes to improve speed is absolutely necessary, because without them, the browser must spend time downloading the image, figuring out its size and then calculating how the rest of the elements on the page must fit into it. When the size of the image is specified, it creates a placeholder for the image and just inserts it without doing all the calculations. While this isn't a big deal on complex, low-traffic web applications, on sites with millions of hits per day, any increase in performance can generate thousands of dollars!

To store the many static images and keep track of them, we've shown how to use property files to store the URLs for retrieval. `<html:img/>` has no way of cleanly transmitting the sizes to the source code. The following snippet shows an entry in a property file with a stored image's URL path:

```
images.anotherOne.logo=/siteRoot/images/logo.gif
```

You can use the stored image in an `<html:img/>` tag with the size attributes filled. The next snippet shows this image being accessed through the `srcKey` attribute (as no bundle is specified, the default message-resources property file is being accessed):

```
<html:img srcKey="images.anotherOne.logo" width="250"  height="125" />
```

The page must therefore "know" something about the image loading, and consequently the developer must know the size of every image that he uses. Even though the URL is stored properly, you must use rather esoteric scripting to properly store the size in the file and retrieve it. The next code snippet shows the entries into the property file:

```
images.anotherOne.logo=/siteRoot/images/logo.gif
images.anotherOne.logo.width=250
images.anotherOne.logo.height=125
```

Now, we'll access the URL, getting the `width` and `height` attributes of the corresponding image with its URL source reference:

```
<bean:define name="logoWidth">
    <bean:messagekey="images.anotherOne.logo.width"/>
</bean:define>

<bean:define name="logoHeight">
    <bean:messagekey="images.anotherOne.logo.height"/>
</bean:define>

<html:img srcKey="images.anotherOne.logo"
          width="<%=logoWidth%>"
          height="<%=logoHeight" />
```

While this might work for a few images, on a large site with hundreds, or even thousands of images, this becomes a maintenance and coding nightmare and is obviously out of the question. The best solution in this case is to rely only on image paths stored in property files for those images that rarely change, and specify the other images with their size attributes directly in the tag until the Struts group decides to support this.

◆ *Related*

- ■ 1.6—Multiple message-resource properties files in an application
- ■ 3.1—Using <html:link/> to increase your application's maintainability
- ■ 3.4—Using <bean:define/>to expose information to your pages
- ■ 3.6—Using <logic:present/> tags to determine page content
- ■ 3.7—Debugging your GUI with the <logic:present/> tag
- ■ 3.8—Using the <logic:equal/> tag for view decisions
- ■ 6.3—Internationalize your images

3.3 *Encoding information with a <bean:write/> tag*

◆ *Problem*

You want to use the `<bean:write/>` tag to encode and unencode information.

◆ *Background*

The `<bean:write>` tag uses the current JspWriter to output the contents of a bean's field or property specified in the tag's `scope` attribute (if the attribute is not set, the default is `page`). The information returned to the page is rendered as a `String`; the way they are rendered in the browser can change, depending upon the `filter` attribute's setting.

There are two ways for the `String` you are requesting to appear. It can be HTML formatted if you wish to render it graphically or with special HTML or XML formatting. You might wish to display special characters as "escaped" (i.e., the < character is `&lt;`, and so on); this is often done when implementing security measures for BBS/forum software, as spurious user input could create havoc in this type of application—a malicious user could create a simple script to create pop-ups, redirect pages, load huge amounts of information and crash browsers, and so on.

When using the `<bean:write>` tag, the `filter` attribute can be set to `true` or `false` to implement this functionality (default value is `true` if the `filter` attribute is not invoked explicitly). When this attribute is set to `true`, any characters that represent HTML markup are escaped. When `false`, the `String`'s characters are rendered by the browser's interpreter as they are coded. The recipe below demonstrates a simple output that retrieves a `String` in both filtered and unfiltered states.

◆ *Recipe*

Consider listing 3.3, rendering an HTML string with a field name of `htmlString`.

Listing 3.3   A simple string of HTML code

```
<table border="1">
<tr><td>This is the first cell</td><td>This is the second cell</td></tr>
<tr><td colspan="2">This is a really wide cell at the bottom</td></tr>
</table>
<h3>End of the HTML String</h3>
```

By employing the code below on your JSP pages, you can alter its presentation by setting the `filter` attribute to `true`:

```
<bean:write name="htmlString" filter="true"/>
```

Below is the browser output of the simple HTML string, `filter` attribute unset *or* set to `true`:

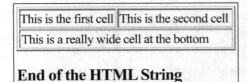

Figure 3.2
Output of a <bean:write/> tag with
the filter set to false, allowing HTML
to be rendered in the browser

```
<table border="1"><tr><td>This is the first cell</td><td>This is the second
    cell</td></tr><tr><td colspan="2">This is a really wide cell at the bottom
    </td></tr></table><h3>End of the HTML String</h3>
```

Now we set the filter attribute set to false:

```
<bean:write name="htmlString" filter="false"/>
```

The browser output of the simple HTML string, with the filter attribute set to false changes the view dramatically, as shown in figure 3.2.

◆ *Discussion*

When the filter attribute is set to false, HTML/XML- formatted Strings can be sent to the browser for further processing or as an end unto itself, creating a powerful tool for the developer to control presentation.

You can use this tool while you are developing your pages to expose the code's values, check for parameters being set and unset, and to validate complicated HTML strings. You might want to show some application where you are applying an XSL translation to an XML String declared in a bean (possibly with JSTL tags). There is no way to do this translation using the <bean:write/> tag without setting the filter attribute to false, exposing the proper characters to the page.

> **BEST**
> **PRACTICE**
> *Beware of sending unfiltered information to the browser*—More often than not you'll want to leave the filter attribute in its default (true) setting; otherwise, you have to write the code for your view in very specific implementations, resulting in the Model and Controller layer "knowing" too much about what needs to be rendered on the View component.

The above is but one example of the filter attribute. You might have a forum or special emailing program or you might be hosting a developer site where you wish to expose code snippets to developers seeking information. There are times when you might have messages or need to render XML or preformatted Strings to your pages. This is when the filter attribute can come in handy for further manipulation or just to expose the raw code.

◆ *Related*

- 1.6—Multiple message-resource properties files in an application
- 3.4—Using <bean:define/>to expose information to your pages
- 3.6—Using <logic:present/> tags to determine page content
- 3.7—Debugging your GUI with the <logic:present/> tag
- 3.8—Using the <logic:equal/> tag for view decisions

3.4 Using <bean:define/> to expose information to your pages

◆ *Problem*

You want to create scripting variables from beans and properties exposed to your JSP pages using <bean:define/> and its associated attributes.

◆ *Background*

A page must "know" as little as possible about your back-end architecture. It should only concern itself with rendering the view and not manipulating any data logic. With this separation, an isolated and consistent connection between the Controller and View components of your application exists. This pipeline for the View needs to be defined in your Struts JSPs using the `<bean:define/>` tag so it can be manipulated into usable GUI components. This tag's job is to act as a contract or API from the server-side to the View component. Without it you can use scripting variables all over your JSPs, getting you into serious trouble if the back end changes. If you've implemented the `<bean:define/>` tag properly, you only need to make your changes in that specific location. This tag allows you to do quite a few things:

- Create a scripting variable from an object you've created on your page.
- Create a scripting variable from a `String` placed in scope.
- Create a scripting variable from the property of a field you've exposed on a bean.
- Set variables into session or page context.
- Cast object types exposed by your beans.

The `<bean:define/>` tag can be used to control most of the data used by the View component in your applications. When combined with other bean, logic, HTML, layout, and other custom tags and simple scriptlets, you can create rich, reusable, and scalable JSPs. Using `<bean:define/>`, as we will see in the recipe to follow, can be simple or quite complex.

◆ **Recipe**

There are many ways to use the `<bean:define/>` tag within our JSP pages. Let's begin with a few simple implementations and then gradually ramp up in complexity.

Defining a page-level variable

This implementation takes a `String` and applies it to the `pageContext`. You can then access this variable using the `<%=theVariableName%>` throughout the page. This is an extremely simple implementation. Using the attributes `id` and `value`, the code follows:

```
<bean:define id="myVariable" value="someValue"/>
```

or you can set the value inside of the tag:

```
<bean:define id="myVariable">someValue</bean:define>
```

You can also set an object defined on the JSP page into `pageContext`. To do this, you use the `name` attribute. First, create your object, then fill out the `<bean:define/>` tag by setting the object's name:

```
<%
    java.util.Map myMap = new java.util.HashMap();      ❶
    myMap.put("value1", "aValue1");
    myMap.put("value2", "aValue2");
    myMap.put("value3", "aValue3");
    myMap.put("value4", "aValue4");

pageContext.setAttribute("myMap",myMap);
%>

    <bean:define id="myVariableMap" name="myMap"/>      ❷
```

In the above snippet, the `java.util.Map myMap` ❶, is placed in `pageContext` by setting the `name` attribute ❷.

Creating a scripting variable from a string in session scope

The real power of the `<bean:define/>` tag is in exposing Java objects to a JSP. In listing 3.4, we're going to create a `String` using a `java.util.StringBuffer` inside a Java class and set its value into session scope.

Listing 3.4   Defining a variable from a bean's field in a Java class

```
String firstStringVar = "pugs";
String secondStringVar = "iguanas";
String favPets = "";
StringBuffer buf = new StringBuffer("I like ");

buf.append(firstStringVar);
buf.append(" and ");
buf.append(secondStringVar);
favPets = buf.toString();              ❶
session.setAttribute("pets",favPets);      ❷
```

Now we can expose the `String myVariable` to our page ❶. The `Action` class "sets" ❷ this variable into session scope (`pets`). Next we expose it to the page by getting it from session with the `<bean:define/>` tag, and outputting the `String` with a simple JSP script.

```
<bean:define id="myVariable" name="pets"/>      ❸
```

```
<h3>I like <%=myVariable%>!</h3>      ❹
```

The above snippets should render in your browser as:

> I like pugs and iguanas!

We define the scripting variable ❸ on the page with the tag's `id` attribute, use the `name` attribute to expose the session attribute (`pets`), and then use it on the page ❹ with the JSP script. You can `type` the definition if you wish. This isn't required, but if you are bringing more than `java.util.String` objects to the page in your tag, you should implement this attribute for safety.

Defining a variable from a bean's property

Let's get a little more detailed and create a scripting variable from a context attribute. You might have many "getters" and "setters" that you want to expose to a page, or just a specific part of the object. The Java class in listing 3.5 defines a variable and various properties associated with it.

Listing 3.5   A simple class with a name property

```
package com.strutsrecipes;
public class Foo{

    private String name;
```

```
    public String getName() {
        return name;
    }
    public void setName(String aVal) {
        name = aVal;
    }
}

Foo fooAttribute = new Foo();
fooAttribute.setName("Bob");
session.setAttribute("myFoo", fooAttribute);
```

Let's assume that the object `fooAttribute` in listing 3.5 is set into `HttpSession` as `myFoo` via an `Action` class, and the `name` property is set. Using `<bean:define/>` in the JSP page for this case would look like the JSP in listing 3.6.

> **Listing 3.6** JSP listing defining a scripting variable specifically from an object's property in session scope

```
<bean:define id="fooName" name="myFoo" property="name"    ❶
    scope="session" type="com.strutsrecipes.Foo"/>
```

The `id` attribute defines a scripting variable based upon the value of the property in the `<bean:define/>` tag . In this case, the tag is basically invoking `fooName.getName()`. When invoking `<%=fooName%>`, whatever `String` that was set through the `setName()` method is rendered on the page.

Note that the `scope` attribute is set to match the Java code in listing in 3.6. We've also `typed` the object as a best practice.

BEST PRACTICE   *Set the `type` and `scope` attribute when using `<bean:define/>`*—As a professional developer, you should `type` your more custom or esoteric Java-Beans to enhance maintainability. While some beans can be obvious, a future developer extending your project will really appreciate the "heads up." If possible, your beans should *always be `typed` to their interface.*

Struts tags have the ability to automatically figure out the bean's type. This is especially true when the tag has inherent expectations of the bean's type (such as `<bean:write/>` or `<layout:collection/>`). You might have problems with Integers and other objects; when this happens, a `ClassCastException` and bean define tag is thrown and your page refuses to load.

<bean:define/> with collections

We often want to expose java.util.Collections to a page for the purpose of rendering dynamic tables, form elements, and so on. Let's take a collection defined in the MyMountains class in listing 3.7 and create a <bean:define/> tag to expose it to a page.

Listing 3.7   Creating a `java.util.Collection` for exposure to a JSP page

```
protected class MyMountains {

protected Collection getMountains() {
  ArrayList el = new ArrayList ();
  el.add("Everest");
  el.add("K2");
  el.add("Kangchenjunga");
  el.add("Lhotse");
  el.add("Makalu");
  el.add("Cho Oyu");
  return el;
  }
}

  // and we set it in session in an Action class…
  session.setAttribute("myMountains",mountains);
```

On the destination JSP page, we use the <bean:define/> tag and <logic:iterate/> tag to create a portion of an HTML page, as shown in listing 3.8. We refer to this collection as myMountains.

Listing 3.8   Exposing a java.util collection to a JSP page using `<bean:define/>`

```
<bean:define id="theMountains" name="myMountains"        ❷
    property="mountains" type= "java.util.Collection" />  ❶

<logic:iterate id="mountain" name="theMountains">        ❸
  <b><bean:write name="mountain"/></b><br/>              ❹
</logic:iterate>
```

Note the type attribute is set ❶. The bean's name myMountains is exposed as a page-scoped variable ❷. The <logic:iterate/> tag iterates over the variable declared in the name attribute, in this case myMountains. During each iteration it creates a variable using the value of the id attribute to expose an element in the collection, in this case mountain ❸. Finally the <bean:write/> tag writes out the String associated with the current iterated member ❹.

The rendered JSP shows the names of the mountains in a list:

Everest

K2

Kangchenjunga

Lhotse

Makalu

Cho Oyu

The use of collections is extremely useful. With a collection exposed on the page, it is possible to render form elements, dynamic tables, and use the functionality of the Struts-Layout tag library, the topic of Chapter 4. The use of Collection is significant in terms of flexibility. You can change the Collection implementation class to any descendant of Collection without touching the JSP.

◆ **Discussion**

It isn't necessary to use the `<bean:define/>` tag for the small stuff. If you have a simple `String` that is already in session and needs to be exposed to a page, just use:

```
"<bean:write name="sessionString" scope="session"/>"
```

This implementation also exposes parameter-level `Strings`, as the `<bean:write/>` tag searches through the available scopes (including request) to find a variable.

Sometimes defining the bean on a page, even redundantly, isn't a bad idea. You might create a page and not refer to it again for some time. If you have the scripting variable instantiated *and typed* on a page, then you can easily keep track of what you've done, what the particular session attribute is, and what you're trying to accomplish. Along with good commenting, you are able to maintain pages that you haven't seen in years. This practice allows you to scale your applications faster if and when you decide to change your pages and expose more properties to the view.

◆ **Related**

- 3.3—Encoding information with a `<bean:write/>` tag
- 3.6—Using `<logic:present/>` tags to determine page content
- 3.7—Debugging your GUI with the `<logic:present/>` tag
- 3.12—Creating a basic Struts Tiles page
- 3.13—Using Tiles with XML definitions

3.5 Use <bean:include/> for the simple server-side includes

◆ **Problem**

You want to use `<bean:include/>` tags to manage "simple" server-side `includes`.

◆ **Background**

Most simple applications' views are handled with a single JSP page, creating a presentation from the top down. Each JSP is a single, rendered, page in the view, without "inserted" or "included" files or any external references (except for the normal CSS, JavaScript, or image files). This type of JSP page isn't a template or skeleton; it contains all it needs for its view with no tiles or complicated externalized structure (Struts Tiles are the subject of a few recipes at the end of this chapter). Tags and beans (and sometimes JSP scripting) deliver the dynamic data; the View component of the JSP is integrated into this structure.

As your code base gets larger and managed content starts to become more segregated and generic, it becomes necessary for your pages to possess homogenized and reusable content. You might find it necessary to include third-party View components on your pages. There is quite a bit of this content available: stock tickers, news, specialized RSS feeds, applets, and so forth. You might need to post copyright notices at the bottom of every page. There might be other applets or widgets that are accessible to users based upon their authentication, accessibility, preference, or state of the application.

Struts provides you with several methods of segmenting your application into different and coherent layers. These include Tiles solutions with JSP and XML, using modules (multiple configuration files), and multiple message-resources. In many cases these solutions may be too complicated for the scale of the project. They require a higher level of maintenance. There are configurations, templates, and possibly multiple struts-config files that must be addressed before this type of solution can be implemented. What happened to the "good old server-side `include`" to handle some of this work?

When developing in Struts, three different `include` methods are available. These are the `include directive`, the `include action`, and Struts' `<bean:include/>` tag. All three are allowed inside the Struts framework, and all three have advantages and disadvantages discussed in the recipe below.

◆ *Recipe*

Let's compare and contrast the two legacy JSP solutions for including information on a page, and then we'll investigate what the Struts `<bean:include/>` tag delivers that is different. If you've been developing JSP solutions for any length of time, you've probably used the two standard JSP `include` methods: the `directive`, and the `action`. While they seem to do the same thing at their most basic level, as you add more and more dynamic content their differences become apparent. Let's look at them separately.

The include directive

The code for an `include` `directive` looks like:

```
<%@ include file="foo.jsp" %>
```

While you can use any other file type here (*.htm,*.html,*.xml, etc), this `include` method allows your included file to contain and reference variables declared in the parent JSP page. This code is rendered *with* the JSP, *before* it is compiled into a single view component. It is an excellent candidate for reusability when you expect your code to compile as part of the general page.

The include action

The code for the `include` `action` looks like:

```
<jsp:include page="foo.jsp" flush="true" />
```

So what's different here? Here's the same page, and it is included in the JSP. But, there is a *big* difference! Rather than being included at compile time, the page is processed when it is requested by the including JSP page; the result of this processing is then included into the JSP page at the point where the tag is located. As this is a full-blown JSP tag, you can dynamically include pages by passing request `Strings` along with the URL into the `page` attribute as shown in listing 3.9.

Listing 3.9 Dynamically including a file with a JSP `include action`

```
<%
   //this is "old school" jsp code on the page
   String jspIncludeVar = "foo";
   String suffix = "jsp";
   String someJspPage= foo +"."+ suffix;
%>

<%-- we'll use the string to define the include --%>
<jsp:include page="<%=someJSPpage%> flush="true"/>
```

You can extend a normal JSP `include` `action` presentation into one that varies not only the page's name, but also the suffix (listing 3.9).

Another difference to note between the two tags is their runtime nature and tolerance to change. The `include` `directive` *does not* render any changes during runtime unless the parent JSP page is changed and/or recompiled. The `include` `action` *does* render any and all changes to its code each and every time; there is a slight performance penalty as all internal pages must be rendered *before* the final page is processed, instead of a "one-time shot" that the `include` `directive` guarantees.

The Struts *<bean:include/>* tag

`<bean:include/>` allows a developer to set a `forward` attribute that will "include" a JSP page mapped to it (along with any corresponding actions, and so on). You can attach an `id` argument instead, which creates a `pageContext()` variable of `java.lang.String` that prints to the page. This tag is similar to the `<jsp:include/>` tag, but has a few Struts features added, such as the ability to pass bean information, or call the `ActionServlet` for different purposes. Let's work with a simple Struts JSP page in listing 3.10. Note that required tag libraries descriptors have been omitted.

Listing 3.10   A simple Struts JSP page that can be used as an `include`

```
<html:html>
<head>
<html:base/>
<title>Struts Test Application</title>
</head>
<body>
<h1>Here's a couple of links</h1>
<ul>
<li><html:link forward="fooLink">a foo link</html:link></li>
<li><html:link forward="anotherFooLink">another foo link</html:link></li>
</ul>
</body>
</html:html>
```

We're now going to include the above JSP using the `<bean:include/>` tag. Let's show the page as a rendered JSP with the following code snip. These two lines of code would be all that the page needs (don't forget the taglibs' descriptors at the top of the page):

```
<bean:include id="fooPage" page="/foo.jsp"/>

<%=fooPage%>
```

This is rendered in your display as shown in figure 3.3.

◆ *Discussion*

All of the include widgets are tools, and should be kept in your repertoire and used when necessary. Often there is static content such as a copyright disclaimer, contact info, a menu, or a complete header or footer that really doesn't change much for long periods of time. Why would you want to maintain this information in every page of your application? Use of an include directive is really the way to go.

You might also have some dynamic content that loads with the page, but is rather static in nature, such as a user's name, the date, and so on. This information is dynamic but "in line" with other information on the page, and doesn't need or "want" to be compiled separately from the rest of the JSP. Again, this is a definite use case for the include directive.

There are other times when the opposite is true. You might need to compile code separately from the JSP page with dependencies upon a particular parameter or page attribute. This is often the case when a page containing different portlets are created and the actual display might be dependent upon whether or not a user has chosen them in his or her preferences. Now there are multiple and independent JSPs on a single container page and more logic might be required to determine what the display is. In the above case you have an excellent reason for using the include action.

<bean:include/> allows for a little more "earth moving" than the above examples. This tag sets the information as a scripting variable so you can define it in one place and use it whenever and wherever you need. It allows you to tie

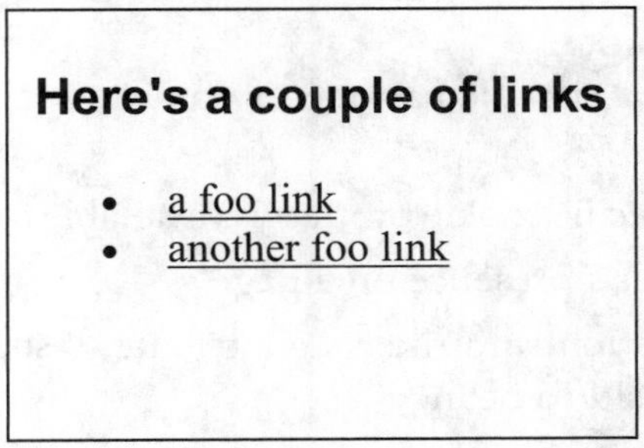

Here's a couple of links

- a foo link
- another foo link

Figure 3.3
Browser view using <bean:include/>
tag from listing 3.10

Actions to an include, multiplying your power exponentially by involving the Controller, allowing you to create richer and more reusable content. What more could we ask for? Well, there are tiles! Tiles take the above ideas and allow the careful and astute developer to create intricate and dynamic pages using templates with predefined insertions. Tiles' definitions can be created individually like regular JSP pages, or they can be produced *en masse* in a single definition page. This power makes it possible to generate applications with similar pages quickly and efficiently. The recipes at the end of this chapter will get you started in this direction.

◆ *Related*

- 3.3—Encoding information with a <bean:write/> tag
- 3.12—Creating a basic Struts Tiles page
- 3.13—Using Tiles with XML definitions

3.6 *Using <logic:present/> tags to determine page content*

◆ *Problem*

You want to use the <logic:present> and <logic:notPresent/> tags to control the content of your JSPs.

◆ *Background*

The body of the Struts <logic:present/> tag is evaluated whenever the JavaBean, or its property, is present within the JSP. If the bean or property exists, even with a null value, the tag is rendered. The attributes available for evaluation are:

- name—Tests for the name or property of a bean object in page, session, or application scope
- parameter—Tests whether or not a specific parameter name is available to the JSP
- cookie—Tests whether or not a specific cookie property is available to the JSP
- header—Tests for a request header's presence on a page
- property—When used in conjunction with the name attribute, tests for the presence of a specific property inside a bean

The <logic:present/> tag has many uses. It can alter the look of your GUI depending upon whether a specific role, parameter, bean, or condition is present; it can expose or hide controls available to users; or it can expose specific errors and error messages when the proper conditions are met. In this recipe, we use this tag to show how to hide elements from users of an application when they are not recognized. We will have a user variable set through an Action class into session, and then retrieve this variable with the <logic:present/> tag in the JSP to show or hide a message. While this particular recipe is simple, one can see how it might be extended to furnish increased functionality to a web application.

◆ *Recipe*

Let's start with the specific Java code in an Action class (listing 3.11) where an application sets the user's name into session. Once this session attribute is set, the Action calls the mapping.findForward() method to direct the Action servlet's response to a specific JSP page.

Listing 3.11   Nonspecific Action class setting a user session attribute

```
public ActionForward execute(ActionMapping mapping,
                             ActionForm form,
                             HttpServletRequest request,
                             HttpServletResponse response)
                             throws Exception {

// … code here executing some business logic and creating a "user" object

    if (user != null){
session.setAttribute("user", user);
}
return mapping.findForward("success");
}
```

Now we can take this user variable from session and check for its presence on a JSP page in listing 3.12. If the user variable is present, we allow some text to be shown.

Listing 3.12   Using the <logic:present/> tags in the JSP

```
<%@ taglib uri="/tags/struts-logic" prefix="logic"%>
<%@ taglib uri="/tags/struts-html" prefix="html"%>

<html:html locale="true">
<head>
```

```
<title></title>
  </head>
<body>
...
<!-- some code above the tag...-->

<logic:present name="user" scope="session">      ❶
<b>THIS TEXT IS HIDDEN FROM PEOPLE I DON'T KNOW</b>   ❷
</logic:present>


...
<!—the rest of the page...-->
</body>
</html:html>
```

The above code in ❷ shows the `<logic:present/>` tags surrounding a simple text `String` nested inside HTML bold tags. Because the `user` parameter is set into session by this `ExecuteFooAction` class, the tag's body and all associated HTML tags are rendered by a browser; the actual logic tags are never seen by the user or rendered in the generated HTML code. If the condition is met in which the `user` attribute isn't set ❶, the message is never evaluated and the generated HTML page is rendered as if this code were never written.

CHECKING FOR NULL VS "EXIST-ENCE" It is important to note that `<logic:present/>` tags only check for the existence of a variable. It doesn't care whether the field has a value or is `null`. If it exists, the tag is rendered. If you have a situation where you must check for `null`, then you should use the `<logic:empty/>` tag. Beware that if the field does not exist, the `<logic:empty/>` tag throws an exception.

It is possible that any variable can be set into session and captured in this manner, and any information can be evaluated within these tags, as long as the tags are open and closed and nested properly inside.

◆ *Discussion*

Struts rewards a good plan, and the `<logic:present/>` tags allow the implementation of complex views with little effort once you've mapped out exactly what you want to accomplish. The boolean evaluation gives you a great deal of flexibility, but it is important to realize that any JSP code that is not captured in tags of this type is *always* compiled and sent to the browser. If you have a specific message for a user when the `<logic:present/>` tag doesn't evaluate, you can use the `<logic:notPresent/>` tag.

A popular use for this tag is in the area of errors and messages. If there are a number of errors that a back-end application might bubble to a View component, it can be useful to propagate them with `present` and `notPresent` tags. Not only can you test for a bean's presence, you can also test the presence of a field on a bean. The bean might have a `getUserId` field that isn't set under a specific circumstance. The following JSP snippet evaluates the `<bean:write/>` tag ❷ only when user ❶ is set.

JSP with `<logic:present/>` tag, property attribute set

```
<logic:present name="user" property="userId" scope="session">     ❶
<b>User Id is: <bean:write name="user" property="userId"/></b>     ❷
</logic:present>
```

This code can be especially helpful in the page development process—To debug your page you can add logic and write tags to ensure the `Action` classes actually placed the bean in scope. This can help you locate the cause of a problem.

BEST PRACTICE   *Logic tags do not implement "try, catch, finally"*—While you can use the `present/notPresent` tags as an analogy for if/else, you really can't easily implement a "try, catch, finally" scenario without planning for and coding it appropriately and specifically in the `Action` class and JSP. While this can be too implementation specific, the `<logic:notPresent/>` or `<logic:present/>` tags can come in handy to keep a view or piece of code from falling through the cracks by acting as your "catch," or even your "finally" statement, depending upon your specific goals.

◆ Related

- 3.3—Encoding information with a `<bean:write/>` tag
- 3.6—Using `<logic:present/>` tags to determine page content
- 3.8—Using the `<logic:equal/>` tag for view decisions
- 3.12—Creating a basic Struts Tiles page
- 3.13—Using Tiles with XML definitions
- 7.6—Protect areas on a page

3.7 Debugging your GUI with the <logic:present/> tag

◆ Problem

You want to use <logic:present/> and <logic:notPresent/> tags to create tests for debugging a GUI.

◆ Background

As applications gain in scope and size, it can become difficult to keep track of parameters and other variables. As your GUI develops, you often wonder if you have all the parameters and fields you need at any given point. If you have missed any variables, you get an error page with a stack trace. While this is fine if the page has only one or two fields or properties to track, if the quantity increases, you might want to pull your hair out as you check to find the missing one.

In the last recipe we discussed the basic use of the <logic:present/> and <logic:notPresent/> tags. These tags are a great way to track multiple variables as you build an application. When you create a new page it is easy to check whether parameters or beans are available to it. Just create tests to check for their presence without "breaking" the page and causing the servlet engine to throw an error.

The following recipe tracks multiple parameters sent to a page. If they are present, it uses them in context. If they are notPresent, then text is displayed showing which ones are missing.

◆ Recipe

Let's start by creating a JSP page with two links. We will pass four parameters to display a userName and send three different CSS style definitions to a style block in the head of the document in listing 3.13. One link sends a page request with multiple parameters. One is the same link with no parameters at all.

> **Listing 3.13 JSP page setting variables into a page attribute for testing on a second page with logic tags**

```
<%
java.util.HashMap params = new java.util.HashMap();      ❶
params.put("userName", "Bill");
params.put("userColor","#001363");
params.put("userFont", "Arial");
params.put("userBackground","#F6FFF4");
pageContext.setAttribute("userInfo", params);
%>
```

```
<head>
<title>Test Parameters</title>
<html:base/>
</head>
<h3>Test for Parameters using &lt;logic:present&gt; tags</h3>
<!--this link carries the parameters-->
<p><html:link forward="testForm" name="userInfo">Pass the parameters test</
    html:link></p>
<!--this link has no parameters -->
<p><html:link forward="testForm">Same link without parameters</html:link></
p>
```

Now let's look at the destination page with the tests. In listing 3.14, the `<logic:present/>` and `<logic:notPresent/>` tags have the `parameter` attribute set to the values in the above `HashMap` ❶ in listing 3.13. If you were doing the same thing for a bean, you would substitute the `parameter` attribute for `name`, and if you were detecting multiple fields on the bean, you would also need to use the `property` attribute.

Listing 3.14   Destination JSP page code using `<logic:present/>` and `<logic:notPresent/>` tags

```
<logic:present parameter="userName">       ❶
<bean:parameter id="userName" name="userName"/>
</logic:present>
<logic:present parameter="userColor">
<bean:parameter id="userColor" name="userColor"/>
</logic:present>
<logic:present parameter="userFont">
<bean:parameter id="userFont" name="userFont"/>
</logic:present>
<logic:present parameter="userBackground">
<bean:parameter id="userBackground" name="userBackground"/>
</logic:present>
<html:html locale="true">
<head>
<title>Test page<logic:present parameter="userName">for:<bean:write
    name="userName"/></logic:present></title>
<html:base/>
<style type="text/css">
<!--
body{
<logic:present parameter="userFont">
font-family:<bean:write name="userFont"/>;
</logic:present>
<logic:present parameter="userColor">
color:<bean:write name="userColor"/>;
</logic:present>
```

```
<logic:present parameter="userBackground">
background-color:<bean:write name="userBackground"/>;
</logic:present>
}
-->
</style>
</head>
<body>
<h3>Are the Parameters "present" <logic:present parameter="userName">for:
   <bean:write name="userName"/></logic:present>?</h3>
If they are, the font should be Arial, The background color should be light
   green and the font color should be dark blue.

<logic:notPresent parameter="userName">           ❷
userName missing<br/>
</logic:notPresent>
<logic:notPresent parameter="userColor">
userColor missing<br/>
</logic:notPresent>
<logic:notPresent parameter="userFont">
userFont missing<br/>
</logic:notPresent>
<logic:notPresent parameter="userBackground">
userBackground missing<br/>
</logic:notPresent>
</body>
</html:html>
```

In listing 3.14, above the head of the document in ❶, we check for each parameter. If each one exists, we define a page-scope bean for it to use the specific variables as we wish on the page. If they do not exist, then the `<logic:notPresent>` tags "catch" this and send out messages in the GUI ❷. This example is somewhat simplified, but it shows the workings of the tags in a complete manner.

You might want to set an object into session context and check its properties as well as determine if the object is present at all. This is accomplished in exactly the same manner, except you use the `<bean:define/>` tag in lieu of `<bean:parameter/>`, and use the `name` attribute instead of the `parameter` attribute in your `<logic:present>`/`<logic:notPresent/>` tags. You are now able to look for and expose fields on the bean instead of the request parameter's simple `String` properties.

◆ *Discussion*

The above code might be overly complete if you are actually developing an application, but it is important to demonstrate how these tags are used in a complete manner. As a developer in the "heat of battle," you might just want to keep it simple and not worry about the presentation so much. You don't need to write so much code to see the results you need. You can put all the code in the body of the document and just check for its presence. In this case a few lines of text can take care of this, not necessarily showing whether a bean is "present" or not. If it's not present, you get nothing, as shown in listing 3.15.

Listing 3.15   JSP testing for the presence of passed parameters

```
<logic:present parameter="userName">
userName detected<br/>
</logic:present>
<logic:present parameter="userColor">
userColor detected<br/>
</logic:present>
<logic:present parameter="userFont">
userFont detected<br/>
</logic:present>
<logic:present parameter="userBackground">
userBackground detected<br/>
</logic:present>
<logic:notPresent parameter="userName">
userName missing<br/>
</logic:notPresent>
<logic:notPresent parameter="userColor">
userColor missing<br/>
</logic:notPresent>
<logic:notPresent parameter="userFont">
userFont missing<br/>
</logic:notPresent>
<logic:notPresent parameter="userBackground">
userBackground missing<br/>
</logic:notPresent>
```

Once the above items are solid and meet your requirements, you can then "add the eye candy" and build out a GUI.

These tags are useful on other levels; you can detect specific "flags" and settings specific to a page, identify previous actions, and create new ones based on previous user input.

<logic:present/>/<logic:notPresent/> tags differ from <logic:empty/> and <logic:notEmpty/> tags in that they do not throw an error if no bean exists; the <logic:empty/> and <logic:notEmpty/> tag *must* have a bean or parameter set or they *will* throw an error.

These tags must be used with the structure of multiple "if" statements. There is no "else" type of tag and it is *vital* to remember this when assembling the logic on the page. You *may* group these tags in the following manner to give a *pseudo* "try/catch/finally" block (listing 3.16), but in the end, you must be judicious as this type of code is very implementation specific.

Listing 3.16   A "pseudo" try/catch block

```
<!-- tries the bean -->
<logic:present name="beanToTry">
<!-- "If bean has a value, it's defined here" -->
   <bean:define id="beanScriptName" name="beanToTry"/>
</logic:present>
<!-- if  bean is null set a "null message" -->
<logic:empty name="beanToTry">
   <bean:define id="beanScriptName" value="Bean Found but is null"/>
</logic:empty>
<logic:notPresent name="beanToTry">
   <bean:define id="beanScriptName" value="No Bean Found at all"/>
</logic:notPresent>
<!-- now a page context variable, "beanScriptName", is set no matter what! -->

<bean:write name="beanScriptName"/>
```

◆ *Related*

- 3.3—Encoding information with a <bean:write/> tag
- 3.6—Using <logic:present/> tags to determine page content
- 3.7—Debugging your GUI with the <logic:present/> tag
- 3.12—Creating a basic Struts Tiles page
- 3.13—Using Tiles with XML definitions

3.8 *Using the <logic:equal/> tag for view decisions*

◆ *Problem*

You want to use <logic:equal/> and <logic:notEqual/> tags to vary your page views.

◆ *Background*

There are quite a few different tags in Struts' logic tag library that check the same type of information in only slightly different ways. One tag that is always an important part of any toolkit is the <logic:equal/> tag, and its sibling, <logic:

notEqual/>. Although other tags, such as <logic:present/>, check for the presence of a bean or bean property, <logic:equal> checks against a specific value in a bean. The <logic:Equal/> and <logic:notEqual/> tags assume the bean exits. These tags will throw an error when the bean has not been set. The <logic:equal/> tag compares the bean's toString() value against the value property. If the property attribute is specified, then the value attribute is compared against that bean's property.

The example recipe below takes a common problem, that is, a presentation with different buttons on a page, depending upon the type of action you might perform. In this case we have a total of three buttons: View, Edit and Delete. This is a typical problem with any type of persisted data (database, session attribute, EJB, and so on) or record storage and retrieval application most often found in user libraries, shopping carts, or document management.

◆ *Recipe*

We start by creating a simple JSP form that contains a drop-down list containing the values view, edit, and delete (listing 3.17).

Listing 3.17   testForm.jsp

```
<html:form action="LogicEqualAction">
   <html:select property="permissionField">
   <html:option value="view"/>
   <html:option value="edit"/>
   <html:option value="delete"/>
</html:select>
<html:submit/>
</html:form>
```

In the corresponding DynaActionForm in the snippet below, we create a single bean attribute, that of permissionField.

```
<form-beans>
<form-bean name="testForm" type="org.apache.struts.action.DynaActionForm">
   <form-property name="permissionField"
                  type="java.lang.String"
                  initial="view"/>
</form-bean>
</form-beans>
```

What we see in this application so far is just a simple form with one field. On the Java side in listing 3.18 we get the passed value and store it in session.

Listing 3.18   LogicEqualTestAction.java

```
// Extract attributes needed
Locale locale = getLocale(request);
String chosenPermission =
      (String) PropertyUtils.getSimpleProperty(form,"permissionField");
      System.out.println("permission chosen:\n"+chosenPermission);

//Save our htmlString in the session
HttpSession session = request.getSession();
session.setAttribute(Constants.PERMISSION, chosenPermission);
//make your application scalable by always mapping an action forward.

return (mapping.findForward("success"));
```

Now we must decide what we want to do with our View component. We decide that we should always be able to view the item in the GUI, except when we're deleting it. The View button must be available in both View and Edit modes. The Edit button is not available in the View or Delete modes (we obviously don't want to edit something that we're deleting). The View and Delete modes only show their respective View and Delete buttons. So we've created a matrix to define this logic visually:

Mode	View button	Edit button	Delete button
View	Show	No show	No show
Edit	Show	Show	No show
Delete	No show	No show	Show

Let's create our GUI with JSP in listing 3.19. We now see the `<logic:equal/>` ❶ and `<logic:notEqual/>` ❷, ❸ tags at work. We've nested some of these tags to alter the view to suit our needs with the smallest amount of code possible.

Listing 3.19   JSP showing the altering of view with `<logic:equal/>` tags

```
<h4>Action chosen: <bean:write name="permission"/></h4>
<logic:notEqual name="permission" value="delete">      ❷
<button style="margin:5px;">View</button>
   <logic:equal name="permission" value="edit">        ❶
      <button style="margin:5px;">Edit</button>
   </logic:equal>
</logic:notEqual>
<logic:equal name="permission" value="delete">         ❸
```

```
        <button style="margin:5px;">Delete</button>
    </logic:equal>
```

By setting the `<logic:notEqual/>` tag first ❷, we've made the Delete button appear alone by setting the value to compare the bean named `permission`. When `permission` equals the `String` value `delete`, then and only then are the items within these tags rendered and evaluated. Inside this `<logic:notEqual/>` tag we also see a nested `<logic:equal/>` tag ❶, which renders the Edit button when the `permission` attribute equals the value `edit`. Notice that the last `<logic:equal/>` tag ❸ has exactly the same values as the `<logic:notEqual/>` tag, to render the Delete button.

◆ *Discussion*

Let's break up the code and show how we did it. We've used the bean's value to show what's been chosen:

```
<h4>Action chosen: <bean:write name="permission"/></h4>
```

Next, we take a look at the first `<logic:notEqual/>` tag:

```
<logic:notEqual name="permission" value="delete">
```

It matches up to the last set of `<logic:equal/>` tags:

```
<logic:equal name="permission" value="delete">
```

We allow both of these tags to process when the page is requested. The content within is rendered in the last tag, or vice versa, depending upon whether or not the `permission` attribute equals `delete`. Now, we look inside the first set of tags, and their nestings.

```
<logic:notEqual name="permission" value="delete">
<button style="margin:5px;">View</button>
    <logic:equal name="permission" value="edit">
        <button style="margin:5px;">Edit</button>
    </logic:equal>
</logic:notEqual>
```

If the `permission` attribute does not equal `delete`, then the inner tags render. At this point, the View button always shows, and the Edit button will show with it when the `permission` attribute equals `edit`.

This scenario comes up often when you are building complex applications, and this recipe will come in handy when you need to discriminate between simple states on a page. These tags can also be combined with tiles to create complex views based on few parameters.

BEST PRACTICE *Beware of null values*—It is important to note that these tags only test equalities. They will often render unexpectedly against null values, and the `<logic:present/>` tag would be a better choice when this occurs. Also you must realize that they do not work on an if/then/else or try/catch/finally mode. There is no "else" or "finally," as every instance must be caught or you must use a combination of logic tags to get the results you expect.

◆ *Related*

- 3.3—Encoding information with a <bean:write/> tag
- 3.6—Using <logic:present/> tags to determine page content
- 3.7—Debugging your GUI with the <logic:present/> tag
- 3.12—Creating a basic Struts Tiles page
- 3.13—Using Tiles with XML Definitions

3.9 Using <bean:resource/> to expose the struts.config.xml to your view

◆ *Problem*

You want to use `<bean:resource/>` to expose your struts-config.xml file for development and possible production purposes.

◆ *Background*

The Struts framework provides a specific tag to expose information from files located in the WEB-INF directory of JSP applications. The three available attributes you can set are:

- `id`—The JSP scripting variable name exposed to the page; this attribute must be set.
- `input`—This attribute is optional, specifying whether or not it is an `Input-Stream` or a `String`. Any value placed in this attribute renders the output of the tag as `InputStream`; otherwise, it defaults to `java.lang.String` (used rarely).
- `name`—The application-relative name of the resource to be loaded into the bean

An example of a `<bean:resource/>` tag used on a jspPage, exposing elements from a struts-config file to a JSP page would be:

```
<bean:resource id="strutsConfig" name="/WEB-INF/struts-config.xml"/>
```

This bean's information can be exposed to the JSP by setting the `input` attribute, which defaults to a `java.lang.String` *if unset*, or an `InputStream` if any arbitrary value is coded into the attribute. Whether or not you want to use an input stream depends on your development needs. The primary output of this tag is a `String`, and you rarely need to specify this attribute unless you have performance issues in production. You would just expose its contents by using `<bean:write/>`:

```
<bean:write name="strutConfig"/>
```

Using this write method you can send your data to the browser with or without the formatting characters escaped, allowing the developer to create rich and informative pages when and *if* you decide to expose this information.

The recipe below creates a bean containing the struts-config file, and then applies an XML/XSLT translation to this string to create a controlled view of this file for use in development.

◆ *Recipe*

The `<bean:resource/>` tag is put to use here by setting the struts-config.xml file of a small application into session as a `String`. We then apply an XML/XSL translation to it so that we can expose its actions, forwards, and mappings to a page for a user or developer.

The JSTL, or Java Standard Tag Library, provides a means of creating this quickly in a JSP with just a few lines of code. The specific tag library is known as xtags. Before we get too deep into the recipe, it is necessary to configure your application to use these tags.

CONFIGUR-ING XTAGS Xtags predate the Java Standard Tag Library and are used to translate XML and XSL/XSLT. While care must be taken to not violate Model-View-Controller architecture (especially in production code), xtags do allow you to present different views based upon the XML or XSL delivered to the page, simply by setting a few attributes or by nesting information in them. As these tags are part of a JSP tag library, they must be configured in your application by adding the appropriate JAR files, placing the tld file in the WEB-INF folder, and finally registering the tld file in the web.xml file so the JSP pages can find the tags. While xtags are no longer being maintained, they are by no means unused and are quite stable. If you wish to use the latest JSTL implementation of XML parsing tags, check out the "x" tag library with the JSTL download. We implement xtags for this recipe, but the JSTL could easily be used to a similar effect.

Go to the Jakarta tag libraries site and download the zip files containing these tags:

http://jakarta.apache.org/taglibs/doc/xtags-doc/intro.html

Install the xtags.jar file into your lib directory. Install the xtags.tld file into your WEB-INF directory and open your web.xml file (listing 3.20) and add the tld descriptor.

Listing 3.20 Configure xtags in the /WEB-INF/web.xml

```
<taglib>
   <taglib-uri>/tags/xtags</taglib-uri>
   <taglib-location>/WEB-INF/xtags.tld</taglib-location>
</taglib>
```

If you have your tld files in a different location you need to modify this listing accordingly. At this point your xtags are configured and ready to use in your JSP pages. This recipe is only one of the many ways that this type of tag may be implemented, and we encourage you to investigate the others thoroughly at the Jakarta site (http://jakarta.apache.org/jstl/ or http://jakarta.apache.org/taglibs/) or with Shawn Bayern's book *JSTL in Action*.

Now that we're configured, let's get down to business. The plan is to expose the global-forwards, form-beans and Actions, along with some of their associated attributes in a browser view while you are developing your application. Because this recipe is only a demonstration and meant to use for development purposes, we limit the number of attributes and information that we expose, and provide our elements in the XSL file in a hard-coded manner. If you wish to expose different attributes and/or elements in your configurations, you can easily do this by just changing the XSL file.

You should now be ready to create the recipe and use the xtags and <bean:resource/> tag to create a rich view of your application's configurations.

The struts-config.xml file we're going to expose is small by any standard. As you develop your application, the particular file you'll expose to your JSP page will probably be much larger. The XML for the recipe's configuration file is shown in listing 3.21.

Listing 3.21   struts-config.xml

```
<?xml version="1.0" encoding="ISO-8859-1"?>
<!DOCTYPE struts-config PUBLIC "-//Apache Software Foundation//DTD Struts
    Configuration 1.1//EN"
            "http://jakarta.apache.org/struts/dtds/struts-config_1_1.dtd">
<struts-config>
<!-- ========================================= Form Bean Definitions -->
  <form-beans>
    <form-bean name="javaForm" type="com.strutsrecipes.BeanWriteTestForm"/>
    <form-bean name="testForm"
                        type="org.apache.struts.action.DynaActionForm">
  <form-property name="htmlString" type="java.lang.String"/>
    </form-bean>
    <form-bean name="anotherTestForm"
                        type="org.apache.struts.action.DynaActionForm">
  <form-property name="htmlString" type="java.lang.String"/>
  <form-property name="address" type="java.lang.String"/>
  <form-property name="city" type="java.lang.String"
                                        initial="Los Angeles"/>
  <form-property name="state" type="java.lang.String" initial="CA"/>
  <form-property name="zip" type="java.lang.String"/>
    </form-bean>
  </form-beans>
  <!-- ================================== Global Forward Definitions -->
  <global-forwards>
    <forward name="welcome" path="/Welcome.do"/>
    <forward name="testForm" path="/FormTest.do" redirect="true"/>
  </global-forwards>
  <!-- ================================== Action Mapping Definitions -->
  <action-mappings>
  <action path="/Welcome" type="org.apache.struts.actions.ForwardAction"
                        parameter="/pages/Welcome.jsp"/>
  <action path="/FormTest" type="org.apache.struts.actions.ForwardAction"
                        parameter="/pages/testForm.jsp"/>
  <action path="/FormAction"  type="com.strutsrecipes.BeanWriteTestAction"
                                name="testForm" scope="session"
                                validate="false">
      <forward name="success" path="/pages/beanAction.jsp"/>
      <forward name="fail" path="/pages/welcome.jsp"/>
    </action>
 </action-mappings>
<!-- ================================== Controller Configuration -->
<controller processorClass="org.apache.struts.tiles.TilesRequestProcessor"/
  >
  <!-- =============================== Message Resources Definitions -->
  <message-resources parameter="resources.application"/>
  <!-- ======================================= Plug Ins Configuration -->
  <!-- ========= Tiles plugin ==================    -->
  <plug-in className="org.apache.struts.tiles.TilesPlugin">
     <set-property property="definitions-config"
```

```
    value="/WEB-INF/tiles-defs.xml"/>
        <set-property property="moduleAware" value="true"/>
        <set-property property="definitions-parser-validate" value="true"/>
    </plug-in>
    <plug-in className="org.apache.struts.validator.ValidatorPlugIn">
        <set-property property="pathnames"
     value="/WEB-INF/validator-rules.xml,/WEB-INF/validation.xml"/>
    </plug-in>
</struts-config>
```

The XSL code is next. Listing 3.22 shows a simple translation with a single template using the `<for-each/>` and `<choose/>` XSL tags to iterate through the various elements in the struts-config.xml, exposing and checking for their required and optional child elements and attributes.

If you are new to XML/XSL translations, use the code as a guide to observe how the various XSL tags act upon the exposed XML file. There are comments in the file, and the code for the translation is complete. The view we're creating is rudimentary but complete; in your application, you might wish to create a far-richer final product by exposing more attributes or adding a richer CSS layer.

Listing 3.22   The XSL code

```
<?xml version="1.0" encoding="UTF-8"?>
<xsl:stylesheet version="1.0"
    xmlns:xsl="http://www.w3.org/1999/XSL/Transform"
    xmlns:fo="http://www.w3.org/1999/XSL/Format">
  <xsl:template match="struts-config">
     <h3>Global Forwards:</h3>
     <hr color="#003163" size="3"/>
    <table class="outertable">
     <tr>
      <th>name</th><th>path</th>
      <th>redirect</th><th>context-relative</th>
     </tr>
    <xsl:for-each select="global-forwards/forward">
      <tr>
        <td><xsl:value-of select="@name"/></td>
        <td><xsl:value-of select="@path"/></td>
        <td><xsl:variable name="REDIRECT">
      <xsl:value-of select="@redirect"/>
      </xsl:variable>
    <xsl:choose>
      <xsl:when test="@redirect"><xsl:value-of select="@redirect"/>
      </xsl:when>
      <xsl:otherwise>na</xsl:otherwise>
      </xsl:choose>
```

```
        </td><td>
      <xsl:choose>
      <xsl:when test="@context-relative">
        <xsl:value-of select="@context-relative"/>
        </xsl:when>
            <xsl:otherwise>na</xsl:otherwise>
        </xsl:choose>
          </td>
      </tr>
   </xsl:for-each>
      </table>
<h3>Form Beans</h3>
<hr color="#003163" size="3"/>
   <xsl:for-each select="form-beans/form-bean">
   <table class="outertable">
      <tr>
        <th>name</th><th>type</th>
      </tr>
      <tr>
         <td><xsl:value-of select="@name"/></td>
         <td><xsl:value-of select="@type"/></td>
      </tr>
    </table>
   <xsl:if test="form-property">
 <p>form properties</p>
    <table class="innertable" width="100%">
      <tr>
         <th>property</th><th>type</th><th>initial</th>
      </tr>
   <xsl:for-each select="form-property">
      <tr>
         <td><xsl:value-of select="@name"/></td>
         <td><xsl:value-of select="@type"/></td>
         <td>
    <xsl:choose>
      <xsl:when test="@initial"><xsl:value-of select="@initial"/>
      </xsl:when>
      <xsl:otherwise>na</xsl:otherwise>
    </xsl:choose>
         </td>
      </tr>
   </xsl:for-each>
      </table>
 </xsl:if>
   </xsl:for-each>
<h3>Actions and Mappings</h3>
<hr color="#003163" size="3"/>
 <xsl:for-each select="action-mappings/action">
    <table class="outertable">
      <tr>
         <th>path</th><th>type</th><th>parameter</th>
```

```
    <th>forward</th><th>validate</th><th>scope</th>
</tr>
<tr>
    <td><xsl:value-of select="@path"/></td>
      <td><xsl:value-of select="@type"/></td>
       <td>
    <xsl:choose>
     <xsl:when test="@parameter"><xsl:value-of select="@parameter"/>
      </xsl:when>
        <xsl:otherwise>na</xsl:otherwise>
      </xsl:choose>
       </td><td>
    <xsl:choose>
    <xsl:when test="@forward"><xsl:value-of select="@forward"/>
     </xsl:when>
     <xsl:otherwise>na</xsl:otherwise>
    </xsl:choose>
    </td><td>
    <xsl:choose>
    <xsl:when test="@validate"><xsl:value-of select="@validate"/>
    </xsl:when>
    <xsl:otherwise>na</xsl:otherwise>
    </xsl:choose>
    </td><td><xsl:choose>
    <xsl:when test="@scope"><xsl:value-of select="@scope"/>
    </xsl:when>
    <xsl:otherwise>na</xsl:otherwise>
    </xsl:choose>
    </td>
</tr>
</table>
<xsl:if test="forward">
<p>forward paths</p>
    <table class="innertable">
      <tr>
       <th>name</th><th>path</th><th>redirect</th>
    </tr>
    <xsl:for-each select="forward">
    <tr>
       <td><xsl:value-of select="@name"/></td>
       <td><xsl:value-of select="@path"/></td>
            <td><xsl:choose>
      <xsl:when test="@redirect"><xsl:value-of select="@redirect"/>
      </xsl:when>
      <xsl:otherwise>na</xsl:otherwise>
      </xsl:choose></td>
      </tr>
      </xsl:for-each>
    </table>
</xsl:if>
</xsl:for-each>
```

```
        </xsl:template>
    </xsl:stylesheet>
```

Both XML and XSL listings are long (whew!). We included the entire listings for both in case you wish to try them in their entirety. We thought about truncating and only exposing a couple of small portions of the struts-config.xml file, but we feel that the usefulness of this recipe would be diminished by doing so.

The JSP code is very simple. We've left out extensive CSS code on the page, but you'd want to add your CSS attributes as a `<style/>` block directly onto the page, as this development widget should be portable to any application you are developing and not dependent upon any part of a specific application (apart from the xtag configuration).

In the View component (listing 3.23) we simply use `<bean:resource/>` to define what we're looking for, set the `id` scripting variable attribute, and set the `name` attribute identifying the configuration file. As the string returned by translating the struts-config file is always XML compliant, we can nest them inside an `<xtags:style/>` tag with the path to the XSL defined in the XSL attribute.

Listing 3.23 The JSP code to expose the struts-config file parsed with the XSL in listing 3.29

```
<%@ page language="java" %>
<%@ taglib uri="/tags/struts-bean" prefix="bean" %>
<%@ taglib uri="/tags/struts-html" prefix="html" %>
<%@ taglib uri="/tags/xtags" prefix="xtags"%>

<html:html>
<head>
<html:base/>
<title>Using &ltbean:resource/&gt; to expose your Struts config file</title>
<style type="text/css">
<!--CSS CODE HERE  Do not import CSS if using for a development widget -->
</style>
</head>
<body>
<div align="center"><h2>Struts Config Form and Action Properties</h2></div>
<bean:resource id="strutsConfig" name="/WEB-INF/struts-config.xml"/>
<xtags:style xsl="exposeConfig.xsl">
<%= strutsConfig %>
</xtags:style>
</body>
</html:html>
```

The output

From figure 3.4 we can see the global-forwards and form beans exposed, along with the form properties in the `DynaActionForm` we've defined. If we scroll further down the rendered HTML page, we'll see:

At this point the usefulness of the `<bean:resource/>` tag becomes apparent. While developing a large application it often becomes necessary to check for any errors that you've made, and to make changes (or at least catalog them) before redeploying the entire application. If you make a small mistake here and there, it can become expensive in time and energy to keep going back and forth, compiling, building, and testing your pages, without having access to your configurations. If you have tiles and validations, you can expose these resources just as easily and with the same effect.

In some cases time might be well spent creating a developer's suite of tools to allow for remote debugging and error checking without immediate access to your source code.

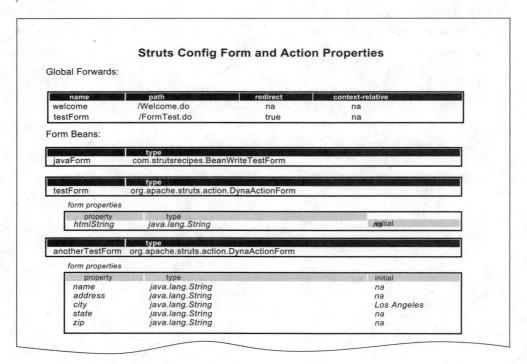

Struts Config Form and Action Properties

Global Forwards:

name	path	redirect	context-relative
welcome	/Welcome.do	na	na
testForm	/FormTest.do	true	na

Form Beans:

	type
javaForm	com.strutsrecipes.BeanWriteTestForm

	type
testForm	org.apache.struts.action.DynaActionForm

form properties

property	type	initial
htmlString	java.lang.String	na

	type
anotherTestForm	org.apache.struts.action.DynaActionForm

form properties

property	type	initial
name	java.lang.String	na
address	java.lang.String	na
city	java.lang.String	Los Angeles
state	java.lang.String	na
zip	java.lang.String	na

Figure 3.4 Exposed struts-config with CSS to using `<bean:resource/>`

◆ *Discussion*

Simply by looking at what an interesting tool only a few lines of code can create, we can explore the possibilities for scaling this product into a complicated but powerful developer's suite. Action classes can be rendered in the GUI as forms with simple text boxes for submitting URL Strings or other parameters that the page needs to render (such a GUI might have a similar look and feel to MX4J, if you have some familiarity with this application). This information can be quickly discovered and viewed by exposing the form beans translated with an XSL stylesheet. Your task is obviously made easier when DynaActionForms or DynaValidatorForms are used instead of JavaForm beans, as less detailed information about the simple form bean's content is available in the struts-config.xml file.

It can be interesting to expose your plug-ins, resource bundles, data-sources, and so on. This only requires a different XSL that can be exposed on this page using logic tags, or rendered on a similar JSP page.

These pages can be grouped into a single developers-only directory and used by you or your team when developing different applications. Simply modify the specific struts-config.xml file to include the Actions you need, and make sure that your xtags are available to your JSP pages.

At some point you might want to expose your configuration(s) to create a site map on your application. This can be as simple or complicated as you wish, depending upon what request parameters or scoped variables are required to render your JSP pages or fire your actions. Using variations on this recipe can create other more specialized solutions as your needs become clear.

◆ *Related*

- 3.3—Encoding information with a <bean:write/> tag
- 3.6—Using <logic:present/> tags to determine page content
- 3.7—Debugging your GUI with the <logic:present/> tag
- 3.12—Creating a basic Struts Tiles page
- 3.13—Using Tiles with XML Definitions

3.10 *Using <html:rewrite/> to resolve URLs*

◆ *Problem*

You want to make sure that all URLs are properly resolved, encoded, and maintainable.

◆ *Background*

If you are new to Struts, or if you are migrating a non-Struts JSP program to the Struts framework, you will soon discover that you can mix and match HTML code, JSP tags, Struts tags, and JSP scriptlets. This can be dangerous if the process is not well thought out. Components we've created will quickly need to be "connected" to beans that we've exposed. New tag libraries extending Struts (like Struts-Layout) might appear. Refactoring might be in order to make existing applications more manageable. If you've mixed and matched code haphazardly, then integration, maintenance, and extension of your software might be impossible without totally rewriting everything.

More often we are called upon to create complex applications while working in team environments. The individuals on a team are going to handle development problems differently. This is especially true with developers that are trying to get up to speed with Struts, or migrate existing JSP applications to Struts before their training is complete. One of the first tags that these "newbie" developers can use to help them understand the rest of the Struts framework is the `<html:rewrite/>` tag.

`<html:rewrite/>` provides "one-stop shopping" for a developer's URL needs, and should be the first tag implemented by a team, especially in a migration environment. Its functionality is simple: it takes a link you wish to use, and appends the proper information to the URL or `Action` you've requested and rewrites it when rendered in a browser. For instance, you want to access the `Action/Foo.do` and your site's URL is:

```
http://www.beets.com/application/
```

By using the tag `<html:rewrite page="/Beets.do"/>`, it renders in the response as:

```
"/application/Beets.do"
```

This tag can be embedded inside normal HTML tags in Struts applications whenever you need to guarantee that your URLs are not only written properly but also in a way that is portable (with the above method, the domain name might change, but you're certain the URLs are always rendered correctly). When writing new Struts programs, many developers find out quickly that URL encoding and base references are required to keep links from breaking. `<html:rewrite/>` inherits from the `<html:link/>` tag, so the following functionality is exposed:

- It provides URL encoding, so you do not need `<%=response.EncodeURL ("myURL")%>` in your code to help you manage your session.

- It provides context path resolving, eliminating the need to add `<%=request.getContextPath()%>` in your code.

- You have access to the global-forwards in the struts-config.xml file by using the `forward` attribute.

- You can request pages through the `page` attribute, as in `<html:link/>` which provides access to the `paramId`, `paramName`, and `name` attributes.

- You can "roll your own" URL using the `href` attribute, which provides client-side access to JavaScript variables that can be added to your URL as a request `String`.

- You may use these tags in conjunction with global-forwards to create links for your js and CSS pages.

- You can attach Collections with name-value pairs to append request `Strings`.

The following recipe shows several different ways to use `<html:rewrite/>` in your code. Although these aren't the only tricks available to you, it is hoped that they are comprehensive enough to get your creative juices flowing. These tricks can be indispensable when migrating applications from other frameworks, or just creating simple JSP applications.

◆ *Recipe*

We're going to use `<html:rewrite/>` on a single JSP page to solve a few different problems:

- Link a style sheet to the page.
- Link a JavaScript file to the page.
- Create a maintainable JavaScript URL variable.
- Create a pop-up page link.
- Create a linked URL attached to a button with an attached `HashMap` as a request `String`.
- Create a URL with an href attribute request `String` attached to a button.

Let's take a look at our JSP page in listing 3.24. `<html:rewrite/>` renders the proper URLs, showing the tag in context within the general JSP page.

Listing 3.24 Jsp page showing `<html:rewrite/>` tags

```
<%
java.util.HashMap params = new java.util.HashMap();      ❶
params.put("param1", "FirstMapParam");
params.put("param2", "SecondMapParam");
params.put("param3", "ThirdMapParam");
pageContext.setAttribute("linkParams", params);
```

```
%>
...

<html:base/>
<script language="JavaScript" type="text/javascript">
<!--
    var urlToOpen = "<html:rewrite forward="popPage"/>";      ❷
//-->
</script>
<script language="Javascript"
        src="<html:rewrite forward="popScript"/>"/>            ❸
<link rel="stylesheet"
type="text/css"  href="<html:rewrite forward="strutsCss"/>">   ❹
</head>
...

<table><tr><td>
<button onclick="<html:rewrite forward="testForm" name="linkParams"/>">   ❺
Reference Link
</button>
</td></tr><tr><td>
<button onclick="parent.location.href='<html:rewrite href=
   "FormTest.do?param1=FirstParameter&param2=SecondParameter&param3=ThirdPa
   rameter"/>';">button with html rewrite href and param string</button>   ❻
</td></tr>
<tr><td>
<button onclick="javascript:newwindow()">popup attached JavaScript
   function</button>
</td></tr>
</table>
...
```

In the first section we've created a java.util.HashMap ❶ to populate three request variables into the first button element ❺. This strategy incorporates multiple parameters in a URL request String. There are many ways to achieve the same result through string concatenation, but this can have serious drawbacks with respect to maintenance. The above method is clean and maintainable because it acts as a "black box" to handle the ?, =, and & characters. The second code fragment is in the <head/> section of the page and references a JavaScript js ❸ file that we've referenced as a global-forward in the struts-config file. This allows for complete portability of your JavaScript source references. We'll also link our style sheet to the page ❹ with a rewrite tag pointing to another forward attribute.

We also have a JavaScript variable as a URL declared on the page ❷. This variable is given the value mapped to the global-forward popScript in the struts-config.xml file when the JSP page is compiled and returned to the browser.

The final examples compare the creation and management of URL parameters: This first one ❺ uses the parameters defined in the head of the page ❶ along with an `Action` defined in the struts-config.xml as a global-forward. The last example ❻ uses another longer URL and request `String` attached directly to a button ❻. The first button references a link with the `HashMap` attached via the `name` attribute. This renders in a browser as:

```
/application/FormTest.do?param1=FirstMapParam&param2=SecondMapPa-
    ram&param3=ThirdMapParam
```

The second button ❻ shows a simple link attached to a button with the URL shown as a `String`. In this case you must use either the `href` or `page` attribute. For demonstration purposes the choice was made to use the `href` attribute because it resolves whatever is in the `String` *literally*, i.e., what you write is what you get on the rendered HTML page:

```
<button onclick="parent.location.href='<html:rewrite href="/FormTest.do?
            param1=FirstParameter
            &param2=SecondParameter
            &param3=ThirdParameter"/>';">
```

Both buttons in ❺ and ❻ link to an `ActionClass` that allows you to manipulate the request parameters passed. The first is much more maintainable, but the second might be needed in certain situations when passing JavaScript parameters on a page.

◆ ***Discussion***

The code for this recipe is demonstrative of various ways to use the `<html:rewrite/>` tag, and many of the examples shown might or might not fit your needs. This tag can work throughout all your HTML tags, allowing for any `src` or `href` attributes to automatically create complete URLs when the page is rendered at the browser. All Struts tags that use URLs for various reasons inherit this functionality, but often there are HTML tags that we want to use in our GUIs that have no Struts equivalent, such as the `<button>` tag, or in any JavaScript URL link, such as:

```
<button onclick="document.location.href='<html:rewrite forward="foofwd"/>'"/>
```

If you're migrating a legacy application to Struts, the `<html:rewrite/>` tag should be one of the first tags used in this migration. Combined with the `<html:base/>` tag, you can easily reference all your links throughout the site, and immediately begin creating a comprehensive struts-config file. This is explained thoroughly below.

BEST PRACTICE *Be careful when using JavaScript and <html:rewrite/>*—`<html:rewrite/>` renders literally whatever is set as the value for the `href` attribute—this means that JavaScript functions that are rendered inside a JSP can use this tag to create their dynamic URLs. Look at the following variable instantiated in

```
JavaScript:var
    bigPath="Foo.do?p1="+jsParam1+"&p2="+jsParam2+"&p3="+jsParam3"
```

To use this in a link, you can write:

```
parent.location.href ='<html:rewrite href="bigPath"/>'.
```

This renders the code with `bigPath` and handles the context correctly. You can then develop your script to populate the JavaScript variables (`jsParam1,jsParam2,JsParam3`).

`<html:rewrite/>` allows you to control any URL on a page—you should implement this tag quickly throughout any migration from a legacy application to Struts. By enforcing the use of `<html:rewrite/>`, you are guaranteed to have solid and portable links within your Struts migration framework. Because other Struts tags that use or manipulate URLs have the same implementation as `<html:rewrite/>`, you can easily take the next steps in your migration plan. The first `Actions` you use in the configuration will probably be simple `org.apache.struts.actions.ActionForwards`. It is important to create these placeholders early, as having links between pages that are not "registered" with the struts-config.xml file will cause nightmares as your application grows and becomes more complicated.

It is important to start using as much of the Struts framework as early as possible in the migration process. This practice allows you to check your functionality early and often to determine when and if anything breaks. Once you're comfortable at this level, you should be able to integrate the rest of the Struts tags and framework with relative comfort and reliability.

◆ *Related*

- 3.4—Using <bean:define/>to expose information to your pages
- 3.6—Using <logic:present/> tags to determine page content
- 3.7—Debugging your GUI with the <logic:present/> tag
- 3.12—Creating a basic Struts Tiles page
- 3.13—Using Tiles with XML Definitions

3.11 *Cleaning up session-scope attributes*

◆ *Problem*

You want to clean up session-scope attributes to improve performance.

◆ *Background*

Complex web applications deployed on J2EE-compliant application servers often use persistent HttpSessions. Though this storage method is invaluable in managing a user's session information, there is a performance penalty. The HttpSession must be read and rewritten whenever it is updated, which means that its data is serialized, read, and then restored. At any given time, a user rarely requires more than a fraction of the data that is available; yet all of this data must be kept, forcing your server to process the entire HttpSession object every time [WBP].

You should remove session state objects when finished with them. Under nominal conditions, upon leaving or logging out of an application, a user's objects that are instantiated in their session are immediately destroyed. On large web applications, or applications interacting heavily with Data Objects and creating overhead that affects server performance, it is wise to keep track of your objects and destroy them when they are no longer needed.

Other reasons for session cleanup are also valid. You might want to start with objects in a null state, or with a preset value. This is relevant when you need to make sure that a JSP is compiled correctly, to determine whether a bean's value is null, or to throw an error if a bean's value is not set at all. You always have the objects' state maintained in the user's session, creating a load that might not be acceptable as the number of users rise; at some point, you may decide that all or part of the objects in session can be safely removed to increase performance.

This recipe details methods you can either use in your Actions to clean up session objects, or you can use them more effectively by extending your Action class and adding these methods to clean up session objects. As you will see, this is particularly easy as the Struts Action contains HttpServletRequest.

◆ *Recipe*

Simply setting an attribute bound to an Object to null does not flag it for garbage collection. The session attribute remains and points to a null value, because the object is not available for garbage collection as long as the session still has a reference to it. This can have adverse results if your goal is to completely remove an object from session. To achieve the removal of an attribute from session, you must call the removeAttribute() method in a Java class:

```
javax.servlet.HttpSession.removeAttribute(attrName);
```

You can call this method when you need it, or create a more global method in an `Abstract Base Action` that you use to extend your `Action` classes. In listing 3.25 is a simple method that can be added to your `Abstract Action` class to clean up session attributes.

Listing 3.25 A method to destroy a session attribute

```
/**
 * destroys a particular session attribute
 * @param request
 * @param name
 */
public void destroyCurrentAttribute(
                  HttpServletRequest request, String name){   ❶
    HttpSession session = request.getSession();      ❷
    session.removeAttribute(name);      ❸
  }
```

You only need to pass the `request` object from the JSP page and the value `String` of the attribute you wish to destroy ❶. By passing `request`, you get a handle to session ❷ that can be used to implement the `removeAttribute()` method ❸. You must encapsulate this code within a try/catch to handle any exceptions. Using this method only requires:

```
destroyCurrentAttribute(request, value);
```

You can have many session attributes that work together in a specific subapplication or category. Because they work together, you might want to destroy all of them simultaneously by creating a method to reset a group of specific variables at once as in listing 3.26.

Listing 3.26 A utility method that cleans up specific session attributes

```
/**
 * Generic "utility" method that cleans up some session attributes
 * which can be huge memory hogs if not taken care of. Note that Constants
 * have been used to synchronize the session attribute names throughout
 * the application
 *
 * @param request
 */
public void destroySomeOfMySessionAttributes(HttpServletRequest request) {
    destroyCurrentAttribute(request, Constants. RESULT);
    destroyCurrentAttribute(request, Constants.LEVEL);
```

```
        destroyCurrentAttribute(request, Constants.FILTER_STRING);
        destroyCurrentAttribute(request, Constants.START_POSITION);
        destroyCurrentAttribute(request, Constants.END_POSITION);
}
```

The code in listing 3.26 implements the method in listing 3.25 for each session attribute you wish to destroy. Again, you must pass `request` into this method, and then call each attribute by name and remove it by using `destroyCurrentAttribute(request, string)`. Groups of these methods can exist in your Controller layer to do "housekeeping" in any area of your application on an as-needed basis.

You might have many of the methods outlined in listing 3.26, each one cleaning up a specific session attribute. At some point, you might decide that all session attributes need to be cleaned up. You can group these methods together into one method to clean up all the session attributes on a global basis. Such a method, outlined in listing 3.27, can also control problems with the back button after a log out, for example.

Listing 3.27 A generic utility method to clean up all specific session attributes

```
/**
 * Generic "utility" method that cleans up all non-essential
 * session attributes. This method SHOULD ONLY BE USED to clean up "session
 * garbage" and not destroy any variable you need.
 *  Be careful not to call it in the wrong place!
 * @param request
 */
public void cleanUpSessionAttributes(HttpServletRequest request) {
    destroySomeOfMySessionAttributes(request);
    destroySomeMoreOfMySessionAttributes(request);
    destroyTheRestOfMySessionAttributes(request);
}
```

Any of these methods can be called from your `Action` class at any time if they are available in a utility class. To access this method, just write:

```
MyUtilityClass.cleanUpSessionAttributes(request);
```

You might wish to make this available to your `Actions` at any given time by placing these utilities in an `Abstract Action`, and then making them available by extending your Action from this one.

◆ *Discussion*

There are a few methods that can be created to compliment those in our recipe, including methods to get values from request, session, or other objects that can be used throughout your application. When grouped together they form a nice set of utilities that can be grouped into a class and used when needed. But why import and instantiate these utilities every single time if you're going to use them in nearly every Action class? It's a much better idea to create an Abstract Action that contains them, and extend your Action class to take advantage of this. The code in listing 3.28 shows such an Abstract Action with the methods from listings 3.25–3.27 contained within.

Listing 3.28 A complete `Abstract Action` class with session cleaning methods

```
package com.strutsrecipes;

import javax.servlet.ServletContext;          ❶
import javax.servlet.http.HttpServletRequest;
import javax.servlet.http.HttpServletResponse;
import javax.servlet.http.HttpSession;

import org.apache.struts.action.Action;
import org.apache.struts.action.ActionForm;
import org.apache.struts.action.ActionForward;
import org.apache.struts.action.ActionMapping;


/** Abstract Base Action for my Applications' Struts Actions */
public abstract class MyBaseAction extends Action {     ❷

/** My Base Action constructor */
public MyBaseAction () {     ❸
        //empty for now.
}

// from listing 3.25
public void destroyCurrentAttribute(HttpServletRequest request, String
   value) {     ❹
        try {
            HttpSession session = request.getSession();
            session.removeAttribute(value);
        } catch (Exception e) {
            System.out.println("attribute :" + value + " not available.\n");
        }
    }

// from listing 3.26
  public void destroySomeOfMySessionAttributes(HttpServletRequest request) {
```

```
        destroyCurrentAttribute(request, Constants. RESULT);      ❺
        destroyCurrentAttribute(request, Constants.LEVEL);
        destroyCurrentAttribute(request, Constants.FILTER_STRING);
        destroyCurrentAttribute(request, Constants.START_POSITION);
        destroyCurrentAttribute(request, Constants.END_POSITION);
    }

//additional to above
    public void destroySomeMoreOfMySessionAttributes(    ❻
                                        HttpServletRequest request){
      //Add another group of attributes here
}

// from listing 3.27
    public void cleanUpSessionAttributes(HttpServletRequest request) {    ❼
      destroySomeOfMySessionAttributes(request);
      destroySomeMoreOfMySessionAttributes(request);
    }
}
```

It is important to show this method from end to end in case you've never used it
before. Once you are familiar with the creation of an Abstract Action, you might
never use the base Struts Action class again. In the above listing, we import all of
the packages that are normally imported by the Struts Action, and also any others
that we might wish to use in other methods, but in this case we don't need any
❶. Next, we declare the abstract MyBaseAction, extending org.apache.struts.
action.Action ❷. Next, we create a constructor method ❸, and then insert the
methods we wish to make available to any Actions extending MyBaseAction ❹, ❺,
❻, ❼. To implement this action in your application, you simply extend it in
your declaration:

```
public class NoParticularAction extends com.mypackage.MyBaseAction {

    ...

}
```

All of the Base Action's methods are now available as native methods to any
Action extending it:

```
destroySessionAttribute(session, "String"); //or some final Constant!!!

destroySomeOfMySessionAttributes(request);

destroyAllOfMySessionAttributes(request);
```

- ◆ *Related*
  - ■ 3.4—Using <bean:define/> to expose information to your pages

- ◆ *References*
  - ■ [WBP] WebSphere Application Server Development Best Practices for Performance and Scalability

3.12 Creating a basic Struts Tiles page

- ◆ *Problem*

You want to create and configure a basic Struts Tiles deployment.

- ◆ *Background*

It has become the latest standard to isolate every piece of an application to increase its scalability, functionality, and long-term maintainability after the initial deployment. The MVC2 paradigm as it is implemented in the Struts framework provides a basis to build loosely coupled applications with reusable objects.

Let's take a quick look at the "V" in MVC (View). Often overlooked by programmers and engineers who scream for functionality and performance, the View can just as easily be built following these same two design principles of functionality and performance. Doing so makes your application look finished and professional—and can often result in the addition of an extra zero in your paycheck!

Most pages have many reusable objects. Menus, copyright notices, frames, layouts, and images are just a few. Isn't the <title></title> tag on every page? If one looks hard enough, it's possible to find many common items throughout a web application.

Only a few years ago, developers implemented ASP, JSP, PHP, and other scripting languages that used server-side includes to load many reusable components of an application into the page. While this got us onto the right track, it offered limited functionality. The earliest versions of these includes had no preprocessing ability. Even as they matured, using includes alone still hamstrung developers that wanted a more efficient system using templates.

Struts Tiles let you define a template (or templates) for your pages. You can then request the desired page by filling out the missing pieces of the template with any information you wish to present. These pieces are snippets of HTML, JSP, Struts, and so on that load into a template and create a GUI. Not only do these templates allow for preprocessing, they also permit the creation of View objects that are loaded and unloaded through the Model and Controller, further isolating every portion of your application and making those last minute changes that always happen more manageable than ever before.

◆ **Recipe**

Let's start by making sure that your struts-config.xml file is configured to use Tiles. At or near the bottom of the file, a `<plug-in>` should be defined as in listing 3.29.

Listing 3.29   Defining the Tiles plug-in inside the struts-config.xml file

```
<plug-in className="org.apache.struts.tiles.TilesPlugin">

</plug-in>
```

If this plug-in exists in your struts-config.xml file (it's in the default struts-config.xml file that ships with Struts), you're ready to continue; otherwise, add it at the bottom of the file, just before the closing `</struts-config>` element node. Make sure the struts-tiles.tld file is in the WEB-INF directory, and the web.xml file has the entry in listing 3.30.

Listing 3.30   Adding the tag library definition to the /WEB-INF/web.xml file

```
<taglib>
   <taglib-uri>/tags/struts-tiles</taglib-uri>
   <taglib-location>/WEB-INF/struts-tiles.tld</taglib-location>
</taglib>
```

This entry belongs with all the other tag library entries. Once these steps are complete you can successfully run Tiles in your Struts applications.

Let's take a quick look at how tiles are used before we start working through a lot of code. The idea behind Tiles is to have a template, a group of tiles that contain various presentation pieces, and a JSP page defining which pieces go where when you actually call them. Consider figure 3.5 below, showing the components and flow of a typical tiled application:

In Figure 3.5, the tiles are nothing more than small, reusable pieces of a page. A "definition" JSP page defines the components mapped to a "Template" page. This definition and template are parsed to produce the final, complete page rendered in the browser. The actual JSP page mapped in the struts-config.xml file is

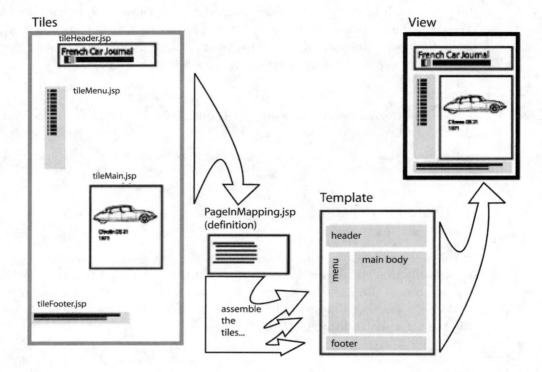

Figure 3.5 A typical tiled application showing the various components and their connections

nothing more than a set of instructions delineating which tiles should be loaded into the template and where. Once the tiles are assembled into the template, the final view is delivered to the browser. Looking at the code from the sample JSP template file below in listing 3.31, we see a simple and complete template.

Listing 3.31   /layouts/testLayout.jsp

```
<%@ taglib uri="/tags/struts-bean" prefix="bean" %>
<%@ taglib uri="/tags/struts-html" prefix="html" %>
<%@ taglib uri="/tags/struts-tiles" prefix="tiles"%>    ❹
<html:html locale="true">
<head>
<title><bean:message key="testForm.title"/></title>
<html:base/>
</head>
<body>
<tiles:insert attribute="header"/>    ❶
<hr/>
```

```
<tiles:insert attribute="body"/>     ❷
<tiles:insert attribute="footer"/>   ❸
</body>
</html:html>
```

Listing 3.31 is a simple page with a header, body, and footer that takes whatever tiles that the definition page sets into the header ❶, body ❷, and footer ❸ attributes. Note that the struts-tiles.tld tag library ❹ is defined at the top.

Looking at the individual tiles, you see they are just small snippets of code assembled into the template and displayed as the view. The header is listing 3.32, the body is listing 3.33, and the footer is listing 3.34.

Listing 3.32   /tiles/titleHeader.jsp

```
<%@ taglib uri="/tags/struts-bean" prefix="bean" %>
<table style="width:100%"></tr>
<td style="padding:10px;"><bean:message key="testForm.header"/></td>
</tr></table>
```

Listing 3.33   /tiles/bodyWithBean.jsp

```
<%@ taglib uri="/tags/struts-bean" prefix="bean" %>
<bean:define id="fooBean" value="this information is from a bean"/>
<table style="border=1px solid #001363;padding:10px">
</tr>
    <td style="background-color:E8E6B9;padding:10px;">
This is text information on the page
    </td>
</tr>
    <td style="background-color:E8E6B9;padding:10px;">
<bean:write name="fooBean"/> 
    </td>
</tr>
</table>
```

Listing 3.34   /tiles/copyright.jsp

```
<hr style="margin-top:80px;color:#001363;"/>
<span style="font-family:Verdana,Arial,sans-serif;font-
size:70%">&copy;Copyright 2004 The Struts Cookbook, all rights reserved.</
span>
```

What we see above is that the individual tiles don't "know" that they are tiles; there is no code on the page that relates to the Tiles framework. The second thing we notice is that everything each page needs to render is in the individual code. This allows for each page to render before it is loaded into the template. Let's now look at the definition page in listing 3.35

Listing 3.35 JSP page using thetestLayout.jsp template, specifying tiles for header, body and footer

```
<%@ taglib uri="/tags/struts-tiles" prefix="tiles"%>
<tiles:insert page="/layouts/testLayout.jsp" flush="true">
    <tiles:put name="header" value="/tiles/titleHeader.jsp"/>
    <tiles:put name="body" value="/tiles/bodyWithBean.jsp"/>
    <tiles:put name="footer" value="/tiles/copyright.jsp"/>
</tiles:insert>
```

BEST PRACTICE *Use Separate directories for file types when implementing Tiles*—Notice that the file types all have separate directories. While this isn't required, it is a best practice and becomes increasingly necessary as your software project grows in size and complexity. After you begin to port your application to Tiles, it can become hard to remember where all the pieces are unless you put them into easily recognizable locations. In this case we have created directories at the same level as the pages directory, those being layouts and tiles, holding the particular objects that coincide with these items. This allows for portability of the JSP pages.

The definitions page basically maps the tiles pages you want to present to the layout template. This happens during runtime. Finally, let's see how this is mapped into the struts-config.xml file in listing 3.36. Note that a global-forward namespace testForm is mapped to the action.

Listing 3.36   struts-config.xml mapping the /pages/testForm.jsp tile definition

```
<global-forwards>
<forward name="testForm" path="FormTest.do"/>
</global-forwards>
<action-mappings>
<action path="/FormTest"
        type="org.apache.struts.actions.ForwardAction"
        parameter="/pages/testForm.jsp"/>
</action-mappings>
```

We call the definition as the Action, as if it were any other JSP page. When the servlet container is started and the page is requested, the browser renders what is shown in Figure 3.6.

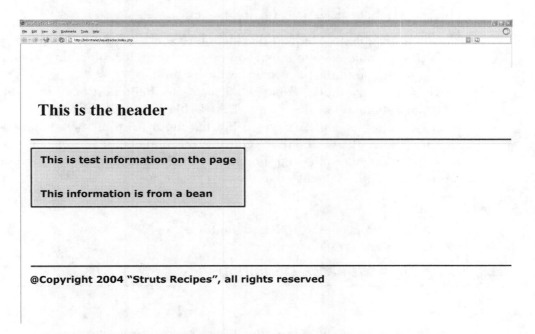

Figure 3.6 Browser view of a tiled page showing the assembled "header, body, and footer" Tiles

◆ *Discussion*

It's important to spend some time deciding how you want to put your Tiles application together, and whether or not you even want to use them at all.

> **BEST PRACTICE** *When to use Tiles*—For applications with a small number of developers and pages, it might never be necessary to use Tiles. For applications with Tiles, create directories to house different elements in the tiles you are creating; definitions, tiles, and layouts would be a good start. If you have many tiles that just control menus or navigation, you might want to create separate directories to handle them.

This recipe is just a basic one to help the developer set up their initial Tiles pages. For more complicated deployments, recipe 3.13, "Using Tiles with XML definitions," can help extend this idea to a robust solution suitable for larger deployments.

It is often easier to build your basic application with the functionality at or near completion before moving your GUI to Tiles. Even then you might want to create simple tiles to handle most of the View's manipulation, and code up more complicated tile definitions and layouts once the project solidifies.

This recipe is a simple example. There's so much more that can be done with Tiles. It is possible to overload tiles definitions, extend them, use them as forwards, pass parameters into them, and even use them for something as simple as sending Strings into the page at a specific location.

You might have noticed that the actual Tiles definition page resembles an HTML page about as much as Java code looks like Fortran. Well, what if you didn't have to actually create these pages as JSP, but simply "list" all the separate definitions into an XML file, thereby reducing the number of files you have lying around, and provide "one-stop shopping" for all the definitions you want to use? This definition file is discussed in the next recipe.

◆ **Related**

■ 3.13—Using Tiles with XML definitions

3.13 Using Tiles with XML Definitions

◆ **Problem**

You want to incorporate XML-defined Tiles in your application.

◆ **Background**

In the previous recipe we laid out how Struts and Tiles work together to extend the possibilities of the Model-View-Controller architecture, allow for greater flexibility and maintainability in your applications, and increase their overall functionality. By creating simple JSP definition pages, a few lines of code become powerful and extensible deployments.

But why have just a few lines of code on several JSP pages that are all similar, except for a few different attributes and values? Some applications may have only a few pages, with many different views and templates. Other times the opposite is true; there are many pages and only one or two templates. There *must* be a better way to manage so many definitions without resorting to a folder full of different JSP-defined definitions that become difficult to compare and control.

XML-based Tiles definitions are the answer. In your WEB-INF directory, you can create a tiles-defs.xml file that allows you to create as many pages as you wish, and then link them to the templates and tiles that you've created in the struts-config.xml file. You can keep track of your entire application's pages in just a few places, often creating many different views with only a few lines of code in a few minutes.

◆ *Recipe*

A quick visit to the struts-config.xml file is required to add the XML configuration details to the Tiles plug-in. Make sure that your code matches the listing in 3.37.

Listing 3.37 The Tiles plug-in for the struts-config.xml file

```
<plug-in className="org.apache.struts.tiles.TilesPlugin">
   <set-property property="definitions-config"
                 value="/WEB-INF/tiles-defs.xml"/>
   <set-property property="moduleAware" value="true"/>
   <set-property property="definitions-parser-validate" value="true"/>
</plug-in>
```

The pointer to the Tiles definition file above is in bold. You can name this file anything, or just leave it with the default name. If you have this code in your struts-config.xml file, we can continue; otherwise, you might need to configure your application for Tiles (this is available in recipe 3.12, "Creating a basic Struts Tiles page," along with a complete explanation of how basic Tiles work).

If you have been using the Struts best practice of putting your JSP pages in a page directory, it is smart to extend this model further by creating a layouts directory to hold your JSP templates, a Tiles directory to hold your various Tiles pages, and any other directories you might wish to create to group certain tiles that have specific roles (such as a menus directory to hold all the tiles that belong to navigation, and so on).

We'll start with the basic testLayout.jsp file in listing 3.38, which acts as our template for the page we're going to create using an XML definition.

Listing 3.38 /layouts/testLayout.jsp

```
<%@ taglib uri="/tags/struts-bean" prefix="bean" %>
<%@ taglib uri="/tags/struts-html" prefix="html" %>
<%@ taglib uri="/tags/struts-tiles" prefix="tiles"%>
<html:html locale="true">
<head>
<title><bean:message key="testForm.title"/></title>
<html:base/>
</head>
<body>
<tiles:insert attribute="header"/>
<hr/>
<tiles:insert attribute="body"/>
<tiles:insert attribute="footer"/>
```

```
</body>
</html:html>
```

The page template above is identical to the JSP-defined page in recipe 3.12, "Creating a basic Struts Tiles page." This template can be used with either JSP or XML Tiles implementations and seamlessly swapped back and forth. We'll now look at the Tile pages, which are nothing more than smaller JSP/Struts/HTML pages that don't really do much alone, but are very informative when put together (also identical to the previous recipe). Because these pages use Struts, all the Actions, beans, and information needed for them to compile correctly must be defined and implemented at their level. A common mistake is to assume the template page interprets these tiles first, but the opposite is true. Here are the JSP tiles showing all the code for each. The header page is listing 3.39, the body page is listing 3.40, and the footer listing is 3.41.

Listing 3.39   titleHeader.jsp

```
<%@ taglib uri="/tags/struts-bean" prefix="bean" %>
<table style="width:100%"></tr>
<td style="padding:10px;"><bean:message key="testForm.header"/></td>
</tr></table>
```

Listing 3.40   bodyWithBean.jsp

```
<%@ taglib uri="/tags/struts-bean" prefix="bean" %>
<bean:define id="fooBean" value="this information is from a bean"/>
<table style="border=1px solid #001363;padding:10px">
</tr>
    <td style="background-color:E8E6B9;padding:10px;">
This is text information on the page
    </td>
</tr>
    <td style="background-color:E8E6B9;padding:10px;">
<bean:write name="fooBean"/> 
    </td>
</tr>
</table>
```

Listing 3.41   copyright.jsp

```
<hr style="margin-top:80px;color:#001363;"/>
<span style="font-family:Verdana,Arial,sans-serif;font-
size:70%">&copy;Copyright 2004 The Struts Cookbook, all rights reserved.</
span>
```

The above tiles are just pieces of a page and a layout. You can literally have hundreds of pieces and one or two layouts, but we need to define how these code snippets all fit together. If we use a JSP page, its definition would look like listing 3.42.

Listing 3.42   Sample JSP definition (see previous recipe)

```
<%@ taglib uri="/tags/struts-tiles" prefix="tiles"%>
<tiles:insert page="/layouts/testLayout.jsp" flush="true">
   <tiles:put name="header" value="/tiles/titleHeader.jsp"/>
   <tiles:put name="body" value="/tiles/bodyWithBean.jsp"/>
   <tiles:put name="footer" value="/tiles/copyright.jsp"/>
</tiles:insert>
```

But we're not going to use JSP. We're going to open the tiles-defs.xml file. The definition we create is nearly identical, but there are subtle differences. Here is the file in its entirety with one definition (listing 3.43).

Listing 3.43   Tile definition entry in the tiles-defs.xml

```
<?xml version="1.0" encoding="ISO-8859-1"?>
<!DOCTYPE tiles-definitions PUBLIC "-//Apache Software Foundation//DTD Tiles
   Configuration 1.1//EN"
        "http://jakarta.apache.org/struts/dtds/tiles-config_1_1.dtd">
<tiles-definitions>
   <definition name=".testForm" path="/layouts/testLayout.jsp">   ❶
      <put name="header" value="/tiles/titleHeader.jsp"/>   ❷
      <put name="body" value="/tiles/bodyWithBean.jsp"/>   ❸
      <put name="footer" value="/tiles/copyright.jsp"/>   ❹
   </definition>
</tiles-definitions>
```

The key differences between the JSP and XML definitions are in the XML namespaces ❶, ❷, ❸, ❹. There aren't that many, really, but when migrating from JSP definitions to XML definitions, it's a good idea to take a second look. It's a fairly common mistake to just cut and paste the JSP code to the XML and forget to change the tag names, and this can obviously cause your project to go haywire until you track it down.

Finally, there's a slight difference in the struts-config.xml file in listing 3.44 as to how you request the page (`parameter` or `forward` attribute in the `<action/>`). Because there's no "JSP" in the definition, there's no "JSP" suffix in the value.

Listing 3.44   Struts-config mapping for a page using XML-based Tiles definition

```
<!-- Form Test XML defined action-mapping -->
<action path="/FormTest"
  type="org.apache.struts.actions.ForwardAction"
  forward=".testForm"/>    ❶
```

The `forward` attribute in the `Action` must match the definition ❶. We call the definition through the `Action`, as if it were any other Struts page. When the servlet container is started and the page is requested, the browser renders what is shown in figure 3.7.

◆ *Discussion*

Definitions in the XML context make rapid development much easier and faster. It's possible to create hundreds of pages very quickly, or define and maintain an entire application from just one or two directories. It is also possible to do many different things inside these definitions besides just "plugging in" pages and calling it a day. You can:

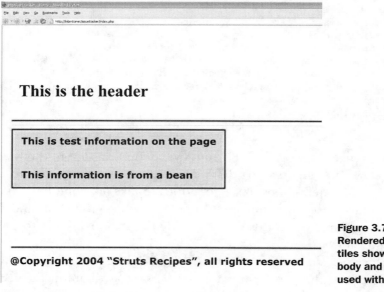

This is the header

This is test information on the page

This information is from a bean

Figure 3.7
Rendered page from tiles showing header, body and footer tiles used with a template

- Send specific `String`s to a page as text.
- Extend definitions by declaring one definition as a subclass.
- Extended definitions can be overloaded.
- Use definitions as `Action Forwards`.
- Declare beans in a defined scope.
- Declare page `Context` attributes.
- Declare lists of `page` attributes.

**BEST
PRACTICE**   *Don't waste time—start with XML-based Tiles as soon as possible*—Many developers tend to create their web applications slowly, migrating to Tiles over time. When creating an application from scratch, it is often a good practice to create XML-based Tiles from the beginning. Tiles isolates the view at a very early stage in the development process. This reinforces good planning and MVC practices within your development group and will go a long way towards keeping your end product componentized.

◆ *Related*

3.12—Creating a basic Struts Tiles page

The Struts-Layout
tag library

I'm tired of all this nonsense about beauty being only skin-deep.
That's deep enough. What do you want, an adorable pancreas?

—Jean Kerr

170

Developers revel in details. Writing "perfect" code means different things to different engineers. Some say that perfect code is that which sticks most closely to Model-View-Controller design patterns. Others argue that performance is the most important thing. Still others insist that maintenance or scalability is paramount, and yet others complain about obtuse code not being understood by teams. Of course, the business managers among us do not get into details: "Whatever works and is quickly developed" becomes a mantra in this world of tight deadlines, looming competition, and high opportunity cost. So who's right?

There is no easy answer. Everyone's right, at least from their perspective. What works and is quickly deployable is extremely important. So is maintainability, which is usually inversely proportional to the deployment time. Some of the more detail-oriented among us shiver at the thought of code that has any compromises. Performance for certain methods cannot be compromised in high-traffic or high-volume deployments. It's important to take a step back and look at the solution from everyone's standpoint.

Le Roi du Pot-au-feu

Le Roi du Pot-au-feu is a small restaurant located at 34, rue Vignon in Paris, near the opera house. The specialty is slow-cooked beef knuckle (Pot-au-feu) in vegetable stock, served with country vegetables and a wonderful plate of marrow bones and freshly baked bread. If your cholesterol level is anything above 200, their amazing house wine can cut through it and stave off the looming heart attack.

Pot-au-feu

For those of you that wish to know, Pot-au-feu is an ancient recipe for stew cooked by the poor in which a pot is left over the fire and bits of meat are added over time:

- 1 beef knuckle bone
- 1 3 lb brisket or rump
- 1 bay leaf
- 2 sprigs parsley
- 1 teaspoon thyme
- 1 4-lb chicken
- 1 pound chicken giblets
- 6 carrots, halved
- 3 leeks, white part only
- 2 onions, stuck with 2 cloves each
- 3 turnips, quartered
- 3 celery ribs, halved
- salt and pepper, to taste

> Combine all ingredients with 3 quarts water and cook on low 8 to 10
> hours. Adjust seasonings. Put meats and chicken on platter with giblets
> and surround with vegetables. Keep warm. Strain broth, skimming off fat,
> and serve separately in cups. Slice meat and serve accompanied with pick-
> les and horseradish, French bread and butter.

The age of this restaurant is unknown, but given the decoration, pictures of
famous customers on the wall, and general atmosphere of the place, its first customer was probably a contemporary of Claude Monet. While this restaurant
might serve something else, Pot-au-feu is what you order when you go there. The
French culture has defined Pot-au-feu, and there is no reason to change it. Consequently, this wonderful restaurant can concentrate on service and presentation.

Struts-Layout tags are similar in this regard. A developer can use them to concentrate on presentation without writing a lot of support code, freeing resources
for development in other areas. Struts-Layout tags are specifically designed to
present business logic in a manner that is suitable, and they are accepted by the
Internet community. As these requirements change, the culture moves them
more into this direction. Just as Le Roi du Pot-au-feu treats the recipe for its signature dish as a "black box," the layout tags can be treated the same way—put
the correct information in, and receive expected results in return. In this chapter, we will show recipes using Struts-Layout tags to create:

- 4.1—An environment for using Struts-Layout tags
- 4.2 & 4.3—Simple and complex dynamic tables
- 4.4—Panels for encapsulating text and GUI areas on your pages
- 4.6—Skins for your application
- 4.7—Creating a complex table with selectable rows
- 4.8—Creating an "Explorer-like" tree menu
- 4.9—Creating "bread crumb" trails
- 4.10—Creating a series of tabbed panes
- 4.11—Paging through long collections of data in a series of dynamically
  created tables

What do layout tags do?

Layout tags are mainly used for presentation. Core to the tags' ability for manipulation is the `java.util.Collection package`. The following recipes show how
to use these tags to create dynamic tables, menu trees, tabbed panes. You can
also use these tags to develop additional capabilities such as sorting columns,

applying dynamic skins to your applications, and organizing your GUI elements into panels. For instance, by simply adding an attribute, such as `sort="true"` to a tag that creates a table column (`<layout:collectionItem/>`), you can automatically sort the items within the column, adding an icon to the header, the necessary methods, and automatically keep track of where you are. Similarly, if you nest the tags creating the table (`<layout:collection/>` and the aforementioned nested `<layout:collectionItem/>`) inside the body of a `<layout:pager/>` tag, you are automatically able to "page" through your results, eliminating the need to add a lot of complicated code to your JSPs and Java files to keep track of and maintain this type of GUI. Similar ease of deployment and configuration exist for creating menus, trees, tabs, and so on. Although this chapter doesn't present every available tag from the Struts-Layout library, the authors have endeavored to provide information on core features and functionality, along with tips and tricks for configuring, extending, and implementing this useful and actively supported framework.

The Struts-Layout tag library is under continuous development and refinement. There are daily builds, release builds, and you may build your library from source if you wish. The site's documentation is good, and these tags promise to continuously support the latest versions of Struts and its related technologies. For more information, the Struts-Layout site's URL is http://struts.application-servers.com. Please note that Struts-Layout is distributed under a GPL license and not under the Apache license that most Struts distributions use.

There is also an active newsgroup hosted by the authors of the library, where development ideas, techniques, and any fixes are actively discussed. It can be found at http://groups.yahoo.com/group/struts-layout/.

Struts-Layout tags are relatively new, but they are already in extensive use, from small sites to enterprise web applications. Their proper implementation allows a developer to condense his or her code base to its smallest and most efficient levels.

Throughout this chapter, we'll use different `java.util.Collections` for our recipes, but almost all will follow a similar pattern, that is, a "list of maps." The following code fragment will be used as our "pseudo persistence layer." In a more robust application your development team will create ways to query objects to arrive at this same functionality:

```
public Collection getCountries) {
  List list = new ArrayList();
    Map m = new HashMap();
```

```
        m.put("COUNTRY", "Kenya");
        m.put("CAPITAL", "Nariobi");
        m.put("ALTITUDE", "1661");
        m.put("POPULATION", "2500000");
        list.add(m);
        m = new HashMap();
        m.put("COUNTRY", "Brazil");
        m.put("CAPITAL", "Brasilia");
        m.put("ALTITUDE", "1161");
        m.put("POPULATION", "2100000");
        list.add(m);
        m = new HashMap();
        m.put("COUNTRY", "Australia");
        m.put("CAPITAL", "Canberra");
        m.put("ALTITUDE", "8");
        m.put("POPULATION", "322000");
        list.add(m);
        return v;
    }
```

This java.util.List is then set into session, defined on the JSP, and then used by the layout tags. To create complex GUI components, we'll iterate through this list, creating columns for COUNTRY, CAPITAL, ALTITUDE, and POPULATION. The recipes in this chapter employ the above structure to demonstrate interesting applications of the Struts-Layout tag library.

In addition, we'll introduce the "skin" tag. While this represents a single line of code in the JSP, a developer can manipulate the configurations and CSS file(s) associated with it to completely control the look and feel of the web application. Once understood and mastered, "skinning" an application becomes dynamic and effortless, and time needed for maintaining a complex site's graphics is reduced dramatically.

Please note that we may often refer to String attributes in some of the code listings through public static final listings from a Constants file. We do this as an example of their use and encourage this practice. For more information on this style of coding, please refer to recipe 1.8, "Manage Constants throughout your application."

Like a good dish of Pot-au-feu, Struts-Layout offers a rich and diverse method of creating GUI "widgets." It has excellent open source community support, and promises forward compatibility to the latest and most useful technologies from the Java community.

4.1 Configuring your application to use Struts-Layout tags

◆ Problem

You need to configure your current application to use the Struts-Layout tag library.

◆ Background

Struts-Layout is an add-in tag library for Struts, following in the footsteps of the now-integrated Struts-Tiles and Struts Validation libraries. Layout tags provide the developer with a rich set of GUI tools to create complicated views with very little code, increasing maintainability and scalability of any given application. There are many tags available in this library, allowing you to create dynamic tables, input fields, tree menus, sortable lists, pop-ups, and so on. There is even a calendar widget! Although the creators of this library state that you don't need to know HTML to get up to speed with these tags, it helps to have a solid knowledge of JSP and HTML to get the most from them.

There are a few things that need to be done to configure this set of tools in your application. Most of this work is just grabbing and putting various JAR files in your class path. (Don't forget to incorporate them into your build.xml file if you use Ant.) There is a little tweaking that must occur to the web.xml file, however. This recipe will discuss configuring your application to use the Struts-Layout tools.

◆ Recipe

Let's start by moving the JAR files you need into your library. If you haven't done so already, download Struts-Layout from http://struts.application-servers.com and unzip it to a temporary area and copy the following files to your library:

- menu.jar
- struts-layout.jar

Both files can be found in the example\struts-layout\WEB-INF\lib folder of the expanded struts-layout download. Note that you need them in your compilation class path at some point, too. Now go ahead and open your /WEB-INF/web.xml file. Insert the following code seen here in listing 4.1, just after the `<web-app>` tag:

Listing 4.1   web.xml with Struts-Layout entries

```
<?xml version="1.0" encoding="ISO-8859-1"?>
<!DOCTYPE web-app PUBLIC "-//Sun Microsystems, Inc.//DTD Web Application 2.2/
   /EN"
   "http://java.sun.com/j2ee/dtds/web-app_2_2.dtd">
<web-app>
   <!--context-param info for Struts-layout pages-->
   <context-param>
      <param-name>struts-layout-config</param-name>          ❶
      <param-value>config</param-value>
   </context-param>
   <context-param>
      <param-name>struts-layout-image</param-name>           ❷
      <param-value>images</param-value>
   </context-param>
   <context-param>
      <param-name>struts-layout-skin</param-name>            ❸
      <param-value>default</param-value>
   </context-param>
   ...
```

The additions in listing 4.1 provide "pointers" to the Struts-Layout configuration property file ❶, the images directory for the skins ❷, and finally the skins directory ❸ where the prebuilt layout widgets, default supporting JavaScript files, and CSS files are located. You also need to make sure that the Layout TLD files are added into the appropriate location in the WEB-INF directory, and that this listing is also added into the web.xml file in the appropriate place. Note the `<taglib-uri>` entry ❶:

```
   ...

   <!-- Struts-Layout config tld descriptor -->
   <taglib>
      <taglib-uri>/tags/struts-layout</taglib-uri>          ❶
      <taglib-location>/WEB-INF/struts-layout.tld</taglib-location>
   </taglib>
</web-app>
```

That's all there is to it. When adding the tags to your pages, don't forget to import the struts-layout tags to your page (notice that the uri attribute below exactly matches the one in the web.xml entry ❶ above:

```
<%@ taglib uri="/tags/struts-layout" prefix="layout" %>
```

You're now ready to begin using the Struts-Layout Libraries.

◆ *Discussion*

The above recipe gives you 90% of the functionality available from the Struts-Layout code. There are a few additional items that must be added for a *complete* installation. These items involve some of the black box JavaScript methods that come with trees, tables and sorting, dynamic menus, dynamic paginations, and skins. Although you can separately configure each of these items when you're ready to use them, it is best to start with these components fully installed, and at a later point you can tweak them as you get to know how they are configured and used.

First, Struts-Layout keeps all of its JavaScript files, skin CSS style sheets, and images associated with its black box widgets in a single config folder under the application root (depending upon the distribution, you may have to move the images into the config folder when you unzip them). At this time you should copy the entire config folder in the Struts-Layout distribution and move it under the root of your application.

You then need to modify the struts-config.xml file to accept the menu, tree, and sorting actions that are available by default with their associated view components. These actions have default `Action` classes associated with them and they should be added and not modified by your development team. When they have been added, you are able to automatically implement many sorting, paging, and menu functions automatically throughout your application by adding only a few lines of code.

Add these lines to your struts-config file in your `<action-mappings/>` as shown in listing 4.2. It is important to comment them ❶ so they do not get deleted later:

Listing 4.2 struts-config.xml

```
<!-- DEFAULT STRUTS APPLICATION MAPPINGS, DO NOT CHANGE OR DELETE -->    ❶
<action path="/sort"
  type="fr.improve.struts.taglib.layout.sort.SortAction"/>

<action path="/treeview"
  type="fr.improve.struts.taglib.layout.treeview.TreeviewAction"/>
```

There's nothing more to do at this point but learn about and use this library to its fullest. Struts-Layout is a newer addition to the Struts family, and as such is undergoing many developmental changes and additions. Frequent their home pages and keep track of new additions and any bug fixes. The author's site is informative and responsive to questions and requests. There are many recipes in this chapter that will get you up to speed in no time.

- ### Related
    - 4.2—Creating a simple table with Struts-Layout tags
    - 4.3—Creating a multicolumn dynamic table with Struts-Layout tags
    - 4.4—Using Struts-Layout panels
    - 4.5—Adding skins to your project with Struts-Layout
    - 4.6—Creating a table with selectable rows using Struts-Layout
    - 4.7—Creating a tree navigation scheme with Struts-Layout
    - 4.8—Creating "bread crumb trails" with Struts-Layout
    - 4.10—Implementing a "pager" with Struts-Layout

4.2 Creating a simple table with Struts-Layout tags

- ### Problem

You want to create a multicolumn table using Struts-Layout tags.

- ### Background

Struts-Layout tags allow you to create rich GUI interfaces without writing lines and lines of code. The most basic use of these tags—creating a simple one-column table with a header, formatted and styled with CSS—follows. We use this recipe to demonstrate the basic use of the `<layout:collection/>` and `<layout:collection-Item/>` tags. Many of the GUI components in later recipes are built upon the use and manipulation of these two tags.

- ### Recipe

We start off by assuming that you've configured your Struts application to use the Struts-Layout library (see recipe 4.1, "Configuring your application to use Struts-Layout tags," if you are unsure about this). The underlying data we want to make viewable is a simple `java.util.ArrayList` of capital cities. We incorporate it into a class file in listing 4.3.

Listing 4.3   IterateTest.java

```java
package com.strutsrecipes;

import java.util.ArrayList;
```

```
import java.util.Collection;

/** A simple list of Capitals for a <logic:iterate/> test */
public final class IterateTest {

    /*Collection of Capitals to iterate through*/
    public Collection getCapitals() {
        Collection el = new ArrayList ();
        el.add("Mexico City");
        el.add("Washington, D.C.");
        el.add("Paris");
        el.add("Nairobi");
        el.add("Canberra");
        el.add("Brasilia");
        el.add("Ulaanbaatar");
        el.add("Tehran");
        el.add("Helsinki");
        el.add("Beijing");
        return el;
    }
}
```

For demonstration purposes the IterateTest class provides a method to create a simple list of capital cities. A fully developed application would probably obtain a record set from a more complex persistence layer.

It's now time to get this information from the back all the way out to our front-end view. Using <jsp:useBean/> we instantiate the page-scope variable iterators through the class com.strutsrecipes.IterateTest (you may also use the <bean:define/> tag as explained in chapter 3, Struts tag libraries):

```
<jsp:useBean id="iterators" class="com.strutsrecipes.IterateTest"/>
```

From this point, we implement the "<layout:collection/>" tag below.
```
    <layout:collection property="capitals"     ❷
            name="iterators"             ❶
            id="capital"            ❸
            styleClass="cities"           ❹
            align="left">          ❻
      <layout:collectionItem title="capital"/>      ❺
    </layout:collection>
```

The name ❶ attribute corresponds to the instantiated bean iterators. The property ❷ attribute matches the field we wish to "get," in this case it is capitals. Finally we need to create a page-scope variable for our <layout:collectionItem/> ❺ to find, this being the id=capital ❸ attribute-value combination. The title attribute is the String value or message-resources key for the table heading.

Struts-Layout attempts to use the `title` attribute as a message-resource key first, and then will use the string literal for its value if there is no value associated with the key. Note that if the `null` value of the message resources definition is set to `false` (default is `true`), the message-resources will return a value bounded with three question marks on each end (i.e., `???this.value???`). For this book, we assume that the message-resources are in their default setting.

 We're not done yet. Because the table is a module of sorts, we need to define the style and layout ahead of time, and then fill out the `styleClass` attribute ❹ in the `<layout-collection/>` tag. The best way to do this is to create a list of CSS classes in a style sheet or style block. We've used a style block here for simplicity:

```
<style type="text/css">
<!--
.cities{text-align:left;background-color:#003366}
th.cities{background-color:#003366;color:white;}
td.cities{background-color:white;}
-->
</style>
```

Finally, the `align` attribute is set ❻. If left out, the table defaults to the `center` value. Often this isn't our best choice, and in this case we've chosen `left`. You may also set a `width` attribute to affect the display, although this is best handled by CSS in most cases. Here is the complete JSP code in listing 4.4; don't forget to import the layout tag library:

Listing 4.4 Complete JSP code listing using `<layout:collection/>` and `<layout: collectionItem/>` to create a single-column dynamic table

```
<%@ taglib uri="/tags/struts-bean" prefix="bean" %>
<%@ taglib uri="/tags/struts-html" prefix="html" %>
<%@ taglib uri="/tags/struts-logic" prefix="logic" %>
<%@ taglib uri="/tags/struts-layout" prefix="layout" %>
<html:html locale="true">
<head>
  <title><bean:message key="testForm.title"/></title>
<html:base/>
<style type="text/css">
<!--
   .cities{text-align:left;background-color:#003366}
   th.cities{background-color:#003366;color:white;}
   td.cities{background-color:white;}
-->
</style>
</head>
```

```
<body>
<h3><bean:message key="testForm.heading"/></h3>
<h4><bean:message key="testForm.instruction"/></h4>
<!-- Iterating through a list of capitals -->
<jsp:useBean id="iterators" class="com.strutsrecipes.IterateTest"/>
<layout:collection property="capitals"
      name="iterators"
      id="capital"
      styleClass="cities"
      align="left">
  <layout:collectionItem title="testForm.capital"/>
</layout:collection>
</body>
</html:html>
```

Several of the tags in this JSP use message resource keys that must be added to the default message resources bundle:

```
testForm.title=A Simple Iteration
testForm.heading=Iteration of Capitals
testForm.instruction=Below is a list of Capital Cities
testForm.capital=Capital
```

When you run your code, the display should be similar to figure 4.1.

Capital
Mexico City
Washington, D.C.
Paris
Nairobi
Canberra
Brasilia
Ulaanbaatar
Tehran
Helsinki
Beijing

Figure 4.1
A browser view of single-column dynamic table created with Struts-Layout tags. The list of capitals has been iterated through, with the "Capital" String in the header element of the table pulled from a message-resource file.

◆ *Discussion*

This is only the most basic of examples. Although simple, it forms the basis of much of the power of this library. What's great about the Struts-Layout tags is their ability to do a large amount of "code churning" with very little "code writing." If we were to create the same table without these tags it would have to incorporate `<logic:iterate/>`, `<bean:write/>`, and numerous HTML tags just to do what three lines of code from this library has made available to us.

We are now ready to create complicated tables with more columns, automatic sorting, and the ability to combine lists, select rows, add links, and create dynamic form elements and other GUI widgets—all accomplished with a few lines of code and the powerful set of Struts-Layout tools.

◆ *Related*

- 4.1—Configuring your application to use Struts-Layout tags
- 4.3—Creating a multicolumn dynamic table with Struts-Layout tags
- 4.5—Adding skins to your project with Struts-Layout
- 4.8—Creating "bread crumb trails" with Struts-Layout
- 4.9—Creating tabbed panes with Struts-Layout
- 4.10—Implementing a "pager" with Struts-Layout

4.3 Creating a multicolumn dynamic table with Struts-Layout tags

◆ *Problem*

You want to create a dynamic, multicolumn table using `<layout:collection>` and `<layout:collectionItem/>` tags from the Struts-Layout library.

◆ *Background*

In the previous recipe we discussed the creation of a dynamic, single-column table using the Struts-Layout tag library. A simple `Collection` containing an `ArrayList` with name-value pairs is one thing, but how do we take the next step up, and create a multicolumn table with multiple rows?

In the Java classes, we need to define this table. Whereas a single column is easily represented with a `java.util.ArrayList`, multiple columns need something with a little more "horsepower," in this case, a `java.util.Collection` (`Vector`) of maps. We can then easily get everything we want to the page, and from there we can let the Struts-Layout tags work their magic.

◆ *Recipe*

We'll need to have our data available to us. For the purposes of this recipe, the underlying information we wish to make viewable is a `java.util.Vector` of maps with COUNTRIES, CITIES, ALTITUDE, and POPULATION as the keys. This particular data is simple in nature, but gives you a proper rendering without having to create different objects and populate them. The first listing, 4.5, shows the `IterateTest` class with the method to obtain the `Collection` we'll be using, `getGeo()` ❶. Each element in the `Collection` contains a `java.util.HashMap()` containing a COUNTRY ❷, its CAPITAL ❸, the capital's ALTITUDE ❹, and the capital's POPULATION ❺. Once the map is created, it is inserted into the `List`.

Listing 4.5   IteratorTest.java

```java
package com.strutsrecipes;

import java.util.Collection;
import java.util.List
import java.util.ArrayList;
import java.util.Map;
import java.util.HashMap;

/**
 * A simple list of Capitals for a <logic:iterate/> test
 */
public class IterateTest {

    public Collection getCountries() {      ❶
      List list = new ArrayList();
        Map m = new HashMap();

        m.put("COUNTRY", "Kenya");          ❷
        m.put("CAPITAL", "Nariobi");        ❸
        m.put("ALTITUDE", "1661");          ❹
        m.put("POPULATION", "2500000");        ❺
        list.add(m);
        m = new HashMap();
        m.put("COUNTRY", "Brazil");
        m.put("CAPITAL", "Brasilia");
        m.put("ALTITUDE", "1161");
        m.put("POPULATION", "2100000");
        list.add(m);
        m = new HashMap();
        m.put("COUNTRY", "Australia");
```

```
                m.put("CAPITAL", "Canberra");
                m.put("ALTITUDE", "8");
                m.put("POPULATION", "322000");
                list.add(m);
                m = new HashMap();
                m.put("COUNTRY", "China");
                m.put("CAPITAL", "Beijing");
                m.put("ALTITUDE", "44");
                m.put("POPULATION", "13800000");
                list.add(m);
                m = new HashMap();
                m.put("COUNTRY", "Mexico");
                m.put("CAPITAL", "Mexico City");
                m.put("ALTITUDE", "2240");
                m.put("POPULATION", "2300000");
                list.add(m);
                m = new HashMap();
                m.put("COUNTRY", "USA");
                m.put("CAPITAL", "Washington, D.C.");
                m.put("ALTITUDE", "9");
                m.put("POPULATION", "572000");
                list.add(m);
                m = new HashMap();
                m.put("COUNTRY", "France");
                m.put("CAPITAL", "Paris");
                m.put("ALTITUDE", "80");
                m.put("POPULATION", "2300000");
                list.add(m);
                m = new HashMap();
                m.put("COUNTRY", "Mongolia");
                m.put("CAPITAL", "Ulaanbaatar");
                m.put("ALTITUDE", "1351");
                m.put("POPULATION", "812000");
                list.add(m);
                m = new HashMap();
                m.put("COUNTRY", "Iran");
                m.put("CAPITAL", "Tehran");
                m.put("ALTITUDE", "1220");
                m.put("POPULATION", "6750000");
                list.add(m);
                m = new HashMap();
                m.put("COUNTRY", "Finland");
                m.put("CAPITAL", "Helsinki");
                m.put("ALTITUDE", "8");
                m.put("POPULATION", "555000");
                list.add(m);

                return list;
        }
    }
```

Although this isn't the most object-oriented code we could use, this file shows the population of the `Arraylist` adding a new `HashMap` instance for each country.

Getting this information to the page becomes a relatively easy process if we use the `<jsp:useBean/>` tag and create a scripting variable of iterators representing the `com.strutsRecipes.IterateTest` object. You can now use the `<layout:collection>` and `<layout:collectionItem>` tags. Here in listing 4.6 is the JSP we use to create our multicolumn table in listing 4.6:

Listing 4.6   JSP showing the use of `<layout:collection/>` and `<layout:collectionItem/>`

```
<jsp:useBean id="iterators" class="com.strutsrecipes.IterateTest"/>      ❶

<layout:collection property="countries"     ❸
                   name="iterators"     ❷
                   styleClass="cities"     ❹
                   align="default">     ❺
   <layout:collectionItem title="testForm.country" property="COUNTRY"/>
   <layout:collectionItem title="testForm.capital" property="CAPITAL"/>
   <layout:collectionItem title="testForm.altitude" property="ALTITUDE"/>
   <layout:collectionItem title="testForm.population" property="POPULATION"/>
</layout:collection>
```

We first instantiate the bean for use on the page using the `<jsp:useBean/>` tag ❶. The attribute that we've set names the page-level scripting variable (iterators), and the referred class is `com.strutsrecipes.IterateTest`.

Next, we need to populate the `<layout:collection/>` tag, which iterates over the named property in the bean to create the table rows. The name of the bean corresponds to our variable, iterators ❷. The `property` ❸ attribute with the value of `geo` is the real workhorse here, as it calls the method `getGeo()` in our bean, and begins the iteration. The `styleClass` attribute ❹ assigns the style information for the entire table (more on this below). Finally, `align` ❺ tells the browser where to put the table on the page, and corresponds to the HTML `<table align="default">`. If left unconfigured, the setting for the `align` attribute in the `<layout-collection/>` tag is center.

After these settings are evaluated, the collection tag hands off to the `<layout:collectionItem/>` tag to create the individual table cells as the iteration commences. The first attribute is `title`, which populates a table header (i.e., `<th>`) in the top row of the table. This can be hard coded, provided your message-resource properties file's `null` attribute is set to `true` (the default) in the struts-config file. You may also use a message bundle key-value pair, as is done here, or a scripting variable.

Country	Capital	Altitude (m)	Population
Kenya	Nairobi	1661	2500000
Brazil	Brasilia	1161	2100000
Australia	Canberra	8	322000
China	Beijing	44	13800000
Mexico	Mexico City	2240	2300000
USA	Washington, D.C.	9	572000
France	Paris	80	2300000
Mongolia	Ulaanbaatar	1351	812000
Iran	Tehran	1220	6750000
Finland	Helsinki	8	555000

Figure 4.2 Browser view of multicolumn dynamic table created using Struts-Layout tags. Using a HashMap() will not guarantee order of these columns – it would be better to use a LinkedHashMap(), available from the Java 1.4 release onwards.

The second attribute, `property`, corresponds to the property key in each `HashMap` item discussed previously (COUNTRIES, CITIES, ALTITUDE, and POPULATION). As the iterations progress, this table is filled out with the proper information, producing a table similar to figure 4.2.

Notice that this HTML information is formatted at this point. To do this we created a simple CSS style block in the code (listing 4.7):

Listing 4.7   CSS listing for dynamic table shown in figure 4.2

```
<style type="text/css">
<!--
.cities{margin-left:10px; background-color:#003366;font-family:Verdana,
        Arial,Helvetica; font-size:75%;}

table.cities{margin-left:10px;background-color:#003366;}

th.cities{background-color:#003366;color:white;}

td.cities{background-color:white;
}
-->
</style>
```

To effectively implement CSS styles within these tags, it is imperative to use the contextual method of declaration, as shown in listing 4.7. Contextual selectors (also known as "descendant selectors") select elements that are descendants of another element in the document tree; for example, `th.cities` would select any `<th/>` HTML element that is located within a `<table/>` whose CSS `class` attribute value is `cities`.

◆ *Discussion*

The above recipe takes dynamic table generation beyond what can be easily delivered using the distributed tags from the Struts tag library (`logic`, `bean`, `html`, and so on.) Struts-Layout tags are extendable in many different ways. By setting a couple of attributes or adding a few extra tags, you can implement sorting on table headers, pagination, option and check box elements, row selection, images, and even add custom JavaScript Actions to table rows with `onRowClick` and `onRowDoubleClick` supporting calls to custom functions. Tables can be embedded in other elements to provide greater power and flexibility, including forms and panels. The next few recipes will show how to capitalize on this specialized table functionality.

◆ *Related*

- 4.3—Creating a multicolumn dynamic table with Struts-Layout tags
- 4.4—Using Struts-Layout panels
- 4.5—Adding skins to your project with Struts-Layout
- 4.6—Creating a table with selectable rows using Struts-Layout
- 4.10—Implementing a "pager" with Struts-Layout

4.4 *Using Struts-Layout panels*

◆ *Problem*

You want to create panels for separating information using Struts-Layout.

◆ *Background*

You often want to create applications with decidedly separate GUI "blobs" on a single page that need distinct segregation from other GUI "blobs": You might be creating a portal page with different information sections that need to be visually separated. You might have a page with a log-in screen and information for users without credentials. You might just have a single screen that needs to organize its information in a manner that is easy to read and understand.

There are many ways to do this—you might want to use nested tables, create a tiles-based solution, or create a custom visual component manager. Although these are clean and workable answers for this type of problem, it is often necessary to remember how everything is produced, what styles you've attached to them, how to manage the title bars of each panel, and finally, what each cell's content should be. It might be much simpler to have a solution based upon a widget that includes a simple table with a title cell and a content cell below, flexible enough to be a template and easy to configure with very little code and predictable results. Finally, if this widget were a simple tag in which other tags could be nested inside to create content, a long-term visual fix for almost any content-managed application may be created.

You needn't use Struts-Layout tags to create panels such as this, but by doing so you can make them much simpler with results that are easily repeatable. Those familiar with Java Swing concepts might grasp `<layout:panel/>` quickly. You can arrange all of your subapplications and group similar view objects into panels that make your web applications more user-friendly, organized, maintainable, and scalable. These panels are created by setting a few attributes, and then nesting your presentation content inside them. Let's take a look at two solutions, one without Struts-Layout and one using the layout tags. A JSP without Struts-Layout's `<layout:panel/>` would look like listing 4.8:

Listing 4.8   A simple JSP panel with Struts-bean tags and no Struts-Layout tags

```
<table class = "panel" align="center" width="50%">
<tr>
   <th><bean:message key="this.is.titlebar"/></th>
</tr>
<tr>
   <td><bean:write  name="theBigInformationString"/></td>
</tr>
</table>
```

In listing 4.8, we've created a simple two-row, one-column table with a header or title ("`<th>`") and a body (`<td>`) element. The title element contains a title from the message-resource properties file, and the lower, or body, element is filled by a `theBigInformationString` bean's value. You've assigned the CSS class `panel` to manipulate the presentation's viewable attributes. Now you can add CSS entries for the class `panel` to your style sheet (listing 4.9) and contextual entries for the table rows and table cells within the `panel` class:

Listing 4.9   CSS attributes of a generic panel

```
/* color of the thin line surrounding the panel**/
table.panel{
    background-color: #1A4D33;
    margin-top: 25px;
    width: 50%;
}

/* CSS attributes of the upper part of the panel **/
th.panel {
    background-color: #1A4D33;
    color: #FFFFFF;
    font-family: verdana;
    font-weight: bold;
}

/* CSS attributes of the lower part of the panel**/
td.panel {
    background-color: #FFFFFF;
    height: 500px;
    padding: 5px;
    vertical-align: top;
}
```

The JSP code in listing 4.8 above is simple, and can be created as a layout with a Tiles solution. But it can be made even simpler, and its usefulness enhanced by using <layout:panel/> tags. Taking the same JSP code in listing 4.8, but using Struts-Layout tags, we end up with code that looks like listing 4.10:

Listing 4.10   A simple panel using Struts-Layout

```
<layout:panel key="this.is.titlebar" styleClass= "panel"
               align="center"    width="50%">
<bean:write  name="theBigInformationString"/>
</layout:panel>
```

There's much less code, no cells and rows to worry about, and it's organized in such a fashion so that many panels can be created easily and quickly. Let's explore this in depth with a recipe for a welcome page containing a couple of links inside a panel.

◆ *Recipe*

We look at the JSP code with <layout:panel/> to create a panel (listing 4.11), and then we examine the CSS used to create its graphic effects (listing 4.12). The actual JSP code to create the panel is amazingly simple, but its interaction with the CSS style sheet is where you can achieve results that create the panel's true look and feel. Note that in the listing, you have to make sure that all of the `action`, `message`, and other various tag attributes used are valid.

Listing 4.11 Sample welcome screen with Struts-Layout panel

```
<%@ taglib uri="/tags/struts-bean" prefix="bean" %>
<%@ taglib uri="/tags/struts-html" prefix="html" %>
<%@ taglib uri="/tags/struts-layout" prefix="layout" %>
<html:html>
<head>
<title><bean:message key="welcome.title"/></title>
<html:base/>
</head>
<body bgcolor="white">

<layout:panel key="welcome.heading"            ❶
              styleClass="welcomepanel">        ❹

<%-- body section of panel --%>
<html:link forward="skinTest" paramId="switcher"    ❷
              paramName="treePage">
<bean:message key="link.tree.test"/>
</html:link>
<br/>
<html:link forward="skinTest" paramId="requestSwitch"   ❸
              paramName="skinPage">
<bean:message key="link.skin.test"/>
</html:link>

<%-- END body section of panel --%>

</layout:panel>

</body>
</html:html>
```

The `<layout:panel/>` tag renders a title bar string set through a `key` attribute corresponding to the value assigned to it in the message-resource properties file of your application ❶. Inside the body of the panel we've created two links, ❷ and ❸, which evaluate inside the lower, or body, section of the panel. The `styleClass` attribute ❹ assigns a CSS value to the entire panel, which is shown in listing 4.12. This CSS class and its contextual elements may either be added as a style block on a page or more dynamically as part of a referenced CSS file. Relevant comments are made in listing 4.12.

Listing 4.12   Relevant CSS code for panel

```
/* color of the thin line surrounding the welcomepanel and general attributes
   for the entire table**/
table.welcomepanel{                    ❶
    background-color: #1A4D33;    ❸
    margin-top: 25px;        ❹
    width: 50%;      ❷
}

/* CSS attributes of the lower part of the default**/
td.welcomepanel {                   ❺
    background-color: #FFFFFF;
    height: 500px;
    padding: 5px;
    vertical-align: top;
}

/* background color of the defaultpanel title**/
th.welcomepanel {                ❻
    background-color: #1A4D33;
    color: #FFFFFF;
    font-family: verdana;
    font-weight: bold;
}
```

Looking at listing 4.12, the formatting is as follows. The name `welcomepanel` is used in context with the table ❶, `<td/>` ❺, and `<th/>` ❻ tags. When any of these tags are encountered within a `welcomepanel` class (the tags are all nested within an HTML table with this class specified), they are put to use in context.

The `<table/>` tag specifies the width of the table ❷, its background color ❸, and the margins determining the placement of the object relative to other items on the page ❹. The `<th/>` tag ❻ specifies the background color and font attributes of the upper, or title, portion of the panel. The `<td/>` tag ❺ does exactly the same for the lower, or body, portion of the panel as the `<th/>` does for the upper. Finally, the slightly dark outline around the bottom of the panel is actually the background color of the table ❸ with a default border width. It is worth experimenting with these combinations until you are comfortable with their use and implementation.

In figure 4.3 is the HTML rendered in the browser, with the specific CSS attributes pointed out.

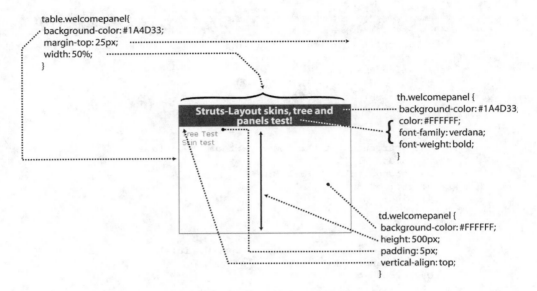

Figure 4.3 Correlation between the rendered page and CSS.

◆ *Discussion*

These panel tags can be easily used as templates with Tiles. Listing 4.13 shows the panel tag used as a JSP tile template. You can then make the panels reusable by inserting different information in the title ❶ and in the body portion ❷. If you have an application with many different panels, you can organize them in the tiles-defs.xml file and manage your components from a single file (see tile recipes in chapter 3 for more information).

Listing 4.13 Panel tag as a tile template

```
<%@ taglib uri="/tags/struts-bean" prefix="bean" %>
<%@ taglib uri="/tags/struts-tiles" prefix="tiles" %>
<%@ taglib uri="/tags/struts-layout" prefix="layout" %>
<bean:define id="panelTitle"><tiles:insert attribute="title" flush="false"/
  ></bean:define>

<layout:panel key="<%=panelTitle%>" styleClass="welcomepanel">      ❶
<%-- You may "cascade" another tile in this with the "insert" property below,
  or at this point insert whatever you wish to render here --%>
<tiles:insert attribute="body"/>      ❷

</layout:panel>
```

◆ **Related**

- ■ 3.12—Creating a basic Struts-Tiles page
- ■ 3.13—Using Tiles with XML definitions
- ■ 4.3—Creating a multicolumn dynamic table with Struts-Layout tags
- ■ 4.5—Adding skins to your project with Struts-Layout

4.5 *Adding skins to your project with Struts-Layout*

◆ **Problem**

You want to use Struts-Layout skins.

◆ **Background**

The initial advent of CSS started web developers on the road to creating a skin, or a cohesive graphic layout and theme, for their applications. CSS has expanded from simple fonts and border classes to complex objects involving position, groupings, and in the CSS-2 specifications, sound and motion. The old days of adding a single style block on a page, or even just a simple reference to a CSS in the head of a document, are nearing an end.

Modern skins are much more than CSS. There are images that must be used throughout your application, such as menu icons, corporate logos, and so forth that can be included in a skin. Often there are simple or even complex JavaScript widgets that are used by most pages, and they too, can be included in a skin. It is even possible to reference skin attributes from a Struts `Action`. This is especially true with Struts-Layout tags, as there are many prebuilt widgets such as menus, trees, table-column-sort, pagers, and so forth that require the referencing of icons, JavaScript, and other prebuilt actions, for these widgets to work seamlessly.

To associate a CSS style sheet with an HTML page, you can simply write in the head of your page:

```
<link rel="stylesheet"
      href="/MySite/CSS/newDefault.css"
      type="text/CSS">
```

Using Struts, we can extend this to include URL rewriting and portability by using Struts' HTML tags inside the code:

```
<link rel="stylesheet"
      href="<html:rewrite forward="mySiteCSS"/>"
      type="text/CSS"/>
```

Similar code for JavaScript works as well:

```
<SCRIPT LANGUAGE="JavaScript" src="/MySite/js/general.js"></SCRIPT>
```

While implementing Struts' tags, and incorporating the above CSS reference code, you have:

```
<link rel="stylesheet"
      href="<html:rewrite forward="mySiteCSS"/>"
      type="text/CSS"/>
<SCRIPT LANGUAGE="JavaScript"
        src="<html:rewrite forward="mySiteCSS"/>"></SCRIPT>
```

If you have a group of CSS, core image references, and JavaScript files that must be made available to your application, things can get complicated to the point that it becomes necessary to register all your global forwards with your struts-config.xml file to make sure that this block of code is imported to each page and in a correct manner. Wouldn't it be nice if all the widgets you use to skin your application could be imported with just one tag?

This tag exists. The Struts-Layout tag library generously includes two different methods of getting your skins working, and best of all, they are highly configurable. Once you have configured your application to use Struts-Layout, you can skin your page by adding the following line of code in the `<head/>` of your HTML:

```
<layout:skin/>
```

The above tag renders:

```
<link rel="stylesheet" href="/MyApp/config/default.css" type="text/CSS">
```

This automatically adds the Struts-Layout skin packages to your page. For the use of basic skins, it is important to note:

- All items used by the Struts-Layout tag library (the default CSS file, pre-written JavaScript, and all images used by the framework in both the JSP and Struts-Layout actions) must reside in the application's /${root}/ config directory. Any deviation from this without custom configurations (explained in the Recipe section) results in loss of functionality and unexpected occurrences.

- When using `<layout:skin/>`, you must include any layout-specific JavaScript through their own references, as shown above.

The default.css file has many references to prebuilt widgets inside the framework. Although the code is well commented, it is important to make sure that you've fully tested everything before deploying, as there are many sample CSS class entries.

There is also a `<layout:html/>` tag that can include all your JavaScript files as well, and does the work of the `<html:html/>`, `<html:base/>`, and `<layout:skin/>` tags in one, plus the `<head>` and `<body>` tags. A drawback to this is you *must* have a prebuilt head with little customization. It is not recommended for use in applications with extensive information and nesting requirements in the `<head>` sections of their documents.

It was stated earlier that skinning an application this way allows for quite a bit of configuration. You may create CSS files with your own namespaces, new directories for your skins and images, and even the prepackaged image names for your application. The following recipe shows you how to create a simple skin configuration with a different skin directory, different images, and a separate directory for these custom skins. The Discussion section briefly covers the other configuration properties available and any current issues that may cause problems with your deployment.

◆ *Recipe*

Configuring your application to use a custom skin is simple. You create a properties file to establish the directories and attributes of your skin, place it in your class path, and finally, reference it in your struts.config.xml as a plug-in, as shown in listing 4.14.

Listing 4.14   Custom skin.propertes

```
directory.config=skinConfig     ❶
directory.images=skinConfig     ❷
skin=newDefault.css     ❸
```

The above properties file in listing 4.14 establishes where to look for the skins directory ❶, where the images directory for the skins can be found ❷, and finally, the name of the new CSS file that is used for the skin ❸. All attributes of the property file are optional, and any that are left out default to the original skins configuration inside the Struts-Layout JAR file. It is important to note that you *may not* specify an attribute in the following way, with an empty value:

```
directory.images=
```

Leaving any attribute blank causes a runtime exception in the JSP the first time it is called. Our new properties created from listing 4.14 are as follows:

- Directory where the skins configuration is found — /MyApp/skinConfig

- Directory where the all of the default images used by your skins' CSS, prebuilt widgets, and associated classes are found ❷— /MyApp/skinConfig/images
- The new name of the CSS file referenced by your skin ❸— newDefault.css

You must register your skin's properties file in your struts-config file's plug-in section, as shown in listing 4.15. The plug-in's `<set-property/>` tag references and sets the `skinResources` property in the layout's class path. The value set in this property is similar to a custom message-resource properties file entry, as it sets the property file in the class path, referenced through a period delimited subpath as in listing 4.14.

Listing 4.15   Custom skin reference in struts-config.xml file

```
<!-- Skin Plug In -->
<plug-in className="fr.improve.struts.taglib.layout.workflow.LayoutPlugin">
 <set-property property="skinResources" value="resources.customSkin"/>
</plug-in>
```

The customSkin.properties file referenced in listing 4.15 should then be placed in the WEB-INF/classes/resources directory, either manually or through an Ant build task. When your servlet container is started, the `skinResources` properties are read into your application and used. Note that this is a runtime environment, and any changes must involve a restart or redeployment of your application. It is not necessary to specify a subdirectory (i.e., resources) in your application, but as a best practice it is wise to group this file with your other Struts and application property files for maintainability.

In the newDefault.css file, (listing 4.16) we've added some entries (for brevity only those items working with the JSP code shown in listing 4.17 are shown):

Listing 4.16   newDefault.css

```
a:hover {color: #CC0000; text-decoration: underline;}
a:active, a, a:visited {color: #6489A0; text-decoration: none;}

body    {
    background-color: #FFFFFF;
    color: #000000;
    font-family: Verdana, Arial, sans-serif;
    margin-left: 0;
    margin-right: 0;
    margin-top: 0;
}
```

```
h1{color: #00696A; font-size: 200%;}
h2{color: #213738; font-size: 140%;}
h3{color: #336633; font-size: 90%;}
h4{color: #791CA2; font-size: 85%;}
h5{color: #000148;font-size: 75%;}

td{
    font-family: Verdana,Geneva,sans-serif;
    font-size: 80%;
    padding: 0px;
    text-align: left;
    white-space: nowrap;
}

/** "defaultpanel" panel attributes **/

table.defaultpanel{background-color: #1A4D33;}

td.defaultpanel {
    background-color: #FFFFFF;
    height: 500px;
    padding: 5px;
    vertical-align: top;
}

th.defaultpanel tr td {
    background-color: #F4F5DC;
    color: #FFFFFF;
    font-family: verdana;
    font-weight: bold;
}

th.defaultpanel {
    background-color: #1A4D33;
    color: #FFFFFF;
    font-family: verdana;
    font-weight: bold;
}

/** attributes of the tree  **/

.treebackground {
    background-color: #F4F5DC;
    border: 1px solid #3333FF;
    height: 100%;
    margin: 0px;
    padding: 10px;
    vertical-align: top;
    width: 100%;
}

.treecell{width: 50%;}

.treerow{height: 100%; width: 100%;}
```

```
.treeview td{
   border: 0px;
   text-align: left;
   vertical-align: top;
   white-space: nowrap;
}
```

All that's left is to create a page and add your skin tag to it, as shown in listing 4.17 (note that a Constants file is being used to normalize the attributes being called from the server side). For more information on how to create and use the `<layout:treeview/>` tag, refer to recipe 4.7, "Creating a tree navigation scheme with Struts-Layout."

Listing 4.17   JSP page with custom skin references

```
<%@ page import="com.strutsrecipes.TestLayoutConstants"%>
<%@taglib uri="/tags/struts-layout" prefix="layout" %>
<%@taglib uri="/tags/struts-html" prefix="html" %>
<html:html>
<head>
<title>Treeview example</title>
<html:base/>
<layout:skin/>              ❶
<script type="text/JavaScript"
        src="<html:rewrite forward="layoutScripts"/>"></script>
</head>
<body>
<center><h2>Skin Test</h2></center>
<table class="skinbackground">         ❷
   <tr>
      <td class="treecell">
         <layout:panel key="tree"
                    styleClass="defaultpanel"         ❸
                    width="100%" align="center">

<!--the image below is  for the top of the
 tree we create from recipe 4.7 -->
         <html:img page="/skinConfig/images/repository.gif"/>
         <layout:treeview align="left"   styleClass="treeview"      ❹
                 name="<%=TestLayoutConstants.TEST_TREE%>" />
      </layout:panel>
   </td>
   <td>    </td>
      <td class="treecell">         ❺
      <layout:panel key="headers"
                    styleClass="defaultpanel"         ❻
                    width="100%"
                    align="center">
```

```
    <p> A second table cell with CSS class="secondcell"</p>    ❼
    <h1> This is an &lt;h1&gt;</h1>
    <h2> This is an &lt;h2&gt;</h2>
    <h3> This is an &lt;h3&gt;</h3>
    <h4> This is an &lt;h4&gt;</h4>
    <h5> This is an &lt;h5&gt;</h5>
  </layout:panel>
  </td>
</tr>
</table>
</body>
</html:html>
```

The `<layout:skin/>` tag ❶ imports the style sheet and JavaScript needed for the page in listing 4.17. The main attributes affected by the skin ❷, ❸, ❹, ❺, ❻, ❼, are embedded HTML code with the CSS `class` attribute set (Struts tags' `style-Class` attribute). The actual page shows a centered title string with two panels— one panel includes a tree with a motiflike look and feel, thanks to customized (+), (–), and path images, located in the /myApp/skinConfig/images directory. One thing to note is that the tree JavaScript is located in the old config directory. At the time of this writing, an issue with the code prevented the relocation of this js file to the skinConfig directory. It is important to check that future releases support a more uniform behavior.

The rendered page follows in figure 4.4.

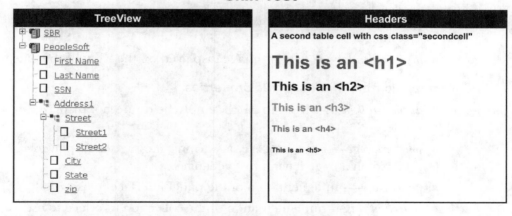

Figure 4.4   A "skinned" application from listing 4.17 in a browser

◆ *Discussion*

The properties that may be set by your skinResources file are as follows:

Graphic effects and directory pointers

- *directory.config*—Web directory which contains the JavaScript and the CSS file for this skin
- *directory.images*—Web directory which contains the images used by this skin
- *skin*—Name of the CSS file to use with this skin
- *layout.sort*—Name of the image to show indicating a sortable column
- *layout.sort.label*—Text to associate with the sort image
- *layout.pager.previous.img*—Name of image used to navigate to the previous page
- *layout.pager.previous.label*—Text to associate with the previous pager image
- *layout.pager.next.img*—Name of image used to navigate to the next page
- *layout.pager.next.label*—Text to associate with the next pager image
- *layout.checkbox.checked*—Image displayed in inspect mode when a check box is selected
- *layout.checkbox.checked.label*—Text to associate with the checked check box image
- *layout.checkbox.unchecked*—Image displayed in inspect mode when a check box is not selected
- *layout.checkbox.unchecked.label*—Text to associate with the unchecked check box image
- *layout.calendar*—Calendar image displayed on the right of the date tag

Nongraphic framework-specific properties

- *display.null.fields*—If set to `false`, empty fields are not displayed in inspect mode.
- *follow.change*—If set to `false`, a warning message is displayed if a link is selected on a page having form changes.
- *panel.class*—Implementation of the panel interface to use
- *collection.class*—Implementation of the collection interface to use
- *tabs.class*—Implementation of the tabbed panel interface to use
- *field.class*—Implementation of the field interface to use

- *formatter.class*—Implementation of the formatter to use
- *policy.class*—Implementation of the policy to use
- *sort.token.required*—Requires a valid token to sort a collection
- *link.token.include*—Includes a transaction token in all links

The nongraphic entries represent Java classes that can extend or overwrite the corresponding prebuilt files for the Struts-Layout widgets. An interesting attribute in this last grouping is also the `sort.token.required` attribute. When set to `true`, a user can experience a page-level error when using the browser's refresh feature on a "sorted" or "paged" JSP page. If this attribute is set to `false`, the page automatically rerenders with the page as it was first rendered. Being set to `true` or `false` has its advantages and disadvantages, and you should decide which is best for your application. The default for this value is `true`.

The Struts-Layout tag library also comes bundled with a few extra CSS skin files, skin1.css, skin2.css, and coincidentally, skin3.css. These skins may be activated on the fly by setting them to a user's session using the method below, available in the `fr.improve.struts.taglib.layout.util.LayoutUtils` class. This method is probably the most used in a Struts `Action` class. For sites that reskin their applications often, this method might best be implemented in an Abstract `Action`.

```
setSkin(HttpSession session, String skinName)
```

Custom skins can be created for user preferences, cobranding of applications, and so on.

◆ Related

- 1.10—Associating Cascading Style Sheets with Struts JSP pages
- 4.3—Creating a multicolumn dynamic table with Struts-Layout tags
- 4.4—Using Struts-Layout panels
- 4.8—Creating "bread crumb trails" with Struts-Layout
- 4.9—Creating tabbed panes with Struts-Layout

4.6 Creating a table with selectable rows using Struts-Layout

◆ Problem

You want to create highlighted and selectable table rows.

◆ *Background*

This recipe enables you to create a complex table that allows a user to select a row and alter its appearance. If another row is selected, the previous row is de-selected, so only one row at a time is changed. This particular trick is accomplished by changing the `background-color` attribute of the table cell's CSS style.

In this recipe, we'll use Struts-Layout tags, `Collections`, and JavaScript to create selectable and deselectable rows. The Struts-Layout tags we use are `<layout: collectionItem>` which is nested inside of `<layout:collection>`, implementing the `onRow-Click` attribute available in the latter tag. The JavaScript we use here is home grown, but this should give you a good idea of what can be accomplished with a few layout tags and some well-placed client-side manipulation. It is even possible to attach actions to these JavaScript functions to make well-formed requests to Struts actions.

◆ *Recipe*

We'll use the familiar `java.util.Vector` of maps with COUNTRIES, CITIES, ALTI-TUDE, and POPULATION as keys corresponding to separate columns in the table we're creating. We've used this same class file in a few different recipes, so we'll truncate it here in listing 4.18. For a more complete example, see listing 4.5 in recipe 4.3, "Creating a multicolumn dynamic table with Struts-Layout tags."

Listing 4.18   iteratorTest.java

```java
package com.strutsrecipes;

import java.util.Collection;
import java.util.Vector;
import java.util.HashMap;

/**
 * @author danilo gurovich
 * A simple list of Capitals for a <logic:iterate/> test
 */
public class IterateTest {

    public Collection getGeo() {
        Vector v = new Vector();
        HashMap m = new HashMap();

        m.put("COUNTRY", "Kenya");
        m.put("CAPITAL", "Nariobi");
        m.put("ALTITUDE", "1661");
        m.put("POPULATION", "2500000");
        v.add(m);
```

```
        m = new HashMap();
        m.put("COUNTRY", "Brazil");
        m.put("CAPITAL", "Brasilia");
        m.put("ALTITUDE", "1161");
        m.put("POPULATION", "2100000");
        v.add(m);

//Continues, add as many as you like...

        m = new HashMap();
        m.put("COUNTRY", "Finland");
        m.put("CAPITAL", "Helsinki");
        m.put("ALTITUDE", "8");
        m.put("POPULATION", "555000");
        v.add(m);

        return v;
    }
}
```

We first need to instantiate a bean for use on the page using the `<jsp:useBean/>` tag. The attribute that we've set names the page-level scripting variable (iterators), and the referred class is `com.stc.strutscookbook.IterateTest`.

Next, we need to populate the `<layout:collection/>` tag, which iterates over the named property in the bean to create the table rows. The name of the bean corresponds to our bean's `id` attribute, iterators. The `property` variable iterates through the `Vector` in the method `getGeo()` in our bean, and starts off the iteration. The `styleClass` attribute assigns the style information for the entire table. For more complete information on layout, please consult the previous recipes on dynamic tables.

After the servlet engine evaluates this tag, the `<layout:collection/>` tag hands control over to the `<layout:collectionItem/>` tag to create individual table cells as the iteration commences. The first attribute is `title` which populates a table header (i.e., `<th>`) in the top row of the table. This can be hard coded as it is here, or you may use a message bundle key or scripting variable.

The second attribute, `property`, corresponds to the property key in each `Hash-Map` item that we discussed previously (COUNTRY ❷, CAPITAL ❸, ALTITUDE ❹, and POPULATION ❺). As the iteration progresses, the table's columns are populated with the proper information.

As we see the `<layout:collection>` and `<layout:collectionItem>` tags in use (listing 4.18), it's crucial to see that we've set an `onRowClick` attribute ❶. Listing 4.19 shows where the selection is actually set up.

Listing 4.19 JSP page showing dynamic table created with Struts-Layout tags and `.onRowClick` attribute set

```
<jsp:useBean id="iterators" class="com.strutsrecipes.IterateTest"/>
  <layout:collection property="geo"
name="iterators"
styleClass="cities"
align="default"
onRowClick="changeRowColor(this)">            ❶
    <layout:collectionItem title="Country" property="COUNTRY"/>     ❷
    <layout:collectionItem title="Capital" property="CAPITAL"/>     ❸
    <layout:collectionItem title="Altitude (m)" property="ALTITUDE"/>   ❹
    <layout:collectionItem title="Population" property="POPULATION"/>   ❺
</layout:collection>
```

We need to add the JavaScript in listing 4.20 to create a function—changeRow-
Color(node):

Listing 4.20   JavaScript to make rows selectable

```
<script language="JavaScript">
<!--
/* Function used to alter the color of the selected element's
children (eg. table row -> cells) */
var lastSelRow = null;      ❶
var node = null;            ❷
function changeRowColor(node) {     ❸
   unSelect();
   children = node.getElementsByTagName("td");
      for (i=0;i<children.length;i++) {
          children[i].style.backgroundColor = '#FBE797';
      }
   lastSelRow = node;
}
function unSelect() {        ❹
   if (lastSelRow) {
      children = lastSelRow. getElementsByTagName("td");
       for (i=0;i<children.length;i++) {
           children[i].style.backgroundColor = '#FFFFFF';
       }
   }
   lastSelRow = null;
}

//-->
</script>
```

Click on this table row to select it.

Country	Capital	Altitude (m)	Population
Kenya	Nairobi	1661	2500000
Brazil	Brasilia	1161	2100000
Australia	Canberra	8	322000
China	Beijing	44	13800000
Mexico	Mexico City	2240	2300000
USA	Washington, D.C.	9	572000
France	Paris	80	2300000
Mongolia	Ulaanbaatar	1351	812000
Iran	Tehran	1220	6750000
Finland	Helsinki	8	555000

Figure 4.5 Dynamic table with selectable rows

Two global client-side variables, `lastSelRow` ❶ and `node` ❷, are the controls for the `background-color`. The function `changeRowColor(node)` ❸ selects each row. `unSelect()` ❹ cleans up any rows that are already selected. If you wish to have multiple selected rows, you must alter the script to reflect this.

Figure 4.5 shows the output with the selected row, "Australia, Canberra" highlighted.

◆ Discussion

There are a few "gotchas" in this recipe. Don't forget the import at the top of the page for the layout tag:

```
<%@ taglib uri="/tags/struts-layout" prefix="layout" %>
```

Struts-Layout tags may present some difficulties with this simple CSS implementation. To effectively use CSS styles within these tags, it is imperative to use the contextual method of declaration, as shown below. As shown in the JSP above, we've added a `styleClass` attribute of `cities` to impart a nicer look and feel. This explanation is more complete in earlier recipes, but an example style block is shown in the code snip below.

```
<style type="text/css">
<!--
.cities{
   margin-left:10px;background-color:#003366;
   font-family:Verdana,Arial,Helvetica;font-size:75%;}
```

```
table.cities{margin-left:10px;background-color:#003366;}

th.cities{background-color:#003366;color:white;}

td.cities{background-color:white;
}
-->
</style>
```

onRowClick allows the implementation of the onRowSelect() JavaScript method on individual rows of a table created in the <layout:collection/>. This client-side scripting may be extended to validate form inputs inside a table, send table node information into the request parameter, and dynamically change the look and feel of the view.

◆ *Related*

  ■ 4.1—Configuring your application to use Struts-Layout tags
  ■ 4.3—Creating a multicolumn dynamic table with Struts-Layout tags
  ■ 4.5—Adding skins to your project with Struts-Layout
  ■ 4.7—Creating a tree navigation scheme with Struts-Layout
  ■ 4.8—Creating "bread crumb trails" with Struts-Layout
  ■ 4.9—Creating tabbed panes with Struts-Layout
  ■ 4.10—Implementing a "pager" with Struts-Layout

4.7 Creating a tree navigation scheme with Struts-Layout

◆ *Problem*

You want to create a navigation menu as an Explorer-type tree.

◆ *Background*

As an Internet user surfing around from site to site, you often find that most sites' navigation schemes are menu-based, with either an "across-the-top" or "down-the-left-side" interface. Every once in awhile you run across a site with a "tree" navigation structure. This type of navigation is rare however, due to the following factors:

- The tree uses JavaScript/DHTML to operate, and browser compatibility issues can come up, especially with sites that need to support the widest variety of browsers.

- There is no de facto standard for the creation of the tree. Many different methods are available to create and operate a tree-navigation view, both server-side and client-side. No particular method has shown itself as a leader in all situations.

- Trees often are overkill for navigation through an application. Many applications do not have the in-depth parent-child relationship necessary to make this type of navigation worthwhile for the user.

- Various frameworks, from Struts, to JSP, PHP, .NET, and so on, have to adapt themselves or completely synthesize a solution to fit a chosen tree widget. Often these compromises violate many architectural rules and accepted practices to get the right look, feel, and functionality.

However, there are specific times when a tree becomes a valid way to navigate through a complex application:

- When there are various vertical elements or subapplications through which to navigate

- When there are well-defined parent-child relationships to views and applications

- When there is a need to show objects and their contents in specific context

When the above conditions exist, a tree type of navigation might be the best solution. Until the Struts-Layout tree was available, there was no Struts-specific solution. It was only possible to adapt JavaScript/DHTML or various home-baked tree implementations to allow for this functionality, which by definition diverted from standardization and often forced compromises that affected the design of the overall application in a negative manner.

BEST PRACTICE *Choose a navigation strategy that is scalable for your application*—Navigation in an application is often one of the first decisions that must be made. Difficulties can be compounded early on by implementing strategies that are specific to your application, not scalable, or those that require a great deal of extra coding to work with your chosen framework. More often than not there are changes, some of them major, as your application's development moves toward completion. As this happens, decisions made early in the cycle that prove to be unscalable or overly complex can stall development, force refactoring, or worst of all, force you into making compromise solutions so a particularly bad component's features can be kept. When choosing how to implement major functional components, you must not only try to get it right for now, but also think ahead and make sure that your decision doesn't hamstring future goals.

In this particular recipe we will show how a Struts-Layout tree is created with the various menu components in the framework. We will create a somewhat static version of a tree inside an `Action` class, show the JSP page that uses the created bean on the page using the `<layout:treeview/>` tag, and include the relevant CSS that manipulates our view of it.

◆ *Recipe*

For the layout tags to successfully use the tree, you must have the tree's default action mapping in your struts-config.xml file. This mapping references the default Struts-Layout class `fr.improve.struts.taglib.layout.treeview.TreeviewAction`, which is found in the menu.jar file in the Struts-Layout distribution .

In listing 4.21 you see the default `/treeview` entry ❷ in the struts-config. xml file with the entry referencing a Struts `Action` class, `TreeManagerAction` ❶, along with the Struts `TreeManagerAction` class (listing 4.22) that we've created to populate the tree.

Listing 4.21 Struts-config file entries

```
<!-- Tree Test action-mapping -->
<action path="/SkinTest"
        type="com.strutsrecipes.TreeManagerAction">      ❶
   <!--if the "skin" link is chosen -->
   <forward name="skinPage" path="/pages/testSkin.jsp"/>
   <!--if the "tree" link is chosen -->
   <forward name="treePage" path="/pages/testForm.jsp"/>
   <!--if the links fail -->
   <forward name="blankPage" path="/Welcome.do"/>
</action>
<!--Default and Tree actions used by Layout jar file -->
<action path="/treeview"       ❷
     type="fr.improve.struts.taglib.layout.treeview.TreeviewAction"/>
```

The `/treeview` action ❷ is the default; and for the Struts-Layout tags to work without modification, this action must be added to your struts-config.xml file verbatim. The upper action, `/SkinTest`, calls the `TreeManagerAction` and passes a parameter to show the tree on a skin page as well as on a standalone tree page. In this particular recipe we are interested only in the `treePage` default `global-forward`, passed from the Welcome JSP page with the correct URL/parameter string:

```
"TreeApp/SkinTest.do?requestSwitch=treePage"
```

At this point, the /`SkinTest` action creates the initial collapsed tree, and the /`treeview` action opens or closes its child nodes when the (+) or (–) is selected, respectively. The `TreeManagerAction` class creates the tree. For those of you with Java Swing experience, you will notice that there are many similarities in the creation of the Struts-Layout tree and many Swing menu components. The code in listing 4.22 shows the events in the creation of the tree. Note the use of Constants when accessing variables from request. For more information on this, please see recipe 1.8, "Manage Constants throughout your application."

Listing 4.22 The `com.strutsrecipes.TreeManagerAction` class

```
package com.strutsrecipes;

import com.strutsrecipes.TestLayoutConstants;

import com.fgm.web.menu.MenuComponent;
import com.fgm.web.menu.MenuRepository;
import org.apache.struts.action.Action;
import org.apache.struts.action.ActionForm;
import org.apache.struts.action.ActionForward;
import org.apache.struts.action.ActionMapping;

import javax.servlet.http.HttpServletRequest;
import javax.servlet.http.HttpServletResponse;

/**
 * Creates a tree for use by the Struts-Layout framework
 * For demonstration purposes. This is a very static method.
 */
public class TreeManagerAction extends Action {

    public ActionForward execute(ActionMapping mapping,
                                 ActionForm form,
                                 HttpServletRequest request,
                                 HttpServletResponse response)
                                 throws Exception {

        //Checks to see if a menu already exists
        if ( request.getSession().getAttribute(
                MenuRepository.MENU_REPOSITORY_KEY) == null) {

            //Represents the Menu       ❶
```

```
MenuComponent menuRoot;

//Represents the highest tree nodes    ❷
MenuComponent mainItem;

//First level node of the tree    ❸
MenuComponent menuItem;

//Second level node of the tree    ❹
MenuComponent subItem;

//Third and lowest node in the tree    ❺
MenuComponent subsubItem;

//Create the Menu Root.
menuRoot = new MenuComponent();
menuRoot.setName(TestLayoutConstants.TEST_TREE);
menuRoot.setTitle(TestLayoutConstants.TEST_TREE);

//This creates the first main menu component -- "Living Spaces"
mainItem = new MenuComponent();
mainItem.setTitle("Living Spaces");
mainItem.setImage("images/stc.gif");

//  Create the "Homes" sub node
menuItem = new MenuComponent();
menuItem.setTitle("Homes");
menuItem.setOnClick(
     "JavaScript:alert('" + menuItem.getTitle() + "');");

//Add this "Homes" to the "Living Spaces"
mainItem.addMenuComponent(menuItem);    ❻

//Add a "house" to the tree
subItem = new MenuComponent();
subItem.setTitle("Oscar's House");
subItem.setLocation("http://www.google.com/");
subItem.setImage("images/house.gif");
menuItem.addMenuComponent(subItem);

//Add components of the house
subsubItem = new MenuComponent();
subsubItem.setTitle("Oscar's Kitchen");
subsubItem.setLocation("http://www.yahoo.com/");
subsubItem.setImage("images/room.gif");
subItem.addMenuComponent(subsubItem);

//Add components of the hous
subsubItem = new MenuComponent();
subsubItem.setTitle("Oscar's Garage");
subsubItem.setLocation("http://www.yahoo.com/");
```

```
subsubItem.setImage("images/room.gif");
subItem.addMenuComponent(subsubItem);

//Add components of the hous
subsubItem = new MenuComponent();
subsubItem.setTitle("Oscar's Library");
subsubItem.setLocation("http://www.yahoo.com/");
subsubItem.setImage("images/room.gif");
subItem.addMenuComponent(subsubItem);

//Add an "Apartments and Condos node"
menuItem = new MenuComponent();
menuItem.setTitle("Apartments and Condos");
menuItem.setOnClick(
        "JavaScript:alert('" + menuItem.getTitle() + "');");

//Add this "Homes" to the "Living Spaces"
mainItem.addMenuComponent(menuItem);
// add a condo to the tree
subItem = new MenuComponent();
subItem.setTitle("Truong's House");
subItem.setLocation("http://www.google.com/");
subItem.setImage("images/house.gif");
menuItem.addMenuComponent(subItem);

// add a room in to the condo's tree
subsubItem = new MenuComponent();
subsubItem.setTitle("Truong's Kitchen");
subsubItem.setLocation("http://www.yahoo.com/");
subsubItem.setImage("images/room.gif");
subItem.addMenuComponent(subsubItem);

// add another condoe
subItem = new MenuComponent();
subItem.setTitle("Suresh's House");
subItem.setLocation("http://www.google.com/");
subItem.setImage("images/house.gif");
menuItem.addMenuComponent(subItem);


// add a room to Suresh's condo
subsubItem = new MenuComponent();
subsubItem.setTitle("Suresh's TV Room");
subsubItem.setLocation("http://www.yahoo.com/");
subsubItem.setImage("images/room.gif");
subItem.addMenuComponent(subsubItem);

//Add the "Living Spaces" node to the tree
menuRoot.addMenuComponent(mainItem);

//Create the second main menuComponent
```

```
        mainItem = new MenuComponent();
        mainItem.setTitle("Java IDEs and APIs");
        mainItem.setOnClick(
            "JavaScript:alert('" + mainItem.getTitle() + "');");

        //Add an IDE
        menuItem = new MenuComponent();
        menuItem.setTitle("IntelliJ");
        menuItem.setLocation("http://www.intellij.com/");
        menuItem.setImage("images/jms.gif");
        mainItem.addMenuComponent(menuItem);

        //Add a J2EE reference
        menuItem = new MenuComponent();
        menuItem.setTitle("J2EE");
        menuItem.setLocation("
        http://java.sun.com/j2ee/sdk_1.3/techdocs/api/index.html"
        );
        menuItem.setImage("images/is.gif");
        mainItem.addMenuComponent(menuItem);

        // Add the "Java IDEs and APIs" to the tree
        menuRoot.addMenuComponent(mainItem);

        MenuRepository menuRepository = new MenuRepository();

// Finally, add the menuRoot to the
// MenuRepository and populate the bean
        menuRepository.addMenu(menuRoot);        ❼

        // put it in the session
 request.getSession().setAttribute(
MenuRepository.MENU_REPOSITORY_KEY, menuRepository);
        }

//call the getForward(request) method to get the right mapping
return mapping.findForward(getForward(request));
    }

    /**
     * Finds a forward depending upon what the viewer has requested.
     * If there are any problems with creating the tree, we can forward
     * to a blank page, otherwise we return the proper mapping.  This may
     * actually be used to create many different trees depending upon the
     * value of "TestLayoutConstants.REQUEST_SWITCH".
     */

    public String getForward(HttpServletRequest request) {
        ActionForward actionForward = null;
        String forward =
                    TestLayoutConstants.BLANK_PAGE;
```

```
        if( request.getParameter(
                TestLayoutConstants.REQUEST_SWITCH) != null){
                    forward =  (request.getParameter(
                TestLayoutConstants.REQUEST_SWITCH));
        }
        return forward;
    }
}
```

While the code in listing 4.22 represents a top-down, semistatic structure, it is important to note the relationship of the objects as shown in listing 4.23.

Listing 4.23   Relationship of tree items from listing 4.22

```
mainItem
    |__menuItem
            |____subItem
                    |__subsubItem
                    |__subsubItem
```

In listing 4.22, the `menuRoot` ❶ component is the main component of the tree (this is the bean name used by the JSP to render the tree on the page—we have set this value to a public static final String that is also used on the JSP page). Its property is set by `mainItem` ❷. Its immediate children are `menuItems` ❸, whose children are `subItems` ❹. The `subItems`' children are `subsubItems` ❺.

Each menu item attaches itself to a specific parent instance through the `Menu-Component.addComponent(menuComponent component)` method, as in annotation ❻. Even though this particular `Action` class has a top-down approach, you can see how a more robust application would extrapolate this and use recursive methods to create its components dynamically.

Once this tree is created, it is added to the bean registered in the `MenuRepository` ❼. When called to the page by the tag, it is referenced by this bean name and declared in the `com.strutsrecipes.TestLayoutConstants` class as:

```
public static final String TEST_TREE = "testTree";
```

Let's now take a look at the JSP page in listing 4.24. There's very little to the code that actually creates the tree, only one tag ❶ with a reference to the Constants String ❷. If you wish to add an image to the top level, you can do it with an `<html:img/>` tag ❸. The rest of the page is dedicated to lining the tree up in the right place, the proper imports, and the use of Struts-Layout's skin tag:

Listing 4.24   The tree code in the JSP

```
<%@ page import="com.strutsrecipes.TestLayoutConstants"%>
<%@taglib uri="/tags/struts-layout" prefix="layout" %>
<%@taglib uri="/tags/struts-html" prefix="html" %>
<html:html>
<head>
<title>Treeview example</title>
<html:base/>
<layout:skin/>
</head>
<body>
<table class="treeBackground">
   <tr>
     <td style="vertical-align:top;padding:15px;">
      <html:img page="/skinConfig/images/repository.gif"/>          ❸
       <layout:treeview align="left"          ❶
                        name="<%=TestLayoutConstants.TEST_TREE%>"    ❷
                        styleClass="treeview"/>
     </td>
    </tr>
</table>
</body>
</html:html>
```

In coordination with the JSP, there are two specific, relevant CSS entries in our skin's corresponding style sheet to create the proper look and feel on our page. In listing 4.25, the treebackground class ❶ controls the size and colors used behind the tree. The contextual listing, treeview.td ❷ takes care of the individual elements. You should start with this CSS listing, or one similar to it, and then experiment until you achieve the desired results.

Listing 4.25   Relevant CSS for the tree view

```
.treebackground {          ❶
   background-color: #F4F5DC;
   border: 1px solid #3333FF;
   height: 100%;
   margin: 0px;
   padding: 10px;
   vertical-align: top;
   width: 100%;
}

.treeview td{          ❷
   vertical-align: top;
   text-align:left;
```

```
    white-space:nowrap;
    border:0px;
}
```

Here in figure 4.6 is the tree as viewed in the browser, fully expanded, with a specific motiflike skin (we've provided our own (+) and (–) images in this example, placing them in the default config directory and replacing the ones that came with the distribution).

The functionality of the tree is nearly identical to an Explorer-type or Swing JTree found in most thick-client applications. The tree's open/closed state persists throughout the session, as it is kept in a session cookie. Note that the (+), (–), and connecting lines between them are configurable and are partly the subject of recipe 4.5, "Adding skins to your project with Struts-Layout."

There are also some JavaScript `onClick` functions defined in listing 4.22 that are called on the Homes, Apartments and Condos, and the Java IDEs and APIs tree nodes. These scripts all fire a sample `alert()` to expose this functionality.

As the Struts-Layout library is expanded, there will be more practical methods available to this tree in the future. Check with the site often and participate in the newsgroup if you wish to stay abreast of the latest changes (references to these are in this chapter's introduction).

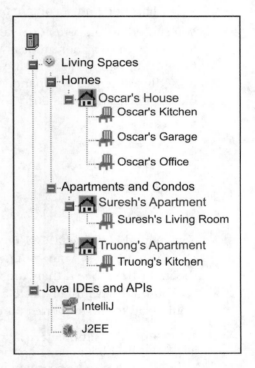

Figure 4.6 The test tree as viewed in a browser

◆ Discussion

When creating your tree, the only thing you need to know is the parent-child relationship of your objects. This is easy if your implementation is static or built through a variety of getter and setter methods that are created in your model. It is important to note that there are many contextual elements that may be added to your tree besides a name and a link. You can assign the following properties

completely at the time of this writing, with more to come as the Struts-Layout library is scaled out:

- *setTitle(String)*—Sets the text name of the node
- *setLocation(String)*—Sets a URL link on the node
- *setImage(String)*—Sets an image to the left of the title
- *setAltImage(String)*—Creates an `alt` attribute for the image
- *setOnClick(String)*—Assigns a JavaScript `onClick` attribute to the node. This node must contain a valid JavaScript statement or function call.

You should assign some CSS values to the tree view because it uses nested tables to create the various nodes. When implementing images with your tree, it becomes apparent that the title text strings tend to be displaced and move unexpectedly as the tree is expanded. This can be minimized to a nearly imperceptible level by using a CSS entry for the `treeview` tag:

```
.treeview td{
    vertical-align: top;
    text-align:left;
    white-space:nowrap;
    border:0px;
}
```

You may also create a CSS entry in the `treeview` class defining a `border:1px solid black` to test your own CSS style sheets. This entry exposes the borders of the inner trees. See if there are ways of making the tree perform as *you* wish.

You might eventually have a need to create something more robust, and that would lead to the implementation of a Visitor pattern.

THE VISITOR PATTERN A Visitor pattern takes predefined operations on a nodal object structure without changing the classes of its member objects. Dedicated methods for each programming task are no longer needed, but you must implement an `accept` method in each class, and then write the action code `visit()` in each class "visited."

A complete implementation of this method is much too detailed for this recipe. A pseudocode Java file showing the `visit()` method for a particular node is shown below in listing 4.26. Every object that uses the `visit()` method has this code implemented upon it, creating an additional `MenuComponent`.

Listing 4.26   Pseudoimplementation of a visitor to dynamically create a tree with node objects

```
public void visit(Node n) {
    if (n == null || n.getName() == null)
            return;
    MenuComponent comp = new MenuComponent();
    comp.setTitle(n.getName());
    comp.setName(n.getName());
    comp.setParent(current);
    comp.setAltImage(n.getAltImage());
    comp.setLocation(n.getLinkPath());
    comp.setImage(n.getImageFileName());
    if (current != null) {
        current.addMenuComponent(comp);
    }
    MenuComponent temp = current;
    current = comp;
    if (topMenu == null) {
        topMenu = comp;
    }
    super.visit(n);
    current = temp;
}
```

◆ *Related*

■ 4.1—Configuring your application to use Struts-Layout

■ 4.5—Adding skins to your project with Struts-Layout

■ 4.8—Creating "bread crumb trails" with Struts-Layout

■ 4.9—Creating tabbed panes with Struts-Layout

4.8 *Creating "bread crumb trails" with Struts-Layout*

◆ *Problem*

You want to use the Struts-Layout framework to create a "crumb trail" list of links that allows the user to revisit pages.

◆ *Background*

Just like Hansel and Gretel left a trail of crumbs to find their way back out of the woods, it is often a good idea to give your users a method to backtrack to pages they have previously visited. Unlike Hansel and Gretel, we need to avoid the mistake of making it edible to birds—and more useful to web applications by creating a trendy and oft-used navigation tool.

Crumb trails are a popular method of providing a backwards navigation system for a web application. They are often used in wizards that have multipage forms that the user may need to back through to change information, or a designer may want to provide a method to show the last *n* pages that a user has visited. Struts-Layout provides a ways to create these crumb trails either dynamically or statically. We'll briefly discuss the static method here, then show a detailed recipe for dynamic crumbs in the Recipe section.

Static crumbs have a limited appeal from a developer's standpoint. There are times when a wizard-type of multipage form needs a crumb trail that is well defined and static. Other times you might want to control how a user backs out of different pages in an application. A simple static crumb trail fills the need for this without creating extra overhead in your code base.

The code in listing 4.27 uses the `<layout:crumbs/>` and `<layout:crumb/>` tags to create a simple crumb trail:

Listing 4.27   Sample static crumbs

```
<%@ taglib uri="/tags/struts-layout" prefix="layout" %>

...

<layout:crumbs styleClass="crumbCSSclass" separator=">">      ❹
    <layout:crumb key="crumb.firstpage" link="/index.jsp"/>      ❶
    <layout:crumb key="crumb.secondpage" link="/NextPage.do"/>      ❷
    <layout:crumb key="crumb.thispage"/>      ❸
</layout:crumbs>
```

The code in listing 4.27 creates a bread crumb trail with Strings referencing a message-resource properties file for crumb.firstpage ❶, crumb.secondpage ❷, and crumb.thispage ❸. Notice that the separator character is set as > ❹, which renders in the browser as:

First Page > Second Page > This Page

<layout:crumbs/> and <layout:crumb/> tag attributes

The attributes that these two crumb tags support are familiar to those experienced with the Struts-Layout tag library, except for a few specific examples. The supported attributes for the `<layout:crumbs/>` tag, which supports the `<layout:crumb/>` tag nested in its body, are:

- *styleClass*—The corresponding CSS class for the crumbs
- *separator*—A character with which to separate the crumbs; the default is a pipe (|)
- *separatorClass*—The CSS class for the separator. When set, the separator character is overridden and an HTML `<div>` tag is inserted, so a `background-image` attribute can be added to the corresponding class in the CSS skin.
- *separatorWidth*—The width of the `<div>` element when the `separator-Class` attribute is set
- *separatorHeight*—The height of the `<div>` element when the `separator-Class` attribute is set

The next two attributes of the `<layout:crumbs/>` tag are used when a scoped bean is set with a crumb object set. When these attributes have values, this tag has no body, and obviously no nested `<layout:crumb/>` tags:

- *crumbsName*—The name of the scoped bean holding the crumb objects
- *crumbsProperty*—The field of the bean containing the collection of the crumb objects

The attributes for the nested `<layout:crumb/>` tags are:

- *key*—Message to display from the resource bundle. If no matching resource bundle is found, the actual text in the attribute is displayed.
- *link*—Link to follow when user clicks on the crumb
- *target*—Window target for the link to open
- *bundle*—Resource bundle associated with the `key` attribute. If this attribute is not set, the default resource bundle used by the struts-config.xml file is associated with the tag.

The `<layout:crumb/>` tag is not used when declaring dynamic tags with `<layout:crumbs/>`. Under certain rare circumstances you might want to use the `<logic:iterate/>` tag with the crumb tags to create dynamic crumbs. The code for this would look like listing 4.28:

Listing 4.28   A possible dynamic crumb solution

```
<%@ taglib uri="/tags/struts-layout" prefix="layout" %>
<%@ taglib uri="/tags/struts-logic" prefix="logic" %>

...
```

```
<layout:crumbs styleClass="crumbCSSclass" separator=">">
   <logic:iterate name="aCrumbClass" id="crumbIterator">
      <layout:crumb key="<%=crumbIterator.getTextKey()%>"
                    link="<%=crumbIterator.getLink()%>"/>
   </logic:iterate>
</layout:crumbs>
```

While the above code in listing 4.28 will work, and you would be able to set all the attributes in the nested tags dynamically, there is a better solution to use, both to lower the amount of code on the page and to move the delineation of the links, crumb titles, and directions into the Controller (Action) class where they belong. The following recipe shows an effective method for creating dynamic crumbs.

◆ *Recipe*

Let's create a simple dynamic crumb using the fr.improve.struts.taglib.crumb. Crumb object. We'll create a list of crumbs as an ArrayList, then populate each crumb's field (listing 4.29), key, and link, using the setKey() ❶ and setLink() ❷ methods. We then set the list into session.

Listing 4.29   Code fragment showing dynamic crumb list

```
List crumbs = new ArrayList();

CrumbImpl crumb1 = new CrumbImpl();
crumb1.setKey("first.page");        ❶
crumb1.setLink("/FirstPage.do");     ❷
crumbs.add(crumb1);

CrumbImpl crumb2 = new CrumbImpl();
crumb2.setKey("second.page");
crumb2.setLink("/SecondPage.do");
crumbs.add(crumb2);

CrumbImpl crumb3 = new CrumbImpl();
crumb3.setKey("submitPage.page");
crumb3.setLink("");
crumbs.add(crumb3);

session.setAttribute("crumbs", crumbs);
```

In the resource bundle for the page, you would add:

```
first.page=Name and Address
second.page=Phone and Email
third.page=Review and Submit
```

Finally, on the JSP for the `submitPage`, you add the following line of code to render the bread crumb:

```
<layout:crumbs crumbsName="crumbs"/>
```

In the rendered page, the view would resemble the following (the default separator (|) is used so no attribute needs to be set):

<u>Name and Address</u> | <u>Phone and Email</u> | Review and Submit

We are propagating the information about the crumbs by using an `Object` in session. While this is acceptable, in practice you might want to make the list even more dynamic and load it as you progress through your application. To do this, add a method to create a crumbs list (it must be a descendant of `java.util.Collection`) in session, and then make sure you can clean it up and reuse it if need be, as in listing 4.30:

> **Listing 4.30** **Action class to retrieve existing `crumbList` from session and add new crumb**

```
package com.strutsrecipes;

import fr.improve.struts.taglib.layout.crumb.CrumbImpl;
import org.apache.struts.action.ActionForm;
import org.apache.struts.action.ActionForward;
import org.apache.struts.action.ActionMapping;

import javax.servlet.ServletContext;
import javax.servlet.http.HttpServletRequest;
import javax.servlet.http.HttpServletResponse;
import javax.servlet.http.HttpSession;
import java.util.ArrayList;
import java.util.Iterator;
import java.util.List;

public class CrumbThirdPageAction {
    public ActionForward execute(ActionMapping mapping, ActionForm form,
  HttpServletRequest request, HttpServletResponse response) {

        HttpSession session = request.getSession();
      //crumbs must be a descendant of Collection
        List crumbs = (List) session.getAttribute("crumbs");
      if (crumbs == null){
       crumbs = new ArrayList();
      }
        String pageLink = request.getRequestURL().toString();
        //add the querystring to the URL...        ❷
        pageLink = pageLink + request.getQueryString();
        String pageName = "submitPage";

        //checks for a back click!        ❸
```

```
        boolean backFlag = checkBackFlag(crumbs, pageName);
        if (backFlag == false) {
            CrumbImpl submitPage = new CrumbImpl();          ❺
            addCrumbAttributes(submitPage, pageName, pageLink);
            crumbs.add(submitPage);
        }
        session.setAttribute("crumbs", pageName);
/*
 * some business logic for the page would go here…       ❶
 */
        return mapping.findForward("submitPage");
}


/**
 * Method for checking for "back clicks" and adjusting List to
 * account for it
 */

private boolean checkBackFlag(List crumbs, String pageName) {    ❹
    Iterator crumbIterator;
    crumbIterator = crumbs.iterator();
    boolean tempBackFlag = false;
    while (crumbIterator.hasNext()) {
        if (crumbIterator.equals(pageName)) {
            //finds out if you already have the page in the list.
            //if you do, it sets the flag and goes to the next record to
            //drop the rest
            tempBackFlag = true;
            crumbIterator.next();
        }
        if (tempBackFlag == true) {
            //if the backFlag is set, remove the ArrayList row
            crumbs.remove(crumbIterator);
        }
    }
    return tempBackFlag;
}


/**
 * Loads the crumb with attributes.
 */
    private CrumbImpl addCrumbAttributes(CrumbImpl crumb,       ❻
String key,
String link) {
    crumb.setKey(key);
    crumb.setLink(link);
    return crumb;
}
}
```

The code in listing 4.30 is embedded in an `Action` class that gets the `submitPage` and sets the crumb—any business logic here is deleted ❶. You probably want to make the private methods in this page protected and move them into their own classes. The `QueryString` is added as a URL as the action is called ❷. The next code snippet ❸ calls `checkBackFlag(List crumbs, String pageName)` and checks for a back-click and eliminates the items forward of the list ❹. Finally, the crumb attributes are added by calling the `addcrumbAttributes(crumb,key,link)` ❺ private method at the bottom of the listing ❻. You might want to eliminate the `checkBackFlag` method if you want to show all the pages, revisited or not.

◆ **Discussion**

Here are some points to help you customize your crumbs to fit your needs:

- When using the crumbs tag, the style class names for the crumb are automatically generated. For example, if the crumbs tag is set to use the Crumb style class, the crumbs tag sets the first link to use the Crumb1 style class, the second link to Crumb2, and so on.

- It is possible to set the separator between the crumbs by using the `separator` attribute. The default separator is (|).

- It is possible to use a skinnable image for the separator. To do this, create a style class with the separator as the background image. Set this style class to be the separator (attribute `separatorClass`) and specify the image size (attributes `separatorWidth` and `separatorHeight`). To finish, set different image URLs in the different CSS files.

A clean up "gotcha"

The above code does leave a gaping hole that can cause problems for the application developer if he or she needs to reuse (and we hope they do) this code in various parts of a complex application. The list of crumbs has no outside boundaries and is at the mercy of the user's session. It can conceivably grow as long as this session is valid. This being the case, you might want to add the method shown in listing 4.31 to limit the size of the crumb list.

Listing 4.31   Method to limit the size of the crumbs list

```
import java.util.ArrayList;

public class CrumbList extends ArrayList {
    private int maxSize = -1;
    private boolean isSet = false;
```

```
    public CrumbList() {
        super();
    }
    public CrumbList(int maxSize) {
        super();
        isSet = true;
        this.maxSize = maxSize;

    }

    public boolean add(Object o) {
        super.add(o);
        int i = this.size();

        if (!isEmpty()) {
            if ((isSet) && (i > maxSize)) {
                remove(0);
            }
        }
        return true;
    }
}
```

BEST PRACTICE   *Implement crumbs in the proper places*—It makes no sense to just drop crumbs throughout most web applications. Just like you'll find in most thick-client implementations, wizards and multipage forms make more sense for this type of GUI widget. Keep the crumbs to only four or so at a time; it makes no sense for anyone to backtrack six or seven views, and the amount of information that would have to be accounted for in a complex application can make it almost impossible to implement.

◆ *Related*

- 4.1—Configuring your application to use Struts-Layout
- 4.5—Adding skins to your project with Struts-Layout
- 4.7—Creating a tree navigation scheme with Struts-Layout
- 4.9—Creating tabbed panes with Struts-Layout

4.9 Creating tabbed panes with Struts-Layout

◆ *Problem*

You want to successfully deploy a tabbed page with Struts-Layout's tag library.

◆ *Background*

Tabbed panes are an extremely popular navigation method used by web-application designers. This style is best used as either an overall navigation scheme when there are a few applications that need to be accessed at any point as the user progresses through a flow, or in a sub-application that has a separate navigation scheme to arrive at the tabbed panes.

> **BEST PRACTICE** *Keep tabs on your Tabs!*—Tabs can get out of control, even on the most well developed of applications. They can end up stretching across a page, in rows, or confusing the user to a high degree by having multiple rows or dissimilar navigation directions from tabs widely scattered throughout an application. It should be considered a best practice to limit your use of tabs to no more than five or so, with care taken to make sure that the navigation and link metaphors are grouped logically and in a user-friendly manner.

There are many ways to create tabbed panes. They can be created using a frameset with tabs across the upper frame and the corresponding application at the bottom. You can also decide to create a single pane with the tabs at the top of each application, cutting and pasting the basic tabbed text and modifying it to show which tab is up or back, depending upon which application or page is selected. Another method is to create tiles to add to a template with the Tab tile corresponding to your selection in one part of the layout, and the application or page tile in another.

There are other methods to achieve this. You may create a single JSP page with struts-logic tags between the tabs. Then you only need one navigation method and one point of maintenance for the page, making them a little more scalable. You can add this page to frames or a tiles-based layout. Having everything on a single page may have some initial advantages in terms of scalability and maintenance. As your application grows in complexity and content, it can be difficult to see into any one of these pages through the struts-logic, struts-html, struts-bean tags, and any other metadata you need to properly render your pages.

Struts-Layout tags have some similarities to the "everything on one page" approach, which works well for compact applications that have a need for tabs. It uses the `<layout:tabs/>` tag and its nested `<layout:tab/>` tags to create a tabbed panel, showing or not showing the content of the tab using JavaScript and DHTML. The content of each tab is in the source code, but its visibility is determined by the tab requested. The code to create the tabs is generic and scalable, making the graphical interface ripe for manipulation with Cascading Style Sheets.

With different CSS classes set in the individual tags by the developer, a properly built style sheet can create an effective tabbed layout.

The following recipe dissects the Struts-Layout tabbed panes on the client-side, and shows in detail how to apply a comprehensive set of CSS classes to them. In the Discussion section we'll show you how to integrate skins, discuss more attributes available in the tags for your use, and briefly cover a server-side implementation of a tabbed pane using Struts-Layout.

◆ *Recipe*

Let's look at a simple set of tabbed panes and see how they relate and nest together in listing 4.32. A simple text String is inserted inside each pane for the demonstration, but you can extrapolate this into any information that might be needed for use by your particular application. Note also that the title of each tab is set by the `key` attribute ❶, accessed through your application's property files. If you have multiple property files, `<layout:tab/>` also accepts a `bundle` attribute that points towards the correct resource bundle. The code below is encased in a simple table ❷ for presentation purposes only; you may want to use a `<layout:panel/>` instead.

Listing 4.32   An extremely simple set of tabbed panes

```
<%@taglib uri="/ tags/struts-layout" prefix="layout" %>
<layout:html>
<!—- "holder" table surrounding tabs for layout purposes -->
<table class="tabtable"><tr><td>    ❷
<layout:tabs styleClass="defaultpanel" width="400">    ❸
<layout:tab key="first.tab" width="50">FIRST PAGE</layout:tab>    ❶
<layout:tab key="second.tab" width="50">SECOND PAGE</layout:tab>
<layout:tab key="third.tab" width="50">THIRD PAGE</layout:tab>
<layout:tab key="fourth.tab" width="50">FOURTH PAGE</layout:tab>
</layout:tabs>
</td></tr></table>
</layout:html>
```

Looking at listing 4.32, we see that there are a few interesting things going on. First of all, the `<layout:tab/>` tag ❶ is nested inside the `<layout:tabs/>` ❸ tag. Each individual tab tag evaluates to a tab in the graphical interface. The `key` attribute to the tab references the property file text for the corresponding tab. The `width<` attribute corresponds to the width of the tab itself. Note that the `<layout:tabs/>` ❸ tag also has a width, setting a value to the `width` of the panel that "holds" the tags. See recipe 4.4, "Using Struts-Layout panels," for more information on panels. Also note the `styleClass` attribute which sets the look and feel of the panel.

The actual HTML browser source code rendered from the above JSP looks like the generated code in listing 4.33. Note the rendered code from the tabs ❶–❷:

Listing 4.33   Generated HTML code from listing 4.25

```html
<html>
  <head>
  <link rel="stylesheet" href='/TreeApp/skinConfig/newDefault.css'
  type="text/css">
  <script type="text/javascript" language="JavaScript" src=
  "/TreeApp/skinConfig/javascript.js"></script>
  <script type="text/JavaScript">
     var imgsrc="/TreeApp/skinConfig/";
   var scriptsrc="/TreeApp/skinConfig/";
   var langue="en";
  </script>
  <base href="http://localhost:8080/TreeApp/pages/testBasicTabs.jsp">
  <title></title>
  </head>
  <body>
  <br>
  <table cellspacing="0" cellpadding="10" width="100%" align=
  "center" border="0">
  <tr>
  <td align="center">
  <table class="tabtable">              ❶
  <tr>
  <td>
  <table border="0" cellspacing="0" cellpadding="0" width="400">
  <tr>
  <td>
<table width="100%" cellspacing="0" cellpadding="0">
  <tr>
<td id="tabs0head0" class="ongletTextEna" width="50" onmouseover=    ❸
  "onTabHeaderOver(0,0,&#39;ongletTextEna&#39;)" onclick=
  "selectTab(0,4,0,&#39;ongletTextEna&#39;,&#39;ongletTextDis&#39;,&#39;on
  gletTextErr&#39;)">
  FIRST</td>
<td width="5" class="ongletSpace"> </td>              ❺
<td id="tabs0head1" class="ongletTextDis" width="50" onmouseover=    ❹
  "onTabHeaderOver(0,1,&#39;ongletTextEna&#39;)" onclick=
  "selectTab(0,4,1,&#39;ongletTextEna&#39;,&#39;ongletTextDis&#39;,&#39;on
  gletTextErr&#39;)">
  SECOND</td>
<td width="5" class="ongletSpace"> </td>              ❺
<td id="tabs0head2" class="ongletTextDis" width="50" onmouseover=    ❹
  "onTabHeaderOver(0,2,&#39;ongletTextEna&#39;)" onclick=
```

```
  "selectTab(0,4,2,&#39;ongletTextEna&#39;,&#39;ongletTextDis&#39;,&#39;on
gletTextErr&#39;)">
  THIRD</td>
<td width="5" class="ongletSpace"> </td>          ❺
  <td id="tabs0head3" class="ongletTextDis" width="50" onmouseover=    ❹
  "onTabHeaderOver(0,3,&#39;ongletTextEna&#39;)" onclick=
  "selectTab(0,4,3,&#39;ongletTextEna&#39;,&#39;ongletTextDis&#39;,&#39;on
gletTextErr&#39;)">
  FOURTH</td>
<td width="5" class="ongletSpace"> </td>          ❺
  <td class="ongletSpace"> </td>
  </tr>
  <tr>
<td height="5" colspan="9" class="ongletMiddle"> </td>      ❻
  </tr>
  </table>
</td>
  </tr>
  <tr>
  <td class="ongletMain">      ❼
<div id="tabs0tab0">FIRST PAGE</div>
<div id="tabs0tab1" style="display:none;">SECOND PAGE</div>
<div id="tabs0tab2" style="display:none;">THIRD PAGE</div>
<div id="tabs0tab3" style="display:none;">FOURTH PAGE</div>
</td>
</tr>
</table>
</td>
</tr>
</table>      ❷
</td>
</tr>
</table>
</body>
</html>
```

Listing 4.33 shows three separate pieces that all work together to form the tabbed panes. The header cell of the table contains all the tabs, nested inside of their own table and identified by an up tab ❸ (ongletTextEna) or down tab ❹ (ongletTextDis) CSS class (the original developers of the Struts-Layout framework are French speaking so that's why the naming convention may not be clear immediately).

The individual tabs are separated by table cells ❺ with a default width of 5 and a nonbreaking space inside. Its CSS class name is ongletSpace.

Next a new table row in the tabs table is added to separate the entire tabs row from the content. The colspan attribute is automatically created to correctly

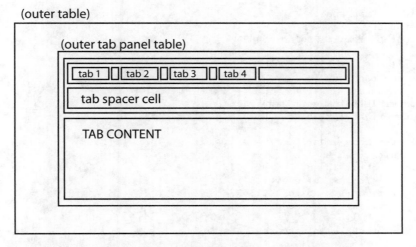

Figure 4.7 Wire diagram of a Struts-Layout tabbed implementation

render a single cell (number of tabs + number of tab spaces + last tab space). This row has a default height of 5 and a CSS class name of `ongletMiddle` ❻.

Finally, the outer table continues to a second row and single cell ❼, holding the content of all the above tabs, ready for their DHTML/JavaScript attribute of `visible` to be set by the corresponding tab above.

A wire diagram of the above code is shown in figure 4.7.

You also need to add CSS to the code to give it a graphical look and feel, as by default there are no hard-coded graphic HTML elements (a default style sheet with the Struts-Layout distribution provides examples). Listing 4.34 shows additions to your CSS file that create a look and feel for your tabbed pane.

Listing 4.34   CSS for tabbed pane

```
/*style for tab up*/
.ongletTextEna{
   border-top:1px solid #001363;
   border-left:1px solid #001363;
   border-right:1px solid #001363;
   padding:2px;
}
/*style for tab back*/
.ongletTextDis{
   border:1px solid #6489A0;
   padding:2px;
   background-color: #E0FFFF;
}
```

```
/*style for tab spaces*/
.ongletSpace{
   border-bottom:1px solid #6489A0;
}
/*style for 5px height connector between
 *tabs and tab body */
 .ongletMiddle{
    border-left:1px solid #001363;
   border-right:1px solid #001363;
 }
/*style for body under tab*/
.ongletMain{
   border-bottom:1px solid #001363;
   border-left:1px solid #001363;
   border-right:1px solid #001363;
   padding:10px;
}
/* style for table holding the tabs */
.tabtable{
   margin:25px;
}
```

Note that in listing 4.34 the CSS classes with the `onglet` prefix are automatically added to the tabbed panes by the Struts-Layout code. Below you can see the information rendered in the browser (figure 4.8), with the second tab selected and the above CSS applied.

The following discussion will delve a little deeper into tabs, explaining more of the tab and CSS class attributes in detail.

◆ *Discussion*

Let's look at table 4.1 showing the `<layout:tabs/>` attributes, which are more global in their implementation. The first table shows the `<layout:tabs/>` tag attributes which are the outer tags in the tabbed panel grouping. These attributes handle the global CSS class for the panel, the attribute to dynamically select the initial panel, and the `width` of the panel table.

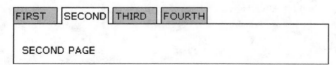

Figure 4.8 A tabbed layout rendered with the CSS from listing 4.35

Table 4.1   A listing of the `<layout:tabs/>` tag attributes

`<layout:tabs/>` — nested `<layout:tab/>` tags inside create a tabbed pane		
`styleClass`	The CSS class for the tabbed panels	Not required
`selectedTabKeyName`	Name of the request parameter or attribute that contains the key of the initially selected tabbed panel. If set, the selected tab is redisplayed after any server-side action calling this page.	Not required
`width`	Width of the panel table, set as an HTML table attribute (`<table width="")`	Not required

Next let's look at table 4.2 to gain an understanding of the attributes implemented by the `<layout:tab/>` tag. These attributes deal with specific tabs as they are set to them. They set the title of the tab, any specific message-resource properties file they might use, the width of the specific tab, or a global forward, page or href to be requested when a tab is clicked:

Table 4.2   A listing of the `<layout:tab/>` tag attributes

`<layout:tab/>`— nested inside `<layout:tabs/>` to create a tabbed panel		
`Key`	The label of the tile, set from a resource bundle. If no matching bundle attribute is found, the value of the string inside the attribute's value is displayed.	Required
`Bundle`	The resource bundle used for the title. When not set, default resource bundle is used.	Not required
`Width`	Width of the tab label cell, set as an HTML table attribute (`<table width="")`	Not required
`Forward*`	If this attribute is set, the global forward specified in the value is selected when the tab is clicked.	Not required
`Page*`	If this attribute is set, the page specified in the value is selected when the tab is clicked. The URL includes the page's `<base/>` attribute.	
`Href*`	If this attribute is set, the `href` tag specified in the value is selected when the tab is clicked. The URL resolves to whatever is set in the value.	

* If one of the `forward`, `href` or `page` attributes are set, the body of the tag is evaluated only if the panel is selected, i.e., its key attribute matches the parameter or request attribute named `selectedTabKeyName`.

Finally, let's look at table 4.3 showing the preset CSS classes that are used by the tabbed panels. Unlike most Struts-Layout tags, there are a few CSS classes that are automatically created when the tag is rendered by the servlet engine.

Table 4.3   Preset CSS classes used by tabbed panels

CSS Classes	
ongleTextEna	CSS class name for a selected tab's table cell
ongleTextDis	CSS class name for an unselected tab's table cell
Ongl:teSpace	CSS class name for the table cell between the tabs
ongletMain	CSS class name for the tab's actual body content
ongletMiddle	CSS class name for the table cell between the tabs and the body content

The above recipe only discusses client-side tabs. This is a great way to work if you have fairly simple content to manage; but often a little more work needs to be done under the covers for a tab's content to be truly dynamic.

Listing 4.35 shows the JSP for a server-side implementation of tabs. By setting the href, page, or forward attribute ❶, ❷ along with a reference to the tab's key, it is possible to create a more dynamic JSP page, as the information located inside the tab's body is *not* evaluated unless it is called by selecting it. You also need to set the selectedTabKeyName ❸ attribute for the <layout:tabs/> tag.

Listing 4.35   Server-side tab code

```
...
<layout:tabs styleClass="FORM" width="400" selectedTabKeyName="tab">      ❸
    <layout:tab key="1" page="/Tabs.do?tab=1">      ❶
       <%@include file="tab1.jsp" %>
    </layout:tab>
    <layout:tab key="2" page="/Tabs.do?tab=2">      ❷
       <%@include file="tab2.jsp" %>
    </layout:tab>
</layout:tabs>
...
```

In this particular case, the tags actually work like Struts-logic tags, evaluating their content only when a specific parameter is met.

◆ *Related*

  ■ 4.1—Configuring your application to use Struts-Layout
  ■ 4.5—Adding skins to your project with Struts-Layout
  ■ 4.7—Creating a tree navigation scheme with Struts-Layout
  ■ 4.8—Creating "bread crumb trails" with Struts-Layout

4.10 Implementing a "pager" with Struts-Layout

◆ Problem

You want to add a pager to your dynamic tables to split their content between pages.

◆ Background

As discussed in previous recipes, using the `<layout:collection/>` and `<layout:collectionItem/>` tags together can create impressive dynamic tables. But what if your table is tens, if not hundreds of lines long? How can we page through them without writing extra code, resorting to other tags, or using JSP scriptlets?

Fortunately the Struts-Layout tag library provides a pager tag to allow for a larger collection in a table to be displayed over many pages. The `<layout:collection/>` and `<layout:collectionItem/>` tags are nested inside them. The pager tag has only three attributes:

styleClass—The corresponding CSS class for the crumbs

maxPageItems—The maximum number of rows per page

width—The width of the table holding the pager's mechanism

An important set of values for the pager tag is its skinnable properties, set in the Struts-Layout skin properties file. These attributes add additional functionality to the pager:

- *layout.pager.previous.label*—Text to display for the previous button
- *layout.pager.next.label*—Text to display for the next button
- *layout.pager.previous.img*—Image to display for the previous button, may be `null` or left empty
- *layout.pager.next.img*—Image to display for the next button, may be `null` or left empty

The following recipe shows how a pager tag is implemented inside a JSP to create a dynamic paged table. In the Discussion section, we'll address an additional tag for paging—`pagerStatus`.

The `pager` tag works by passing the number of items per page into the collection and indexing them. As the collection is paged, the number of items is incremented by the number of pages plus one. A similar implementation can be created using the `<logic:iterate/>` tags and setting the `indexId` and `offset` attributes, but it is necessary to handle the paging logic, similar to what is available in the Struts-Layout pager tag's source (index value for first, index value plus one for last displayed).

◆ *Recipe*

Let's look at our familiar table with countries and capitals (listing 4.36). If we display a long table here, it might need to be scrolled inside the browser. Under certain circumstances, we might not want this behavior. The Countries.java file is our persistence layer with all the information we need. Notice that we've created a list of maps. Each item in the list contains four fields (columns for our table)—COUNTRY ❶, CAPITAL ❷, ALTITUDE ❸, POPULATION ❹.

Listing 4.36   Countries.java

```java
package com.strutsrecipes;

import java.util.ArrayList;
import java.util.Collection;
import java.util.HashMap;
import java.util.List;

/**
 * A list of countries with their capitals,altitude of capitals and
   * populations for demonstration purposes.
 */
public class Countries {

    public Countries() {
    }

    public Countries(Collection mountains) {
        this.countries = getCountries();
    }

    /**
     * countries is field for populating the dynamic tables
     */
    public Collection countries = null;

    /**
     * Getter for countries, returns Vector of Maps
     * @return Vector v
     */
    public Collection getCountries() {
        List countryList = new ArrayList();
        HashMap m = new HashMap();
```

```
            m.put("COUNTRY", "Kenya");        ❶
            m.put("CAPITAL", "Nariobi");        ❷
            m.put("ALTITUDE", "1661");        ❸
            m.put("POPULATION", "2500000");        ❹
            countryList.add(m);

            m = new HashMap();
            m.put("COUNTRY", "Brazil");
            m.put("CAPITAL", "Brasilia");
            m.put("ALTITUDE", "1161");
            m.put("POPULATION", "2100000");
            countryList.add(m);

    //... Add more, you need 10-12, see listing 4.5 ...

            m = new HashMap();
            m.put("COUNTRY", "Finland");
            m.put("CAPITAL", "Helsinki");
            m.put("ALTITUDE", "8");
            m.put("POPULATION", "555000");
            countryList.add(m);

            return countryList;
    }
}
```

Next we'll review our `Action` class, `PagerAction.java`, shown in listing 4.37. In it we see that the Controller has instantiated the Countries object ❶, and then set it into session ❷, and finally directed the page to a mapping ❸:

Listing 4.37   PagerAction.java

```
package com.strutsrecipes;

import org.apache.struts.action.Action;
import org.apache.struts.action.ActionForm;
import org.apache.struts.action.ActionForward;
import org.apache.struts.action.ActionMapping;

import javax.servlet.http.HttpServletRequest;
import javax.servlet.http.HttpServletResponse;
import javax.servlet.http.HttpSession;

import com.strutsrecipes.Countries;

import java.util.Collection;
```

```
/**
 * Creates a paged table for use by the Struts-Layout framework
 */
public class PagerAction extends Action{

    /** PagerAction Class to create a paged table  */

    public ActionForward execute(ActionMapping mapping,
                                 ActionForm form,
                                 HttpServletRequest request,
                                 HttpServletResponse response) {
    HttpSession session = request.getSession();
    Countries countries = new Countries();               ❶

    //TestLayoutConstants.Countries = "countries"
    session.setAttribute(TestLayoutConstants.COUNTRIES,  ❷
 countries.getCountries());

    return mapping.findForward("pagerTest");             ❸
    }
}
```

BEST PRACTICE *Keep your Actions as short as possible*—Your Actions should be short and contain little or no business logic, taking the information from the persistence layer model and then setting it into a bean of your choosing. The Action class should then delineate the correct page for viewing. For a Controller (Action class) to do its job correctly, it must control the flow of information between objects, and control the flow of a user's progress, and manipulate data as little as possible.

Now let's look at the JSP file in listing 4.38. We've imported all the tag definitions and the LayoutUtils at the top of the page ❶, set some styles for the table we're creating ❷, and then used <bean:define/> to create a page context variable ❸ from the session attribute (countries) ❹ that contains our Object, typed as a java.util.Collection ❺.

We then define our pager tag and its attributes ❻. The maxPageItems in this case specifies that four rows of the table are shown on every paged table. The styleClass attribute is specific to how the pager's display is rendered. We use the <layout:collection/> and <layout:collectionItem/> tags ❼, ❽, to create the table, just as in recipe 4.3, "Creating a multicolumn dynamic table with Struts-Layout tags."

Listing 4.38   pagerTest.jsp

```
<%@ taglib uri="/tags/struts-bean" prefix="bean" %>
<%@ taglib uri="/tags/struts-html" prefix="html" %>
<%@ taglib uri="/tags/struts-logic" prefix="logic" %>
<%@ taglib uri="/tags/struts-layout" prefix="layout" %>
<%@ page import="fr.improve.struts.taglib.layout.util.LayoutUtils" %>   ❶
<html:html locale="true">
<head>
<title><bean:message key="testForm.title"/></title>
<html:base/>
<style type="text/CSS">   ❷
<!--
.titles{font-family:Verdana, Arial,Helvetica;font-size:75%;}
.cities{margin-left:10px;background-color:#003366;font-family:Verdana,
   Arial,Helvetica;font-size:95%;}
table.cities{margin-left:10px;background-color:#003366;}
th.cities{background-color:#003366;color:white;}
td.cities{background-color:white;}
.pager{font-family:Verdana,Arial,Helvetica;font-size:75%;text-
   align:center;)
-->
</style>
</head>
<body>
<center>
<h3><bean:message key="pagerTest.heading"/></h3>
<!-- Iterating through a list of capitals -->
<p class="titles">
A Simple Paged Table</p>
<bean:define id="countries"          ❸
             name="countries"        ❹
             type="java.util.Collection"/>   ❺
<layout:pager maxPageItems="4" styleClass="pager">   ❻
<layout:collection name="countries" id="info"
                   styleClass="cities" align="default">   ❼
        <layout:collectionItem title="Country" property="COUNTRY"/>   ❽
        <layout:collectionItem title="Capital" property="CAPITAL"/>
        <layout:collectionItem title="Altitude (m)" property="ALTITUDE"/>
        <layout:collectionItem title="Population" property="POPULATION"/>
</layout:collection>
</layout:pager>
</p>
<center>
</body>
</html:html>
```

Still, care must be taken with your CSS to get everything looking "just so,"
   especially with the pager tag. Notice the CSS style block at the top of
   the page:

```
<style type="text/CSS">
<!--
...
.pager(font-family:Verdana, Arial,Helvetica;font-size:75%; text-
  align:center)
-->
</style>
```

In listing 4.39, by declaring the `styleClass` CSS attribute for the pager ❶, we can manipulate the information's view within it, as the tag propagates the `style-Class` (in this case, pager) throughout the HTML rendered by it ❷. This is especially important as the pager's GUI is its own HTML table ❶.

Listing 4.39   JSP page with `<layout:page/>` tag in use

```
<table border="0" cellspacing="1" cellpadding="1" class="pager">        ❶
  <tr>
   <td width="33%" class='pager'></td>
   <td width="33%" class='pager'>1
     
    <a href="/TreeApp/sort.do?layoutCollection=0
                     &layoutCollectionProperty=
                     &layoutCollectionState=0
                     &pagerPage=1"                                       ❷   ❸
                     class="pager">2</a>
    <a href="/TreeApp/sort.do?layoutCollection=0
                     &layoutCollectionProperty=
                     &layoutCollectionState=0
                     &pagerPage=2"
                     class="pager">3</a>
    
   </td>
   <td width="33%" class='pager'>
   <a  href="/TreeApp/sort.do?layoutCollection=0        ❹
           &layoutCollectionProperty=
           &layoutCollectionState=0
           &pagerPage=1">&gt;&gt;</a>
   </td>
  </tr>
</table>
```

Notice in listing 4.39 that the request Strings in the anchor tabs all call the `/sort.do` action in the individual pages ❸ or in the >> link ❹, signifying the "go to next page" link. When you can navigate to an earlier page, a << link appears to handle this. Remember that the `/sort.do` action is a default mapping that must

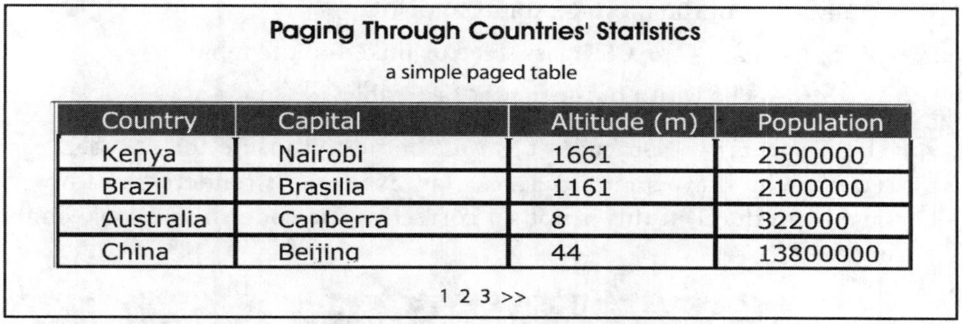

Paging Through Countries' Statistics			
a simple paged table			
Country	Capital	Altitude (m)	Population
Kenya	Nairobi	1661	2500000
Brazil	Brasilia	1161	2100000
Australia	Canberra	8	322000
China	Beijing	44	13800000

1 2 3 >>

**Figure 4.9 View of pager GUI. Navigation is through the links at the bottom of the page. A "<<"
link will automatically appear when a "previous" page becomes available to view.**

be included in your struts-config.xml file when configuring Struts-Layout (see
recipe 4.1, "Configuring your application to use Struts-Layout tags").

Using the information in the style block in the JSP code, figure 4.9 shows our
GUI rendered.

There are 10 total Country Items in the list created for figure 4.9. By clicking
the numbers at the bottom, a user can page through the information by invoking
the /sort.do action. Remember that this is a built-in action required by the
Struts-Layout framework.

◆ *Discussion*

Sometimes just being able to page through your list isn't enough. There might
be larger lists in which more information about where you are in the list is
required. Fortunately, the Struts-Layout library also has a tag, <pagerStatus/>,
that is used to display more information keyed to arguments passed into it:

- *arg {0}*—The current page number
- *arg {1}*—The total number of pages
- *arg {2}*—The total number of items
- *arg {3}*—The number of the first displayed item
- *arg {4}*—The number of the last displayed item

The default arguments message is {0}/{1} if the <layout:pagerStatus/> tag is
used but the key attribute isn't set. There are three other attributes available to
the pagerStatus tag along with the key:

key—Key of the message status to display

styleClass—The CSS class selector linked to the table

width—The width of the *styleClass* table

The `<layout:pagerStatus/>` tag *must* be nested inside the `<layout:pager/>` tag set, *after* the `<layout:collection/>` tag. Nothing is rendered and no error message is produced if this is not set correctly. The code should look similar to listing 4.40.

Listing 4.40   JSP page showing `<layout:pagerStatus/>` tag embedded inside `<layout:pager/>`

```
<bean:define id="countries" name="countries" type="java.util.Collection"/>
<layout:pager maxPageItems="4" styleClass="pager">
  <layout:collection name="countries" id="info" styleClass="cities"
  align="default">
        <layout:collectionItem title="Country" property="COUNTRY"/>
   <layout:collectionItem title="Capital" property="CAPITAL"/>
   <layout:collectionItem title="Altitude (m)" property="ALTITUDE"/>
   <layout:collectionItem title="Population" property="POPULATION"/>
  </layout:collection>
  <!-- you can remove the pagerStatus tag to only show the pager. -->
<layout:pagerStatus key="pagerTest.pagerStatus" styleClass="pager"/>
</layout:pager>
```

The `<layout:pagerStatus/>` tag is properly located after the `</layout:collection>` tag. It has a `key` property set to pass arguments that are predefined in a message-resource properties file. The entry into the message-resource properties file is:

```
pagerTest.pagerStatus={0} of {1} Total Pages.<br/> total items:{2}.
```

This entry passes { *the current page number* } of { *the total number of pages* } *total pages* – line break– *total items*: { *the total number of items* }. The final table with pager tags appears in figure 4.10.

Currently there is no way of moving the widget that contains the page links and pager status from the bottom of the table. Future versions of Struts-Layout will address this.

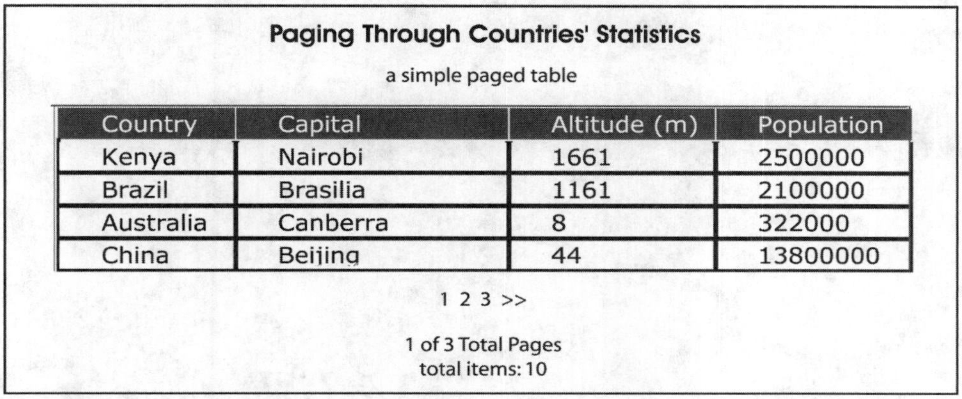

Paging Through Countries' Statistics

a simple paged table

Country	Capital	Altitude (m)	Population
Kenya	Nairobi	1661	2500000
Brazil	Brasilia	1161	2100000
Australia	Canberra	8	322000
China	Beijing	44	13800000

1 2 3 >>

1 of 3 Total Pages
total items: 10

Figure 4.10 Paged example with `<pagerStatus/>` tag implemented – the display is below the "page" links. arg{0} is the page displayed, arg{1} is the total pages, arg{2} equals the total items in all the pages.

◆ *Related*

- 4.2—Creating a simple table with Struts-Layout tags
- 4.3—Creating a multicolumn dynamic table with Struts-Layout tags
- 4.6—Creating a table with selectable rows using Struts-Layout

Validation within the Struts framework

I'm the Dude, so that's what you call me—ya know ah, that or "His Dudeness," or "Duder," or "El Duderino" if you're not into the whole brevity thing.

> —*The Big Lebowsky,*
> written by Ethan and Joel Coen,
> performed by Jeff Bridges

242

It is so very important to let users know what you are expecting from them. Large high-volume sites can spend hundreds of thousands of dollars just to make sure that the information traded between the user and the vendors is absolutely correct and validated. They tailor their forms to make sure that the user will be more likely than not to fill them out. If the user puts information into a field, machinery in the background can actually correct the spelling or punctuation of the input if it "knows" what to look for. Consequently, it is important that any input that fails the business-side validation of an application should be sent back to the user for clarification.

Enterprise software companies manage this posted information at many levels. They have teams of human factors engineers creating forms that users will find easy and entertaining to fill out. This look and feel of an application is created and maintained mostly in the View layer. Filtering applications deep in the back end of applications manage the persistence layer's "hygiene," acting as another line of defense. Struts provides numerous ways of doing both client-side and server-side validation in an efficient and safe manner.

The simplest validations are available in the form bean's `validate()` method, but you can also create messages and errors in the `Action` classes. The latest validation strategy available is the Struts Validator framework, which allows for client-side and server-side validation through preconfigured XML files, implemented as a plug-in node in your Struts configuration file. This framework extends commons-validation, and allows for data confirmation on the client-side and server-side through the form beans `ValidatorForm` and `ValidatorActionForm`. `ValidatorForm` will validate the form against multiple actions, and `ValidatorActionForm` is mapped to the `Action` class of a form. You are then able to extend your `Action` form using one of these two types.

The recipes in this chapter cover:

- *Basic form validation*—Validating input in an `Action` form
- *Simple server-side validation using the Struts Validator framework*—Implementing server-side validation and understanding the content and relationship of validator-rules.xml and validation.xml.
- *Simple client-side validation using the Struts Validator framework*—Implementing client-side (`JavaScript`) validation with the Struts Validator framework
- *Exception handling*—Using Struts' declarative exception handling
- *Creation of an aggregate exception handler*—Using Struts' declarative exception handling with an aggregate of exceptions

- *Create a* `DispatchAction` *form*—Forms employed by `DispatchActions` calling validate methods associated with their `Action` counterparts
- *Validator constants*—Using Validator constants
- *Validation of a wizard*—Using the Validator in a wizard type of application

Validation is often overlooked until the last minute. Time and business constraints often emphasize functionality and features, and only some lightweight or implementation-specific validation is created as a placeholder for more robust methods later. Struts Validator framework allows the developer to create both basic and complex validation solutions quickly and effectively, allowing for reuse and ease of maintenance. The recipes that follow will help the developer create specific validation implementations, whether they are creating a new application or performing a complex migration from a legacy container.

5.1   Use an ActionForm to validate

◆ *Problem*

You want to validate input using an `ActionForm`.

◆ *Background*

`ActionForm`s are the first lines of defense in validation. The Struts controller extracts HTTP parameters from the request to populate the `ActionForm` associated with an `ActionMapping`. Before passing the `ActionForm` to the `Action`, the controller has the opportunity to validate it.

In this recipe we show you the few simple steps required to trigger `Action-Form` validation.

◆ *Recipe*

There are five steps required to use `ActionForm` validation.

1   Override the `ActionForm`'s validate method to perform validation to potentially create `ActionErrors`.

2   Declare error key/value pairings in the default resource bundle for the errors you created.

3   Set the `validation` attribute to `true` on the `ActionMapping` (this is optional as the default is `true`).

4 Set the `input` attribute on the `ActionMapping` to define the JSP used to correct the errors.

5 Present the errors to the user.

With the above plan in mind, we'll illustrate this recipe using a simple logon page. Let's get started by overriding the `ActionForm`'s validate method, as shown in listing 5.1.

Listing 5.1 `ActionForm` **validate method**

```
public ActionErrors validate(
   ActionMapping mapping,
   HttpServletRequest request) {
   ActionErrors errors = new ActionErrors();

   if (null == getUserId() || 0 == getUserId().length()) {
      errors.add(
         ActionErrors.GLOBAL_ERROR,
         new ActionError("error.required.userid"));
   }

   if (null == getPassword() || 0 == getPassword().length()) {
      errors.add(
         ActionErrors.GLOBAL_ERROR,
         new ActionError("error.required.password"));
   }

   return errors;
}
```

All Struts forms must extend `ActionForm`. If you look at this base class you will notice it has an empty implementation of the validate method that simply returns `null`. This is the method you need to override in order to exercise form validation. In listing 5.1 you see that we check that something was entered in both the password and userId fields. If either of these fields is empty, an `ActionError` is aggregated into `ActionErrors`. You can either return an `ActionErrors` of length zero or `null`, the choice is yours. You avoid object creation if you wait to create `ActionErrors` until you are sure you have an `ActionError`. The constructor to the `ActionError` class accepts a key to a localized message. Let's see how to register text messages against those keys (listing 5.2).

Listing 5.2 **application.properties resource file**

```
errors.header=<h3 style="color:red">Error</h3><ul>
errors.footer=</ul><hr>
```

```
error.required.userid=<li>user id required</li>
error.required.password=<li>password required</li>
```

In listing 5.2 we add the properties used to look up error messages. Later we will show you how to render these messages on the page, but for now the errors generated by the validate method are wrapped in the `errors.header` and `errors.footer` key values and rendered on the page.

Next we see how to turn on form bean validation, as shown in listing 5.3.

Listing 5.3 Action mapping in struts-config.xml file

```
<action     path="/logon"
            name="logonForm"
            type="com.strutsrecipes.formbean.actions.LogonAction"
            validate="true"     ❶
            input="/logon.jsp">     ❷
            <forward name="success" path="/main.jsp"/>
</action>
```

The action mapping presented in listing 5.3 is very typical of many action mappings, except for two differences. The action mapping contains two new attributes—validate and input. Whenever the validate attribute is set to true ❶ the Struts RequestProcessor invokes the validate method. If you don't set this attribute to true, the validate method is not called. If the validate method returns ActionErrors containing at least one ActionError, the RequestProcessor automatically directs the response to the path specified in the input attribute ❷.

The last step is to display the error messages on the page, as shown in listing 5.4.

Listing 5.4 JSP using <html:error> tag

```
<%@ taglib uri="/WEB-INF/struts-html.tld" prefix="html" %>

<html:html>
  <body>
    <html:form action="logon">
        <p>UserId:<html:text property="userId"/></p>
        <p>Password:<html:password property="password"/></p>

        <p><html:submit /></p>

        <p><html:errors/></p>     ❶
    </html:form>
```

```
    </body>
  </html:html>
```

In listing 5.3, we used the `input` attribute to direct the user back to the input page to attempt data entry once again. In listing 5.4, we present the logon.jsp used for input. Notice we have inserted an `<html:errors/>` tag ❶. This tag automatically iterates over the list of `ActionErrors` returned in listing 5.1 and looks up the key values against the default resource bundle populated in listing 5.2. Remember that header and footer keys wrap the `ActionError`'s key values. The errors are formatted by placing `<ul>` tags in the header and footers, and `.<li>` tags in the error key values. Otherwise, you could use `errors.prefix` and `errors.suffix` to hold the `<li>` tags.

◆ *Discussion*

In this recipe we explored using form bean validation. Form bean validation is useful when you want simple validation without using the Validator. Form bean validation is often used for simple "sanity" checks.

Alternatively, you can use the Validator to perform server-side and client-side validation. The Validator offers the ability to define your validation rules declaratively.

Many developers believe that simple form bean validation is dead. This is not true. Form bean validation is a good choice for simple "sanity" checks, or when you don't have time to develop expertise with the Validator. Many developers like to get their feet wet with form bean validation when first starting out with Struts. Regardless, form bean validation is a good technique to keep in your back pocket.

◆ *Related*

  ▪ 5.6—Tailor a form for a DispatchAction

5.2 *Struts Validator files explained (server-side)*

◆ *Problem*

You want to implement server-side validation and need to understand the content and relationship of validator-rules.xml and validation.xml.

◆ *Background*

The Struts Validator framework is a mature product included with the Struts 1.1+ release at the Struts site. Thanks to David Winterfeldt, validation can now be completely object oriented, scalable, and easy to maintain throughout an application. Two files, validator-rules.xml and validation.xml, give a complex web deployment the ability to reference many standard validations that come packaged within the download, presenting the astute developer with a logical platform to create custom validations for specific needs.

It's important to note that the Struts Validator framework provides the developer with two different types of validation: client-side and server-side. The differences between these two are quite important.

Client-side validation occurs at the browser level and is almost always associated with JavaScript. It provides the user with immediate feedback and, when implemented correctly, guides the user's inputs into forms without calls to the server, which can be expensive.

Server-side validation occurs in the back end after posting information, usually from a form. When an error in the input is caught, the page ideally returns with messages instructing the user how to fill out the form correctly. While client-side validation can "filter" your data well before submission, server-side validation is important to ensure that all your data is correct, no matter how it has been entered in a browser.

◆ *Recipe*

Let's look at the two XML reference files and see how they interact with each other and the rest of a Struts application. The validator-rules.xml file provides a group of functions that allow for many of the general validations needed on thin-client forms:

- Credit card
- Date
- Email
- Integer
- Min length
- Max length
- Required field
- Float

- Range
- Short value
- Long value
- Double value
- Regular expression mask
- Byte

Any or all of these methods can be invoked on any form input or application *at any time without any modification*. If you want to create custom validations that extend or add to these validations, it is wise to do so in a separate custom validator-rules file so that upgrades and changes by the Jakarta team to the validator-rules.xml file can be seamlessly integrated into your project.

The validation.xml is the next configuration file you need for your web application. This file acts as a bridge between the validator-rules.xml (and other custom XML rules configurations) and your deployed application:

- It assigns the individual validation rules to a specific form.
- It channels specific validations into generic rules.
- It allows for internationalization of your forms.
- It allows for "dependencies" and multiple validations in single fields.

We need to make sure that the Validator framework is installed in the struts-config.xml file. This framework is instantiated through a plug-in, inserted into the XML after the `<action-mappings/>`, `<controller/>`, and `<message-resources/>` nodes, as seen in listing 5.5:

Listing 5.5 Plug-in for StrutsValidator in struts-config.xml

```
<plug-in className="org.apache.struts.validator.ValidatorPlugIn">
  <set-property property="pathnames"
          value="/WEB-INF/validator-rules.xml,/WEB-INF/validation.xml" />
</plug-in>
```

Let's look at a specific implementation of the Validator framework as a *server-side* check of an email input. The check covers a "required" field, whether it is `null`, and/or whether the sequence of characters has the proper syntax to qualify it as a proper email address. This code inside the validator-rules.xml file looks like:

Listing 5.6   validator-rules.xml (email validation node, server-side validation)

```
<validator name="email"        ❶
        classname="org.apache.struts.validator.FieldChecks"     ❷
        method="validateEmail"      ❸
        methodParams="java.lang.Object,      ❹
                        org.apache.commons.validator.ValidatorAction,
                        org.apache.commons.validator.Field,
                        org.apache.struts.action.ActionErrors,
                        javax.servlet.http.HttpServletRequest"
        depends=""     ❺
        msg="errors.email">     ❻
        <javascript>

/* Note: JavaScript validation for email is also written into this validator,
   but the code for it is not shown here as it is out of the scope of this
   particular recipe. */...
        </javascript>
</validator>
```

We'll examine the attributes in listing 5.6. The namespace used to identify the rule is name ❶. className ❷ is the fully qualified class that the rule needs to execute the validation. method ❸ is the method called in the classname's class. method-Params ❹ represents the list of parameters used by the specified method.

The last two attributes used in this rule are depends ❺ and msg ❻. depends is interesting because if there are multiple rules that need to be called before this specific rule, the depends attribute allows for these rules to be called and evaluated first. For example, if

```
depends="minLength"
```

is specified, the validation checks for a minimum length before checking whether email syntax is correct (in this case, this is part of the validateEmail method, redundant for this particular case). For readers who use Ant on a regular basis, this attribute should look familiar!

Finally, the msg attribute refers to the corresponding value in your application.properties resource bundle. In this case, the errors.email value defaults to the key/value pair in your properties file as:

```
errors.email={0}is an invalid email address
```

The {0} argument is passed into the message from the arg0 key attribute ❶ in the snippet below. It is time to build a bridge from your rules to the application. Take a look at the validation.xml file with an email entry:

```
<form-validation>
    <formset language="en" country="US">    ❶
        <form name="emailFooForm">    ❷
            <field property="emailField" depends="required,email">    ❸
                <arg0 key="registrationForm.email.displayname"/>    ❹
            </field>
        </form>
    </formset>
</form-validation>
```

This is a very simple validation but it provides an easy transition to the framework if you've never implemented it. Let's decompose this nodeset and understand it completely. The `<formset>` node ❶ contains one or more form nodes. Each `<formset>` node can specify a language and country to allow the validations to be specific to the user's locale. The `<form>` ❷ node references the form in the JSP page.

Looking at the `<form>`'s child node, `<field>` ❸, the property `email` refers to the field in the form bean to check with our validator-rules.xml file, and creates a dependency of `required,email`, which means that we will check the "required" rule in the validator-rules.xml first, and then the email rule if there is information present. If the field is left blank by the end user, it fails and propagates the `errors.required` key (listing 4.5, annotation 6) in the property file.

Finally, we might want to pass an argument into this field to further customize our default error message, or just override the message completely. We have chosen in this case to modify the message with the addition of an argument, `arg0` ❹, that is passed into the default error message

```
errors.email={0}is an invalid email address
```

in the `{0}` position. This message is referenced by the key value `registration-Form.email.displayname` also found in the resource bundle.

This validation works for standard form beans and dynamic forms equally (in this case `emailFooForm`). We now have referenced a form in our application, `emailFooForm`, internationalized it, referenced the specific field, defined it as a required field with a proper email syntax, and created a specific custom error message for it!

◆ Discussion

The Struts Validator framework decreases the number of lines of code you need to write, and this recipe is designed to whet your appetite to use the framework as your application grows in size and scope, allowing you to reuse code, internationalize your application, and create a scalable, portable and maintainable thin-client solution.

As you start to create your own validations, you need a good understanding of regular expressions, and it won't hurt to "get your arms around" JavaScript to the fullest extent possible when working with client-side solutions. The Validator framework is by far the best method to use when creating your applications from scratch, and you can find many more code snippets in your virtual travels across the web. There are times when you might want to use the older form bean method of validation instead of the Validator framework as well—often this happens during large-scale migrations from other application formats, or when there are legacy Java-enabled validation schemes already in place.

◆ **Related**

- 5.1—Use an Action Form to Validate
- 5.3—Struts Validator files explained (client-side)
- 5.4—Use declarative exception handling
- 5.5—Aggregate Exceptions

5.3 Struts Validator files explained (client-side)

◆ **Problem**

You want to implement client-side (JavaScript) validation with the Struts Validator framework.

◆ **Background**

The previous recipe explained the basic Struts Validator framework with respect to server-side data-checking. This recipe builds upon this foundation and discusses the embedding of JavaScript into the validator-rules.xml file to create an object-oriented, reusable, and maintainable client-side solution.

◆ **Recipe**

We'll start off by introducing a JSP tag that is needed to connect our page to the validation rules we are about to create:

```
<html:javascript formName="yourEmailForm"/>
```

This tag can be inserted anywhere on the JSP page, although it is best to locate it near the form you are validating for later reference. We're going to validate an email address on the client-side in a similar manner to the previous recipe's server-side validation for the sake of continuity and simplicity. The attribute, formName, should contain as a value the name of the ActionForm. The JSP form declaration must also be modified to:

```
<html:form action="yourEmailAction" onSubmit="return validateYourEmail-
    Form(this);">
```

This tag creates an onSubmit JavaScript action that calls the validateYourEmail-Form() function. If validation fails, a JavaScript alert() message box populated by appropriate message(s) pops into view. The function, validateYourEmail-Form(), is created on the fly by Struts (i.e., validate+FormBeanName).

Let's take a new look at the validator-rules.xml file and the JavaScript-embedded code ❶, as shown in listing 5.7:

Listing 5.7   validation-rules.xml

```
<validator name="email" classname="org.apache.struts.validator.FieldChecks"
    method="validateEmail"
    methodParams="java.lang.Object,
                org.apache.commons.validator.ValidatorAction,
                org.apache.commons.validator.Field,
                org.apache.struts.action.ActionErrors,
                javax.servlet.http.HttpServletRequest"
    depends="" msg="errors.email">        ❷

    <javascript><![CDATA[     ❶
        function validateEmail(form) {
            var bValid = true;
            var focusField = null;
            var i = 0;
            var fields = new Array();
            oEmail = new email();
            for (x in oEmail) {
                if ((form[oEmail[x][0]].type == 'text' ||
                    form[oEmail[x][0]].type == 'textarea') &&
                    (form[oEmail[x][0]].value.length > 0)) {
                    if (!checkEmail(form[oEmail[x][0]].value)) {
                        if (i == 0) {
                            focusField = form[oEmail[x][0]];
                        }
                        fields[i++] = oEmail[x][1];
                        bValid = false;
                    }
                }
            }
            if (fields.length > 0) {
                focusField.focus();
                alert(fields.join('\n'));
            }
            return bValid;
```

```
                }

    /**
     * Reference: Sandeep V. Tamhankar (stamhankar@hotmail.com),
     * http://javascript.internet.com
     */
    function checkEmail(emailStr) {
        if (emailStr.length == 0) {
            return true;
        }
        var emailPat=/^(.+)@(.+)$/;
        var specialChars="\\(\\)<>@,;:\\\\\\\"\\.\\[\\]";
        var validChars="\[^\\s" + specialChars + "\]";
        var quotedUser="(\"[^\"]*\")";
        var ipDomainPat=/
^(\d{1,3})[.](\d{1,3})[.](\d{1,3})[.](\d{1,3})$/;
        var atom=validChars + '+';
        var word="(" + atom + "|" + quotedUser + ")";
        var userPat=new RegExp("^" + word + "(\\." + word + ")*$");
        var domainPat=new RegExp("^" + atom + "(\\." + atom + ")*$");
        var matchArray=emailStr.match(emailPat);
        if (matchArray == null) {
            return false;
        }
        var user=matchArray[1];
        var domain=matchArray[2];
        if (user.match(userPat) == null) {
            return false;
        }
        var IPArray = domain.match(ipDomainPat);
        if (IPArray != null) {
            for (var i = 1; i <= 4; i++) {
                if (IPArray[i] > 255) {
                    return false;
                }
            }
            return true;
        }
        var domainArray=domain.match(domainPat);
        if (domainArray == null) {
            return false;
        }
        var atomPat=new RegExp(atom,"g");
        var domArr=domain.match(atomPat);
        var len=domArr.length;
        if ((domArr[domArr.length-1].length < 2) ||
            (domArr[domArr.length-1].length > 3)) {
            return false;
        }
        if (len < 2) {
            return false;
```

```
        }
        return true;
     }]]></javascript>
  </validator>
```

Wow. We didn't have to write a single line of code, as this particular check ships with the Struts validation package. The JavaScript validation script ❶ is located below the server-side validation entry ❷ and entered into the XML file as a `<[CDATA[` entry. When called from the page with the `<html:javascript/>` tag and the `onSubmit` attribute's setting in the `<form/>`, it overrides the server-side and immediately implements the JavaScript validation.

You can also implement server-side validation for the same field to further ensure your information is correct, or to apply different checks that might be needed for your data layer to operate correctly.

BEST PRACTICE *Don't trust JavaScript as your only means of validation!*—There are times when a user cannot access your web application through a browser, or the more astute (and often nefarious) users might just type the information they want to post in a request string to circumvent your client-side checks and post information to your persistence layer that could seriously damage it. You could disable GET requests, but even this isn't perfect as a user could simulate a browser if he or she know how to do it. Never assume that your users have your best interests at heart, and always plan for validation to help you with security. Only server-side validation can guarantee data posted to your persistence layer is valid and safe.

◆ ***Discussion***

One can begin to see how it is possible to create complex JavaScript validations and easily reuse them throughout an application. It is easy to integrate JavaScript into a form by using the `<html:javascript>` tag. Once done, you only need to modify the `<html:form>` tag to include the `onSubmit` attribute with a `validate+ FormBeanNameHere` value.

You can obviously "roll your own" validations using the above framework, and create or modify JavaScript functions to meet your needs. If you do create custom JavaScript validations, beware that you will "own" this code, and will not have the open source community to help you maintain it and guarantee forward compatibility. It is imperative when creating custom JavaScript functions that you research the existing code base to be sure that they are not suitable for your need first, as improved versions of what is currently available are eventually released into the community.

◆ Related

- 5.1—Use an Action Form to Validate
- 5.3—Struts Validator files explained (server-side)
- 5.4—Use declarative exception handling
- 5.5—Aggregate Exceptions

5.4 *Use declarative exception handling*

◆ Problem

You want to use Struts declarative exception handling.

◆ Background

Declarative exception handling is one of the most powerful features introduced in Struts 1.1. Used correctly, declarative exception handling can save developers many hours of effort, and contribute to a robust and maintainable application.

`Action`s tend to have a narrow focus. They use `request` information to access the business layer to formulate a response to the client. When things go right, the business layer carries out its responsibilities without any issues. Often the business layer returns a Data Transfer Object [PEAA], but other times a silent response is appropriate. However, things do not always run so smoothly. The business layer can discover business errors, such as an invalid business condition. Other times the business layer encounters system errors, such as the inability to access a database. Indeed, the `Action` can encounter errors attempting to communicate with the business layer. The Struts developer needs to spend a considerable effort managing exceptions and determining the appropriate response under the various error scenarios. Many diligent developers have created mechanisms to consolidate exception-handling logic, but Struts has factored this into the framework by implementing an `ExceptionHandler`.

EXCEPTION HANDLING Struts declarative exception handling is a framework mechanism to ease the burden of managing exceptions. The controller plays a key role in exception handling. Whenever exceptions are thrown by an `Action`, the default `ExceptionHandler` creates and stores an `ActionError` in scope before forwarding the request to the appropriate page. You can define the `ActionError` key, and the `ActionForward`, by creating exception tags in the struts-config.xml file. The `ExceptionHandler` attempts to match the exception's class name against the one you defined in the exception tag. Similar to `ActionForwards`, exceptions are either local or global. As is the case with `ActionForwards`, local exceptions supercede global ones. Interestingly, exceptions also match on their class hierarchy. If an exception fails to match on the class name, it attempts to match against any of the exceptions super types by navigating up the class hierarchy. This allows you to handle exceptions by using a classification of exceptions rather than requiring you to match on each individual exception type. This is useful when you want to provide the same behavior for a class of exceptions, such as system exceptions.

Let's illustrate this recipe by devising a use case (see figure 5.1). Our use case calls for a small application to persist information about cities. The user is presented with a menu page containing a single link to a page to enter city information. The city page accesses the business layer to save data, but it can receive exceptions. Our exception strategy classifies all exceptions as either system or business. `SystemException` represents technical errors such as the inability to

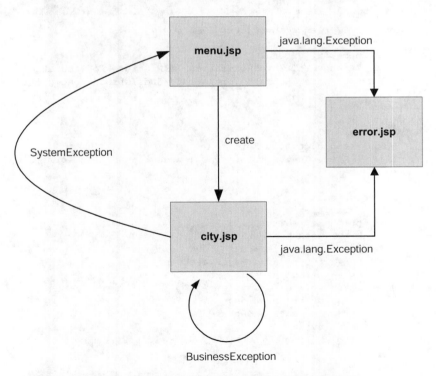

Figure 5.1 Illustrative use case demonstrating an exception strategy

communicate with the business or resource layers. BusinessException represents business rule violations. Our use case stipulates that all SystemExceptions return the user to the menu page. On the other hand, BusinessExceptions send the user back to the input page to attempt the request again. All of our exceptions must descend from one of these two abstract exception types. Therefore, any other exception must be the result of a programming bug. In that circumstance we send the user to a generic error page.

◆ *Recipe*

In this recipe we create one business exception: InvalidCityName, which extends BusinessException. We also create two system exceptions: ConnectionException and SecurityException, both of which extend SystemException. All exceptions are potentially thrown by CityAction. Let's have a look at the struts-config.xml file in listing 5.8.

Listing 5.8   struts-config.xml

```xml
<?xml version="1.0" encoding="ISO-8859-1" ?>

<!DOCTYPE struts-config PUBLIC
        "-//Apache Software Foundation//DTD Struts Configuration 1.1//EN"
        "http://jakarta.apache.org/struts/dtds/struts-config_1_1.dtd">

<struts-config>

    <form-beans>
        <form-bean name="cityForm"
                type="com.strutsrecipes.exceptionhandling.forms.CityForm"/>
    </form-beans>

  <global-exceptions>
        <!-- default exception -->
        <exception key="error.default"           ❹
                path="/error.jsp"
                scope="request"
                type="java.lang.Exception"/>
            <!-- default system exception -->
        <exception key="error.system"           ❸
                path="/menu.do"
                scope="request"
                type=
"com.strutsrecipes.exceptionhandling.exceptions.SystemException"/>


        <!-- default business exception -->
        <exception key="error.business"          ❷
```

```
                    path="/menu.do"
                    scope="request"
                    type=
     "com.strutsrecipes.exceptionhandling.exceptions.BusinessException"/>

    </global-exceptions>

    <global-forwards type="org.apache.struts.action.ActionForward">
        <forward   name="city"        path="/city.do"/>
        <forward   name="menu"        path="/menu.do"/>
    </global-forwards>

<action-mappings>
    <action
            path="/citysubmit"
            type="com.strutsrecipes.exceptionhandling.actions.CityAction"
            name="cityForm"
            scope="request"
            input="/WEB-INF/pages/city.jsp">
            <exception key="error.business.city"           ❶
                    path="/city.do"
                    scope="request"

    type="com.strutsrecipes.exceptionhandling.exceptions.InvalidCityName"/>
    </action>

    <action    path="/city"
               type="org.apache.struts.actions.ForwardAction"
               parameter="/WEB-INF/pages/city.jsp"/>

    <action    path="/menu"
               type="org.apache.struts.actions.ForwardAction"
               parameter="/WEB-INF/pages/menu.jsp"/>

</action-mappings>

<message-resources
    parameter="com.strutsrecipes.exceptionhandling.application"/>
</struts-config>
```

To handle our sole business exception we nest an exception tag ❶ under the Action tag. We also create a global exception ❷ to handle any unexpected business exceptions which might be introduced in the future. All system exceptions are handled by a global exception ❸ that matches on the system exception super type. To ensure we have a very robust application, we create a global exception ❹ to catch any exceptions that happens to slip through.

Listing 5.9 application.properties

```
errors.header=<h3><font color="red">Error</font></h3>
error.default=An unknown error has occurred
error.system=A system error has occurred
error.business=A business error has occurred
error.business.city=A city business error has occurred
```

In listing 5.9 we create key/value pairs to match the key attributes or the exception tags.

◆ *Discussion*

Our use case is intended to handle both business and system exceptions. The business exception is caught as a local exception, but we create a global exception in case one slips through the cracks. All system exceptions are caught as a global exception.

Let's review the code. The beauty behind Struts exception handling is that all of your work is restricted to the struts-config.xml file and a properties file. We nest a local exception tag under the city Action tag ❶. This exception tag is matched whenever CityAction throws InvalidCityName. Because the Exception-Handler matches super types, as well as the type itself, any subclass of Invalid-CityName also matches. In this small application our single business exception is caught by the local exception tag. However, if any business exceptions happen to sneak through, we catch them as global exceptions matching the business exception super type ❷. Notice that the exception tag path attribute directs the user to the City page. The key attribute is used to identify the key to use in the creation of an ActionError. Declaring local exceptions against specific exception types allows us to create meaningful error messages tailored to specific business errors.

Our use case states that all system exceptions must return to the menu page. Generally, its not appropriate to communicate detailed system messages to the client. That task is generally relegated to the logger. It is sufficient to inform the user a system error has occurred. We catch system errors as a global exception ❸, which allows us to deal with system errors as a class of errors. Additional system exceptions can be added, and handled appropriately, without a code change. The path and key attributes are used to send the appropriate page with the desired error message.

At ❹ we define a global exception to catch any exception that happens to slip through. Because the Action execute method can return any exception extending Exception, you need to be careful to return only intended exceptions. Failure to do so generates a "Server Error 500" page. A good practice is to create a global exception tag to catch `java.lang.Exception`.

In listing 5.9, we added our error message to the application.properties file. Although we chose to use application.properties, you are free to use other bundles by defining a bundle attribute stating a servlet context attribute to a message resources bundle – your choice. Error messages are rendered on the page in the usual way using `<html:errors/>`.

You will find that exception handling has the potential to save you many development hours. In addition, devoting effort to planning out an exception strategy yields more savings as you minimize your maintenance effort.

BEST PRACTICE   *Always create a global exception tag to catch java.lang.Exception*—Under Struts 1.1, an `Action`'s execute method allows an unintentional return of an exception descending from `java.lang.Exception`. Unless these exceptions are caught by the `ExceptionHandler`, the user receives a "Server Error 500" page. A graceful way to handle this unexpected condition is to create a global exception tag to handle `java.lang.Exception`.

◆ **Reference**

- ■ [PEAA] Patterns of Enterprise Application Architecture

5.5 *Aggregate exceptions*

◆ **Problem**

You want to use declarative exception handling with an aggregation of exceptions.

◆ **Background**

In recipe 5.4 we showed you how you can use declarative exception handling to save yourself many hours of development time. In that recipe we demonstrated the use of the default `ExceptionHandler` to dispatch the user to a page displaying an appropriate error message. Using the exception returned from the `Action`'s execute method, the default exception handler uses the information found in a matching exception tag in the struts-config.xml file to create an `ActionError` and sends the user to a page.

In a nutshell, the default exception handler uses a single exception to generate a single `ActionError` on a page. However, the user experience is much less frustrating when all validation errors are discovered and reported by the business layer in one call. The user can fix all validation errors before resubmitting the page. A common approach to bulking the returning group of exceptions is to create an exception that is able to aggregate a collection of other exceptions. The business layer discovers all business rule violations, aggregates them into an aggregate exception before throwing the aggregate exception back to the Action.

In this recipe we show you how to create your own exception handler to generate error validation messages for each exception in the aggregation, before forwarding the user to the appropriate page. To illustrate this recipe we modify the use case scenario demonstrated in recipe 5.4. If you have not already done so, we recommend that you read that recipe before tackling this material.

◆ *Recipe*

Let's start by creating the AggregateException class to hold a collection of exceptions (listing 5.10).

Listing 5.10 AggregateException class

```
package com.strutsrecipes.aggregateexceptionhandler.exceptions;

import java.util.ArrayList;
import java.util.List;

public class AggregateException extends Exception {

    private ArrayList exceptions = new ArrayList();

    public void add(Exception e) {
        exceptions.add(e);
    }

    public List getExceptions() {
        return exceptions;
    }
}
```

Next, we create a custom exception handler to process the AggregateException (listing 5.11).

Listing 5.11 AggregateExceptionHandler class

```
package com.strutsrecipes.aggregateexceptionhandler.controller;

import java.util.Iterator;
import java.util.List;
```

```java
import javax.servlet.ServletException;
import javax.servlet.http.HttpServletRequest;
import javax.servlet.http.HttpServletResponse;

import org.apache.struts.Globals;
import org.apache.struts.action.ActionError;
import org.apache.struts.action.ActionErrors;
import org.apache.struts.action.ActionForm;
import org.apache.struts.action.ActionForward;
import org.apache.struts.action.ActionMapping;
import org.apache.struts.action.ExceptionHandler;
import org.apache.struts.config.ExceptionConfig;
import org.apache.struts.util.ModuleException;

import
   com.strutsrecipes.aggregateexceptionhandler.exceptions.AggregateException;

public class AggregateExceptionHandler extends ExceptionHandler {

    public ActionForward execute(
        Exception ex,
        ExceptionConfig ae,
        ActionMapping mapping,
        ActionForm formInstance,
        HttpServletRequest request,
        HttpServletResponse response)
        throws ServletException {

        ActionErrors storedErrors = null;

        //process aggregate        ❺
        ActionForward forward = super.execute(ex, ae, mapping,
                    formInstance, request, response);


        if (ex instanceof AggregateException) {
            AggregateException age = (AggregateException) ex;

            if ("request".equals(ae.getScope())){        ❻
                storedErrors = (ActionErrors)
                            request.getAttribute(Globals.ERROR_KEY);
            } else {
                storedErrors = (ActionErrors)
                        request.getSession().getAttribute(Globals.ERROR_KEY);
            }

            List exceptionList = age.getExceptions();
            Iterator errors = exceptionList.iterator();

            while (errors.hasNext()) {
```

```
            Exception e = (Exception) errors.next();
            ExceptionConfig config =
                        mapping.findException(e.getClass());       ❼

            ActionError error = null;
            String property = null;

            if (e instanceof ModuleException) {
                error = ((ModuleException) e).getError();
                property = ((ModuleException) e).getProperty();
            } else {
                error = new ActionError (config.getKey(),
                                            e.getMessage());
                property = error.getKey();
            }

            storedErrors.add(property, error);       ❽
        }
    }

    return forward;       ❾
}
}
```

Now, we create exception tags in the struts-config.xml file (listing 5.12).

Listing 5.12   struts-config.xml

```xml
<?xml version="1.0" encoding="ISO-8859-1" ?>

<!DOCTYPE struts-config PUBLIC
          "-//Apache Software Foundation//DTD Struts Configuration 1.1//EN"
          "http://jakarta.apache.org/struts/dtds/struts-config_1_1.dtd">

<struts-config>

    <form-beans>
        <form-bean name="cityForm"
 type="com.strutsrecipes.aggregateexceptionhandler.forms.CityForm"/>
    </form-beans>

  <global-exceptions>
        <!-- default exception -->
        <exception key="error.default"
                   path="/error.jsp"
                   scope="request"
                   type="java.lang.Exception"/>

        <!-- default business exception -->
```

```
    <exception key="error.business"
              path="/menu.do"
              scope="request"

type="com.strutsrecipes.aggregateexceptionhandler.exceptions.BusinessExc
eption"/>

    <!-- business exception: invalid city name -->
    <exception key="error.business.name"        ❶
              path="/menu.do"
              scope="request"

type="com.strutsrecipes.aggregateexceptionhandler.exceptions.InvalidCity
Name"/>


    <!-- business exception: Invalid City Population-->
    <exception key="error.business.population"        ❷
              path="/menu.do"
              scope="request"

type="com.strutsrecipes.aggregateexceptionhandler.exceptions.InvalidCity
Population"/>

    <!-- business exception: Invalid State-->
    <exception key="error.business.state"        ❸
              path="/menu.do"
              scope="request"

type="com.strutsrecipes.aggregateexceptionhandler.exceptions.InvalidStat
e"/>

</global-exceptions>

<global-forwards type="org.apache.struts.action.ActionForward">
   <forward    name="city"         path="/city.do"/>
   <forward    name="citySubmit"   path="/citysubmit.do"/>
   <forward    name="menu"         path="/menu.do"/>
</global-forwards>

<action-mappings>
  <action
         path="/citysubmit"

 type="com.strutsrecipes.aggregateexceptionhandler.actions.CityAction"
         name="cityForm"
         scope="request"
         input="/WEB-INF/pages/city.jsp">
         <exception key=""
                   path="/city.do"
                   scope="request"
```

```
                        handler=
 "com.strutsrecipes.aggregateexceptionhandler.controller.AggregateExceptionH
   andler"    ❹

    type="com.strutsrecipes.aggregateexceptionhandler.exceptions.AggregateEx
    ception"/>
      </action>

    <action     path="/city"
                type="org.apache.struts.actions.ForwardAction"
                parameter="/WEB-INF/pages/city.jsp"/>

    <action     path="/menu"
                type="org.apache.struts.actions.ForwardAction"
                parameter="/WEB-INF/pages/menu.jsp"/>

  </action-mappings>
  <message-resources

    parameter="com.strutsrecipes.aggregateexceptionhandler.application"/>
  </struts-config>
```

Notice that we have added three new global exception tags, ❶, ❷, ❸. To catch the `AggregateException` we create a local exception. Notice the tag handler attribute ❹ is used to declare the exception handler used in lieu of the default exception handler. If you have read recipe 5.4, "Using declarative exception handling," this will seem familiar to you.

Listing 5.13   application.properties file

```
errors.header=<h3><font color="red">Error</font></h3>
errors.suffix=<br>
error.default=An unknown error has occurred
error.business=A business error has occurred
error.business.aggregate=A aggregate business error has occurred
error.business.name=A city business error has occurred
error.business.population=A population business error has occurred
error.business.state=A state business error has occurred
```

The final step is to define the error messages to be rendered on the pages by adding key/value pairs to the application.properties file (listing 5.13). Notice that the property keys match the exception tag's key attribute.

It is interesting that the code changes required to implement aggregation exceptions are not much greater than those for the default exception handler.

◆ *Discussion*

The business layer is responsible for discovering, and aggregating, business exceptions into the AggregateException. The Action simply invokes the business layer without catching business layer exceptions. Since the Action throws Exception, AggregateException is thrown to the controller. In this case, the controller matches the local exception tag that specifies the AggregateException-Handler as the exception handler. The AggregateExceptionHandler behaves very much like the default exception handler except that it uses each aggregated exception to build an ActionError. The path on the AggregateException is used to forward the user to the appropriate page.

Using your knowledge of basic exception handling [DEH], let's take another pass over the sequence of events, this time taking a detailed look at the code. First, we need a class to hold the aggregate of exceptions (listing 5.10). The AggregateException is an ordinary exception class providing an add method to add exceptions to a private collection. The getException method is provided to retrieve the entire private collection.

In this use case, the AggregateException is caught by the nested exception tag under the Action tag ❹. The exception tag specifies a handler attribute to override the default exception handler with the AggregateExceptionHandler. Extending AggregateExceptionHandler from ExceptionHandler allows us to leverage existing exception handling logic. We override the execute method to intercept exception handling (listing 5.11).

Here's the heart of the recipe. We use the default handler's execute method to process the AggregateException in the usual way. This determines the Action-Forward and stores an instance of ActionErrors in context. We obtain a reference to the ActionErrors just created and store it in the storedErrors variable. Using the mapping findException method, we look up everything we need to create additional ActionErrors for each of the aggregated exceptions. The stored-Errors contains ActionErrors for all of the aggregated exceptions.

Let's see how this is done.

At ❺ we call the super's execute method to obtain the ActionForward and set up ActionErrors in context.

At ❻ we obtain a reference to the ActionErrors created at ❺. If the exception is an AggregateException we obtain the list of exceptions by calling the Aggregate-Exception getExceptions method.

Iterating over the collection of exceptions, we use the ActionMapping to find the appropriate exception tag ❼. In this case, we find them as global exceptions.

We then add them to the collection of ActionErrors ❽ created by ❺ and retrieved at ❻.

Before exiting we return the ActionForward for the AggregateException ❾.

The last step is to add the error messages to the application.properties file (listing 5.13). You are free to use another bundle by defining a bundle attribute on the exception tag.

Listing 5.12 shows the declarative exception-handling recipe struts-config. xml file adjusted for this recipe. You can see how relatively easy it is to implement an AggregateException. We simply create a global exception for each aggregated exception ❶, ❷, ❸; and change the local exception to trap the AggregateException using the AggregateExceptionHandler ❹. If you are not planning on reusing exception tags, you are free to make the global aggregated exceptions local.

Aggregate exceptions are a popular way to validate your web page. Discovering as many errors in a single submit is usually less frustrating for users. This recipe shows you how to manage aggregate exceptions in an easy fashion by extending the default exception handler.

◆ Related

- 5.4—Use declarative exception handling

5.6 Tailor a form for a DispatchAction

◆ Problem

You want forms employed by your DispatchActions to call validate methods associated with their Action counterparts.

◆ Background

The principal role of an ActionForm is to shuttle request parameters from the HTTP request to the Action associated with the request. In addition to being a Data Transfer Object [PEAA], ActionForms can optionally assume responsibility for data validation. Only two steps are required to take advantage of Action-Form validation.

Listing 5.14 ActionMapping triggering form validation

```
<action path="/auto"
        type="com.strutsrecipes.dispatchform.actions.AutoAction"
        name="AutoForm"
```

```
scope="request"
input="/Auto.jsp"
validate="true"
parameter="method"/>
```

First, you need to set the action mapping `validate` attribute to `true` (listing 5.14).

Listing 5.15 `ActionForm` **validate method signature**

```
public ActionErrors validate(ActionMapping mapping,HttpServletRequest
request)
```

Second, the validate method must be implemented (listing 5.15).

Whenever the action mapping `validate` attribute is set to `true`, the Struts controller uses reflection to call the `ActionForm`'s validate method. If the `validate` method has not been implemented, the controller continues along its merry way, oblivious to the fact that validation was not performed. Should the `validate` method return `ActionErrors`, the controller uses the `input` attribute to direct the response. The response uses the `<html:errors>` tags to present the error messages to the client.

Some people code all of their data validation in the `ActionForm` validate method. Other people use the `validate` method to invoke business layer validations. Yet others constrain `ActionForm` validation to "sanity" checks, completing validation once the `Action` invokes the business layer. Whichever strategy you settle on, `ActionForm` validation can be an effective means to ensure input data is correct.

Listing 5.16 **Client request to** `DispatchAction`

```
http://127.0.0.1:8080/myapp/auto.do?method=read
```

Listing 5.17 `DispatchAction` **dispatch methods**

```
public ActionForward create(ActionMapping mapping,
                            ActionForm form,
                            HttpServletRequest request,
                            HttpServletResponse response)
        throws IOException, ServletException

public ActionForward read(ActionMapping mapping,
                          ActionForm form,
                          HttpServletRequest request,
                          HttpServletResponse response)
```

```
        throws IOException, ServletException

   public ActionForward update(ActionMapping mapping,
                               ActionForm form,
                               HttpServletRequest request,
                               HttpServletResponse response)
        throws IOException, ServletException

   public ActionForward delete(ActionMapping mapping,
                               ActionForm form,
                               HttpServletRequest request,
                               HttpServletResponse response)
        throws IOException, ServletException
```

Another seemingly unrelated and useful Struts feature is the DispatchAction. The DispatchAction is a specialized abstract Action class designed to dynamically invoke methods based on a client request parameter. As a best practice, methods should share a logical relationship supporting the decision to encapsulate them in a single Action class. The classic example extends DispatchAction to provide CRUD (create, read, update, delete) on some business entity. The client passes a request parameter known to the DispatchAction, as shown in the URL (listing 5.16). The DispatchAction consults the action mapping parameter attribute to obtain the name of the request parameter containing the method to be invoked. The DispatchAction uses reflection to invoke a method whose name matches the parameter value (listing 5.17). In the example illustrated through listings 5.14, 5.16 and 5.17, the action mapping stipulates the method HTTP request parameter as the name of the dispatch method. The client request provides a method request parameter populated with read. Consequently, the DispatchAction invokes the read method on the concrete implementation of the DispatchAction.

The DispatchAction and form validation are two common Struts features often used together. In this scenario, the DispatchAction's associated form bean employs the same validate method for all dispatch methods. Using the CRUD example, create, read, update, and delete all call the same ActionForm validate method to perform validation. In practice, each method has unique validation requirements. One solution is to embed "if" statements in the validate method to meet the needs of the DispatchAction methods. Under this solution the validate method obtains the method name in the same manner as the DispatchAction, and then using "if" statements it targets validation logic specific to the dispatch method.

To reduce this complexity we need an `ActionForm` capable of dispatching form validation in much the same way as the `DispatchAction`. The separation of validation logic provides a degree of "low coupling" within the `ActionForm` [UML].

In this recipe we show you how to create an abstract `DispatchActionForm` capable of dispatching form validation using the same client-provided parameter used by the `DispatchAction`. With `DispatchActionForm` added to your arsenal, you can "dispatch-enable" your current `ActionForms` by extending `DispatchActionForm` instead of `ActionForm` and implement the required validate methods.

◆ *Recipe*

Let's start by creating the `DispatchActionForm`. The objective of the `Dispatch-ActionForm` is straightforward—override the `validate` method to dispatch validation based on the method name used by the `DispatchAction` (listing 5.18).

Listing 5.18 Abstract `DispatchActionForm`

```
package com.strutsrecipes.dispatchform.forms;

import java.lang.reflect.InvocationTargetException;
import java.lang.reflect.Method;
import java.util.HashMap;
import javax.servlet.http.HttpServletRequest;

import org.apache.struts.action.ActionErrors;
import org.apache.struts.action.ActionForm;
import org.apache.struts.action.ActionMapping;

abstract public class DispatchActionForm extends ActionForm {
    private static final String VALIDATE_METHOD_NAME_PREFIX =
            "validate";        ❶
    protected Class clazz = this.getClass();        ❷
    protected HashMap methods = new HashMap();        ❸
    protected Class types[] = { ActionMapping.class,
                                HttpServletRequest.class };        ❹

    public ActionErrors validate(        ❺
        ActionMapping mapping,
        HttpServletRequest request) {

    ActionErrors actionErrors = new ActionErrors();        ❻

    String parameter = mapping.getParameter();        ❼
    if (parameter == null) {
        return null;
    }

    String name = request.getParameter(parameter);        ❽
```

```
        if (parameter == null) {
            return null;
        }

    Method method = null;
    try {
        StringBuffer sb = new StringBuffer(name);
        String s = sb.substring(0, 1);
        sb.replace(0, 1, s.toUpperCase());
        name = sb.insert(0,VALIDATE_METHOD_NAME_PREFIX).toString();

        method = (Method) methods.get(name);
        if (method == null) {
            method = clazz.getMethod(name, types);
            methods.put(name, method);
        }
    } catch (NoSuchMethodException e) {
        return null;           ❿
    }

    return dispatch(method, mapping, request);        ⓫
}

private ActionErrors dispatch(
    Method method,
    ActionMapping mapping,
    HttpServletRequest request) {
    ActionErrors errors = null;
    try {
        Object args[] = { mapping, request };
        errors = (ActionErrors) method.invoke(this, args);
    } catch (ClassCastException e) {
        return null;
    } catch (IllegalAccessException e) {
        return null;
    } catch (InvocationTargetException e) {
        return null;
    }

    return errors;
    }
}
```

❾

⓬

Create an abstract class extending from `ActionForm`.

❶ Define the method prefix required by all of our `validate` methods.

❷ Obtain this class's `Class` object. This will be used later on to obtain the `Method` object representing the validation method.

❸ Create a cache to store the validate Method objects created further down. Because Struts allows ActionForm beans to be cached, there is an advantage to caching the Method objects, thereby avoiding repeated reflection work. Although significant gains have been made in reflection performance [REFPERF], it is prudent to cache our reflection work.

❹ Create an array of the Class objects we need as arguments to the validate methods.

❺ Override the validate method called by the Struts controller. It is in the validate method where we dispatch form validation.

❻ Create ActionErrors in preparation for the dispatch validation.

❼ Use the action mapping to obtain the name of the request parameter used for dispatching.

❽ Get the request parameter for the parameter name obtained at ❼.

❾ Here we do a little fancy foot work to determine the validation method name. We prefix the method name with validate before uppercasing the first letter of the parameter value. For example, a parameter value of read yields validateRead. Once we have determined the method name, we check to see if it is cached before creating a Method object.

❿ Swallow the NoSuchMethodException because we are not required to implement all validation methods.

⓫ Invoke a private method to dispatch the validation.

⓬ Use reflection to invoke the appropriate validation method.

Listing 5.19   Concrete form using DispatchActionForm

```
package com.strutsrecipes.dispatchform.forms;

import javax.servlet.http.HttpServletRequest;

import org.apache.struts.action.ActionError;
import org.apache.struts.action.ActionErrors;
import org.apache.struts.action.ActionForm;
import org.apache.struts.action.ActionMapping;

public class CarForm extends DispatchActionForm {     ❶

    private String id;
    private String make;
    private String model;
    private String year;
    private String rating;

    public String getId() {
```

```java
            return id;
        }

        public String getMake() {
            return make;
        }

        public String getModel() {
            return model;
        }

        public String getRating() {
            return rating;
        }

        public String getYear() {
            return year;
        }

        public void setId(String id) {
            this.id = id;
        }

        public void setMake(String make) {
            this.make = make;
        }

        public void setModel(String model) {
            this.model = model;
        }

        public void setRating(String rating) {
            this.rating = rating;
        }

        public void setYear(String year) {
            this.year = year;
        }

        public ActionErrors validateCreate(        ❷
            ActionMapping mapping,
            HttpServletRequest request) {
            ActionErrors errors = new ActionErrors();
            if (getId().compareTo("5") > 0) {
                errors.add(
                    ActionErrors.GLOBAL_ERROR,
                    new ActionError ("error.validate.create"));
            }
            return errors;
        }
```

```
public ActionErrors validateUpdate(        ❸
    ActionMapping mapping,
    HttpServletRequest request) {
    return validateCreate(mapping, request);
}

public ActionErrors validateDelete(        ❹
    ActionMapping mapping,
    HttpServletRequest request) {
    ActionErrors errors = new ActionErrors();
    if (getId().compareTo("2") < 0) {
        errors.add(
            ActionErrors.GLOBAL_ERROR,
            new ActionError ("error.validate.delete"));
    }
    return errors;
}
}
```

Now that we have created our abstract `DispatchActionForm`, let's put it into play!
Let's step through listing 5.19 to see how this is done.

❶ Extend from `DispatchActionForm` instead of `ActionForm`.

❷ Implement the `create` validation method.

❸ Implement the `update` validation method.

❹ Implement the `delete` validation method.

In each case, the validation methods take responsibility for their own validation.

◆ *Discussion*

The `DispatchAction` is one of the most useful `Action`s in the Struts framework.
Consolidating business functionality pertinent to a logical business entity helps
reduce your development and maintenance effort. Unfortunately, Struts doesn't
extend this same feature to `ActionForm` validation. Coalescing the `Dispatch-Action` with form validation mandates nasty "if" statements in the `ActionForm`
validate method. The abstract `DispatchActionForm` overcomes this oversight by
bringing the same usefulness of the `DispatchAction` to `ActionForms`. Because the
design of the `DispatchForm` mimics the `DispatchAction`, you can use the same
action mapping parameter attribute to serve both masters, resulting in consis-
tency in the naming of methods.

> **BEST PRACTICE** *Apply high cohesion to* `DispatchAction`—Dispatch methods should support the management of a single entity. The relationships between the methods and the entity support the decision to encapsulate them in a single `DispatchAction` class. The High Cohesion GRASP principle is one of the design principles you should consult when designing classes. [UML].

◆ Reference

- ■ [DISPACT] Struts DispatchAction java doc
- ■ [PEAA] Patterns of Enterprise Application Architecture
- ■ [REFPERF] Java programming dynamics, Part 2: Introducing reflection, IBM DeveloperWorks
- ■ [UML] Applying UML and Patterns: An Introduction to Object-Oriented Analysis and Design and the Unified Process, GRASP: Design Objects with Responsibilities, High Cohesion, Low Coupling

5.7 Use Validator constants

◆ Problem

You want to use Validator constants.

◆ Background

Writing maintainable applications is one of the best ways to increase productivity, minimize defects, and lower the delivery costs of future enhancements. Using constants has been a trademark of maintainable applications for quite some time. The concept of constants has been implemented in the Validator to make sure validation rules are as maintainable as the rest of the application. In this recipe we explore Validator constants by showing you how to define and employ them.

◆ Recipe

The Validator supports global constants and formset constants. As you might expect, global constants are available to the contents of all formsets, whereas formset constants are visible only to a specific formset. Formset constants override global constants whenever they share the same name.

Constants are used to replace four types of values within the validation.xml file.

- ■ `<field>` tag property attribute
- ■ `<var-value>` tags body value

- `<msg>` tag key attribute
- `<arg>` tags key attribute

In listing 5.20 we show you an example of Validator constants.

Listing 5.20   validation.xml file using Validator constants

```
<form-validation>

    <global>
        <constant>
          <constant-name>constantProperty</constant-name>           ❶
          <constant-value>registrationNumber</constant-value>
        </constant>

        <constant>
          <constant-name>constantVarValue</constant-name>           ❷
          <constant-value>^0</constant-value>
        </constant>

        <constant>                                                   ❸
          <constant-name>constantMessageKey</constant-name>
          <constant-value>error.invalid.registrationNumber</constant-value>
        </constant>

        <constant>
            <constant-name>constantArgumentKey</constant-name>       ❹
           <constant-value>sampleForm.registration</constant-value>
        </constant>
    </global>


    <formset>
        <form name="sampleForm">
          <field property="${constantProperty}" depends="required,mask">  ❺
              <msg name="mask" key="${constantMessageKey}"/>          ❻
              <arg0 name="required" key="${constantArgumentKey}"/>    ❼
              <arg0 name="mask" key="${constantArgumentKey}"/>        ❽
              <var>
                 <var-name>mask</var-name>
                 <var-value>${constantVarValue}</var-value>          ❾
              </var>
            </field>
        </form>
    </formset>
</form-validation>
```

Constants are created using the <constant> tag. The <constant> tag wraps <constant-name> tag to give the constant a name, and <constant-value> tag to specify its value. The value of the constant is extracted by referring to the constant name as ${myconstant} where myconstant is the value in the body of <constant-name> tag. Global constants are nested inside a <global> tag under the <form-validation> tag, whereas formset constants are nested inside the <formset> tag.

Let's step through an example to see how this is actually done. In listing 5.20 we create a constant for all four replacement types.

At ❺ we use a constant to parameterize the <field> tag property attribute. The constant's name is book-ended by ${ and }. The value in between is taken from the constant value defined at ❶. Similarly, the <msg> tag key attribute at ❻ uses the constant declared at ❸.

At ❼ and ❽ we use the constantArgumentKey constant declared at ❹ to populate the <arg> tag key attribute.

At ❾ the <var-value> tag's body is replaced with the constantVarValue defined at ❷.

Listing 5.21 is an example of concatenating constants in the replacement value.

Listing 5.21 Concatenate replacement values

```
<form-validation>

   <global>
       <constant>
           <constant-name>constantPhoneAreaCode</constant-name>
           <constant-value> ([0-9]{3})</constant-value>              ❶
       </constant>

       <constant>                                                    ❷
           <constant-name>constantPhoneNpaNxx</constant-name>
           <constant-value>[0-9]{3}-[0-9]{4}</constant-value>
       </constant>
   </global>
<formset>

 <form name="sampleForm">

    <field property="phoneNumber" depends="required,mask">
       <arg0 name="required" key="sampleForm.phone"/>
       <arg0 name="mask" key="sampleForm.phone"/>
       <var>
         <var-name>mask</var-name>
```

```
            <var-value>^${constantPhoneAreaCode}${constantPhoneNpaNxx}$
            </var-value>    ❸
          </var>
       </field>

    </form>
  </formset>


</form-validation>
```

■

In the previous example we replaced a value with just one constant, but that does not need to be the case. In listing 5.21 we show you an example where two constants, ❶ and ❷, are concatenated ❸. This technique allows us to share validation building blocks. For example, this technique allows us to reuse the validation mask on phone number validations not requiring areas codes by defining the mask as <var-value>^${constantPhoneNpaNxx}$</var-value>.

In listing 5.22 we concatenate validation constants.

Listing 5.22   Concatenate validation constants

```
<form-validation>

   <global>
        <constant>
           <constant-name>constantPhoneAreaCode</constant-name>
           <constant-value> ([0-9]{3})</constant-value>           ❶
        </constant>

        <constant>
           <constant-name>constantPhoneNpaNxx</constant-name>
           <constant-value>[0-9]{3}-[0-9]{4}</constant-value>      ❷
        </constant>

        <constant>
           <constant-name>constantPhoneNumber</constant-name>
           <constant-value>
^${constantPhoneAreaCode}${constantPhoneNpaNxx}$</constant-value>  ❸
        </constant>
    </global>


    <formset>

      <form name="sampleForm">

        <field property="phoneNumber" depends="required,mask">
           <arg0 name="required" key="sampleForm.phone"/>
```

```
                    <arg0 name="mask" key="sampleForm.phone"/>
                    <var>
                        <var-name>mask</var-name>
                        <var-value>${constantPhoneNumber}</var-value>
                    </var>
                </field>

        </form>
    </formset>

</form-validation>
```

Constants can be built from other constants. In listing 5.22 we build constant-PhoneNumber ❸ from constantPhoneAreaCode ❶ and constantPhoneNpaNxx ❷. This technique allows you to refactor constantNpaNxx into constantNpa and constant-Npx with minimal impact.

Validation rules tend to be shared across applications. There is no need to duplicate validation rules or constants among several applications. You can share constants between applications by breaking out constants (listing 5.23) into a separate file from the formsets (listing 5.24). The two are merged together by listing multiple validation files with the Validator plug-in (listing 5.25).

Listing 5.23   validation-constants.xml file

```
<form-validation>
    <global>
        <constant>
            <constant-name>constantPhoneAreaCode</constant-name>
            <constant-value> ([0-9]{3})</constant-value>
        </constant>

        <constant>
            <constant-name>constantPhoneNpaNxx</constant-name>
            <constant-value>[0-9]{3}-[0-9]{4}</constant-value>
        </constant>

        <constant>
            <constant-name>constantPhoneNumber</constant-name>
            <constant-value>
^${constantPhoneAreaCode}${constantPhoneNpaNxx}$</constant-value>
        </constant>
    </global>

</form-validation>
```

Listing 5.24   validation-without-constants.xml file

```
<form-validation>
   <formset>

      <form name="sampleForm">

         <field property="phoneNumber" depends="required,mask">
            <arg0 name="required" key="sampleForm.phone"/>
            <arg0 name="mask" key="sampleForm.phone"/>
            <var>
               <var-name>mask</var-name>
               <var-value>^${constantPhoneAreaCode}${constantPhoneNpaNxx}$
                  </var-value>
            </var>
         </field>
      </form>
   </formset>
</form-validation>
```

Listing 5.25   Validator plug-in tag in struts-config.xml file

```
<plug-in className="org.apache.struts.validator.ValidatorPlugIn">
      <set-property property="pathnames"
          value="/WEB-INF/validator-rules.xml,
                 /WEB-INF/validation-constants.xml,
                 /WEB-INF/validation-without-constants.xml"/>

</plug-in>
```

◆ *Discussion*

In this recipe we looked at Validator constants. You need to spend a little more time setting things up, but you can yield the dividends only found in maintainable applications. Constants can be used to replace a single parameter, or they can be concatenated at replacement time. Some circumstances warrant creating smaller constants as foundation pieces for larger ones. This technique comes in handy when you want to mix and match the smaller constants. Moreover, splitting out constants into their own file allows you to reuse constants across multiple applications. If you want to share constants, but keep your constants file nice and trim, you can take it to the next level by keeping a library of constants in a master file and using an XSL style sheet to pull off the ones you need for your application.

BEST PRACTICE *Use Validator constants to increase maintainability*—Factor out common and reusable field property names, message keys, arg keys, and var-values into Validator constants to consolidate maintenance points. Consider encapsulating constants into a single file as a means to share them across applications.

◆ **Related**

■ 5.2—Struts Validator files explained (server-side)

5.8 *Validation in a wizard*

◆ **Problem**

You want to use the Validator in a wizard application.

◆ **Background**

The Validator is a popular way to validate user input in Struts applications. Validation rules are defined in the validation.xml file by creating `<formset>` tags. Each `<formset>` tag wraps one or more `<form>` tags. Each `<form>` tag corresponds to an `ActionForm` and contains `<field>` tags for every field to be validated on the page.

Single form wizards present a special validation problem because one form is used for all pages participating in the wizard. If we applied Validator in the usual way, each page would validate all form fields. Fields would be validated even before the user had the chance to input data! Fortunately, the Validator has built-in support for single form wizards. In this recipe we will show you how to set up validation rules for wizards. Moreover, we present a secure and robust technique for managing the wizard page validation.

◆ **Recipe**

Let's get started by creating validation rules. If you have not already done so, we suggest you read recipe 2.7, "Create a wizard."

> **Listing 5.26   validation.xml using page attributes**

```
<form-validation>
    <formset>
        <form name="sampleForm">
            <field property="firstName" depends="required" page="0">      ❶
                <arg0 name="required" key="sampleForm.firstName"/>
            </field>

            <field property="lastName" depends="required" page="0">       ❷
                <arg0 name="required" key="sampleForm.lastName"/>
            </field>
```

```
<field property="productNumber" depends="required,mask" page="1">  ❸
    <arg0 name="required" key="sampleForm.productNumber"/>
    <arg0 name="mask" key="sampleForm.productNumber"/>
    <var>
        <var-name>mask</var-name>
        <var-value>^3</var-value>
    </var>
</field>

<field property="quantity" depends="required" page="1">      ❹
    <arg0 name="required" key="sampleForm.quantity"/>
</field>

<field property="comment" depends="required" page="2">       ❺
    <arg0 name="required" key="sampleForm.comment"/>
</field>
        </form>
    </formset>
</form-validation>
```

The validation.xml file in listing 5.26 is typical of something you might find when validating a single form. In a wizard application the same form is used across several pages. Therefore, we need a way to tell the Validator to limit validation to the fields on a particular page. The <field> tag's page attribute satisfies this need. Each time the page is submitted, the Validator selects only those <field> tags with a page attribute value less than or equal to the form's page attribute. On each wizard page the previous page validations are reexecuted as a safety check to ensure a page was not skipped.

Let's look at listing 5.26 to see how this is done

- firstName and lastName are on the first page. At ❶ and ❷ we set the page attribute to "0".

- productNumber and quantity are on the second page. At ❸ and ❹ we set the page attribute to "1".

- Comment is on the last page. At ❺ we set the page attribute to "2".

Notice the clearForm action mapping sets the parameter attribute to "−1". This has the effect of turning off validation because there are no <fields> tag page attributes less than or equal to "−1". See recipe 2.7, "Create a wizard," for further details on the clearForm action mapping.

The Validator expects the page number to be on the form. It is the developers' responsibility to make sure the page property is set appropriately on the form. You don't need to create a page property because ValidatorForm and its subclass `ValidatorActionForm` have already done that for you. We have decided to specify the page number on the action mapping. We will subclass `Validator-Form` to look at the action mapping to get and set the page number just before the Validator validates.

Listing 5.27   struts-confi.xml file with `ActionMapping` specifying page number

```xml
<?xml version="1.0" encoding="ISO-8859-1"?>
<!DOCTYPE struts-config PUBLIC "-//Apache Software Foundation//DTD Struts
   Configuration 1.1//EN"
            "http://jakarta.apache.org/struts/dtds/struts-config_1_1.dtd">

<struts-config>

    <form-beans>
        <form-bean name="sampleForm"
                    type="com.strutsrecipes.wizard.forms.SampleForm"/>
    </form-beans>

    <global-forwards>
        <forward name="sample" path="/clearForm.do"/>
    </global-forwards>

    <action-mappings>
            <action
                path="/clearForm"
                type="com.strutsrecipes.wizard.actions.ClearForm"
                name="sampleForm"
                scope="session"
                parameter="-1">

                <forward name="next" path="/pages/page1.jsp"/>
            </action>

            <action
                path="/SampleAction1"
                name="sampleForm"
                scope="session"
                input="/pages/page1.jsp"
                forward="/pages/page2.jsp"        ❶
                parameter="0"/>        ❷

            <action
                path="/SampleAction2"
                name="sampleForm"
                scope="session"
                input="/pages/page2.jsp"
                forward="/pages/page3.jsp"        ❸
                parameter="1"/>        ❹
```

```
                <action
                    path="/SampleAction3"
                    type="com.strutsrecipes.wizard.actions.Submit"
                    name="sampleForm"
                    scope="session"
                    input="/pages/page3.jsp"
                    parameter="2">       ❺

                    <forward name="next" path="/clearForm.do"/>
                </action>
        </action-mappings>

        <message-resources parameter="resources.application"/>


        <plug-in className="org.apache.struts.validator.ValidatorPlugIn">
                <set-property property="pathnames"
                    value="/WEB-INF/validator-rules.xml,/WEB-INF/validation.xml"/>
        </plug-in>

</struts-config>
```

Let's see how this works. The struts-config.xml file presented in listing 5.27 is very similar to the wizard recipe (recipe 5.8). At ❷, ❹ and ❺ we hijacked the `parameter` attribute to specify the page number associated with the form being received. Soon we will see how this parameter is used to control validation. Because we don't need to process the form, we simply forward the user to the next page (see listing 5.27 ❶ and ❸). However, you are free to use whichever `Action` class you like as long as the parameter attribute is available.

Listing 5.28   WizardValidatorForm

```java
package com.strutsrecipes.wizard.forms;

import javax.servlet.http.HttpServletRequest;

import org.apache.commons.lang.math.NumberUtils;
import org.apache.struts.action.ActionErrors;
import org.apache.struts.action.ActionMapping;
import org.apache.struts.validator.ValidatorForm;

public class WizardValidatorForm extends ValidatorForm {

    public ActionErrors validate(
        ActionMapping mapping,
        HttpServletRequest request) {
```

```
        String page = mapping.getParameter();        ❶
        setPage(NumberUtils.stringToInt(page));       ❷
        return super.validate(mapping, request);      ❸
    }
}
```

The `WizardValidatorForm` works by intercepting the validation process just before the Validator is called. The `ValidatorForm` `validate(..)` method calls the Validator. Therefore, all we need to do is set the page number before the Validator does its job.

Let's step through listing 5.28 to see how it works.

❶ The `parameter` attribute is obtained from the action mapping.

❷ Convert from `String` to `int`, and set the `page` attribute using the `setPage(..)` method inherited from `ValidatorForm`. Using `org.apache.commons.lang.math.NumberUtils` [JCL] saved us a few steps.

❸ Use the `ValidatorForm`'s `validate` method to invoke the Validator in the usual way.

The page number is automatically set as long as you extend your `ActionForm` from the `WizardValidatorForm` in listing 5.28. To use the `WizardValidatorForm`, simply extend it in the usual way.

◆ *Discussion*

This recipe shows you how to take advantage of Struts' built-in validation support for wizards. We showed you a straightforward technique to set the page number using the action mapping. Another approach is to set the page number on the JSP as a request parameter—possibly using a hidden field. Because all subclasses of `ValidatorForm` inherit the `page` property, that technique works. Although it can get the job done, it has a couple of drawbacks. First, changing the wizard sequence involves changing the JSP for the page number and the struts-config.xml file for the new sequence. This means you have two points of maintenance instead of one. The second reason is that it exposes a security risk. Because the page number is being sent to the server as a request parameter, a clever user can spoof the request to set the page number to a low number to bypass validation. A more secure and robust solution is to set the page number on the server-side, outside the reach of the digitally misguided.

◆ *Related*

  ▪ 2.7—Create a wizard

  ▪ 5.2—Struts Validator files explained (server-side)

◆ *Reference*

  ▪ [JCL] Jakarta Commons Lang component

5.9 *Create a pluggable validator for cross-form validation*

◆ *Problem*

You want to create a pluggable validator to validate a field in the current form against a field in a different form.

◆ *Background*

The Validator is a valued asset in the war against data entry error. Using the Validator you can validate user input by using a standard set of validators accessible through Struts. Behind the scenes, Struts employs the Jakarta Commons Validator framework to do the heavy lifting. The flexible and rich set of validators are quite capable of addressing most needs. However, there are times when you need to create your own custom validator. In this recipe we show you how to do just that! To make matters a little more interesting, we present a technique to perform cross-form validation suitable in a multiform wizard-style application. A multiform wizard application is designed such that form beans are cached in the session context until the last page in the wizard is reached. Form beans are cached by setting the scope attribute to session on the action mapping. On the last page, the application persists the information and clears the forms in preparation for the next input cycle.

We present this recipe in the context of a real-life use case. Assume we have a multiform wizard style application to enter customer and driver information. The customer page records the given name and surname, address, and other similar information. The user navigates the wizard to a driver page. Along with other information, the user enters his or her driver's license number. In Ontario, Canada, driver license numbers must adhere to a number of rules. One of the rules is that the first character of the driver license number must match the first letter of the driver's surname. In our illustrative application, we create a custom pluggable validator to ensure the first character of the driver license number entered on the driver page matches the first character of the surname entered on the customer page and the length is 15 characters.

◆ *Recipe*

Let's quickly enumerate the steps.

- Declare the custom validator in validator-rules.xml.
- Associate the validator with the form bean's property in validation.xml.
- Add validation error keys to the default resource bundle.
- Extend the form bean to use the Validator framework.
- Create the custom `Validator` class.

We start by showing you how to declare and configure the custom pluggable validator presented in this recipe. With a clear understanding of the configurable runtime parameters under your hat, we show you how to create a custom pluggable validator to perform cross-form validation.

The Validator mandates that we declare all pluggable validators, either standard or custom, in validator-rules.xml (listing 5.29). The validation rule is then associated with one or more fields on the form using the validation.xml file (listing 5.30).

Listing 5.29   validator-rules.xml

```
<validator name="driverLicenseRule"        ❶
 classname="com.strutsrecipes.customvalidator.validators.
   InsuranceValidator"         ❷
                method="validateDriverLicense"        ❸
                methodParams="java.lang.Object,
                        org.apache.commons.validator.ValidatorAction,
                        org.apache.commons.validator.Field,        ❹
                        org.apache.struts.action.ActionErrors,
                        javax.servlet.http.HttpServletRequest"
                msg="errors.driver.licence">        ❺
    </validator>
```

We declare our "yet to be created" `InsuranceValidator` pluggable validator in the validator-rules.xml file.

❶ Here we give our validator a logical name.

❷ State the fully qualified class name of the custom validator.

③ Because the class defined at **❷** can contain several methods capable of providing validation services, we declare here the name of the method responsible for validating driver license numbers.

④ Enumerate the method parameters to the method declared at **❸**.

⑤ Declare the error message key used whenever this validation fails.

Next, we update the validation.xml file to associate the pluggable validator with the desired form field, as shown in listing 5.30.

Listing 5.30   validation.xml

```
<form name="driverForm">          ❶
   <field property="driverLicense"   ❷
          depends="driverLicenseRule">   ❸
      <arg0 key="driverForm.driver"/>   ❹
      <var>
         <var-name>formName</var-name>
         <var-value>customerForm</var-value>   ❺
      </var>
      <var>
         <var-name>lastNameFieldName</var-name>
         <var-value>lastName</var-value>   ❻
      </var>
   </field>
</form>
```

The definition of the form tag in the validation.xml file is very typical. The only difference is the reference to the validator declared in listing 5.29.

❶ Define the form name.

❷ Here we state the field name on the form to be validated.

❸ Reference the validation rule to be executed to validate the field at **❷**. Note that the value in this attribute must match the value at **❶** in listing 5.29.

❹ Specify the key name used to look up the replacement parameter in the message declared at **❺** in listing 5.29.

❺ The pluggable validator requires two parameters to find a field on the form containing the surname used to validate the driver license number. Here we declare the form name containing the surname. The form name is the one specified on the `<form-bean>` name attribute in the struts-config. xml file.

❻ Specify the field name containing the surname. Specifying runtime parameters allows us to reuse this validation rule on other forms without being forced to use predetermined form and field names.

At ❺ in listing 5.29 and ❹ in listing 5.30 we declare keys to the default resource bundle. In listing 5.31 we provide example messages for those keys.

Listing 5.31   Default resource bundle

```
errors.driver.license=invalid {0} number
driverForm.driver=Ontario driver's license
```

The `ActionForm` must extend `ValidatorActionForm` or `ValidatorForm`. Listing 5.32 is a very simple form containing the driver license number.

Listing 5.32   ActionForm

```
package com.strutsrecipes.customvalidator.forms;

import org.apache.struts.validator.ValidatorForm;

public class DriverForm extends ValidatorForm {
   private String driverLicense;

 public String getDriverLicense() {
      return driverLicense;
   }

   public void setDriverLicense(String driverLicense) {
      this.driverLicense = driverLicense;
   }
}
```

Lastly, we create the pluggable validator, as shown in listing 5.33.

Listing 5.33   Custom `Validator` class

```
package com.strutsrecipes.customvalidator.validators;

import java.io.Serializable;

import javax.servlet.http.HttpServletRequest;

import org.apache.commons.validator.Field;
import org.apache.commons.validator.ValidatorAction;
import org.apache.commons.validator.ValidatorUtil;
import org.apache.commons.validator.Var;
import org.apache.struts.action.ActionErrors;
import org.apache.struts.validator.Resources;

public class InsuranceValidator implements Serializable {      ❶
```

```
public static boolean validateDriverLicense(        ❷
                    Object thisForm,
                    ValidatorAction validatorAction,       ❸
                    Field field,
                    ActionErrors errors,
                    HttpServletRequest request) {

    String driverLicense =                              ❹
            ValidatorUtil.getValueAsString(thisForm, field.getProperty());

    if (null == driverLicense) {
        errors.add(field.getKey(),                      ❺
            Resources.getActionError(request, validatorAction, field));
        return false;
    }

      //get "formName" validation parameter
    Var validationParameter = field.getVar("formName");       ❻
    String formName = validationParameter.getValue();

    //get "lastNameFieldName" validation parameter
    validationParameter = field.getVar("lastNameFieldName");      ❼
    String lastNameFieldName = validationParameter.getValue();

    Object crossReferenceForm =
request.getSession().getAttribute(formName);        ❽

      if (null == crossReferenceForm) {
        errors.add(field.getKey(),                       ❾
              Resources.getActionError(request, validatorAction, field));
          return false;
      }

      String lastName =                                  ❿
ValidatorUtil.getValueAsString(crossReferenceForm,lastNameFieldName);

    //apply validation rule
  if ((null == lastName)
  || (15 != driverLicense.length())                     ⓫
  || !(driverLicense.substring(0, 1).equals(lastName.substring(0, 1)))){
      errors.add(field.getKey(),
            Resources.getActionError(request, validatorAction, field));
      return false;
  }

  return true;

  }
}
```

Let's step through listing 5.33 line by line.

❶ Declare the class. Notice we don't need to extend a base class, and the only interface we need to implement is `Serializable`.

❷ Create a method matching the name we declare at **❸** in listing 5.29.

❸ Define the same method arguments declared at **❹** in listing 5.29.

❹ Obtain the driver's license on the `driverForm`.

❺ If the driver license doesn't exist on this form, we place an error in the errors object and return false.

In order to validate the driver license against the surname, we need to obtain the form and field names holding the surname. This information was declared at **❺** and **❻** in listing 5.30. We obtain the `formName` parameter at **❻** and the `lastName-FieldName` at **❼** in listing 5.33.

Now, we are ready to access the `customerForm` in the session context at **❽**. If the form doesn't exist, we fail the validation at **❾**.

❿ Extract the surname from the customer form obtained at **❽** using the parameters obtained at **❻** and **❼**.

⓫ We apply the validation rule. The license number must be 15 characters long and the first character of the surname must match the first character of the license number. If these conditions are not met, an error is added to the errors object. False is returned to fail the validation.

If the validation passed, `true` is returned

Listing 5.34   Validator plug-in

```
<plug-in className="org.apache.struts.validator.ValidatorPlugIn">
  <set-property property="pathnames"
    value="/WEB-INF/validator-rules.xml,/WEB-INF/validation.xml"/>
</plug-in>
```

Lastly, you must add the Validator plug-in to the struts-config,xml file, as shown in listing 5.34.

◆ *Discussion*

The Validator framework's support for pluggable validators allows you to create your own custom validators for whatever situation is at hand. By adding to the standard set of pluggable validators you can build up a library of reusable validation rules available to your entire organization.

All of the standard validators validate information on the current form. In this recipe we show you a technique to access another form cached in the session context. This technique is ideal when you are employing a multiform wizard. You then will use the form bean to cache your input until the last page in the wizard is reached. This technique can be easily adapted to access any other session context attribute you desire.

◆ ***Related***

 ■ 5.2—Struts Validator files explained (server-side)

Internationalization

*I was gliding along smoothly and without obstruction or accident,
until I came to that word "spalleggiato," then the bottom fell out.*

—Mark Twain, *Italian without a Master*

Internationalization is an interesting topic, given the prevalence of applications and information on the Internet that are only available English. Even in the United States it is somewhat perilous to ignore different languages and cultures. Many ethnic neighborhoods in America use English as their second language, and the most popular U.S. radio stations in 2003 were in Spanish! As the world comes closer together through wires and airwaves, and companies have to compete in a highly competitive market, solid internationalization and localization solutions could provide the edge to profitability.

The "national language" of the United States

If one vote had been cast the other way, the "official" language of the United States government would have been German! Well, not really. It is just a myth. What actually happened was a proposal was sent to Congress in 1795 recommending the printing of federal laws in German as well as English, and no bill was ever actually voted upon. A group of German-Americans from Augusta, Virginia, petitioned Congress, and in response to their petition a House committee recommended publishing three thousand sets of laws in German and distributing them to the states (with copies of statutes printed in English as well). The House debated this proposal on January 13, 1795, without reaching a decision, and a vote to *adjourn and consider the recommendation at a later date* was defeated by one vote, 42 to 41. There was no vote on an actual bill, merely a vote on whether or not to adjourn. Because the motion to adjourn did not pass, the matter was dropped. The House debated translating federal statutes into German again on February 16, 1795, but the final result was the approval of a bill to publish existing and future federal statutes in English only.

In this chapter we will present recipes for using Struts' internationalization tools to:

- *Set the locale of your application*—Letting the user choose the locale for the application
- *Internationalize text and images*—Setting the language of your application's text, and setting image references based upon specified internationalization parameters
- *Internationalize* Forwards—Forwarding to different layouts and pages based upon internationalization settings
- *Internationalize tiles*—Using tiles based on locale
- *Internationalize validation*—Varying field validation rules based on locale

This chapter cannot discuss all the issues and solutions for the developer, but we've tried to present solutions that can be extrapolated and extended to any area you might need. Although we do not discuss the JSTL in this book (we do, however, highly recommend Sean Bayern's *JSTL in Action*, Manning, 2003), it is worthy to note the internationalization available through the formatting tag library. These tags take information and correctly format them based on the browser's locale setting, leaving little or no work for the developer. The developer can then format numbers, currency, dates, times, and so forth with ease. You can also localize messages and parameters to your application as well, helping you to target your pages to users around the world.

What makes any tag library so nice to work with is its convenience and open source community support. It's still rather new in the Struts world and we hope that you investigate it. One of the truly great things about Struts is the fact that it doesn't mandate your "view" strategies—you can use Struts' tags, JSTL tags, and other extensions of the framework as your needs arise.

6.1 *Set locale dynamically*

◆ *Problem*

You want to let the user choose the locale.

◆ *Background*

The default Struts `RequestProcessor` is responsible for setting the locale in the user's session under the `org.apache.struts.Globals.LOCALE_KEY` key. If the `<struts-config>` controller tag `locale` attribute has not been set to `false`, or the locale has not been previously set in the session, the `RequestProcessor` places the `Locale` returned by the servlet container in the user's session.

In practice, the locale needs to be set programmatically based on information entered by the user. In this recipe we show you a simple technique to do just that.

◆ *Recipe*

Listing 6.1 is an example of an `Action` setting the `Locale` programmatically.

> **Listing 6.1   Set locale in an `Action`**

```
package com.strutsrecipes.i18nsetlocale.actions;

import java.util.Locale;
```

```
import javax.servlet.http.HttpServletRequest;
import javax.servlet.http.HttpServletResponse;
import javax.servlet.http.HttpSession;

import org.apache.struts.Globals;
import org.apache.struts.action.Action;
import org.apache.struts.action.ActionForm;
import org.apache.struts.action.ActionForward;
import org.apache.struts.action.ActionMapping;

import com.strutsrecipes.i18nsetlocale.forms.SampleForm;

public class SampleAction extends Action {

    public ActionForward execute(
        ActionMapping mapping,
        ActionForm form,
        HttpServletRequest request,
        HttpServletResponse response)
        throws Exception {

        SampleForm sampleForm = (SampleForm) form;
        String countryCode = sampleForm.getCountryCode();        ❶
        String languageCode = sampleForm.getLanguageCode();

        HttpSession session = request.getSession(true);   ❷
        Locale locale = new Locale(languageCode, countryCode);   ❸
      session.setAttribute(org.apache.struts.Globals.LOCALE_KEY, locale);   ❹
        return mapping.findForward("success");
    }
}
```

Let's step through the Action in listing 6.1.

At ❶ we cast the Form and extract the user-inputted language and country codes. Then we obtain a reference to the session ❷, and create a new locale ❸ using the language and country code obtained at ❶. Because Locale is immutable, there is no point in retrieving the locale from the session in an attempt to change its language and country codes. At ❹ we set the locale in session. org.apache.struts.Globals.LOCALE_KEY is used by Struts locale-sensitive features to determine the locale.

That's all there is to it! You have now taken control of the locale used by locale-sensitive tags, Tiles, and the Validator.

◆ Discussion

In this recipe we showed you a simple way to set the locale using language and country code entered by the user. This technique is tried and true and used by many applications. The Action is the most common place to set the locale. Alternatively, you can set the locale in the Form's validate method (see recipe 6.6, Internationalize validation) or reset method. Neither method is an intuitive location to set locale. In particular, coupling locale setting with form validation might lead to inadvertently turning off locale setting whenever Form validation is disabled.

◆ Related

- 6.6—Internationalize validation

6.2 Internationalize your text

◆ Problem

You want to internationalize text on your web page.

◆ Background

The Internet has empowered us with the means to communicate around the globe. A truly globalized application delivers web pages in multiple languages. Maintaining multiple versions of web pages, or dynamically building text to support multiple languages quickly eats up valuable programming resources. Fortunately, Struts has built-in support to make this job a snap. In this recipe we show you how to set up and use resource bundles to internationalize your applications.

◆ Recipe

Four steps are required to internationalize an application:

- Create a properties file.
- Declare the properties file to Struts.
- Access a properties file key.
- Add a new language.

Listing 6.2   applications.properties

```
welcome=Greetings!
title=The Welcome Page
```

Creating a properties file is very easy. Using your favorite text editor, create a file with a key value pair. The key and the value are separated with an equal sign, with the key on the left and the value on the right. You can choose any file name you like but the file suffix must be .properties. Listing 6.2 is an example of a typical properties file. Once the properties file has been created it must be placed anywhere on the class path. This can be in the WEB-INF/classes directory or subdirectory under classes. It can also be in a JAR file in your lib directory.

Listing 6.3 `<message-resources>` **tag in struts-config.xml file**

```
<message-resources parameter="resources.application"/>
```

The second step is to declare the properties file to Struts by creating a `<message-resources>` tag under the `<struts-config>` tag in the struts-config.xml file. The `parameter` attribute is used to indicate the location of the properties file. In listing 6.3 the `parameter` attribute says that application.properties is found in the resources directory. The "." is used to delineate the directories. Although we use "application," you are free to use any name you like.

Listing 6.4   JSP using message-resource properties file

```
<%@ taglib uri="/tags/struts-bean" prefix="bean" %>
<%@ taglib uri="/tags/struts-html" prefix="html" %>

<html:html>
<head>
<title><bean:message key="title"/></title>    ❶
<html:base/>
</head>
<body>
    <bean:message key="welcome"/><br>           ❷
</body>
</html:html>
```

After starting up the servlet container we are ready to access the properties file key. In listing 6.4 we use the `<bean:message>` tag to write out the properties file key values. At ❶ we write out the value of the `title` key. At ❷ we write out the value of the `welcome` key. All changes to values are made to the properties file— no JSP changes are required. Any Struts tag accepting a key attribute is capable of obtaining values from a properties file in this way.

Listing 6.5   applications_fr_CA.properties

```
welcome=Bonjour!
title=Bienvenue
```

The last step provides support for additional languages. To support another language all you need to do is create a new properties file appending the language and country to the base name, and place the file in the same directory as the first one created. In listing 6.5 we add support for Canadian French. Struts looks at the locale to find the appropriate properties file. See recipe 6.1, "Set locale dynamically," for details on setting the locale.

Struts uses the locale's language and country codes to find the appropriate properties file by using the following sequence. The search terminates as soon as it finds the key.

> base_language_country.properties
>
> base_language.properties
>
> base.properties

Qualifying language by country provides for language differences between countries. For example, a properties file for France French is application_fr_FR.properties. Using the rules above, a properties file for all French translations regardless of country is application_fr.properties. All you need to do to support another language is to create a new properties file! The translations are automatically written to the page.

Listing 6.6   `<message-resources>` tag in struts-config.xml file

```
<message-resources parameter="resources.application"/>    ❶
<message-resources key="animal" parameter="myanimals"/>    ❷
<message-resources key="plant" parameter="myplants"/>    ❸
<message-resources key="mineral" parameter="myminerals"/>    ❹
```

In listing 6.3 we created the default message resource, but you are free to create and use others. In listing 6.6 we show you how to declare "alternate" message resources. You create the properties files in the same manner described earlier. However, declaring them to Struts and using them is slightly different. In listing 6.6 we create 3 new message resources in addition to the default message resource. The default message resource is declared at ❶. The three new message resources are created at ❷, ❸, and ❹. Since these are not the default message resource you must specify the key attribute.

Listing 6.7   JSP using other message-resource properties file

```
<%@ taglib uri="/tags/struts-bean" prefix="bean" %>
<%@ taglib uri="/tags/struts-html" prefix="html" %>

<html:html>
<head>
<title><bean:message key="title"/></title>
<html:base/>
</head>
  <h1><bean:message key="title"/></h1>
    <bean:message key="welcome"/><br>
    <bean:message bundle="animal" key="horse"/><br>       ❶
    <bean:message bundle="plant" key="maple"/><br>        ❷
    <bean:message bundle="mineral" key="marble"/><br>     ❸
</body>
</html:html>
```

In listing 6.7 we show you how to access "alternate" message-resource properties files. You must specify which message-resource properties file you want to access by specifying the bundle attribute. In listing 6.7 we access the alternate message resources at ❶, ❷, and ❸. Notice the `bundle` attribute matches the key attribute in listing 6.6. If you don't specify the `bundle` attribute, then only the default message-resource properties file is searched. Alternate message-resource properties files are internationalized in the same way as the default.

◆ *Discussion*

Strut's built-in support for internationalization saves a great deal of effort and maintenance down the road. By using this feature you can quickly and easily add support for additional languages. You can even support language variances among countries. Using the key search sequence you can keep the most generic keys near the base and apply the variances near the top of the search sequence.

Alternate message-resource properties files allow you to group keys in a logical fashion. For example, you could keep images in one bundle (as shown in recipe 6.3, "Internationalize your images"), and business keys in another.

There is one "gotcha" to keep in mind. Message-resource properties files are loaded into memory on startup. Changes to the properties files do not take effect until the next time the message-resource properties files are loaded.

◆ *Related*

- 6.1—Set locale dynamically
- 6.3—Internationalize your images

◆ *Reference*

■ [CTRYCODES] ISO 3166 Codes (Countries)

6.3 *Internationalize your images*

◆ *Problem*

You want to choose an image based on locale.

◆ *Background*

A picture might be worth a thousand words, but some pictures might have a few words embedded inside of them. For example, a corporate logo image might contain a summarized mission statement. The logo needs to be localized to meet the language needs of users from other locales. Other times, textless images, such as road signs, might need to vary based on locale. In either case, the application needs to select the right image for the intended locale.

Before digging into the recipe, let's take a moment to review the locale-sensitive resource bundle [RB] [I18NBASIC] search sequence. Struts uses the locale's language and country codes to search for a key through the properties files in the following order.

application_language_country.properties

application_language.properties

application_.properties

The search terminates as soon as it runs across the key it's looking for. The search order requires a country code, but is prequalified by language code. Once a match on language code is found, the search continues on country code. This would lead you to believe that you must specify the language code even when you want to localize on country code alone. In the discussion section we show you a simple trick to get around this problem.

In this recipe we present a very simple, yet useful way to localize images.

◆ *Recipe*

Images are rendered using the `<html:img>` and `<html:image>` tags. Localizing images works the same way for both tags, but for brevity's sake we illustrate this recipe using the `<html:img>` tag. Image tags have four properties of interest to localization (see table 6.1).

Table 6.1 `<html:img>` and `<html:image>` `alt, title, src, page` nonkey attributes

Property	Description
alt	The alternate text of this element
title	The advisory title for this element
src	The URL of this image
page	The application-relative URI for the image

Instead of hard coding the text values of these properties in the tag you can use the key equivalents to pull them from your application's message-resource properties file (see table 6.2).

Table 6.2 `<html:img>` and `<html:image>` `altKey, titleKey, srcKey, pageKey` key attributes

Property	Description
altKey	The message resource key of the alternate text of this element
titleKey	The message resource key of the advisory title for this element
srcKey	The message resource key of the URL of this image
pageKey	The message resource key of the application-relative URI for the image

Getting the `<html:img>` tag's properties values from the message-resource properties file means you automatically get localization of those key values. All that's left is to create properties files for the locales in which you are interested. As long as the locale has been set in session context's `org.apache.struts.Globals.LOCALE_KEY` attribute, the key's values are obtained by searching through the properties files in the order described above. See recipe 6.1 for further details on how to do this.

Let's roll up our sleeves and look at a working example to see how this is done. In the example in listing 6.8, we assume you have declared a message resource for "application."

Listing 6.8 `<html:img>` tag using keyed properties

```
<html:img pageKey="image.house.page"
          altKey="image.house.alt"
          titleKey="image.house.title"/>
```

In listing 6.8 we present an `<html:img>` tag using key properties instead of literal values. Not only does this allow you to localize the `<html:img>` tag, but you get the added benefit of changing those values externally without making a code change to the JSP.

> **BEST PRACTICE** *Prefer keyed tag properties*—It is preferable to use keyed tag properties instead of specifying a literal in the nonkey equivalent. Externalizing property values promotes maintainability and provides the opportunity to localize.

Now, let's populate the properties files, shown in listing 6.9.

Listing 6.9   application.properties

```
image.house.page=/images/house.gif
image.house.alt=house
image.house.title=house
```

Listing 6.9 is the default properties file. This properties file is used when the matching locale-specific properties files do not exist, or the key doesn't exist higher in the search sequence.

Listing 6.10 is used when the locale contains the "fr" language, but not the country codes.

Listing 6.10   application_fr.properties

```
image.house.page=/images/maison.gif
image.house.alt=maison
image.house.title=maison
```

Listing 6.11 is used when the locale contains the "fr" language and the "CA" country codes.

Listing 6.11   application_fr_CA.properties

```
image.house.page=/images/maisonencanada.gif
image.house.alt=maison
image.house.title=maison
```

◆ *Discussion*

Localizing images is very straightforward. Simply use the `<html:img>` and `<html:image>` key properties instead of the nonkey equivalents, and you get localization

automatically. As a side benefit your application becomes more maintainable by externalizing the values.

The image tags uses the session context under the `org.apache.struts.` `Globals.LOCALE_KEY` key to find the locale used for localization. You can override this behavior by specifying the `locale` attribute. The `locale` attribute is the name of the request, or session, key the `locale` attribute used to look up the image tag key properties.

Sometimes you need to localize on country code without prequalifying on language. For example, you might want to localize textless images of road signs. Because very few modern road signs contain text, there is no need to localize based on language. However, road signs generally vary by country. Creating properties files for every language within a country results in an undesirable maintenance burden. You can circumvent this problem by concatenating two underscore characters before the country code. It is equivalent to using an empty `String` as the language code value. For example, the properties file for `Locale("","CA")` is application__CA.properties. Notice, there are two underscore characters between "application" and "CA".

◆ **Related**

  ■ 6.2— Internationalize your text

◆ **Reference**

  ■ [I18NBASICS] Java Internationalization Basics
  ■ [RB] ResourceBundle API

6.4 *Create a locale-sensitive ActionForward*

◆ **Problem**

You want to choose an `ActionForward` based on locale.

◆ **Background**

Internationalized applications must respond differently based on locale. Most applications present translations for field labels, drop-down lists, and option buttons, as shown in recipe 6.2. Other applications must rearrange page layouts for different locales, as shown in recipe 6.5, "Internationalize your tiles." In this recipe we show you how to choose an `ActionForward` based on locale. This is useful when locale demands a radically different way of interacting with the business layer—so different that a new Action is appropriate. Other times it is easier to maintain a view dedicated to a locale rather than implement complex conditional logic in a single view for all locales.

◆ *Recipe*

In this recipe we overload the findForward method in the ActionMapping class to consider locale when choosing an ActionForward. Locale-sensitive forwards search for ActionForwards using the tried and true strategy employed by resource bundles. The ActionMapping appends the locale's language code and country code to the ActionForward's name. If it fails to find an ActionForward it attempts again, this time without the country code. Should that fail, it tries once more with just the ActionForward name. Name, language, country must all be separated by an underscore. Because Struts does not support "variant" in resource bundle searching, neither have we.

For example, assuming the language is "fr", the country is "CA", and the name of the ActionForward is "success", the search would be executed in the following order until a match is found.

- success_fr_CA
- success_fr
- success

The best way to customize forward-locating behavior is by extending Action-Mapping and telling Struts to use this new class instead of ActionMapping. In listing 6.12 we show you how to extend ActionMapping.

Listing 6.12 LocaleSensitiveActionMapping

```java
package com.strutsrecipes.i18nforward.controller;

import java.util.Locale;

import org.apache.struts.action.ActionForward;
import org.apache.struts.action.ActionMapping;

public class LocaleSensitiveActionMapping extends ActionMapping {      ❶

    public ActionForward findForward(String name, Locale locale) {     ❷

        ActionForward localeForward =
            findForward(                                               ❸
                name +
                    "_" + locale.getLanguage() +
                    "_" + locale.getCountry());
```

```
        if (localeForward != null) {
           return localeForward;                    4
        }

        localeForward = findForward(name + "_" + locale.getLanguage());    5
        if (localeForward != null) {
           return localeForward;
        }                                            6

        return findForward(name);    7
     }
  }
```

Let's step through the code:

❶ Create the `LocaleSensitiveActionMapping` by extending from the Struts default.

❷ Overload the `findForward` method to accept both name and locale.

❸ This is the first attempt to find the `ActionForward` by appending the language and country. Notice we leverage the super class's `findForward(String name)` method. This allows us to benefit from any changes made to this method in the future.

❹ Return an `ActionForward` when the search at ❸ was successful.

❺ Search again when the search at ❸ was unsuccessful–this time by appending just the language.

❻ If the search at ❺ was successful, return the `ActionForward`.

❼ If both ❸ and ❺ were unsuccessful, we try using the default behavior.

Let's look at an example <action-mappings> in a struts-config.xml file (listing 6.13) to see how it should be set up.

Listing 6.13 Sample `ActionMappings`

```
<action-mappings

type="com.strutsrecipes.i18nforward.controller.LocaleSensitiveActionMapp
ing">
    <action path="/sample"
            type="com.strutsrecipes.i18nforward.actions.SampleAction"
            name="sampleForm">
             <forward name="success"     path="/userDefault.jsp"/>
             <forward name="success_fr"  path="/userfr.jsp"/>
            <forward name="success_en_US" path="/userenUS.jsp"/>
    </action>
</action-mappings>
```

Notice the action-mapping tag has a type attribute in listing 6.13. This attribute tells the Struts controller to use this class instead of org.apache.struts.action. ActionMapping. The fully qualified class name specified by the type attribute must subclass org.apache.struts.action.ActionMapping.

Notice the naming convention of the forward tags. The forward tag for English United States (en US) is success_en_US. The other forward tags are named accordingly.

Lastly, let's look at an example of how to use locale-sensitive forwarding. Listing 6.14 presents a very trivial Action.

Listing 6.14 SearchAction

```
package com.strutsrecipes.i18nforward.actions;

import java.util.Locale;
import javax.servlet.http.HttpServletRequest;
import javax.servlet.http.HttpServletResponse;
import javax.servlet.http.HttpSession;

import org.apache.struts.Globals;
import org.apache.struts.action.Action;
import org.apache.struts.action.ActionForm;
import org.apache.struts.action.ActionForward;
import org.apache.struts.action.ActionMapping;

import com.strutsrecipes.i18nforward.controller.LocaleSensitiveActionMapping;

public class SampleAction extends Action {

    public ActionForward execute(
        ActionMapping mapping,
        ActionForm form,
      HttpServletRequest request,
        HttpServletResponse response)
        throws Exception {

        LocaleSensitiveActionMapping lsam =
            (LocaleSensitiveActionMapping) mapping;         ❶
        HttpSession session = request.getSession(true);     ❷
        Locale locale = (Locale)
    session.getAttribute(org.apache.struts.Globals.LOCALE_KEY);   ❸
        return lsam.findForward("success", locale);         ❹
    }
}
```

Let's step through listing 6.14.

LocaleSensitiveActionMapping was passed as an execute method argument as the ActionMapping super class. In order to use it we must cast at ❶. At ❷ we obtain the HttpSession, and at ❸ we use the session obtained at ❷ to obtain the locale from the session context using Struts' known key. At ❹ we call the Locale-SensitiveActionMapping class findForward method to return the ActionForward associated with the locale retrieved at ❹.

◆ *Discussion*

There are alternative ways of providing localized forwarding than the method shown in this recipe. We could code the decision logic into the Action class. This might be appropriate if this were a "one off" situation—although "one offs" tend to become "two off" and "three off." Alternatively, we could have extended our Struts Action from a base class implementing similar logic. That strategy would be useful when you need to provide this behavior to selected Actions. This recipe is appropriate when you want to provide this behavior to all Actions.

◆ *Related*

- 6.2—Internationalize your text
- 6.5—Internationalize your tiles

◆ *Reference*

- [I18NBASICS] Java Internationalization Basics

6.5 *Internationalize your tiles*

◆ *Problem*

You want to use a tile based on locale.

◆ *Background*

Internationalizing applications can be more than just localizing text. You might need to rearrange the layout. Cultural differences transcend simple language text translations. Often color choices, organization of material, font types, and styles contribute to making an application "culturally friendly." In this recipe we show you how Tiles supports locale sensitivity.

◆ *Recipe*

Localizing Tiles is simple, straightforward, and mimics the strategy employed by resource bundles. To localize a Tile definition you create a new Tiles configuration file and append the language and country code to the file name. For example, given that the Tiles definition file is tiles-defs.xml, the French Canadian Tiles definition file is tiles-defs_fr_CA.xml. Similar to resource bundles, the language code is appended before the country code. The codes are delineated with an underscore character. For example, the search sequence for a French Canadian Tile definition is as follows:

- tiles-defs_fr_CA.xml
- tiles-defs_fr.xml
- tiles-defs.xml

Struts searches for each Tiles definition in the Tiles definition files in the order described above. This means you only need to override the locale-sensitive Tiles definitions, not all of them. Struts continues to search for the other Tiles definitions until it reaches the bottom of the order. Let's look at an example to make this clearer.

Listing 6.15 presents the default Tiles definition file. Notice this file contains two definitions; .testForm and .othertestForm.

Listing 6.15   tiles-def.xml—default Tiles defintion file

```xml
<?xml version="1.0" encoding="ISO-8859-1"?>
<!DOCTYPE tiles-definitions PUBLIC "-//Apache Software Foundation//DTD Tiles
   Configuration 1.1//EN"
       "http://jakarta.apache.org/struts/dtds/tiles-config_1_1.dtd">

<tiles-definitions>
   <definition name=".testForm" path="/layouts/defaultlayout.jsp">
       <put name="header" value="/tiles/myheader.jsp"/>
       <put name="body"   value="/tiles/mybody.jsp"/>
       <put name="footer" value="/tiles/myfooter.jsp"/>
   </definition>
   <definition name=".othertestForm" path="/layouts/defaultlayout.jsp">
       <put name="header" value="/tiles/myotherheader.jsp"/>
       <put name="body"   value="/tiles/myotherbody.jsp"/>
       <put name="footer" value="/tiles/myotherfooter.jsp"/>
   </definition>
</tiles-definitions>
```

In listing 6.16 we override the .testForm definition for French Canada.

Listing 6.16   tiles-def_fr_CA.xml—French Canada Tiles defintion file

```
<?xml version="1.0" encoding="ISO-8859-1"?>
<!DOCTYPE tiles-definitions PUBLIC "-//Apache Software Foundation//DTD Tiles
   Configuration 1.1//EN"
        "http://jakarta.apache.org/struts/dtds/tiles-config_1_1.dtd">

<tiles-definitions>
   <definition name=".testForm" path="/layouts/frenchlayout.jsp">
        <put name="header" value="/tiles/myheader.jsp"/>
        <put name="body"   value="/tiles/mybody.jsp"/>
        <put name="footer" value="/tiles/myfooter.jsp"/>
   </definition>
</tiles-definitions>
```

Listing 6.16 presents the French Canada override for the `.testForm` Tiles definition. The Tiles definition in listing 6.16 is automatically picked up when the French Canada locale is stored in session context under `org.apache.struts.Globals.LOCALE_KEY`. See recipe 6.1, "Set locale dynamically," to see how to set the locale in your application. Notice there is no need to repeat `.othertestForm` in listing 6.16. An application populated with a French Canada locale will search listing 6.16 for the `.othertestForm` Tiles definition. Failing to find it in listing 6.16, it will find it in listing 6.15.

In listing 6.17 we override the layout.

Listing 6.17   Locale override of the layout

```
<tiles-definitions>
   <definition name=".testForm" path="/layouts/frenchlayout.jsp"/>
</tiles-definitions>
```

Another interesting feature of Tiles localization is that you don't need to override the entire definition. In listing 6.17 we override the layout, but the `put` tags are taken from the default Tiles definition.

Listing 6.18   tiles-def_fr_CA.xmlFrench Canada Tiles defintion file

```
<tiles-definitions>
   <definition name=".testForm" path="/layouts/frenchlayout.jsp">
   <put name="body" value="/tiles/myheader.jsp"/>
   </definition>
</tiles-definitions>
```

Listing 6.18 shows you how to override the layout and just one of the three put tags. The other three put tags are taken from the default Tiles definition. Notice that there is no need to repeat the .othertestForm definition in listing 6.18. If .othertestForm is not found in tiles-def_fr_CA.xml, Tiles will continue to look in tiles-def_fr.xml and finally in tiles-def.xml.

◆ *Discussion*

Localizing Tiles is straightforward because it employs the same strategy as resource bundles. This strategy is an effective approach when the layout or the put tags vary under different locales. Although you might decide to use certain Tiles and layout for specific locales, you should continue to localize the text within them to allow you to reuse them over several locales.

◆ *Related*

- 3.13—Using Tiles with XML definitions
- 6.2—Internationalize your text
- 6.4—Create a locale-sensitive ActionForward

◆ *Reference*

- [I18NBASICS] Java Internationalization Basics

6.6 *Internationalize validation*

◆ *Problem*

You want field validation rules to vary by locale.

◆ *Background*

The Validator is an important asset in implementing field-level validation logic. You only need to declare the Validator plug-in to extend your form from org.apache.struts.validator.ValidatorForm or org.apache.struts.validator. ValidatorActionForm, and register field validation rules against your form in the validation.xml file to get field validation off the ground. Changes to field validation rules are restricted to the validation.xml file—no code changes required!

There are 14 basic validators at your disposal including range validation, required checking, data validation, and mask validation using regular expressions. If none of these basic validators meet your needs, you can plug in your own custom validator.

In practice, application developers sometimes need to vary field validation by locale. Mailing addresses must be validated against US zip codes or Canadian postal codes. Requesting a document-by-document number might make validation vary based on language. Other times it is the combination of both country and language. In this recipe we show you how to configure your validation rules to meet these needs.

◆ *Recipe*

Localization of text messages and Tiles is implemented by creating files suffixed with language and country codes, but the Validator is different. All of the changes required to localize your validation rules are made within the validation.xml file. This file contains one or more `<formset>` tags. Each `<formset>` tag contains one or more `<form>` tags. A `<form>` tag corresponds to the form bean used by an `Action`. Each `<form>` tag has one or more `<field>` tags. Each `<field>` tag represents validation to be applied to a field. The validation rule is registered within the `<field>` tag. Please see recipe 5.2, "Struts-Validator files explained (server-side)," on how to get started with the Validator.

Localizing validation is achieved by creating another `<formset>` specifying language and country attributes, creating `<form>` tags for the forms you want to localize, and overriding only the `<field>` tags pertinent to that locale.

Let's step through an example. In our example we validate the registration number field on the `sampleForm Form` to ensure that it has been entered and conforms to the rules laid out in table 6.3

Table 6.3   Rules implemented in validation.xml file (listing 6.19)

Language	Country	Regular expression	Rule	Example
fr	CA	^1	Must start with "1"	**1**2345
none	CA	^2	Must start with "2"	**2**234586
fr	none	^3	Must start with "3"	**3**47374
any or none	Any or none	^4	Must start with "4"	**4**34

How does the Validator find a localized field validation rule? The Validator tries to find a formset form matching both language and country codes. Failing to find a match, the Validator tries again using only the language code. If that fails too, it attempts to match using just the country code. If the match is still unsuccessful, the Validator resorts to the default formset.

Listing 6.19 contains formsets for several country and language code combinations. Notice the mask values vary among the various combinations.

Listing 6.19   validation.xml file with localized formsets

```
<form-validation>

    <!-- formset language="fr" country="CA" -->
    <formset language="fr" country="CA">      ❶
        <form name="sampleForm">
            <field property="registrationNumber" depends="required,mask">
                <arg0 key="sampleForm.registration"/>
                <var>
                    <var-name>mask</var-name>
                    <var-value>^1</var-value>      ❷
                </var>
            </field>
        </form>
    </formset>

    <!-- formset country="CA" -->
    <formset country="CA">      ❸
        <form name="sampleForm">
            <field property="registrationNumber" depends="required,mask">
                <arg0 key="sampleForm.registration"/>
                <var>
                    <var-name>mask</var-name>
                    <var-value>^2</var-value>      ❹
                </var>
            </field>
        </form>
    </formset>

    <!-- formset language="fr" -->
    <formset language="fr">      ❺
        <form name="sampleForm">
            <field property="registrationNumber" depends="required,mask">
                <arg0 key="sampleForm.registration"/>
                <var>
                    <var-name>mask</var-name>
                    <var-value>^3</var-value>      ❻
                </var>
            </field>
        </form>
    </formset>

    <!-- default formset -->
    <formset>      ❼
        <form name="sampleForm">
            <field property="registrationNumber" depends="required,mask">
```

```
            <arg0 key="sampleForm.registration"/>
            <var>
               <var-name>mask</var-name>
               <var-value>^4</var-value>          ❽
            </var>
         </field>
      </form>
   </formset>

</form-validation>
```

Let's look at listing 6.19 by trying out a few scenarios.

Let's consider the case where the session context's `org.apache.struts.Globals.LOCALE_KEY` attribute is set to `Locale("fr","CA")`. The Validator searches through the list of formsets to find the formset at ❶ matches both language and country code. The validation rule at ❷ is applied.

Let's consider another case where the session context's `org.apache.struts.Globals.LOCALE_KEY` attribute is set to `Locale(","CA")`. The Validator searches through the list of formsets, but discounts the formset at ❶ because the `country` attribute has not been defined. The next nearest match is the formset at ❸. The validation rule at ❹ is applied.

Yet another case is where the session context's `org.apache.struts.Globals.LOCALE_KEY` attribute is set to `Locale("fr")`. The formset at ❶ and ❸ are discounted because the `formset` tags contain `country` attributes, but the `Locale` object does not contain a country code. The formset at ❺ qualifies because the formset matches on the language, and the `country` attribute has not been declared. The validation rule at ❻ is applied.

Finally let's consider the case where the session context's `org.apache.struts.Globals.LOCALE_KEY` attribute is set to `Locale("en","US")`. Neither ❶, ❸, or ❺ match. In this case the Validator chooses the default formset at ❼. The validation rule at ❽ is applied.

The localized formsets behave in an inheritance-like fashion. Formsets specializing on locale need only override the locale sensitive fields. All other fields can be left alone.

◆ *Discussion*

Varying validation rules by locale is a common situation among web applications with a global reach. The Validator's locale-sensitivity feature makes this problem easy to deal with. All you need to do is set the locale in the session context's `org`.

apache.struts.Globals.LOCALE_KEY attribute and override the locale-sensitive field validation in the formsets. Because everything is done declaratively, you can localize validation rules without changing a single line of Java code.

If you are setting the locale on the same page you are performing locale sensitive validation, you will run into a "gotcha." The Validator's org.apache.struts. validator.ValidatorForm and org.apache.struts.validator.ValidatorAction-Form classes trigger validation by overriding the form's validate method. This implies validation occurs before the Action is called. If you set the locale in the Action, validation will have occurred before the locale has been set. Validation would not have taken the intended locale into consideration. The workaround is to override the form's validate method yourself and set the locale there, then call the parent's validate method (see listing 6.20).

Listing 6.20 Workaround on setting locale in the same page as locale-sensitive validation

```
public ActionErrors validate(
    ActionMapping mapping,
    HttpServletRequest request) {

    HttpSession session = request.getSession(true);
    Locale locale = new Locale(languageCode, countryCode);
    session.setAttribute(org.apache.struts.Globals.LOCALE_KEY, locale);

    return super.validate(mapping, request);
}
```

◆ *Related*

- 5.2—Struts-Validator Files explained (server-side)
- 6.2—Internationalize your text
- 6.5—Internationalize your tiles

◆ *Reference*

- [I18NBASICS] Java Internationalization Basics

Logging in, security, and guarding

Security is mostly a superstition. It does not exist in nature, nor do the children of men as a whole experience it. Avoiding danger is no safer in the long run than outright exposure. Life is either a daring adventure, or nothing.

—Helen Keller

Are you who you are? Since you *are* who you are, who are you in relation to my application?

If you understand the above line completely, then you know the difference between authentication and authorization. It's really not that simple when you delve deeply into the workings of an application. There are many questions that need to be answered, both at the level of the intent and nature of the application and at the architectural underpinnings you wish to employ.

Let's look at authentication first. We'll take the example out of the electronic world of 1s and 0s and use a human interaction example. Let's say you're sitting in a crowded coffee house at a table with two chairs. You're reading the paper and not interacting with anyone, and one of the few seats left in the entire establishment is at your table. Somebody comes up with a cup of coffee and asks if they can sit at your table since you have an empty seat. You say, "Sure, go ahead. If you'd like to read some of my paper, I'm through with the Sports and Entertainment sections." You are now sharing information with an anonymous user.

Time marches on, and you're sipping your coffee, and you look up from your paper about the same time as your tablemate. After an awkward second, the stranger says "Thanks so much for the spot at your table, it was very crowded here today and I needed to sit for a minute. My name is Dean." Dean is no longer anonymous, and you now know something about him. At this point you need to decide whether to trust him or not, and for the purposes of sharing a table and a paper, Dean's name is about all you need to know. You have a pleasant conversation.

A few days later you go to the coffee shop, order your usual latté and sit down with your paper. Dean comes in a few minutes later, and although the place is not very busy, he comes over to your table, and brings a different paper and offers to share. As you two sit quietly and read your papers, you trade a few comments and get to know each other a little better, and it becomes routine to sit together over coffee and conversation whenever you both are at the coffee shop at the same time. You trade personal information and details over a period of weeks, and you now know quite a bit about Dean, so when you see him, the interaction between you is more personalized, and there are fewer "barriers" than if Dean were a complete stranger. You might buy the coffee, or Dean might pick up an extra biscotti. You now know Dean from other strangers, and he is welcome at your table at any time. He is "authenticated" as Dean, and "authorized" as someone with whom you share a table, paper, and conversation.

You've made quite a few decisions in the above scenario: You've decided to let someone share your space and information; further, you've decided to expand this decision into a specific person and interact with him based upon who he is and what he does. Let's now draw some parallels with a web application.

In our "coffee shop" web application, we have a web site with information available to all users (strangers that ask to sit at the table and share the newspaper). As the person gives a few details and requests, we offer more information. At this point we've decided the level of "security" that we need to have is a name, as the person is not asking to borrow a thousand dollars and we're not offering it anyway. As we decide to share more information, we know who "Dean" is, and because we know more about him than just his name, we have also "authorized" him to share in more information based upon "who" he is *specifically*. If another person asked to sit at your table, he or she might have to go through the same procedure as Dean.

In this chapter we're going to reveal different ways to implement security strategies for general and specific areas of an application. We'll involve ourselves in the following four areas:

- A simple log-in/log out authentication strategy—This is a lightweight security model, as it has low security and is very generic in nature. This is a very basic model that is not container based, and is expandable and scalable.

- Integrating domain authentication with Struts—Becoming more common and a little more "industrial strength," container-based authentication would compare to our coffee shop being a members-only establishment: anyone getting in has to be authenticated following an understandable and agreed-upon policy, and is then given a name badge by the management. When Dean asks to sit at your table, you already "know" his name and that he's an "authentic" member of the coffee shop.

- Protecting individual fields from a group of users—This is similar to meeting someone for the first time. As you get to know them more, they have "access" to more information. Even if you have many people at your table, they *might* have access to different information with respect to a conversation's context.

- Protecting areas on a page from certain groups of users—A similar recipe to the above field-level approach, but at the page level.

- Using Struts to protect your `Actions` from unauthorized access. You don't want a stranger at the coffee shop to drink from your mug or take a bite out of your cookie! We've devised a couple of different recipes to address specific methods for guarding `Actions` with various mechanisms to do this.

The recipes in this chapter give the user a choice—from very simple to quite complex—of methods to control access, protect information, and guide the user. While authentication and authorization is usually implemented to keep out unwanted or malicious users, it's also well advised to think of these strategies as a way to "guide" specific users to information that is more usable and pertinent to their needs. More often than not a user isn't malicious, they are just looking for the most germane information, and authorization and authentication is an accepted standard to make this happen.

7.1 Tomcat domain authentication and Struts

◆ Problem

You want to integrate domain authentication with Struts.

◆ Background

Security is a hot topic with respect to web applications. It is not uncommon for many enterprise-level projects to expose sensitive business logic and processes to a browser. It is important that this type of information be kept from malicious or "wandering" users.

Tomcat and other servlet containers have an excellent domain-level authentication system that can be integrated with databases or a flat file to authenticate the user and establish the level of access to different areas through the "role" assigned to the user. This system is part of the Servlet 2.2 specification:

There are currently four separate mechanisms for user authentication in a servlet container.

- *HTTP Basic*—This is by far the simplest type of authentication to implement. As a browser makes a request to an area protected by the container, a system-level authentication box appears, requesting a user name and password (users of many web-based mail applications will recognize this dialog box immediately). This box is triggered through a response from the container in the form of a "401 unauthorized" message, which triggers the dialog box from any HTTP-compliant browser. The log-in and password information is sent back to the server via Base64 authentication. Once this information is processed, access is granted to the page and all pages are protected by the container and the level of access set up in the container's configuration. HTTP Basic is extremely easy to set up and its support is universal, but its look and feel is fixed and although it is Base64 encoded, this is not a secure encryption method.

- *HTTP Form*—Consider this type of authentication as HTTP Basic authentication with a "friendly face." Instead of the system-level box, the user is presented with an HTML page with a log-in and password text box containing an HTML form (this is outside of the Struts application) with specific form and field names for posting to the server. If authentication fails, a specified error page is displayed. It is important to note that this method should only be implemented when a session is maintained using cookies or HTTPS.

- *HTTPS Client*—This is HTTP authentication through a Secure Sockets Layer. All data is transmitted using public-key cryptography and developers don't have to know about the encryption to implement the system. It requires a certificate from an authority such as VeriSign. More information is available on this type of authentication in the last recipe of this chapter.

- *HTTP Digest*—This is the same as HTTP Basic except that the password is encrypted as well as encoded. This provides the advantages of Basic authentication with more security, but is only supported on Internet Explorer 5 and newer versions. Not all servlet containers implement this, as it is not mandated by the Servlet specifications.

This recipe will discuss Basic and Form-based authentication and their integration into the Struts framework. Other recipes in this chapter will expand on this information.

A servlet container can secure an entire application or part of it from users through the use of user names and the roles assigned to them. This definition is created in the web application *and* in the servlet container's configuration files. The servlet container can be configured to use any type of persistence layer available, from a simple XML file to an open source database or fully functional LDAP that conforms to the Servlet security model. The directories and pages secured by the application are defined in the web.xml file at the container or application level, whichever is applicable. If you are securing one application or many, you have a consistent and well-defined method in which to complete your task.

With respect to Struts, security using this method is accessed from outside of the framework. With Basic Authentication you can secure your entire application. When using a form-based mechanism it is important to create directories that are not secured by the container's configuration, as any servlets, images, CSS files, or HTML pages will not render if they are "behind" the secured areas of your application, and, in most cases, you wouldn't want them to be.

◆ *Recipe*

Two methods are discussed here. First is the HTTP Basic authentication method, which opens an Alert dialog box with a log-in and password text line, similar to the box in figure 7.1.

This method eschews any HTML code and immediately loads the index or designated welcome file as soon as Tomcat decides who you are and what role you have. For our second method (HTTP Form-based authentication), you need to create a log-in and log-in error page using standard HTML When any protected page is requested by an unauthorized user, the log-in page is requested and the designated welcome file is displayed. If the user fails to authenticate, the error page you've created is sent to the browser.

We must first decide what we wish to protect. If you wish to protect an entire application with absolutely no access until the user is known, you must use the Basic method, as it uses an Alert box and needs nothing in the way of HTML pages, images, or links to do its job. If we wish to use the Form method, then two simple HTML or JSP pages must be created, and any files (such as images, `includes`, and so on) that we want to use on these pages must also be made available in an unprotected area.

Figure 7.1 Dialog box used with Basic authentication.

NOTE This recipe shows the use of a flat-file authentication. More robust applications are simple to adapt but are out of the scope of a Struts recipe. Many sources have information as to how to configure your specific data source to the container's system.

To begin, open the web.xml file in the WEB-INF directory of your application. Find the end of your file at the `</web-app>` tag and insert the following information (tailored to your directory needs) in front of it. Both Basic and Form types are shown below in listing 7.1:

Listing 7.1 Basic authentication in web.xml file

```
  </taglib>
  <!--Security for entire application-->
  <security-constraint>
    <web-resource-collection>
      <web-resource-name>My web application</web-resource-name>
      <url-pattern>/*</url-pattern>
      <http-method>GET</http-method>
      <http-method>POST</http-method>
      <http-method>PUT</http-method>
      <http-method>DELETE</http-method>
      <http-method>HEAD</http-method>
      <http-method>OPTIONS</http-method>
      <http-method>TRACE</http-method>
    </web-resource-collection>
    <auth-constraint>
      <role-name>applicationuser</role-name>
      <!--more roles can be added here -->
    </auth-constraint>
  </security-constraint>
  <login-config>
    <auth-method>BASIC</auth-method>
  </login-config>
</web-app>
```

The above method protects your entire directory, but there is no custom log-in or error screen provided. To provide your log-in and error screen, it is crucial to specify the directories and files that are protected, as shown below in listing 7.2:

Listing 7.2 Form authentication listing in web.xml file

```
</taglib>
  <!--Security for application with custom log-in and error pages -->
  <security-constraint>
    <web-resource-collection>
```

```
            <web-resource-name>My Custom Page Application</web-resource-name>
            <url-pattern>/index.jsp</url-pattern>
            <url-pattern>/pages/*</url-pattern>
            <http-method>POST</http-method>
            <http-method>PUT</http-method>
            <http-method>DELETE</http-method>
            <http-method>HEAD</http-method>
            <http-method>OPTIONS</http-method>
            <http-method>TRACE</http-method>
            </web-resource-collection>
            <auth-constraint>
            <!--more roles can be added here -->
            <role-name>customuser</role-name>
            </auth-constraint>
        </security-constraint>
        <login-config>
            <auth-method>FORM</auth-method>
            <form-login-config>
            <!--These are the two pages that must be created, if you attach
                images, css, or include files it is important that they be in a
                non-protected area or your results will not be what you intend -->
            <form-login-page>/login.html</form-login-page>
            <form-error-page>/error.html</form-error-page>
            </form-login-config>
        </login-config>
    </web-app>
```

Next, let's take a look at the server.xml file in the {Tomcat-directory}/conf/ folder. It is heavily commented, but we are looking for the section after the <engine> and <logger> tags in the default file. For flat-file realm authentication, uncomment the line:

```
<Realm className="org.apache.catalina.realm.MemoryRealm"/>
```

Make sure that any other realm tags are commented out. Note that this uncommenting procedure is uneccessary when using Tomcat 4.1+, since the UserDatabaseRealm is enabled by default. You are now ready to name your users in the tomcat-users.xml file, also located in the {Tomcat-directory}/conf/ folder. Listing 7.3 demonstrates a sample tomcat-users.xml file that creates a couple of users for the Form-based login described in the above web.xml file listed in 7.2:

Listing 7.3   tomcat-users.xml file employing form-based authentication

```
<?xml version="1.0" encoding="utf-8"?>
<tomcat-users>
    <role rolename="customuser"/>
    <user username="aguy" password="thisPassword" roles="customuser"/>
```

```
<!-- you may comma delimit more roles in the "roles" attribute-->
    <user username="anotherguy" password="thisGuysPwd" roles="customuser"/>
</tomcat-users>
```

Finally, let's look at the JSP log-in and error pages in listings 7.3 and 7.4. The bold variable names in the HTML form used here are recognized by your container and **must** be used.

Listing 7.4 Login.html for form-based authentication

```
<html>
<head>
<title>My Log In Page</title>
</head>
<body>
<form action="j_security_check">
<table style="width: 50%">
   <tr>
      <td>Username:</td>
      <td><input type="text" name="j_username" /></td>
   </tr>
   <tr>
      <td>Password:</td>
      <td><input type="password" name="j_password" /></td>
   </tr>
   <td> </td>
   <td><input type="submit" value="Login" /></td>
   </tr>
</table>
</form>
</body>
</html>
```

Listing 7.5 error.html page for handling any login errors for above login page

```
<html>
<head>
<title>Log in error</title>
</head>
<body>
<p style="font-size: 125%; color: red">Log-In Error</p>
<p>The user name and/or password are incorrect.</p>
<p><a href="login.html">try again</a></p>
</body>
</html>
```

◆ *Discussion*

There might be a situation where you just wish to protect your `Actions` instead of—or in addition to—individual pages. This is simply done by adding

```
<url-pattern>*.do</url-pattern>
```

within the `<web-resource-collection/>` xml tags. This implementation protects your methods, but a security hole exists without additional pattern-mappings, as a user could type a URL in directly—http://www.mysite.com/pages/myFooPage.jsp and possibly access it.

This is a great place to discuss the options for solving that particular problem:

1 Place all JSPs under WEB-INF.

2 Secure *.jsp with a constraint that *no* user has permission to use, thereby preventing direct access.

Although the limitations of the flat file are apparent when compared to what can be achieved with a database, it really depends upon the size and scope of the application you're creating. As more roles and realms are needed, it is possible to protect areas in your site from certain roles as they are created. This is explained and extended in the recipes related to this one.

Finally, you might want to secure your entire site by listing some or all of your JSP files inside the WEB-INF directory. This type of security allows you to use the *.do security constraint with ease, as only those files that you wish to protect can be accessed through the Struts `Action`. Please see "Best Practice: Use the container to protect resources" for details.

◆ *Related*

- 7.2—Handling log out
- 7.4—Secure an action mapping using the container
- 7.5—Customized action mapping security
- 7.6—Protect areas on a page
- 7.7—Protect fields

7.2 *Handling log out*

◆ *Problem*

You want to implement log out in your application.

◆ *Background*

We've discussed logging into an application, but once you're there, you're eventually going to need to make a clean break with the page upon leaving. It's important to judge the level of security you want for your web application; not just to prevent hacking, but to control the user's Actions within it. Just sticking a logout button on a page and round-tripping it to the welcome screen might be good for a test application, but let's look at the handling of some real-world problems.

First, let's decide in advance just how far out you need to go. A great deal of this decision depends upon the security your application needs. If you are interested only in capturing a user name, authenticating and recording entry and exit, and controlling "how" a user can come into your application or bookmark it, then that's a lighter-weight solution than one that regulates what a user sees, does, or accesses.

But if you're implementing container-managed security through your application server or a servlet container such as Tomcat, then you need to make a more robust and secure solution that not only ensures that entry into your site is controlled, but it also makes sure that the user can't just "hit the back button" and waddle back into the application.

◆ *Recipe*

Either way, there's not a lot of code to logging out, it just depends on what you want to do and what you get in return for your trouble. First, you might just want to control a small application by using <logic:present/> or <logic:if> tags to evaluate whether a user is logged in or not. This is often done by detecting the presence of a user variable, or by detecting a flag with a role, group, or Boolean variable. With such a simple log-in or security method as this is, it is only a matter of using an Action class with the following code in the execute() method to set the user's name and any user-specific session information to null.

```
// we already have access to HttpRequest
HttpSession session = request.getSession();
session.setAttribute(Constants.YOUR_LOGIN_FLAG_OR_USER_KEY,null);

//you may want to set other session and/or request variables to null here
//forward to a log-out page or back to welcome or whatever...

return mapping.findForward("logout");
```

If you are using a J2EE-compliant application server or servlet container and wish to use container-managed security, you need a more "industrial-strength" solution. Interestingly, such a solution involves writing less code:

```
HttpSession session = request.getSession();
session.invalidate();

//forward to a log-out page or back to welcome or whatever...

return mapping.findForward("logout");
```

The above code completely invalidates the session and forwards to a logout page. When the method requesting a page is detected, the user cannot enter back into any part of the defined realm without having to completely log back in.

◆ *Discussion*

The first method prevents the user from backing into an application, or walking into a side door. It also requires the developer to add some security-based code into every page he or she creates, or extend the Action servlet and create a custom security model. While this can be handled quite easily through the use of Tiles, includes, and other similar methods, it still requires some conscious effort. This effort is rewarded by very tight control and the ability to create small-to-large views based upon developer-defined schemes. By using this method, you "own" your security model and may configure it to your application in the manner you see fit—creating views, controllers and applications that discriminate between roles, users, and other custom groupings.

The J2EE container-managed security is much more global, as you can control access to one or many applications in the servlet container, and is much more common with web applications because of its ease of implementation and the fact that you don't have to implement any page-level security measures. Everything is handled by the server as it tracks your session. Of course, you give up tight control on the view and navigation without resorting to additional measures that might have some overlap and redundancy, but are often needed and required. These types of controls are explained further in the remaining recipes of this chapter.

It just depends upon what you need. Sometimes a little security is just fine, sometimes your requirements are global, and then again you might need something very specific. The remaining recipes in this chapter discuss securing applications in simple and complex manners. There are many more ways of securing an application than there are for logging out, and the above recipe takes care of most of a developer's needs as long as the strategies implemented are not very esoteric.

◆ *Related*

- ▪ 1.3—What is "jsessionid" and why do I need it?
- ▪ 7.1—Tomcat domain authentication and Struts

7.3 *Switch to SSL and back again*

◆ *Problem*

You want to use SSL in your application.

◆ *Background*

Most organizations consider information their most valuable asset. Guarding information is more than a full-time job for developers and administrators alike. The protection of information must be approached from many different angles. The database, user interface, and business layer are just a few of the critical areas that need your attention. Even the door to the server room must be kept locked. More importantly, once the data has left the building via the Internet, it can be compromised by some very talented people electronically poking and prodding data on the wires.

In this recipe we demonstrate how to enable Secure Socket Layer (SSL) in your container. In addition, we introduce you to the Struts SSL extension for HTTP/HTTPS switching (ssl-ext) library—a package allowing you to declare which `Actions` are SSL enabled. This very easy-to-use package allows you to convert between SSL-enabled `Actions` and disabled ones with ease.

Before diving into the recipe, let's cover some SSL basics. SSL is a network protocol originally developed by Netscape to provide authentication and transmission security. The SSL protocol resides in a layer above TCP/IP, but below application protocols such as HTTP, LDAP, and IMAP. Prior to transmission, the client verifies the identity of the server. Similarly, the server might optionally verify the identity of the client. To thwart the efforts of digital eavesdroppers, the two hosts agree upon a cryptographic algorithm, commonly called a cipher, to encrypt and decrypt transmissions. In addition to providing confidentiality, SSL audits the transmission to ensure it remains untampered enroute. The entire workings of SSL are beyond the scope of this recipe, but we encourage you to explore SSL using some of the resources mentioned in the resource section.

Most containers, including Tomcat, provide SSL services. Enabling SSL on your container ensures your communication is secure and not tampered with. The container is able to recognize SSL communication by inspecting the URL scheme. The URL scheme is the portion of the URL preceding the colon. An HTTP unsecured protocol is identified with "http" before the colon. For example, http://127.0.0.1 indicates an unsecured HTTP protocol. An "s" is placed after http to indicate the request wishes to communicate using SSL. For example, https://127.0.0.1 is the appropriate URL for an SSL HTTP request.

Many applications have both SSL and non-SSL links. The challenge is to format your links for SSL when you want a secure communication. By default, the Struts link tag uses the same URI scheme as the current page you are viewing. So, how can you build a link from a secured page to an unsecured one, and vice versa? One option is to build your own link tag to draw SSL links, but this can quickly lead to a maintenance burden whenever you need to convert from one to the other. Now, if you could do this declaratively in the struts-config.xml file, then you would be a happy camper. You could use tags to paint your link, but you could change them declaratively in the struts-config.xml file as things change. Fortunately, that's exactly what the Struts SSL extension for HTTP/HTTPS switching (ssl-ext) library does for you. In this recipe we show you how to set up SSL with Tomcat. We then show you how to set up and use ssl-ext in your application to encrypt your data over the wire. A complete explanation of SSL authentication is beyond the scope of this book; instead, we focus on the Struts development aspect of SSL.

◆ *Recipe*

Implementing this recipe is divided into three sections. In the first section we show you how to enable SSL on Tomcat. Next, we describe exactly what needs to be done to install ssl-ext in your application. Lastly, we apply ssl-ext into your code. Let's get started!

Step 1: enable SSL in Tomcat

1   Download and install JSSE 1.0.2 (or later) from http://java.sun.com/products/jsse/. This web site tells you everything you need to know to install JSSE. Note that the Java 2 SDK Standard Edition v 1.4 has prebundled JSSE for you. If you are using JDK v 1.4, then you can skip this step.

2 Create a certificate keystore. Enter one of the following commands:

For Windows: %JAVA_HOME%\bin\keytool -genkey -alias tomcat -keyalg RSA

For UNIX: $JAVA_HOME/bin/keytool -genkey -alias tomcat -keyalg RSA

You will be asked a number of questions. For the purposes of this exercise, simply enter whatever makes sense to you. See your system administrator when the time comes to implement into a controlled environment.

3 Uncomment the SSL HTTP/1.1 Connector from conf/server.xml. The uncommented connector should look like this (take special note of the port number, you are going to need to know it later):

```
<Connector className="org.apache.coyote.tomcat4.CoyoteConnector"
           port="8443"
           minProcessors="5"
           maxProcessors="75"
           enableLookups="true"
           acceptCount="10"
           debug="0"
           scheme="https"
           secure="true"
           useURIValidationHack="false">
<Factory
   className="org.apache.coyote.tomcat4.CoyoteServerSocketFactory"
      clientAuth="false"
      protocol="TLS" />
</Connector>
```

4 Restart Tomcat. Point your browser at https://127.0.0.1:8443 to make sure everything went as planned. If Tomcat renders the page, then you are successful.

Congratulations, you have enabled SSL on Tomcat.

Step 2: set up Struts SSL extension for HTTP/HTTPS switching (ssl-ext) for your application

Because ssl-ext is a Struts extension library, it's not surprising that its installation is similar to Struts. If you have installed Struts, the following instructions will seem familiar.

1 Download the ssl-ext binaries from http://sslext.sourceforge.net. The download contains a working sample application. Unzip the download to the Tomcat webapps directory. In the following steps you will copy over many of the files from the sample application to create your own ssl-ext application.

2 Copy over sslext.jar from the sample app to your WEB-INF/lib directory.

3 Copy over sslext.tld from the sample app to your WEB-INF/lib directory.

4 Place the following snippet with the other taglibs in the web.xml file:

```
<taglib>
  <taglib-uri>/WEB-INF/sslext.tld</taglib-uri>
  <taglib-location>/WEB-INF/sslext.tld</taglib-location>
</taglib>
```

5 Add the plug-in tag to the struts-config.xml file. Take special note of the
httpsPort property. It must be the same one used to configure Tomcat
(step 1, instruction 3). As you might expect, the httpPort property should
match the Tomcat configuration found in the conf/server.xml. The two
values defined below are the Tomcat default values.

```
<plug-in className="org.apache.struts.action.SecurePlugIn">
    <set-property property="httpPort" value="8080"/>
    <set-property property="httpsPort" value="8443"/>
    <set-property property="enable" value="true"/>
</plug-in>
```

That's it! You are ready to start using ssl-ext.

Step 3: build an application using ssl-ext

Let's build an application to demonstrate ssl-ext in action. In this step, we'll
show how ssl-ext is used to format the URL for links targeting SSL-secured pages.
Conversely, we'll demonstrate URL formatting for links targeting ordinary non-
SSL pages. We'll see that securing the page is done by making a small change to
the struts-config.xml file. Listing 7.6 show the struts-config.xml action mapping
for a sample application.

Listing 7.6 Struts-config.xml

```
<?xml version="1.0" encoding="ISO-8859-1" ?>

<!DOCTYPE struts-config PUBLIC
          "-//Apache Software Foundation//DTD Struts Configuration 1.1//EN"
          "http://jakarta.apache.org/struts/dtds/struts-config_1_1.dtd">

<struts-config>

  <global-forwards type="org.apache.struts.action.ActionForward">
     <forward    name="unsecured"    path="/unsecured.do"/>
     <forward    name="secured"      path="/secured.do"/>
     <forward    name="menu"         path="/menu.do"/>
  </global-forwards>

  <form-beans>
```

```
    <form-bean name="dummyForm" type="com.strutsrecipes.ssl.forms.Dummy" />
  </form-beans>

  <action-mappings type="org.apache.struts.config.SecureActionConfig">    ❶
    <action     path="/menu"
                type="org.apache.struts.actions.ForwardAction"
                parameter="/WEB-INF/pages/menu.jsp">
                <set-property property="secure" value="false"/>
    </action>

    <action     path="/unsecured"
                type="org.apache.struts.actions.ForwardAction"
                parameter="/WEB-INF/pages/unsecured.jsp">
                <set-property property="secure" value="false"/>    ❷
    </action>

    <action     path="/secured"
                type="org.apache.struts.actions.ForwardAction"
                parameter="/WEB-INF/pages/secured.jsp">
                <set-property property="secure" value="true"/>    ❸
    </action>

    <action     path="/securesubmit"
                type="org.apache.struts.actions.ForwardAction"
                name="dummyForm"
                parameter="/WEB-INF/pages/securesubmit.jsp">
                <set-property property="secure" value="true"/>    ❹
    </action>

    <action     path="/unsecuresubmit"
                type="org.apache.struts.actions.ForwardAction"
                name="dummyForm"
                parameter="/WEB-INF/pages/unsecuresubmit.jsp">
                <set-property property="secure" value="false"/>    ❺
    </action>
  </action-mappings>

  <plug-in className="org.apache.struts.action.SecurePlugIn">
    <set-property property="httpPort" value="8080"/>
    <set-property property="httpsPort" value="8443"/>
    <set-property property="enable" value="true"/>
  </plug-in>

</struts-config>
```

To secure an `Action` with SSL, you nest a `<set-property>` tag inside the `Action`
tag. The value of the `property` attribute is always `secure`. A `true` value of the
`value` attribute indicates we want URLs to issue an SSL request by setting the URI
scheme to "https". Similarly, a `false` value indicates the page is an ordinary,
unsecured page; and the URI scheme should be "http". A value of `any` defaults to
the current page's scheme. Although you can achieve the same effect using an

ordinary Struts link tag, the any value let you change it to true or false by making a change to the struts-config file.

Because the secure property is not supported by the default action mapping, we need to override it at ❶. Listing 7.7 demonstrates how ssl-ext link tags are used to generate a protocol formatted URL.

Listing 7.7 menu.jsp: JSP using ssl-ext link tags

```
<%@ page language="java" %>
<%@ taglib uri="/WEB-INF/struts-html.tld" prefix="html"%>
<%@ taglib uri="/WEB-INF/sslext.tld" prefix="sslext"%>       ❻

<html:html>
<h1>SSL: Menu</h1>

<h2>Links</h2>
<br><sslext:link forward="unsecured">unsecured</sslext:link>   ❼
<br><sslext:link forward="secured">secured</sslext:link>   ❽

<h2>submit to secured</h2>
<sslext:form action="/securesubmit" >   ❾
<br><html:text property="name" value=""/>
<html:submit/>
</sslext:form>

<h2>submit to unsecured</h2>
<sslext:form action="/unsecuresubmit" >   ❿
<br><html:text property="name" value=""/>
<html:submit/>
</sslext:form>

</html:html>
```

The links to secured pages are prefixed with https, and the links to unsecured are formatted with the usual http. For example, the link at ❼ is rendered "unsecured" as http://127.0.0.1:8080/ssl/unsecured.do, whereas the link at ❽ is rendered "secured" as https://127.0.0.1:8443/ssl/secured.do.

The most striking observation in listing 7.7 is that we never specify whether or not the page is secured with SSL. That information is defined in the struts-config. xml file. The link tag at ❼ in listing 7.7 maps to ❷ in listing 7.6. Analogously, ❽ maps to ❸, ❾ maps to ❹, and ❿ maps to ❺. The ssl:ext link tag consults the struts-config.xml file when painting the URL protocol segment. To use the ssl-ext taglib you need to declare it as we have done at ❻.

Submits work in much the same way, except you must use the form tag from the ssl-ext namespace ❾❿.

There you have it. Applying ssl-ext is completely unraveled in the preceding steps.

◆ *Discussion*

Because Step 1 and Step 2 are self-explanatory we dispense with reviewing those sections. Step 3 is far more interesting and worthy of closer inspection. The JSP work is straightforward, and despite the sslext namespace, it looks pretty much the same as any Struts JSP. Instead of painting the links with the Struts link tag, we use the same tag from the sslext namespace. Behind the scenes, the tag is using the action mapping to set the URI scheme to either http or https. To paint the URL with https, you set the `secure` property on the action mapping to `true`. To paint the URL as "http", you set it to `false`. The submit works in the same way, except you use the form tag from the sslext namespace instead of the Struts html namespace.

There is one more tag we haven't discussed. The `pageScheme` tag uses the `secure` attribute to force a redirect to http or https. For example, an https request to a page with `<sslext:pageScheme secure="false">` redirects the request to http, despite the fact the request was made to https.

The job of ensuring the URL is prefixed with the right scheme would certainly be more difficult if it were not for ssl-ext. Instead of tackling this problem in the JSP by tailoring each link for SSL, we can manage it from the struts-conf.xml file. The maintenance payback is substantial. For example, if we had 20 links to the same Struts `Action`, then 20 JSP changes would be required to change a link to use SSL. The identical change under ssl-ext requires just one change to the struts-config.xml! Too err is human, to avoid errors is divine.

> **BEST PRACTICE** *Use SSL judiciously*—SSL is a proven, reliable, flexible, and popular way to authenticate and secure applications, but you should use it only when you need it. All SSL transmissions encrypt and decrypt data. Depending on the chosen cipher, these operations can impact your performance.

◆ *Reference*

- [SSLDOC] SSL Overview
- [SSLEXT] SSL Extension for Struts HTTP/HTTPS switching
- [SSLSPEC] SSL Specification
- [SSLTOM] SSL Tomcat Configuration
- [URI] W3 URI Specification

7.4 *Secure an action mapping using the container*

◆ *Problem*

You want to protect an action mapping from unauthorized access.

◆ *Background*

Suppose you want to restrict update access to users with a supervisor role, but provide inquiry access to all other users. Removing the user's ability to navigate to the unauthorized page impedes their ability to submit the update using the application, but a clever user can spoof a URL using the web browser's location bar. Another solution is to use the container to define security constraints in the web. xml file. However, as the number of URLs grows, this strategy becomes unwieldy and difficult to maintain. This recipe shows you how to use inherent Struts functionality to protect your action mappings by registering roles against them.

REQUEST PROCESSOR Struts supports the Model-View-Controller (MVC) design paradigm. MVC demands that all requests are dispatched to a controller. The controller becomes the single point of entry to the entire application, forcing all requests to be handled in a consistent manner. The Struts `ActionServlet` fulfills the MVC controller responsibilities, but delegates the real work to the `RequestProcessor`. The default `RequestProcessor` is responsible for finding the appropriate `ActionMapping`, populating the `ActionForm` with request parameters, validating the `ActionForm` when required, and invoking the `Action` before forwarding the response to the appropriate `ActionForward`. In addition to this busy work load, the `RequestProcessor` ensures request processing is restricted to authorized users.

◆ *Recipe*

First, you need to configure the container to challenge the user for their user name and password when they attempt to access the application. Once authenticated, the container has the means to help you determine a user's role. See recipe 7.1, "Tomcat domain authentication and Struts," to add users and roles to the container's security mechanism.

To restrict access to an action mapping for a list of roles, you simply add a list of comma-delimited roles to the `roles` attribute on the `Action` tag inside the struts-config.xml file. The `roles` attribute specifies which roles are authorized to access the action mapping. The omission of the `roles` attribute leaves the action mapping unprotected. It's that simple!

Listing 7.8   The `Action` tag `roles` attribute

```
<action-mappings>
    <action    path="/unprotected"    ❶
               type="org.apache.struts.actions.ForwardAction"
               parameter="/WEB-INF/pages/unprotected.jsp"/>
    <action    path="/protected"    ❷
               roles="supervisor,appladmin"
               type="org.apache.struts.actions.ForwardAction"
               parameter="/WEB-INF/pages/protected.jsp"/>
    <action    path="/menu"
               type="org.apache.struts.actions.ForwardAction"
               parameter="/WEB-INF/pages/menu.jsp"/>
</action-mappings>
```

Let's step through listing 7.8.

At ❶ we show an unprotected action mapping. At ❷ we protect the action mapping by adding a `roles` attribute. Users possessing either supervisor or appladmin are authorized to access this action mapping.

◆ ***Discussion***

A good practice to secure your JSPs from direct client access is to place them under the WEB-INF directory. Once secured, the `ActionServlet` becomes your vehicle to access your JSPs. Whenever a request is received by the `ActionServlet`, the `RequestProcessor` is called into duty to ensure the user is authorized to invoke the requested `Action`. The `RequestProcessor` consults the container's security mechanism by calling the `isRoles()` on the request object to validate the user's container-defined role against the list of roles specified in the `Action` tag's `roles` attribute. Authorized users are cleared to process the `Action` in the usual way. Those users denied access are presented with the standard "HTTP Status 400 – User is not authorized to access *resource name*."

This recipe secures action mapping from request spoofing. It provides an effective means of securing action mappings using the container's built-in security mechanism with very little effort on your part.

Although this recipe is an effective strategy of securing JSPs and pages, there are a couple of limitations. First, you are tied to the containers security mechanism to define your users and roles. Second, users precipitating security violations are presented with the standard server error screen and left without navigability back to the main application. These limitations are addressed in recipe 7.5, "Customized action mapping security."

This recipe takes a coarse-grained approach by securing the entire page. See recipe 7.6, "Protect areas on a page," and recipe 7.7, "Protect fields," for a fine-grained approach to a similar problem.

BEST PRACTICE *Use the container to protect resources*—If your container supports Servlet specification 2.3, an excellent practice is to force all client requests through the `ActionServlet`. Simply place all your JSPs under the WEB-INF directory. The servlet engine denies client access to all resources stored below the WEB-INF directory. With your JSPs protected by the servlet engine, all requests must be marshaled through the `Action-Servlet` and processed by the `RequestProcessor`.

◆ Related

- 7.1—Tomcat domain authentication and Struts
- 7.5—Customized action mapping security
- 7.6—Protect areas on a page
- 7.7—Protect fields

◆ Reference

- [CORE] Core J2EE Patterns, Best Practices, and Design Strategies, Controlling Client Access

7.5 Customized action mapping security

◆ Problem

You want to use Struts to protect your `Action`s from unauthorized access, but you want to use your own security mechanism. Furthermore, you want to send the user to a page of your choice when security violations are detected.

◆ Background

In recipe 7.4, "Secure an action mapping using the container," we explored inherent Struts functionality to detect unauthorized access of `Action`s. Using this Struts feature can be very effective, but there are some limitations. First, you are forced to use the container's security mechanism. Second, the user was left without navigability back to the application. In this recipe we show you how to address these two limitations by extending the `RequestProcessor` and leveraging Struts' ability to process exceptions declaratively. See recipe 5.4, "Use declarative exception handling."

Let's review the controller. The Struts ActionServlet receives all requests, but delegates the real work to the RequestProcessor. The default RequestProcessor is responsible for finding the appropriate ActionMapping, populating the Action-Form with request parameters, validating the ActionForm when required, and invoking the Action before forwarding the response to the appropriate Action-Forward. Moreover, the RequestProcessor ensures request processing is restricted to authorized users. For a description of the RequestProcessor and its relationship to the ActionServlet, we recommend you read recipe 7.4.

The hallmark of a good framework is one that allows you to tailor its behavior by extending and overriding *hot spots*. Hot spots are framework methods which can be overridden to implement customize behavior. Struts 1.1 refactored the ActionServlet to introduce the RequestProcessor to empower developers with 15 hot spots. In this recipe we override the RequestProcessor processRoles method to change the behavior of Action authorization.

◆ *Recipe*

Let's begin by creating a brand new RequestProcessor to utilize a different authorization mechanism than the one provided by the default RequestProcessor. Because we want to keep most of the default implementation intact, we extend RequestProcessor and override the processRoles method, as shown in listing 7.9.

Listing 7.9 SecurityRequestProcessor

```
package com.strutsrecipes.customguardaction.controller;

import java.io.IOException;

import javax.servlet.ServletException;
import javax.servlet.http.HttpServletRequest;
import javax.servlet.http.HttpServletResponse;

import org.apache.struts.action.ActionForward;
import org.apache.struts.action.ActionMapping;
import org.apache.struts.action.RequestProcessor;

import com.strutsrecipes.customguardaction.business.SecurityComponent;
import
    com.strutsrecipes.customguardaction.exceptions.SecurityViolationException;
public class SecurityRequestProcessor extends RequestProcessor {

    protected boolean processRoles (
        HttpServletRequest request,
        HttpServletResponse response,
        ActionMapping mapping)
```

```
        throws IOException, ServletException {

        // Obtain the list of roles from action config
        String roles [] = mapping.getRoleNames();
        if ((roles == null) || (roles.length < 1)) {          ❶
           return (true);
        }

        // verify user possesses role
        for (int i = 0; i < roles.length; i++) {
           if (isUserInRole (request.getRemoteUser(), roles [i])) {   ❷
              return (true);
           }
        }

        // invoke declarative exception handling              ❸
        ActionForward forward =    processException(request,response,
                 new SecurityViolationException(),null,mapping);
        // forward user
        if (forward != null) {                                ❹
           process ForwardConfig(request, response, forward);
        }
        return (false);

     }

   protected boolean isUserInRole (String user, String role) {
      // invoke proprietary security mechanism
      return new SecurityComponent().isAuthorized(user, role);
   };

   }
```

Now, let's register `SecurityRequestProcessor` with the `ActionServlet` by adding the controller tag to the struts-config.xml file, as shown in listing 7.10.

Listing 7.10 Controller tag

```
<controller processorClass=
"com.strutsrecipes.customguardaction.controller.SecurityRequestProcessor"/>
```

To declare the response our application should take when a `SecurityViolation-Exception` is encountered, we register an exception with exception handler by nesting an exception tag under the `Action` tag in the struts-config.xml file.

Finally, we register roles against the `Action` tag.

Listing 7.11 `<action-mapping>`

```
<action-mappings>
    <action     path="/unprotected"
                type="org.apache.struts.actions.ForwardAction"
                parameter="/WEB-INF/pages/unprotected.jsp"/>

    <action     path="/protected"
                roles="supervisor,appladmin"      ❺
                type="org.apache.struts.actions.ForwardAction"
                parameter="/WEB-INF/pages/protected.jsp">
                // declare exception to exception handler
                <exception key="error.security"
                        path="/menu.do"
                        scope="request"                              ❻
                        type="com.strutsrecipes.
                            customguardaction.exceptions.
                            SecurityViolationException"/>

    </action>

    <action     path="/menu"
                type="org.apache.struts.actions.ForwardAction"
                parameter="/WEB-INF/pages/menu.jsp"/>
</action-mappings>
```

Let's step through the code to see how it all works. We start by creating a new `RequestProcessor`. By extending `SecurityRequestProcessor` from `RequestProcessor`, all of the default `RequestProcessor` hot spots execute, except `processRoles`. At ❶ we obtain a list of all the roles we declared at ❺. At ❷ we verify that the user possesses at least one of the roles by calling the `isUserInRole` private method. The `isUserInRole` method validates the user and role by invoking our proprietary security mechanism.

In the event that the user does not possess the authority to invoke the `Action`, we call the `processException` method ❸ to obtain the `ActionForward` defined declaratively to the exception handler ❻. The default `RequestProcessor` normally calls this method to deal with exceptions returning when processing an `Action`, but we are using it to deal with `SecurityViolationException`. We then invoke the `processActionForward` method ❹ to direct the response to the appropriate `ActionForward`.

All of the information required to handle the exception is defined in the exception tag ❻. The `type` attribute is used to identify the exception to be handled, and the `path` attribute identifies the destination page. The exception handler automatically places an `ActionError` in context using the value declared in the key attribute. The receiving page can use `<html:errors/>` to present an error message to the user.

We tell the `ActionServlet` to use `SecurityRequestProcessor` instead of the default `RequestProcessor` by creating a controller tag with a `processorClass` attribute (listing 7.10).

Roles are registered against the `Action` by adding a `roles` attribute to the `Action` tag nested inside the `<action-mappings>` tag ❺ (listing 7.11).

◆ **Discussion**

The `ActionServlet` intercepts the request in the usual way. However, the `Action-Servlet` employs the `SecurityRequestProcessor` instead of the default `Request-Processor` to process the request. The `RequestProcessor` invokes all the hot spots in the usual way, except that our `SecurityRequestProcessor` hijacks the way `Actions` are authorized. `Action` authorization has been modified to use our own proprietary security mechanism instead of the container. Whenever a security violation is detected, the Struts exception handler is invoked, using a newly minted `SecurityViolationException`. The exception handler determines the appropriate `ActionForward` used for the request response. The user is informed of the security violation because the exception handler automatically creates an `Action-Error`. The menu page picks up the error through the `<html:errors>` tag and renders the error message on to the page. All of the limitations have been addressed! We can use our proprietary security mechanism to authorize our `Actions`, and the user is sent to the menu page to attempt his request once more.

One "gotcha" rears its ugly head. The exception handler handles all exceptions the same, irrespective of their origin. This means that a `SecurityViolation-Exception` originating from the `SecurityRequestProcessor` is treated the same as one originating from the `Action`. If you need to handle these two scenarios differently, then you need to throw a unique exception from `SecurityRequestProcessor`.

This recipe shows you how to override `Action` authorization to provide a clean way of using your own authentication mechanism. It also presents an alternative way to employ declarative exception handling.

◆ **Related**

- 5.4—Use declarative exception handling
- 7.1—Tomcat domain authentication and Struts
- 7.4—Secure an action mapping using the container

◆ **Reference**

■ [CORE] Core J2EE Patterns, Best Practices, and Design Strategies, Controlling Client Access

7.6 Protect areas on a page

◆ **Problem**

You want to protect areas on the page. Some areas on the screen need to be hidden from certain groups of users.

◆ **Background**

Web pages can contain diverse sets of information; you might not want all users to see all information. You want all users to access the page, but you would like to hide certain portions of the page from various types of users. For example, you want to hide employment information from some users, benefit information from another group of users; but make basic information available to all users.

One possible solution is to build a page for each type of user and use the Action to forward the user to the appropriate page for their security role. This might be fine for a small application with a very small number of roles, but it doesn't scale well as the number of roles and areas increase. As the number of pages increases, the maintenance effort quickly becomes unmanageable. A better solution is to create a single page and declare which areas are accessible by which roles. This solution reduces your maintenance effort to a single page.

The Struts Tiles framework provides an easy way to divide your screen into smaller, reusable pieces. Tiles allows you to create a mosaic of tiles which can be assembled into a larger tile. Each tile is declared with a definition tag. You specify accessibility of the tile by adding a role attribute to the definition tag. Only users possessing the appropriate role can see the portion of the screen rendered from a Tiles definition.

To refresh your memory on Tiles basics, we recommend you read recipe 3.12, "Creating a basic Struts Tiles page."

◆ **Recipe**

The first thing we need to do is add roles and user IDs to your container's configuration. See recipe 7.1, "Tomcat domain authentication and Struts," for complete instructions on how to do this.

The next step is to create a web page using Tiles by dividing your page into the areas you want to protect (see listing 7.12).

Listing 7.12 user.jsp using tiles

```
<%@ taglib uri="/WEB-INF/struts-tiles.tld" prefix="tiles" %>
<%@ taglib uri="/WEB-INF/struts-form.tld" prefix="form" %>
<%@ taglib uri="/WEB-INF/struts-bean.tld" prefix="bean" %>
<%@ taglib uri="/WEB-INF/struts-html.tld" prefix="html" %>
<%@ taglib uri="/WEB-INF/struts-logic.tld" prefix="logic" %>

<HTML>
  <HEAD>
    <title><tiles:getAsString name="title"/></title>
  </HEAD>
  <h1><tiles:getAsString name="title"/>: User Information</h1>
  <body>
      <tiles:insert attribute='basic'/>
      <tiles:insert attribute='personal'/>
      <tiles:insert attribute='employment'/>
      <tiles:insert attribute='benefits'/>
      <p>
      <html:link forward="search">search</html:link>
    </body>
</html>
```

Each of these areas becomes a tile. This example illustrates four areas; basic, personal, employment, and benefits. Each of these areas is encapsulated in a tile. In listing 7.13 we create Tile definitions.

Listing 7.13 tiles-def.xml file

```
<!DOCTYPE tiles-definitions PUBLIC
      "-//Apache Software Foundation//DTD Tiles Configuration//EN"
      "http://jakarta.apache.org/struts/dtds/tiles-config.dtd">

<tiles-definitions>
<definition name="site.user" path="/layouts/user.jsp">          ❶
    <put name="title"       value="Protect Area Recipe" />
    <put name="basic"       value="site.basic" />               ❷
    <put name="personal"    value="site.personal" />
    <put name="employment"  value="site.employment" />
    <put name="benefits"    value="site.benefits" />
</definition>

<definition name="site.basic"       path="/tiles/basic.jsp"/>
<definition name="site.personal"    path="/tiles/personal.jsp"/>
<definition name="site.employment"  path="/tiles/employment.jsp"
                                    role="mgr">                  ❸
```

```
<definition name="site.benefits"   path="/tiles/benefits.jsp"
                                    role="hr"/>

</tiles-definitions>
```

In listing 7.13 we declare each tile in the tiles-def.xml file and assemble them into the site.user tile **❶**. The tiles are inserted into the main tile at **❷**. To limit the access to a user role we add a `role` attribute to definition tag **❸**. The absence of a `role` attribute leaves the tile unprotected. That's it! You can easily add or remove roles from the tiles by modifying the definition tag in the tiles-def.xml file.

◆ *Discussion*

The implementation of this recipe is simple and straightforward. First you need to analyze your page to identify the areas you want to protect. Each of these areas is encapsulated in a tile, and a master tile is used to assemble the smaller tiles. Whenever, the master tile is referenced in an `ActionForward`, the user's container defined roles are consulted before rendering the tile to the user.

There is a "gotcha" lurking in the shadows. Notice that the `role` attribute name is "role" and not "roles". This means you cannot provide a comma-delimited list of roles. If you do, Tiles thinks that the comma is part of the role name and access is denied. You can work around this limitation by creating additional roles for the combinations you require. Note that this is not consistent with the `roles` attribute on the `Action` tag in the struts-config.xml file.

There are two limitations worth noting. First, you are restricted to the container security mechanism. Second, you cannot practically limit access to individual fields.

The Tiles framework is instrumental in providing modularity and reuse in the View [MVC], but this recipe shows you how the Tiles definition tag's `role` attribute implements security in a maintainable and robust fashion.

◆ *Related*

- 3.12—Creating a basic Struts tile page
- 3.13—Using Tiles with XML definitions
- 7.1—Tomcat domain authentication
- 7.7—Protect fields

◆ *Reference*

- [MVC] Model-View-Controller

7.7 *Protect fields*

◆ *Problem*

You want to protect individual fields from a group of users. You also want to make some fields private so they are only visible to the user logged on.

◆ *Background*

Circumstances arise in which you need to protect an individual field. Often you want to restrict access to a set of users possessing a security role. One option is to use the approach outlined in recipe 7.6. Using tiles certainly does the job, but it might lead to a plethora of tiles. This recipe will show you a better way to deal with fine-grained protection of fields.

In addition to showing you how to restrict field access to a group of users, we will also show you how to provide private fields. Private fields are only visible to the user logged into the application.

◆ *Recipe*

Add roles and user IDs to your container's configuration. See recipe 7.1 for complete instructions on how to do this.

In listing 7.14 we use the Struts `<logic:present>` tag to restrict access to users possessing the "mgr" role.

Listing 7.14   Restrict access to a group of users

```
<logic:present role="mgr">
   Phone number: <bean:write name="user" property="phoneNumber"/><br>
</logic:present>
```

In listing 7.15 we use the Struts `<logic:present>` tag to restrict access to the user logged on.

Listing 7.15   Private fields restrict access to the user logged on

```
<bean:define id="userName" name="user"      ❶
              property="userId"
              type="java.lang.String"/>

<logic:present user="<%= userName %>">      ❷
   Password: <bean:write name="user" property="password"/><br>
</logic:present>
```

◆ **Discussion**

The code samples in the recipe section present two techniques for protecting individual fields. Listing 7.14 uses the `<logic:present>`tag to ensure only managers can access the phone number field. The present tag `role` attribute consults the container security mechanism to ensure the user viewing the page possesses the "mgr" role. All other users will not see the phone number. The obvious limitation is that you must use the container security mechanism to authenticate the user.

Listing 7.15 presents a technique to limit access to the user currently logged on. The user's name, password, and other information is created by the business tier and encapsulated in a user bean. This bean contains the information we want to display and the name of the user who owns that information. At ❶ we create a scripting variable to hold the owner's user name. Again, as in listing 7.14, we use the `<logic:present>` tag to implement security. This time we use the `user` attribute ❷ to validate that the user name, represented with the `userName` scripting variable, is the same as the user logged on. The `<logic:present>`tag consults the container's security mechanism to determine the name of the user logged on. If the name on the user bean matches the logged on user, the field is presented. Once again, this technique requires that you use the container's security mechanism to authenticate the user.

This recipe demonstrates two new techniques for your security toolbox. Armed with these techniques, you are able to deliver fine-grained security access at the field level.

◆ **Related**

  - 7.1— Tomcat domain authentication and Struts
  - 7.6—Protect areas on a page

◆ **Reference**

  - [CORE] Core J2EE Patterns, Best Practices, and Design Strategies, Controlling Client Access

Advanced recipes

8

Everything should be made as simple as possible, but not simpler.
—Albert Einstein

Many problems encountered by developers require complex solutions. At first glance the solution seems obvious, but implementing it in Struts may seem elusive—at least until someone can point the way. As you progress in your career as a developer, new challenges will always appear, and what might seem self-evident, clear, and concise can suddenly reveal the amazing intricacy of its details.

A complex business-to-consumer (B2C) web application may seem transparent at the beginning of development: a consumer comes to the site, picks out something that he or she wants, and purchases it through a secure mechanism. The site, even though it is involved, seems straightforward in its requirements. You need certain functionalities:

- A home, or "landing" page for each vertical or product channel
- A mechanism to dynamically display each product
- A shopping cart application for tracking the purchases of products
- A mechanism to record and transfer the order for the products to the suppliers
- A method of confirming the order for the products ordered

That would seem to be all there is for the site. Once this functionality is delivered, the site will obviously become a complete success and every member of the company will be on the way to a millionaire lifestyle—well, not really. There are details and dependencies for the above functionalities. Each item needs supporting functionality that may have tertiary dependencies, and so on. At some point a development group, with input from the business managers, will decide on a technology and specific implementation. At that point the complexity and risk is probably the highest.

No technology or implementation is a panacea. All technologies, frameworks, and languages have plusses and minuses. It's where these minuses occur that things can get muddled; this is when other technologies, frameworks, and even languages need to be adapted to the original solution. Simple at first, the details increase in complexity, and Struts isn't immune to this—but its ability to adapt and "plug-in" other technologies makes it an ideal candidate for many business solutions. Let's take a look at the following case study.

Case study—a modern luxury hotel

A modern luxury hotel seems to have functions that are completely well defined through centuries of evolution:

- Provide a selection of luxury rooms for guests.
- Provide amenities for these guests.
- Provide a concierge to facilitate requests from guests.
- Provide a wonderful food and beverage program for guests.
- Provide a method of cleaning rooms on a timely and efficient basis.
- Provide a method for taking care of guests' luggage.
- Provide things for guests to do during their stay.
- Provide a method to find employees.
- Provide an accounting department for receivables and payables.

There may be a few other items here, but the list seems very short. If a company can accomplish the above with success, they will receive a 5-star rating and people will come from all over the world just to stay at this modern luxury hotel. To deliver the above items, there are lots of details with dependencies. With these details new and complex functionalities are revealed:

- How do you feed all the employees? Do they eat at once or in shifts? How do you schedule this and work it into employee schedules so they aren't eating in the first hour that they come to work? What about union rules? You need to have some kind of sophisticated rules engine that allows for all of these parameters. This engine will have to interface with a table of employees, then manipulate this table based upon HR rules and work within the available times posted by the food and beverage groups for feeding employees.

- How do you track your guests? How can you remember that Ms. Finchley always brings her three Pugs and they have special diets? How do you know that it is *worth* remembering this? You must be able to retrieve guest records and history. This may be quite minimal, but frequent or very wealthy guests may have needs that they are more than willing to pay for. You may also want to award perks that are reserved for guests that spend a certain amount of money with the hotel. This being the case, we have the basic requirements for a different rules engine.

- What do you do with all the dirty linens? You need to inventory and track linens, from towels and sheets to the napkins used in the restaurant, not to mention employee uniforms. At some point inventories will decrease and orders should be automatically placed to bring them back to predetermined nominal levels.

- Do you belong to a worldwide hotel chain and need to interface with their reservations system? What about meeting their rules and regulations? How do you deal with their registration system? What communication protocols do they use? Do you need to have things automatically hooked to both CRM and accounting systems?

- What do you do with all the cars in which your hundreds of guests and employees arrive in every day? Often you'll need to bill customers for their parking, but conversely compensate employees parking in a different lot.

- What do you do with seasonal business? Do you hire temp employees? A more sophisticated hotel will have logic built into its HR system to predict when to hire more employees. It might have automatic connections to employment agencies or web sites.

- Who creates and maintains all HR rules for working in front of guests? Who trains new hires? A library of standard operating procedures and HR rules must be developed and maintained.

- What do you do about maintaining all the hard facilities such as plumbing, air conditioning, and electrical? Who fixes all the stuff when a rock band comes and trashes a floor? When something breaks, a purchase order must be generated to buy the new part. Preapproved vendors must have connections to the accounting system to ensure purchases are authorized and to streamline transactions. Maintenance schedules must be created and maintained.

This is a simplified example. What seems like a completely straightforward and not too involved system becomes tied up in details. Dependencies suddenly become complex. Disparate and often far-flung persistence layers may need to "talk" to each other seamlessly. Rules engines may need to be defined and built to handle tasks that, while not obvious in the beginning, will create large savings or even generate profit. Functionalities that were never envisioned become extremely important.

Let's revisit our B2C web application

A modern B2C web application has many details that become obvious as development continues. As these requirements are defined by business development personnel, an ordered list can be created. Here are examples of additional functionality that a successful consumer-oriented web application might need to remain competitive:

- Functionality needs to be available to recognize returning users.
- Connections to the data layer must be secure and pooled.

- The application must allow for users' entry from sites that are trading partners. You don't want to show competing products when a user is sent to you from a particular partner.

- Support for testing new and different GUIs, flows, and products need to be available to the site's marketing team. A certain number of users may be directed to a parallel grouping of pages to see a form with different input fields, to test whether or not they would be more or less likely to complete it.

- As the site expands, a complete and automatic system must be in place to transfer information, orders, and other metrics to trading partners, completely working within their protocols.

- Disaster recovery, real-time monitoring, and redundancy need to be addressed.

- Standards must be in place to manage marketing, architecture, change, and fixes throughout the system, which involves the "clashing" of sometimes hundreds of engineers and marketing persons (very different thinking!)

There are hundreds of underlying functions in a modern B2C site. From special deals that may be short lived or available only to special customers, to managing customer reviews, surveys and marketing emails—having increased and vital functionality reveals deeper layers of requirements that must be met to realize a prosperous future.

Struts can never hope to deliver all the functionality that you need for every situation, but many times there are other technologies available that can meld into this framework. Other times, you might simply need to extend one of the existing Struts packages to meet your needs.

The recipes within this chapter show solutions to both the obvious and obtuse, and provide a path and framework that, it is hoped, will solve some issues that you as a developer may encounter as you create larger and more complex Struts-related applications.

8.1 Caching using a Struts plug-in

◆ Problem

You want to increase performance by caching application resources.

◆ *Background*

Caching application resources is one of the most common ways to improve application performance. There are a number of strategies to achieve this, but one of the techniques available to the Struts developer is the plug-in interface.

A plug-in is a Java class, which implements the `org.apache.struts.action.PlugIn` interface, and is registered with the `ActionServlet` using the struts-config. xml file. The `ActionServlet` invokes all registered plug-ins when the `ActionServlet` is loaded, and once again when `ActionServlet` is unloaded by the servlet engine. A plug-in is most often used to acquire and release resources on these events.

As we will see in this recipe, utilizing the plug-in interface requires only two steps; implementing the `org.apache.struts.action.PlugIn` interface and registering the plug-in implementation with the `ActionServlet`. Performing those two simple steps allows you to load and cache resources when the `ActionServlet` processes the plug-in.

A clear understanding of the `ActionServlet` interaction with plug-ins equips you with the knowledge to effectively manage common resources. The key to understanding the life cycle of plug-ins lies in the fact that the plug-in life cycle shadows that of the `ActionServlet`. As you will see in the Discussion section, a couple of "gotchas" are related to `Servlet` life cycle.

SERVLET LIFE CYCLE Typical of all servlets, the `ActionServlet` has three states. The first state is the initialization state. When the servlet engine loads a servlet, it is obligated to call the servlet's `init(ServletConfig)` method. This method provides the servlet with the opportunity to perform any initialization work required, including loading and caching of servlet resources. The servlet remains in memory and becomes available to service client requests. The second state is the service state. Client requests are serviced by the `service()` method. Whenever the client requests servicing, the servlet engine invokes the `service()` method on the in-memory servlet. The service method has access to any of the resources cached during the invocation of the `init()` method. HTTP servlets generally use the `javax.servlet.http.HttpServlet` class to automatically invoke `doPost` and `doGet` whenever those HTTP methods are received. The third state is the destroy state. The servlet engine, upon its discretion, removes the servlet from memory. The servlet specification demands that the `destroy()` method be called just prior to removing the servlet from memory. The `destroy()` method provides the servlet with the opportunity to remove any of the resources cached during its lifetime.

The ActionServlet uses init(ServletConfig), service(ServletRequest req, ServletResponse res), and destroy() to manage its own resources. The init(ServletConfig) method is used to convert the struts-config.xml file into Java object representations of all Struts configurations, including plug-ins. More importantly, from the perspective of this recipe, the ActionServlet init(ServletConfig) method instantiates plug-in implementations, populates any properties on the plug-in, and invokes init() on the plug-in interface. The ActionServlet finds all the information it needs by accessing the plug-in configuration object. This provides the plug-in implementation with the opportunity to load resources and makes them available in the application context.

When the ActionServlet is removed from memory by the servlet engine, the ActionServlet destroy() invokes the plug-in destroy() method which provides the plug-in with the opportunity to remove cached resources.

◆ *Recipe*

As stated earlier, only two steps are required to implement a plug-in. The first step is to implement the org.apache.struts.action.PlugIn interface. The second step is to register it with the ActionServlet and set any properties using the struts-config.xml file.

Let's explore this recipe by stepping through an example. In this example we present a page of the most populated cities in the United States. To increase performance we use a plug-in to cache a list of CityStatistic objects in the servlet context. The plug-in obtains the CityStatistic objects by invoking the business layer. The number of cached CityStatistic objects is defined dynamically by using a plug-in parameter. Once in memory, JSPs have access to the list of cities to render the page without incurring the cost of accessing the business layer.

Before getting started let's have a look at the plug-in interface, as shown in listing 8.1.

Listing 8.1 The PlugIn interface

```java
public interface PlugIn {

    // Receive notification that our owning module
    // is being shut down
    public void destroy();

    // Receive notification that the specified module
    // is being started up
```

```
public void init(ActionServlet servlet, ModuleConfig config)
        throws ServletException;
}
```

Notice that the init method takes in the ActionServlet and ModuleConfig as arguments. Struts allows you to create plug-ins for individual modules. This allows you to ensure your plug-ins are as modular as the rest of your application.

Now, let's have a look at the implementation of the PlugIn interface (listing 8.2).

Listing 8.2   A PlugIn implementation

```
package com.strutsrecipes.plugin.plugins;

import java.util.List;
import javax.servlet.ServletException;

import org.apache.struts.action.ActionServlet;
import org.apache.struts.action.PlugIn;
import org.apache.struts.config.ModuleConfig;

import com.strutsrecipes.plugin.business.BusinessFacade;

public class ApplicationPlugIn implements PlugIn {
    private int count = 0;
    private String keyName = null;
    private List cities = null;

    public ApplicationPlugIn() {
        super();
    }

    public void setCount(int count) {
        this.count = count;
    }

    public void setKeyName(String keyName) {
        this.keyName = keyName;
    }

    public void destroy() {
    }

    public void init(ActionServlet servlet, ModuleConfig config)
        throws ServletException {
        BusinessFacade businessFacade = new BusinessFacade();
        cities = businessFacade.getMostPopulatedCities(count);
        servlet.getServletContext().setAttribute(keyName, cities);
    }
}
```

The last step is to register the plug-in with the `ActionServlet` by adding the plug-in tag in the struts-config.xml file, as shown in listing 8.3.

Listing 8.3   The plug-in element

```
<plug-in className="com.strutsrecipes.plugin.plugins.ApplicationPlugIn">
    <set-property property="keyName" value="citystats"/>
    <set-property property="count" value="35"/>
</plug-in>
```

Your JSP can access the list of cities in the usual way (listing 8.4).

Listing 8.4   Accessing the list of cities

```
<table>
<logic:iterate id="row" name="citystats">
   <tr>
   <td><bean:write name="row" property="name"/></td>
   <td><bean:write name="row" property="population2000"/></td>
   <td><bean:write name="row" property="population1990"/></td>
   <td><bean:write name="row" property="numberChange1990To2000"/></td>
   <td><bean:write name="row" property="percentChange1990To2000"/></td>
   <td><bean:write name="row" property="rank1990"/></td>
   <td><bean:write name="row" property="rank2000"/></td>
   </tr>
</logic:iterate>
</table>
```

◆ Discussion

Let's step through all the pieces to see how they interact during the sequence of events. When the `ActionServlet` is loaded by the servlet engine, it processes the struts-config.xml file to create Struts configuration object representations, including plug-ins. Prior to accepting any requests, the `ActionServlet` uses reflection to instantiate the class specified in the `className` attribute. It then calls the setters identified by the `set-property` tag's property attribute using the value specified in the value attribute. The plug-in has these properties at its disposal when `init` and `destroy` are invoked. Because plug-in properties are considered immutable, only setters are implemented. The `init` method invokes the business layer to obtain the list of cities and places them in the servlet context under the desired key.

Using plug-ins is an effective way to cache common resources with Struts. However, understanding the relationship between the plug-in and the `Action-Servlet` surfaces a couple of "gotchas."

The servlet engine retains the `ActionServlet` in memory to reduce the overhead of creating a new `ActionServlet` on each request. Whenever a new request is received, the servlet engine relays the request to the same instance of the `Action-Servlet`. This means that multiple requests have concurrent access to resources stored as instance and class variables. If you have placed references to these objects in context, then you have compounded the opportunity for these objects to be unknowingly modified.

You have a couple of remedies at your disposal. One solution is to limit access to read-only and protect yourself by making the objects "immutable" [Bloch], or by making a "defensive copy" [Bloch]. Another solution is to prudently synchronize your code, or use a synchronized collection such as `Vector`, to regulate access to the areas of the code you want to protect. The best approach is to consider cached resources as read-only objects.

Another "gotcha" reveals itself when one considers that the plug-in `destroy()` method may not execute. A server crash may bring down the servlet engine, but leave the JVM up. This condition will bypass the call to the `ActionServlet` `destroy()` method. Because the `ActionServlet` `destroy()` method calls the plug-in `destroy()` method, any cached resources that cannot be purged by the garbage collector remain in memory.

**BEST
PRACTICE** *Consolidate resource references*—A good practice is to encapsulate resource references into a single object before storing it in context. This minimizes, but does not eliminate, the chances of plug-ins clobbering one another. The same thing can be achieved by implementing and enforcing a servlet context attribute key-naming convention. This is a good practice to follow when you are placing many objects in context.

One important recognized limitation of this recipe is its inability to refresh static data once it has been cached. The servlet engine must be brought down and restarted to force the plug-in to repopulate the cache.

Plug-ins can be used to cache files, XSL stylesheets, database connections, JMS connections, EJB home interfaces, and many other types of resources. Plug-ins provide the capability to cache resources, but does not pool resources. Pooling of resources allows the same resource to be shared among one or more applications. Plug-ins provide a means to cache a resource for your web application. Your own architectural needs help you determine the appropriateness of a caching solution.

Plug-ins are currently being employed by the Validator and Tiles and have proven to be an effective way to cache resources. By reducing the cost of creating and recovering expensive objects, you can boost your performance.

◆ *Reference*

- [BLOCH] *Effective Java Programming Language Guide,* Item 13: Favor immutability, and Item 24: Make defensive copies when needed.
- [JSBE] *Java Servlets by Example*
- [JSR000154] JSR-000154 Java Servlet 2.4 Specification
- [SOS] Story of a Servlet: An Instant Tutorial

8.2 *Use the Tiles controller*

◆ *Problem*

You want to use the Tiles controller to preprocess information.

◆ *Background*

The Tiles controller allows you to intercept the "View" process just before the tile is processed. This allows you to modify and augment data enroute. You can think of the Tiles controller as a preprocessing hook just before a tile is rendered.

The Tiles controller is triggered by associating the Tiles controller to a Tiles definition in the tiles-defs.xml file. Whenever that Tiles definition is accessed, the controller executes. You can do whatever you like in the controller, but normally you massage the data in some way. You can also create new data and place it in the Tiles context under an attribute name of your choosing.

There are two types of Tiles controllers: `Class` and `Action`. Both types work equally well; we will discuss the pros and cons of each type in the discussion section.

◆ *Recipe*

We explore both types of controllers by intercepting a list of announcement messages in the request context and prune off those announcements which are not deemed "important" before the `.header` tile is rendered.

There are only two steps required to use a `Class` Tiles controller. First, you must create the controller class and second you must associate it with a tile definition. Let's see how this is done by looking at the `.header` definition in listing 8.5.

Class Tiles controller

There are two ways to create `Class` type controllers. You can either implement the `org.apache.struts.tiles.Controller` interface, or you can extend the `org.apache.struts.tiles.ControllerSupport` class. The `ControllerSupport` class is nothing more than an empty implementation of the `Controller` interface. Registering the controller with the tile definition is easy to do. Let's see how it is done by looking at listing 8.5.

Listing 8.5   Definition tag using `controllerClass` attribute in tiles-def.xml

```
    <definition name=".header"
                path="/tiles/myheader.jsp"
    controllerClass="com.strutsrecipes.tilesctrl.controller.
                     AnnouncementTilesController">     ❶
    </definition>
```

In listing 8.5, at ❶ we define a `controllerClass` attribute on the definition tag and specify the fully qualified name of our `Controller` class in the attribute's value.

Let's have a look at the `AnnouncementTilesController` class in listing 8.6 to see the controller in action.

Listing 8.6   `AnnouncementTilesController` Tiles controller class

```
package com.strutsrecipes.tilesctrl.controller;

import java.io.IOException;
import java.util.Iterator;
import java.util.List;

import javax.servlet.ServletContext;
import javax.servlet.ServletException;
import javax.servlet.http.HttpServletRequest;
import javax.servlet.http.HttpServletResponse;

import org.apache.struts.tiles.ComponentContext;
import org.apache.struts.tiles.Controller;

public class AnnouncementTilesController implements Controller {

    public void perform(
        ComponentContext tileContext,        ❶
        HttpServletRequest request,
        HttpServletResponse response,
        ServletContext servletContext)
        throws ServletException, IOException {
```

```
        List announcements = (List) request.getAttribute("announcements");    ❷

        Iterator i = announcements.iterator();
        while (i.hasNext()) {
           String announcement = (String) i.next();
           if (announcement.toLowerCase().indexOf("important") == -1) {        ❸
              i.remove();
           }
        }

        tileContext.putAttribute("title", "important announcements");          ❹

      }
   }
```

The `AnnouncementTilesController` class in listing 8.6 implements the controller interface by defining a single `perform` method. Although it is not required to do so, the signature of the `perform` method closely resembles its deprecated cousin in the `Action` class, with one noticeable difference. The `perform` method signature accepts a reference to the tile's context by receiving a reference to `Component-Context` ❶. The data placed in the `ComponentContext` allows us to pass information to the tile. Stepping through the rest of the `perform` method, we obtain a reference to the list of announcements from the request object ❷, and then we massage the list of announcements by removing any announcement not embedded with the `important` literal ❸. Finally, we create a `String` in the tile's context under the `title` key ❹.

Listing 8.7 shows you how to achieve the same effect by extending the `Control-ler-Support` class instead of implementing the `Controller` interface.

Listing 8.7 `AnnouncementTilesControllerSupport` **Tiles controller class**

```
package com.strutsrecipes.tilesctrl.controller;

import java.io.IOException;
import java.util.Iterator;
import java.util.List;

import javax.servlet.ServletContext;
import javax.servlet.ServletException;
import javax.servlet.http.HttpServletRequest;
import javax.servlet.http.HttpServletResponse;

import org.apache.struts.tiles.ComponentContext;
import org.apache.struts.tiles.ControllerSupport;
```

```
public class AnnouncementTilesControllerSupport extends ControllerSupport {

    public void perform(
        ComponentContext tileContext,
        HttpServletRequest request,
        HttpServletResponse response,
        ServletContext servletContext)
        throws ServletException, IOException {

        List announcements = (List) request.getAttribute("announcements");

        Iterator i = announcements.iterator();
        while (i.hasNext()) {
            String announcement = (String) i.next();
            if (announcement.toLowerCase().indexOf("important") == -1) {
                i.remove();
            }
        }

        tileContext.putAttribute("title", "important announcements");

    }

}
```

AnnouncementTilesControllerSupport and AnnouncementTilesController in listing 8.7 can be used interchangeably.

In listing 8.8 we present the JSP used to access the list of important announcements.

Listing 8.8   myheader.jsp

```
<%@ taglib uri="/tags/struts-bean"   prefix="bean" %>
<%@ taglib uri="/tags/struts-logic"  prefix="logic" %>
<%@ taglib uri="/tags/struts-tiles"  prefix="tiles" %>
<%@ taglib uri="/tags/struts-html"   prefix="html" %>

<h3><tiles:getAsString name="title"/></h3>        ❶

<logic:iterate id="row" name="announcements">
    <bean:write name="row"/><br>                  ❷
</logic:iterate>
```

Data is retrieved in the usual way.

❶ Access the `title` String from the tile's context.

❷ Iterate over the announcements. The controller has trimmed the list to just the announcements containing the String `important`.

Action Tiles controller

Let's look at the second way of creating a Tiles controller. There are three steps required to create an `Action` Tiles controller. In addition to creating the controller class and associating it with a definition tile, you must register the `Action` Tiles controller in the struts-config.xml file. In listing 8.9 we see how to configure the tiles-def.xml file.

Listing 8.9 Definition tag using `controllerUrl` attribute in tiles-def.xml

```
<definition name=".footer"
            path="/tiles/myfooter.jsp"
            controllerUrl="/QuoteAction.do">
</definition>
```

The Tiles controller is declared in the tiles-defs.xml file in much the same way as a `Class` Tiles controller, except that we use a `controllerUrl` attribute on the definition tags instead of `controllerClass` (see listing 8.9).

A controller is created by extending `org.apache.struts.tiles.actions.Tiles-Action`. A `TilesAction` behaves just like any other Struts `Action`, except that it has a reference to the tile's context. Any data placed in the tile's context is available to the tile. The subclass of the `TilesAction` must be registered as an action-mapping in the struts-config.xml file in the usual way. In listing 8.10 we present an `Action` Tiles controller.

Listing 8.10 `QuoteTilesControllerAction` Action Tiles controller

```
import java.util.List;

import javax.servlet.http.HttpServletRequest;
import javax.servlet.http.HttpServletResponse;

import org.apache.struts.action.ActionForm;
import org.apache.struts.action.ActionForward;
import org.apache.struts.action.ActionMapping;
import org.apache.struts.tiles.ComponentContext;
import org.apache.struts.tiles.actions.TilesAction;

public final class AnnouncementTilesControllerAction extends TilesAction {
```

```
public ActionForward execute(
    ComponentContext tileContext,        ❶
    ActionMapping mapping,
    ActionForm form,
    HttpServletRequest request,
    HttpServletResponse response)
    throws Exception {

    List announcements = (List) request.getAttribute("announcements");

    Iterator i = announcements.iterator();
    while (i.hasNext()) {();
        String announcement = (String) i.next();
        if (announcement.toLowerCase().indexOf("important") == -1) {    ❷
            i.remove();
        }
    }

    tileContext.putAttribute("title", "important announcements");

    return null;  | ❸
    }
}
```

Listing 8.10 presents the Action type Tiles controller equivalent to the Class type Tiles controllers in listings 8.6 and 8.7. This Action is identical to a typical Action except it extends TilesAction, receives a ComponentContext argument ❶ in the execute method, and returns a null ActionForward ❸. The code at ❷ is identical to listings 8.6 and 8.7.

Because Tiles attempts to invoke the Action, we need to define it in the struts-config.xml file, as shown in listing 8.11.

Listing 8.11   struts-config.xml

```
<action path="/QuoteAction"
        type="com.strutsrecipes.tilesctrl.controller.
                QuoteTilesControllerAction"/>
```

In listing 8.11 we present the action-mapping in the struts-config.xml file. Notice the value of the controllerUrl attribute in listing 8.9 matches the value of the path attribute in listing 8.11. The myheader.jsp JSP doesn't care which type of controller is used. Therefore, the myheader.jsp in listing 8.8 works well with this Action Tiles Controller.

◆ *Discussion*

Both `Class` and `Action` Tiles controller types work equally well. Which one you use is largely a matter of personal preference. However, `Action` Tiles controllers allow you to chain controllers together.

The `Class` type Tiles controllers offers an implementation choice. You can either implement the `Controller` interface or extend the `ControllerSupport` class. Which one should you use? Interfaces make it difficult to add new features. An upgrade to Tiles controller functionality may cause you to implement new methods to meet the contract dictated by the `Controller` interface, or may deny you access to new features. This means you might need to make a code change when upgrading to a new release. It is more likely that the Struts development team will use the `ControllerSupport` as an adapter, providing you with backwards compatibility and the ability to take advantage of new Tiles controller features. It also means you won't be forced to make a code change. Therefore, we recommend you extend `ControllerSupport`, instead of implementing the `Controller` interface.

Tiles controllers allow you to intercept processing at a point in time. What you do at that point in time is up to you. However, this doesn't mean you can throw caution to the wind. For example, accessing the business layer within the Tiles controller is probably not a good idea. The business layer may need to undertake the expense of establishing database connections, issuing remote calls or other resource-expensive activities on each request. A well-known architectural best practice is to minimize the number of fine-grain calls to the business layer by adopting fewer coarse-grain calls [CORE]. Using Tiles controllers to access the business layer may result in multiple fine-grain calls. You need to consider the possible performance consequences of making multiple fine-grain calls instead of fewer course-grain ones.

As a rule of thumb, Tiles controllers should be considered when: (1) you are committed to Tiles, (2) you expect the functionality to be coupled to the tile, and (3) you don't have to worry about performance problems caused by accessing the business layer multiple times.

◆ *Related*

- 3.13—Using Tiles with XML definitions

◆ *Reference*

- [CORE] Core J2EE Patterns, Best Practices, and Design Strategies
- [TILECEDRIC] Cedric Dumoulin's Tiles Library Documentation

8.3 *Generate a response with XSL*

◆ *Problem*

You want to generate a page using XSL.

◆ *Background*

There is more than one way to skin a catfish, and even more ways to generate an HTTP response. Some organizations are making information available in XML format. Indeed, your business tier may be doing just that. In those cases, XSLT allows you to transform XML into an HTML page.

XSLT is used for more than just creating HTML pages. We tend to be myopic when we think about HTTP requests. An HTTP request can return any variation of XML, not just HTML. In fact, we can use HTTP to transfer data in XML format. The job of transmitting XML is not solely the domain of Web services. Ordinary HTTP requests can return XML to browsers, servlets, and a variety of other clients. In those instances, we can use XSLT to manipulate and massage XML into the form expected by clients. Struts is up to the task of delivering XML.

Let's cover some terminology and concepts. XML Stylesheet Language (XSL) is composed of three parts. XSL-FO, XSLT, and XPath. Only XSLT and XPath are relevant to this recipe, but you can read up on XSL-FO using the reference provided at the end of the recipe [XSLFO]. The XML Stylesheet Language for Transformation (XSLT) characterizes a way of converting one XML structure to another. XSLT transforms XML at selected points in the source XML to some target format. XPath is the syntax used to identify those points. A stylesheet is a grouping of XSLT commands used to transform XML from one structure to another. To transform an XML structure, you invoke an XSLT transformation processor with XML and the XSL stylesheet. The processor churns out XML in the desired format. There is a variety of XSLT transformation tools available, but your choice will depend on the job at hand [XMLPERF].

In this recipe we show you how to use Java, Struts, XML, and XSLT to generate an HTTP response.

◆ *Recipe*

Before you get started you are going to need an XSLT processor. We recommend Xalan [XALAN] http://xml.apache.org/xalan-j/. Some versions of Tomcat have an XSLT processor already bundled inside, so there is no need to place anything inside the lib folder. Check with Tomcat documentation to determine if you need to add an XSLT processor to the lib folder.

Most Struts `Actions` return an `ActionForward` to the controller. The controller delegates the responsibility for generating the response to a JSP, a Velocity template, or whatever you are using on your project. We are going to mimic the approach taken in recipe 8.4, "Generate a PDF." Instead of returning an `Action-Forward`, our `Action` is going to take responsibility for generating the entire response by writing to the `HttpServletResponse` directly. We don't use a JSP at all! The reasoning for this decision can be found in the discussion section of recipe 8.4. As there is quite a bit of synergy between this recipe and recipe 8.4, we encourage you to read them both.

Listing 8.12 Base `Action`

```
package com.strutsrecipes.pdf.actions;

import java.util.List;
import javax.servlet.http.HttpServletRequest;
import javax.servlet.http.HttpServletResponse;

import org.apache.struts.action.Action;
import org.apache.struts.action.ActionForm;
import org.apache.struts.action.ActionForward;
import org.apache.struts.action.ActionMapping;

import com.strutsrecipes.pdf.business.BusinessFacade;

public abstract class BaseQuoteAction extends Action {

    public ActionForward execute(
        ActionMapping mapping,
        ActionForm form,
        HttpServletRequest request,
        HttpServletResponse response)
        throws Exception {

        BusinessFacade businessFacade = new BusinessFacade();
        List quotes = businessFacade.getQuotes();
        return createResponse(quotes, response);
    }

    protected abstract ActionForward createResponse(          ❶
        List quotes,
        HttpServletResponse response)
        throws Exception;
    {

    }
}
```

In listing 8.12 we create an abstract class to encapsulate our business logic. The BaseQuoteAction invokes the business façade to obtain a list of quotes, and delegates the responsibility of the response to the abstract createResponse method ❶. Factoring out the business logic into an abstract class allows us to reuse business logic whenever we need to implement another Action to support a different media type.

Listing 8.13 XSLQuoteAction concrete Action

```
package com.strutsrecipes.xsl.actions;

import java.io.ByteArrayInputStream;
import java.io.ByteArrayOutputStream;

import java.io.InputStream;
import java.util.Iterator;
import java.util.List;

import javax.servlet.ServletOutputStream;
import javax.servlet.http.HttpServletResponse;
import javax.xml.transform.Transformer;
import javax.xml.transform.TransformerConfigurationException;
import javax.xml.transform.TransformerException;
import javax.xml.transform.TransformerFactory;
import javax.xml.transform.stream.StreamResult;
import javax.xml.transform.stream.StreamSource;

import org.apache.struts.action.ActionForward;

import com.strutsrecipes.xsl.beans.Quote;

public class XSLQuoteAction extends BaseQuoteAction {
    private static final String XSL_FILE = "quotes.xsl";

    protected ActionForward createResponse(
        List quotes,
        HttpServletResponse response)
        throws Exception {

        StringBuffer sb = new StringBuffer();
        sb.append("<quotes>");

        Iterator i = quotes.iterator();
        while (i.hasNext()) {
            Quote quote = (Quote) i.next();
            sb.append("<quote>");
            sb.append(quote.getQuote());
            sb.append("</quote>");
        }

        sb.append("</quotes>");
```

❶

```
    ByteArrayInputStream bais =
        new ByteArrayInputStream(sb.toString().getBytes());     ❷
     StreamSource source = new StreamSource(bais);

    ByteArrayOutputStream baos = new ByteArrayOutputStream();
    StreamResult result = new StreamResult(baos);     ❸

    try {
      InputStream inputStream =
       this.getClass().getClassLoader().getResourceAsStream(XSL_FILE);     ❹
       TransformerFactory factory = TransformerFactory.newInstance();     ❺
       Transformer transformer =
           factory.newTransformer(new StreamSource(inputStream));     ❻
       transformer.transform(source, result);     ❼

    } catch (TransformerConfigurationException e) {
       throw new Exception(e);
    } catch (TransformerException e) {
       throw new Exception(e)[1];
    }

    response.setContentType("text/html");     ❽
    response.setContentLength(baos.size());     ❾
    ServletOutputStream stream = response.getOutputStream();
    baos.writeTo(stream);     ❿
    stream.flush();     ⓫

    return null;     ⓬
  }
}
```

In listing 8.13 we create the XSLQuoteAction concrete class by extending the abstract BaseQuoteAction class. We are required to implement the create-Response method to generate our response. XSLQuoteAction is fully equipped to use XSL to generate HTML.

Let's run through the code in listing 8.13 to see how this is done.

In ❶ we build our XML by iterating over the list of Quote beans. Converting JavaBeans to XML can be done using any one of a number of tools including Castor [CASTOR] and JAXB [JAXB], but we have elected to keep things simple. We have employed a loop to concatenate <quote> tags enclosed in a single <quotes> tag. In ❷ we create an input stream to hold our XML. We then create an output stream to hold our target XML ❸. Now, we need an XSL stylesheet. Recall that the

---

[1] Chained exceptions are introduced in JDK 1.4. You can create your own chained exception when using earlier JDK versions.

stylesheet contains XSLT commands used to transform source XML to target XML. In this case, our target XML is an HTML page. Let's keep moving through listing 8.13 and defer discussion of the stylesheet itself. See "How XSL Works" in this recipe callout box.

Next, we load the stylesheet using the class loader ❹. This technique allows you to place the stylesheet anywhere in your class path. We use a constant to define the file name, but you might want to place the file name in a properties file for maintainability purposes. The Transformer is the workhorse used to do the actual XML transformation. We use a factory to obtain an XSLT transformer, but first we need to obtain the factory.

We create a `TransformerFactory` ❺, and we use the factory to manufacture a `Transformer` ❻. Then we transform the source XML to the target XML ❼. At this point in time the `ByteArrayOutputStream` created at ❸ contains the target XML. Now that we have the HTML, it's time to write it out to the response ❽. First we need to set the response `ContentType` to "text/html" to tell the browser the kind of file it is going to receive. We also need to tell the browser the size of the file by setting the `ContentLength` ❾. The last step is to write the file to the response output stream ❿ and flush the buffer ⓫. Because we have taken care of the response, we return null to the controller to indicate that it does not need to forward a response ⓬.

Listing 8.14 shows the generated XML/HTML.

Listing 8.14 Target XML file

```
<html>
<h1>Albert Einstein Quotes</h1>
<ol>
<li>I want to know God's thoughts... the rest are details.</li>
<li>Anyone who has never made a mistake has never tried anything new.</li>
<li>The most beautiful thing we can experience is the mysterious.
    It is the   source of all true art and science.</li>
<li> Everything should be made as simple as possible, but not simpler.</li>
<li>I am enough of an artist to draw freely upon my imagination.
    Imagination is more important than knowledge. Knowledge is limited.
    Imagination encircles the world.</li>
<li>Common sense is the collection of prejudices acquired by age 18.</li>
<li>Do not worry about your problems with mathematics, I assure you mine
    are far greater.</li>
<li>Gravitation can not be held responsible for people falling in love.</li>
<li>Reality is merely an illusion, albeit a very persistent one.</li>
<li>The only reason for time is so that everything doesn't happen at
    once.</li>
</ol>
</html>
```

Listing 8.15   Stylesheet

```
<xsl:stylesheet xmlns:xsl="http://www.w3.org/1999/XSL/Transform"
    version="1.0">
    <xsl:template match="/">  ❶
        <html>
            <h1>Albert Einstein Quotes</h1>
                <ol>
                    <xsl:apply-templates />  ❷
                </ol>
        </html>
    </xsl:template>
    <xsl:template match="quotes/quote">  ❸
        <li><xsl:value-of select="." /></li>  ❹
    </xsl:template>
</xsl:stylesheet>
```

HOW XSL WORKS IN THIS RECIPE   To complete our discussion, we need to turn our attention to the stylesheet in listing 8.15. The stylesheet is very simple, but still gives us a little insight into what it can do. Despite its relatively compact vocabulary [XSLTSPEC], XSLT is surprisingly agile at transforming XML.

A complete review of XSLT is beyond the scope of this recipe, but we'll cover this small slice as an illustration. The XSLT transformer parses the source XML tree from top to bottom and left to right. As it parses you can trap an event by specifying an `<xsl:template match="/">` tag. You declare the XML node you want to trap by specifying a `match` attribute. The `match="/"` attribute matches the root, regardless of the root's tag name. When a match is found, the XSLT transformation processor executes all the commands under the `<xsl:template>` tag, until it meets the closing tag. If the tag does not belong to the XSL namespace, it simply writes it out to the target. At ❶ in listing 8.15, we write out the `<html>` tag followed by an `<h1>` tag and an ordered list. If the XSLT transformation processor meets a tag from the XSL namespace, it processes the tags between the open and closing `<xsl:template>` tag as XSLT. Notice that between the `<ol>` tags there is an `<xsl:apply-templates/>` tag ❷. When the XSLT transformation processor meets this tag, it tries to match the remaining XML document against other `<xsl:template>` tags. In this case it matches `<xsl:template match="quotes/quote">`. In our XML structure the root tag `<quotes>` encloses `<quote>` tags. The `match` attribute ❸ specifies the "path" to match. At ❸ it matches any `<quote>` tag directly under a root tag called `<quotes>`. Each time it finds a match, it executes that template. At ❹ we extract the value of the current node and wrap it with a `<li>` tag. Listing 8.14 shows the target XML/HTML.

◆ *Discussion*

In this recipe we introduced you to XML transformations. We showed you how to use Java, Struts, XML, and XSLT to generate an HTTP response without using a JSP. While it's entirely possible to generate XML using XSLT in a JSP, it binds us to JSP technology. The best use of an MVC architecture is one that allows us to migrate to a new "View" technology with minimal effort. If you are strongly committed to JSP, or it's the best way to expedite your project, then you may need to waver from MVC purity. Regardless of your approach, this recipe is one example of how you can achieve XML transformations with Struts.

◆ *Related*

- 8.4—Generate a PDF recipe

◆ *Reference*

- [CASTOR] Castor
- [JAXB] JAXB
- [XALAN] Xalan
- [XMLPERF] XML Performance Benchmarks
- [XMLSPEC] XML Specification
- [XSLFO] XSL-FO Specification
- [XSLTSPEC] XSLT Specification

8.4 *Generate a PDF*

◆ *Problem*

You want to generate a PDF.

◆ *Background*

HTML is undoubtedly the ubiquitous document standard, but it does have its limitations. Often, content authors must resign themselves to the browser's inability to render the document as intended. Skilled HTML designers can work magic, but the browser's limitations can be an uphill battle. Things only get worse when you factor in the disparate and nonstandard support among browsers. Creating professional looking documents in HTML is a challenge.

Portable Document Format (PDF) [PDFRM] has become a popular choice for delivering professional looking documents. PDF technology was created by Adobe

[ADOBE] in 1993 to electronically distribute information while faithfully maintaining the integrity of the intended look and feel. Unlike HTML, internal PDF format is unintelligible to the human eye, but PDF browsers do a wonderful job of translating content into beautifully rendered documents. Fortunately, PDF browsers are widely available by downloading a free PDF browser from Adobe.

Using PDF, content authors are able to create professional looking documents with headers, footers, watermarks, searching capabilities, security, and much more. Originally PDFs could only be created using the Adobe creation software, but recently a number of alternative technologies have emerged to create PDFs programmatically. One of the best programmatic tools to enter this arena is an open source project called iText [ITEXT]. iText is currently available under MPL and LGPL license agreements, which means that you can download and use it for free, but you should consult their web site to get the details. If iText doesn't meet your fancy, there is an array of tools which may be more to your liking.

In this recipe we show you how to create PDF documents programmatically using Java and Struts. We'll show you how to do it in such a way that you can switch from PDF to another View technology without design mayhem.

◆ *Recipe*

In this recipe we will create a simple PDF document to list famous Einstein quotes. Let's get started by downloading the iText JAR file from http://www.lowagie.com/iText, then dropping the JAR into the WEB-INF/lib folder. In order to view your PDF creation you need a PDF browser. If you have not already done so, download it from Adobe http://www.adobe.com.

Generally, Struts applications use the `Action` to access the business layer, then pass the controller an `ActionForward` to target a response. The controller's job is to issue a call to a JSP, a Velocity template, or whatever you are using on your project. I'm sure this is a strategy you are quite comfortable with. This time, we are going to do things a bit differently. The PDF document is created and sent directly to the response from the `Action`. No JSP is used to generate a response. This is likely atypical of most of the Struts applications you have seen. Although it is possible to generate a PDF from a JSP, we have elected to do it from the `Action`. We'll defer our reasoning for that decision to the discussion section.

Listing 8.16 Base `Action`

```
com.strutsrecipes.pdf.actions;

import java.util.List;
```

```
import javax.servlet.http.HttpServletRequest;
import javax.servlet.http.HttpServletResponse;

import org.apache.struts.action.Action;
import org.apache.struts.action.ActionForm;
import org.apache.struts.action.ActionForward;
import org.apache.struts.action.ActionMapping;

import com.strutsrecipes.pdf.business.BusinessFacade;

public abstract class BaseQuoteAction extends Action {

    public ActionForward execute(
        ActionMapping mapping,
        ActionForm form,
        HttpServletRequest request,
        HttpServletResponse response)
        throws Exception {

        BusinessFacade businessFacade = new BusinessFacade();
        List quotes = businessFacade.getQuotes();
        return createResponse(quotes, response);
    }

    protected abstract ActionForward createResponse(    ❶
        List quotes,
        HttpServletResponse response)
        throws Exception;
    {

    }
}
```

In listing 8.16 we create an abstract class to encapsulate our business logic. The class `BaseQuoteAction` invokes the business façade to obtain a list of quotes and delegates the responsibility of the response to the abstract `createResponse` method ❶. Although it is not pertinent to creating a PDF using Struts, we use the discussion section to explore the use of an abstract class as a means to increase reuse and maintainability.

Listing 8.17 Concrete `Action`

```
package com.strutsrecipes.pdf.actions;

import java.io.ByteArrayOutputStream;
import java.util.Iterator;
import java.util.List;
```

```
import javax.servlet.ServletOutputStream;
import javax.servlet.http.HttpServletResponse;

import org.apache.struts.action.ActionForward;

import com.lowagie.text.Document;
import com.lowagie.text.ListItem;
import com.lowagie.text.Paragraph;
import com.lowagie.text.pdf.PdfWriter;
import com.strutsrecipes.pdf.beans.Quote;

public class PDFQuoteAction extends BaseQuoteAction {

    protected ActionForward createResponse(
        List quotes,
        HttpServletResponse response)
        throws Exception {

        ByteArrayOutputStream baos = new ByteArrayOutputStream();   ❶
        PdfWriter writer = null;   ❷
        Document document = new Document();   ❸

        try {
            writer = PdfWriter.getInstance(document, baos);   ❹

            document.addAuthor(this.getClass().getName());   ❺
            document.addCreationDate();
            document.addProducer();
            document.addCreator("Albert Einstein");
            document.addTitle("Einstein Quotes");

            com.lowagie.text.List list = new   ❻
                com.lowagie.text.List(true, 20);

            document.open();   ❼
            document.add(new Paragraph("Albert Einstein Quotes"));   ❽

            Iterator i = quotes.iterator();
            while (i.hasNext()) {   ❾
                Quote quote = (Quote) i.next();
                list.add(new ListItem(quote.getQuote()));
            }

            document.add(list);   ❿
            document.close();   ⓫

        } finally {   ⓬
            if (document != null) {
                document.close();
            }
            if (writer != null) {
```

```
        writer.close();
    }
}

response.setContentType("application/pdf");           ⑬
response.setHeader("Content-disposition",              ⑭
    "inline; filename=quote.pdf");
response.setContentLength(baos.size());                ⑮

ServletOutputStream stream = response.getOutputStream();  ⑯
baos.writeTo(stream);        ⑰
stream.flush();        ⑱

return null;        ⑲
    }
}
```

In listing 8.17 we create a concrete class extending the BaseQuoteAction. Note that PDFQuoteAction implements the createResponse method. By virtue of inheritance, PDFQuoteAction has everything it needs to generate a PDF. This is where it starts to get interesting!

We have chosen to use the iText [ITEXT] API to create a PDF document to list famous Einstein quotes. The createResponse method creates an iText document which ultimately becomes a PDF. Instead of delegating the job of creating the request to a JSP, we format the entire response ourselves.

Let's step through the createResponse method nice and slowly, line by line (listing 8.17).

Create a ByteArrayOutputStream to store the PDF until we are ready to send it back to the browser ❶. Declare a PdfWriter ❷, which is used to associate the PDF document with the ByteArrayOutputStream. Next, create a new PDF Document ❸, which will hold all the PDF constructs, such as lists and paragraphs, and then create an instance of PdfWriter ❹. This creates the association between Byte-ArrayOutputStream and Document. As PDF constructs are added to the Document, the resulting PDF is added to the ByteArrayOutputStream.

The next step is to create meta data for the PDF document ❺. The Author is the person who wrote the document content. By default the Producer is iText. The Title appears in the outer border of the document. The Creator is the person, or thing, that created the document. As you might expect, CreationDate is the date the document was created. Create an iText List ❻. It takes two arguments; a true Boolean declares a numbered ordered list (1, 2, 3, etc.). A value of false indicates an unordered list using bullets. The second argument is a value indicating the type of bullet. Open the PDF document in preparation of adding `Lists`, `Paragraphs`, and so on ❼. Add a `Paragraph` ❽. We use it to create a title for the list of quotes. Next we iterate over the list of quote beans ❾. For each quote we create a `ListItem`. Each `ListItem` is added to the `List` created at ❻. At ❿ we add the `List` to the `Document`. All the `ListItems` have been added to the List. We are finished with building the PDF `Document` ⓫. Close the `Document`.

We make sure the `Document` and the `PdfWriter` close when exceptions are thrown ⓬. We also want to set the content type on the response to tell the browser it is receiving a PDF ⓭. It is important to set `ContentType`, `Headers`, and `ContentLength` before you start writing data to the browser.

Next we set the content disposition header ⓮. The first parameter tells the browser what to do with the stream it is sending; `inline` instructs the browser to launch the PDF browser in the browser. `attachment` pops up a windows to save the file to the file system or open the PDF browser. Then we set the length of the response ⓯, get the `ServletOutputStream` from the response ⓰, and write the `ByteArrayOutputStream` to the `ServletOutputStream` ⓱. This sends the PDF document to the browser.

Flush the stream's cache to the browser ⓲. Because we are building the response ourselves, there is no `ActionForward` to send back ⓳.

◆ Discussion

This recipe uses the iText open source project to create a simple PDF. Upon issuing a request to this `PDFQuoteAction`, the user's browser launches the PDF browser to display a document of famous Einstein quotes.

The `PDFQuoteAction` uses the inherited `execute` method to access the business layer, but relies on its implementation of the `createResponse` method to generate the PDF. This `Action` does not return an `ActionForward`. Instead, it uses the iText API to populate the `ByteArrayOutputStream` with the PDF document. Once the PDF document has been built, the response headers and the `ByteArrayOutput-Stream` are written to the response output stream.

Perhaps you want your PDF document to be a template for dynamic data—such as a form. This can be done by using the `MessageFormat` [MFORMAT] API to merge your static content with dynamic data. Then it's simply a matter of adding the resulting text to the PDF in much the same way as we have done above.

You may be wondering why we didn't create the PDF in the JSP. It is entirely possible to create a JSP scriptlet to achieve the same effect as the `PDFQuoteAction`. In fact, some people consider the format of the presentation to be a responsibility of the JSP. However, doing so couples [UML] you to the implementation of the

View. Although we can do this with a JSP, it may not be possible with other View technologies. Today, JSP and Velocity are popular, but things change rapidly. Tying the solution to the View results in an implementation-dependent design impeding the solution's portability. It is for this very reason we created an abstract class to factor out the business logic. Refactoring the above implementation to use a JSP is straightforward: create `HTMLQuoteAction` extending `BaseQuoteAction` and implement the `createResponseAction` to return an `ActionForward` pointing to a JSP. To prove our point we invite you to read recipe 8.3, "Generate a response with XSL."

We have only scratched the surface of PDF programmatic functionality. You are invited to review the iText [ITEXTJ] Java documentation or other competitive products to explore the rich set of features available to you. Before long you will be practicing the fine art of PDF wizardry.

> **BEST PRACTICE** *Create solutions independent of View implementation*—Wherever possible, implement designs that don't rely on a single technology. Solutions relying on "tech tricks" are red flags indicating you may have painted yourself into a corner. Technology moves fast. You need to keep your options open.

◆ **Related**

- 8.3—Generate a response with XSL

◆ **Reference**

- [ADOBE] Adobe
- [ITEXT] iText
- [ITEXTJ] iText Java Docs
- [MFORMAT] Message Format Java API
- [PDFRM] Portable Document Format Reference Manual
- [UML] Applying UML and Patterns: An Introduction to Object-Oriented Analysis and Design and the Unified Process

8.5 Hibernate and Struts

◆ **Problem**

You want to use Hibernate in your Struts application.

◆ *Background*

Persistence is a fundamental piece of an application. Obviously, without persistence all work would be lost. However, persistence means different things to different people. The length of time something must be persisted is a fundamental qualifier in choosing a persistence storage medium. For example, the HTTP session may be suitable when the life of a piece of data is limited to the user's session. In contrast, persistence over several sessions, or several users, requires a database. The volume of data is another important qualifier. For example, best practices [WBP] suggest large amounts of data should not be stored in an HTTP session. In those circumstances, you need to consider a database. In this recipe we target persistence in a database.

The type of database you choose has an important influence on your architecture and design. As object-oriented developers we tend to represent data as an interconnected web of objects as a means to describe the business problem at hand—this is often called a domain model. However, the most common storage medium is based on a relational paradigm. Unless our object model mirrors a relational structure, the in-memory representation of our data is at odds with the means to persist it. This problem is called the *mismatch paradigm*. One of the most popular tools to address the mismatch problem is a category of tools called Object-Relational Mappers. An Object-Relational Mapper is software used to transform an object view of the data into a relational one, and provide persistence services, such as create, read, update and delete (CRUD). Many good papers have been written on Object-Relational Mappers, but in essence they all speak to the Data Mapper pattern [PEAA]. One of the most popular Object-Relational Mappers is the open source Hibernate project.

In this recipe we show you how to employ Hibernate in a Struts application. In addition, we will show you how to create a Struts plug-in to give your Hibernate-powered Struts applications a performance boost.

HIBERNATE "Hibernate is a powerful, ultrahigh-performance object/relational persistence and query service for Java. Hibernate lets you develop persistent objects following common Java idiom—including association, inheritance, polymorphism, composition, and the Java collections framework. Extremely fine-grained, richly typed object models are possible. The Hibernate Query Language, designed as a "minimal" object-oriented extension to SQL, provides an elegant bridge between the object and relational worlds. Hibernate is now the most popular ORM solution for Java.

"Hibernate rejects the use of build-time code generation/bytecode processing. Instead, reflection and runtime bytecode generation are used and SQL generation occurs at system startup. This decision ensures that Hibernate does not affect IDE debugging and incremental compile.

"All major relational database management systems are supported: Oracle, DB2, MySQL, PostgreSQL, Sybase, SAP DB, HypersonicSQL, Microsoft SQL Server, Informix, FrontBase, Ingres, Progress, Mckoi SQL, Pointbase, and Interbase."

From the Hibernate home page, http://www.hibernate.org/

◆ *Recipe*

In this recipe we use an example to illustrate everything you need to do to use Hibernate in a Struts application. We create an application to retrieve and display elements from the chemical periodic table. The application offers the user a search page to look for an element by element symbol. The application responds by searching the database for an element matching the symbol name and returns information about the element.

We'll start by showing you how to get the Hypersonic database server up and running. With the database server started, we create the table and data required to exercise the application. Once the database is ready to go, we'll create all the Hibernate artifacts required to execute this application by using the Hypersonic database server. The next step is to respond to search requests by calling upon Hibernate to handle database access from inside our `Action`. Because creating Hibernate factory objects is expensive, we'll create a Struts plug-in to create the factory and store it in context.

Let's start by bringing up the Hypersonic database server. You need to download Hypersonic from http://hsqldb.sourceforge.net/. Place hsqldb.jar in your class path and launch Hypersonic by entering the following command in your DOS prompt:

```
java org.hsqldb.Server
```

Although the server's response varies from one version of Hypersonic to another, the following response is a typical indication that Hypersonic is ready to serve database requests.

```
Server 1.6 is running
Press [Ctrl]+{c} to abort
```

With the database server up and running, we are ready to create the elements table and populate it with data, as shown in listing 8.18.

Listing 8.18   Create and populate elements table

```
create table elements (id integer(3) IDENTITY,
                               name char(30),
                               number char(30),
                               mass char(30),
                               symbol char(2));

CREATE UNIQUE INDEX ui_elements_pk ON elements (symbol)

insert into  elements ( name,  number, mass, symbol)
  values ('Manganese','25','55','Mn');
insert into  elements ( name,  number, mass, symbol)
  values ('Zinc','30','65','Zn');
insert into  elements ( name,  number, mass, symbol)
  values ('Thulium','69','169','Tm');
insert into  elements ( name,  number, mass, symbol)
  values ('Californium','98','251','Cf');
insert into  elements ( name,  number, mass, symbol)
  values ('Gold','79','197','Au');
insert into  elements ( name,  number, mass, symbol)
  values ('Ytterbium','70','173','Yb');
insert into  elements ( name,  number, mass, symbol)
  values ('Molybdenum','42','96','Mo');
insert into  elements ( name,  number, mass, symbol)
  values ('Palladium','46','106','Pd');
```

❶ ❷ ❸

Listing 8.18 presents the SQL commands necessary to create the elements table ❶, create a unique index on symbol ❷, and insert data ❸. We have only presented a few of the periodic elements. We'll leave it to you to dust off your high school chemistry textbook to create data for the remaining elements.

Listing 8.19 presents the Element JavaBean used to store data retrieved from the database.

Listing 8.19   Element JavaBean

```
package com.strutsrecipes.hibernate.beans;

public class Element {
    private String name;
    private String symbol;
    private String number;
    private String mass;
    private int id;

    public Element() {
        super();
    }
```

```java
    public Element(String name, String symbol, String number, String mass) {
        this.name = name;
        this.symbol = symbol;
        this.number = number;
        this.mass = mass;

    }

    public int getId() {
        return id;
    }

    public void setId(int id) {
        this.id = id;
    }

    public String getMass() {
        return mass;
    }

    public String getName() {
        return name;
    }

    public String getNumber() {
        return number;
    }

    public String getSymbol() {
        return symbol;
    }

    public void setMass(String mass) {
        this.mass = mass;
    }

    public void setName(String name) {
        this.name = name;
    }

    public void setNumber(String number) {
        this.number = number;
    }

    public void setSymbol(String symbol) {
        this.symbol = symbol;
    }
}
```

Hibernate is an Object-Relational Mapping tool. Its job is to map objects to relational tables and vice versa. Therefore, we must tell Hibernate how to map the columns in the "elements" table to the properties of the Elements JavaBean. This is done using the Element.hbm.xml file. The information embodied in this file is required to empower Hibernate to copy data from the table to the Elements JavaBean. If we were using Hibernate to update data, the information in the Element.hbm.xml file would be used to extract data from the Elements JavaBean to generate SQL update statements. Listing 8.20 presents Element.hbm.xml.

Listing 8.20   Element.hbm.xml

```xml
<?xml version="1.0"?>
<!DOCTYPE hibernate-mapping PUBLIC
   "-//Hibernate/Hibernate Mapping DTD//EN"
   "http://hibernate.sf.net/hibernate-mapping-2.0.dtd">

<hibernate-mapping>
   <class name="com.strutsrecipes.hibernate.beans.Element"      ❶
            table="elements">      ❷

      <id name="id" column="id">                ❸
         <generator class="native"/>
      </id>

      <property name="name" column="name"/>
      <property name="number" column="number"/>      ❹
      <property name="mass" column="mass"/>
      <property name="symbol" column="symbol"/>
   </class>
</hibernate-mapping>
```

Let's step through listing 8.20

At ❶ we declare the full package name of the class to be associated with the "elements" table. At ❷ we declare the name of the table associated with the class declared at ❶. Next we declare the mapping from the id JavaBean property to the id column ❸. Because the property and column name have the same value, we could have omitted the column attribute, but we have explicitly declared the column for clarity purposes. The <id> tag is a special tag. It is used to declare the primary key for the table. The enclosing <generator> tag instructs Hibernate to generate the key in whichever way is most appropriate for the database implementation. You should consult Hibernate documentation for more information on the <id> tag. Finally, at ❹ we have declared mapping for the remaining JavaBean properties. Once again the column attribute was declared for clarification purposes.

Once the mapping file has been broken down in detail, it's all rather straightforward. It simply describes which table maps to which class and which JavaBean properties map to which column names. Later on we will tell you where to place this file.

Next, we configure Hibernate by declaring environmental information. In listing 8.21 we present hibernate.cfg.xml file.

Listing 8.21   hibernate.cfg.xml

```xml
<?xml version='1.0' encoding='utf-8'?>
<!DOCTYPE hibernate-configuration
     PUBLIC "-//Hibernate/Hibernate Configuration DTD//EN"
     "http://hibernate.sourceforge.net/hibernate-configuration-2.0.dtd">

<hibernate-configuration>
 <session-factory>
 <property name="dialect">net.sf.hibernate.dialect.HSQLDialect
    </property>         ❶
 <property name="connection.driver_class">org.hsqldb.jdbcDriver
    </property>         ❷
 <property name="connection.username">sa</property>         ❸
 <property name="connection.password"></property>         ❹
 <property name="connection.url">jdbc:hsqldb:hsql://127.0.0.1
    </property>         ❺
 <property name="show_sql"> </property>         ❻
 <property name="">true</property>

 <mapping resource="/com/strutscookbook/hibernate/beans/Element.hbm.xml"/>
 </session-factory>
</hibernate-configuration>
```

Let's step through listing 8.21.

We start by specifying the database implementation dialect that allows Hibernate to take advantage of implementation-specific features. At ❶ we declare the Hypersonic dialect. You should consult the Hibernate documentation to choose the appropriate dialect for your database. At ❷ we declare the database driver. You must ensure this driver is in your application's class path. We then declare the database username ❸, the database password ❹, and the database connection URL ❺. At ❻ we instruct Hibernate to display the SQL generated at runtime in the log.

The hibernate.cfg.xml file must be placed in your class path.

The procedure to use Hibernate within your application requires the following steps:

1   Create a Hibernate configuration object.

2   Use the Hibernate configuration object to create a Hibernate factory object.

3   Use the Hibernate factory object to create a Hibernate session object.

4   Use the Hibernate session object to start a transaction (optional).

5   Employ the Hibernate session object to create, read, update, and delete data on the database.

6   Commit the transaction (optional).

7   Close the session.

A Hibernate best practice is to create and cache the Hibernate factory to enhance performance. Therefore, we will create a Struts plug-in to perform steps 1 and 2 and cache the Hibernate factory in the Servlet context, as shown in listing 8.22.

Listing 8.22 HibernatePlugin.java

```java
package com.strutsrecipes.hibernate.plugin;

import java.net.URL;
import javax.servlet.ServletException;

import net.sf.hibernate.HibernateException;
import net.sf.hibernate.MappingException;
import net.sf.hibernate.SessionFactory;
import net.sf.hibernate.cfg.Configuration;

import org.apache.commons.logging.Log;
import org.apache.commons.logging.LogFactory;
import org.apache.struts.action.ActionServlet;
import org.apache.struts.action.PlugIn;
import org.apache.struts.config.ModuleConfig;

public class HibernatePlugin implements PlugIn {
    private Configuration config;
    private SessionFactory factory;
    private String path = "/hibernate.cfg.xml";
    private static Class clazz = HibernatePlugin.class;

    public static final String KEY_NAME = clazz.getName();      ❶

    private static Log log = LogFactory.getLog(clazz);

    public void setPath(String path) {      ❷
        this.path = path;
    }
```

```
public void init(ActionServlet servlet, ModuleConfig modConfig)
   throws ServletException {

   try {
      URL url = HibernatePlugin.class.getResource(path);        ❸
      config = new Configuration().configure(url);        ❹
      factory = config.buildSessionFactory();        ❺
       servlet.getServletContext().setAttribute(KEY_NAME, factory);        ❻

   } catch (MappingException e) {
      log.error("mapping error", e);
      throw new ServletException();

   } catch (HibernateException e) {
      log.error("hibernate error", e);
      throw new ServletException();
   }
}

public void destroy() {
   try {
      factory.close();        ❼
   } catch (HibernateException e) {
      log.error("unable to close factory", e);
   }
}
}
```

Creating a Struts plug-in requires only two steps. First, create a class implementing `org.apache.struts.action.PlugIn` (listing 8.22). Second, define a `<plug-in>` tag in the struts-config.xml file (listing 8.23).

Let's step through listing 8.22.

At ❶ we create a constant to hold the name of the Servlet context attribute key. We have chosen to use the `HibernatePlugin` class name. Notice the constant is static public final. We use the `HibernatePlugin` class to access the key name in the `Action` (listing 8.24). At ❷ we define the path property. By default the `Hibernate-Plugin` looks for the Hibernate configuration file at /hibernate.cfg.xml. You can use this property to load the Hibernate configuration file from another file name and directory anywhere on the classpath. Next we use the class loader to find the Hibernate configuration file ❸, and then we create the Hibernate configuration object ❹. At ❺ we use the Hibernate configuration object to create a Hibernate factory object, and then we store the Hibernate factory object in the Servlet context ❻. The factory is now available to any code with a reference to the servlet.

As a good practice we close the factory in the destroy method at ❼.

Listing 8.23 presents the application struts-config. The only thing out of the ordinary here is the `<plug-in>` tag. This is where we declare the Hibernate plug-in which creates and caches the Hibernate factory object.

Listing 8.23   struts-config.xml

```xml
<?xml version="1.0" encoding="ISO-8859-1" ?>

<!DOCTYPE struts-config PUBLIC
        "-//Apache Software Foundation//DTD Struts Configuration 1.1//EN"
        "http://jakarta.apache.org/struts/dtds/struts-config_1_1.dtd">

<struts-config>
  <form-beans>
      <form-bean name="searchForm"
                 type="com.strutsrecipes.hibernate.forms.SearchForm"/>
  </form-beans>

  <global-forwards>
     <forward  name="search" path="/search.jsp"/>
     <forward  name="searchsubmit" path="/searchsubmit.do"/>
  </global-forwards>

  <action-mappings>
    <action path="/searchsubmit"
          type="com.strutsrecipes.hibernate.actions.SearchAction"
          name="searchForm"
          scope="request"
          input="/search.jsp">
          <forward name="success" path="/element.jsp"/>
    </action>
  </action-mappings>

  <plug-in className="com.strutsrecipes.hibernate.plugin.HibernatePlugin">
    <set-property property="path" value="/hibernate.cfg.xml"/>
  </plug-in>
</struts-config>
```

Listing 8.24 presents the `SearchForm` used to search for an element. It's very simple because the user can only search by element symbol.

Listing 8.24   SearchForm.java

```java
package com.strutsrecipes.hibernate.forms;

import org.apache.struts.action.ActionForm;
public class SearchForm extends ActionForm {
   String symbol;
```

```
   public String getSymbol() {
      return symbol;
   }

   public void setSymbol(String symbol) {
      this.symbol = symbol;
   }
}
```

Let's have a look at the SearchAction in listing 8.25. Although you may decide to employ Hibernate in other areas of your application architecture, we have chosen to use it in the Action. We'll defer the discussion of the other alternatives to the discussion section.

Listing 8.25 SearchAction.java

```
package com.strutsrecipes.hibernate.actions;

import java.util.List;

import javax.servlet.http.HttpServletRequest;
import javax.servlet.http.HttpServletResponse;

import org.apache.commons.logging.Log;
import org.apache.commons.logging.LogFactory;

import net.sf.hibernate.Hibernate;
import net.sf.hibernate.HibernateException;
import net.sf.hibernate.Session;
import net.sf.hibernate.SessionFactory;

import org.apache.struts.action.Action;
import org.apache.struts.action.ActionError;
import org.apache.struts.action.ActionErrors;
import org.apache.struts.action.ActionForm;
import org.apache.struts.action.ActionForward;
import org.apache.struts.action.ActionMapping;

import com.strutsrecipes.hibernate.beans.Element;
import com.strutsrecipes.hibernate.forms.SearchForm;
import com.strutsrecipes.hibernate.plugin.HibernatePlugin;

public class SearchAction extends Action {
 private static Log log = LogFactory.getLog(SearchAction.class);

    final public static String HQL_FIND_ELEMENT =
 "from com.strutsrecipes.hibernate.beans.Element as e where e.symbol = ?";  ❶
```

```
public ActionForward execute(
    ActionMapping mapping,
    ActionForm form,
    HttpServletRequest request,
    HttpServletResponse response)
    throws Exception {

    SearchForm searchForm = (SearchForm) form;        ❷
    Element element = null;
    List elements = null;
    SessionFactory factory = null;
    Session session = null;

    try {

        factory =
            (SessionFactory) servlet.getServletContext()    ❸
                .getAttribute(HibernatePlugin.KEY_NAME);

        session = factory.openSession();      ❹

        elements =
            session.find(
                HQL_FIND_ELEMENT,                ❺
                searchForm.getSymbol(),
                Hibernate.STRING);

        if (!elements.isEmpty()) {                    ❻
            element = (Element) elements.get(0);
        }

    } catch (HibernateException e) {          ❼
        log.error("Hibernate error", e);
        } finally {
            log.error("Hibernate exception encountered");   ❽
        session.close();
    }

    if (element != null) {                             ❾
        request.setAttribute("element", element);
        return mapping.findForward("success");
    }

    ActionErrors errors = new ActionErrors();

    errors.add(ActionErrors.GLOBAL_ERROR,              ❿
        new ActionError("error.notfound"));
    saveErrors(request, errors);
    return mapping.getInputForward();
    }
}
```

Let's take a quick overview of what happens in the `SearchAction`. The `Search-Action` uses the `SearchForm.getSymbol()` method to obtain the element symbol entered by the user on the search page. Hibernate is used to search the database and convert the data stored in the database to an `Element` object. The `Element` object is placed in request context for the JSP. Let's step through listing 8.25 line by line to see how it's done in detail.

First we declare a constant to search the database ❶. We'll delve more deeply into this at ❹. We next cast the form to `SearchForm` ❷, and then we obtain the Hibernate factory ❸. Recall the Hibernate plug-in has already created the factory and cached it in the Servlet context. Next, we obtain a session ❹. The session obtains a connection to the database. Hibernate uses the configuration information we created in listing 8.21 to connect to the database. At ❺ we search the database. There are other ways to employ Hibernate to search the database, but the `find` method is appropriate whenever a search doesn't use the primary key. Notice, we have the `HQL_FIND_ELEMENT` constant declared at ❶. The SQL defined in `HQL_FIND_ELEMENT` looks somewhat like standard SQL, but not quite. The SQL used by Hibernate is proprietary to Hibernate and reflects an object-oriented version of SQL, rather than the relational SQL to which you are accustomed.

Let's delve into the Hibernate SQL (HQL) code snippet.

```
from com.strutsrecipes.hibernate.beans.Element as e where e.symbol = ?
```

This statement tells Hibernate to select all `Element` objects residing in the com. strutsrecipes.hibernate.beans package. The `where` clause filters the list to only those elements whose symbols match a runtime parameter. The `as e` indicates that e may be used as an alias elsewhere in the HQL, as we have done in the `where` clause. You can see that we are selecting objects, not rows, in the database. Hibernate uses the information in listing 8.21 to map the class we are interested in to its associated table. In this example the relationship between the table and the object are very close, but that does not necessarily need to be the case. For more information on HQL and other creative ways to use Hibernate we suggest you refer to the Reference section of this recipe.

The second and third arguments to the `find` method are the value and data type of the HQL replacement parameter. The Hibernate reference material describes other ways to replace runtime parameters.

The `find` method always returns a `List`. In this case we obtain a list of `Element` objects. We are confident that a maximum of one instance is returned because the "elements" table has a unique key constraint on the `symbol` column (see listing 8.18 ❷).

Returning to listing 8.25, at ❻ we copy the element reference in the first position in the list to the element variable. To deal with any Hibernate exceptions, we have chosen to log the exception and present the user a "not found" message ❼, but you may decide to present a different message or use declarative exception handling. See recipe 5.4, "Use declarative exception handling." Next, we close the session ❽. Closing the session in the `finally` clause guarantees it is attempted even when exceptions are thrown. At ❾ we store the `Element` object in the request context, and finally we build the `ActionError` when the symbol can't be found ❿.

For the sake of completeness, we have presented the search.jsp (listing 8.26) and the element.jsp (listing 8.27).

Listing 8.26   Search.jsp

```
<%@ page language="java" %>
<%@ taglib uri="/WEB-INF/struts-html.tld" prefix="html" %>

<html:html>
<body>
  <h1>Search for an Element</h1>

  <html:form action="/searchsubmit.do">
    symbol <form:text property="symbol"/>
  <html:submit value="Search"/>
  </html:form>

  <html:errors/>

</body>
</html:html>
```

Listing 8.27   Element.jsp

```
<%@ page language="java" %>
<%@ taglib uri="/WEB-INF/struts-bean.tld" prefix="bean" %>
<%@ taglib uri="/WEB-INF/struts-html.tld" prefix="html" %>

<html:html>
  <h1>Periodic Element</h1>
  Name: <bean:write name="element" property="name"/><br>
  Symbol: <bean:write name="element" property="symbol"/><br>
  Number: <bean:write name="element" property="number"/><br>
  Mass: <bean:write name="element" property="mass"/><br>

  <html:link forward="search">Search</html:link><p>
</html:html>
```

Before putting Hibernate to work, consult the Hibernate documentation to ensure you have all the required Hibernate JAR files in your class path.

◆ *Discussion*

Persistence of data is a tedious and laborious job. To make matters worse, a considerable effort must be spent transforming an object-oriented representation of the data to a relational one, and vice versa. Fortunately, several good Object-Relational Mappers exist to ease this burden. In this recipe we explore Hibernate—one of the most popular open source Object-Relational Mappers available to Java programmers.

Hibernate is a very rich product with many unexplored features left for you to discover. Our simple example is limited to `read` behavior, but the rest of the CRUD family is just as easy. Update functionality is as simple as accessing the desired element, calling the desired JavaBean setter, and calling the session commit method. Hibernate takes care of generating the SQL and updating the table. A `delete` is also rather simple—`session.delete(element)` is all it takes! Finally, `create` only requires instantiating the object, calling the setters, and calling `session.save(element)`.

Hibernate best practices recommend caching the Hibernate factory object. We chose to create and cache the factory using a Struts plug-in. Alternatively, you could have chosen to cache using any other means in your arsenal.

Although this recipe can serve you well, there are some drawbacks. First, we have exposed Hibernate to the Struts `Action`. Migrating to another persistence layer framework requires us to change every `Action` employing Hibernate. Second, our persistence is tightly coupled to the presentation layer. This coupling denies us the opportunity to reuse the persistence logic in some other presentation mechanism, such as a batch program. We invite you to read recipe 8.6, "Create a layered application," to address these shortcomings.

Although there is room for improvement, this recipe is suitable when you do not expect to reuse your persistence logic. Your may find yourself in this situation developing prototypes or small throwaway applications.

◆ *Related*

- 5.4—Use declarative exception handling

◆ *Reference*

- [HIA] *Hibernate In Action*
- [HIB] Hibernate home page

- [PEAA] *Patterns of Enterprise Application Architecture*
- [PL] The Design of a Robust Persistence Layer for Relational Databases
- [WBP] WebSphere Application Server Development Best Practices for Performance and Scalability

8.6 Layering applications

◆ Problem

You want to apply the Layers pattern to your application.

◆ Background

"A place for everything, and everything in its place" is a good motto to consider whether you are tackling a nasty closet filled with long forgotten treasures or a software application. A well-designed application keeps everything neat and tidy to position itself to deliver future enhancements quickly and effectively.

Oddly, this recipe is not so much about what you can do with Struts, but what you shouldn't do. In this recipe we show you how to apply the Layers pattern to create maintainable and flexible applications. Along the way we employ the Factory, Data Access Object, and Façade patterns to support our goal of a well-designed application. We will be focusing on good design practices and borrowing on well-known object-oriented design (OOD) principles to do that. We will go slowly, but you can always consult material listed in the Related section as a refresher.

Creating layered applications requires a broad knowledge of patterns. Here is a summary of the patterns used in this recipe.

- *Data Access Object pattern*—The Data Access Object pattern encapsulates data access logic within an object (DAO). Data access implementation details are hidden from the client of the DAO. The DAO knows which data source to use and how to access it. The encapsulation quality of DAOs contributes to code reuse and maintainability.

- *Façade pattern*—The Façade pattern ensures the complexities of a subsystem are hidden from its clients by exposing a simple interface. Implementation details within the façade can be changed without impacting the clients of the façade. The façade represents the subsystem's contractual obligation to its client.

- *Factory pattern*—The factory pattern delegates object creation responsibility to an object dedicated to that purpose. Implementation details and conditional logic is hidden from the factory's client. The pattern contributes to lower maintenance costs by consolidating creational logic to a single point of maintenance. An object-oriented principle advocating an object's responsibilities is labeled by identifying groups of related responsibilities among a larger set of responsibilities.

- *Layers pattern*—The Layers pattern organizes the architecture of the system using the principle of Separation of Concerns in such a way that the specialized concerns are separated from the generic ones.

Many applications are built in layers to support the notion of Separation of Concerns. By separating applications based on their responsibilities within the overall architecture, we can protect applications from pervasive and invasive changes. Changes are easily traced to a single area, thereby promoting a more effective use of programming resources and lowering the risk of instability to the application. In addition, by segregating code by responsibility we provide more opportunity for reuse. Strut's Model-View-Controller (MVC) pattern is one of the best examples of Separation of Concerns [MVC].

A well-designed application is divided into three layers: presentation, business (domain), and persistence (data source) [PEAA]. The presentation layer is responsible for handling interactions with the client. Struts clearly belongs in the presentation layer. The business layer manages business logic. Its job is to ensure business validation is applied, and business processes are executed. The persistence layer is responsible for data storage and retrieval.

Designing your application into these three layers allows you to reuse business logic from another presentation framework, such as line commands or a batch program. Keeping business and persistence logic out of your Struts `Actions` enables you to reuse that logic elsewhere.

We will use an application to illustrate a layered application. We borrow upon the application in recipe 8.5, "Hibernate and Struts," as a foundation for the example in this recipe. In recipe 8.5, Hibernate is exposed to the Struts `Action`. This means that migrating to another persistence layer framework requires changing every `Action` employing Hibernate. In addition, persistence is tightly coupled to the presentation layer. This coupling denies us the opportunity to reuse the persistence logic in some other presentation mechanism. These weaknesses are addressed in this recipe.

Let's take a moment to sketch out the architecture of this application using a layered approach (see figure 8.1). Struts is used to manage the user interaction. It accepts requests for information on the chemical periodic table and displays

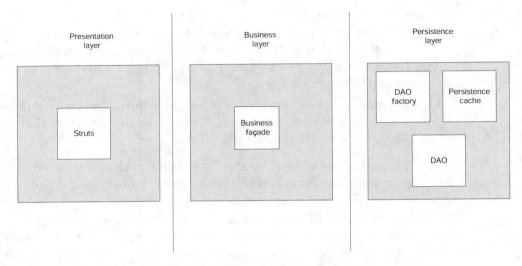

Figure 8.1 Example application layering diagram.

the results to the user using a JavaServer Page (JSP). The application is split into three layers: Struts in the presentation layer, a business layer to hold our business logic, and a persistence layer. Struts interacts with the business layer by calling a business façade. The business façade interacts with the persistence layer by creating and invoking a DAO.

The difference between this recipe and the Hibernate recipe is that the `Action` will obtain its information from a special class called a `BusinessFacade`, instead of Hibernate directly. The business façade is responsible for performing any business logic and accessing the persistence layer. The persistence layer is responsible for talking to the database, but does not expose the database implementation to the business layer. In fact, it doesn't even expose Hibernate. This layer of abstraction allows us to unplug the presentation layer from the business layer. We can also unplug the business layer from the persistence layer. It's like using the Java equivalent of Lego blocks. In this application we create a façade as a single point of entry to the business layer. Other applications may want to create multiple façades to the business layer.

We are going to increase the flexibility of the persistence layer by using a Data Access Object pattern and a Factory pattern to empower us to swap out Hibernate in favor of TopLink or JDBC declaratively! Let's get started!

◆ *Recipe*

At first glance, a layered application appears to introduce complexity—perhaps unnecessary complexity prior to indoctrination. The application appears to be more complex because you must drill down to find functionality. There is even more digging to do. Trying to keep the whole thing in your head can be overwhelming. In fact, layered applications reduce complexity by separating concerns, but you need to adjust your thinking. As you comb through the code, you need to focus on the functionality at hand. You need to trust that the supporting functionality fulfills its responsibility. Later, once you have a good understanding of the base functionality, you can drill down into the supporting logic to see if your trust is well founded. With that mind-set, let's get going.

Presentation layer

Naturally, Struts plays a key role in the presentation layer. We kick things off by looking at the `SearchAction` Struts `Action`, shown in listing 8.28.

Listing 8.28 `SearchAction`

```
package com.strutsrecipes.layers.actions;

import java.util.List;

import javax.servlet.http.HttpServletRequest;
import javax.servlet.http.HttpServletResponse;

import org.apache.commons.logging.Log;
import org.apache.commons.logging.LogFactory;
import org.apache.struts.action.Action;
import org.apache.struts.action.ActionForm;
import org.apache.struts.action.ActionForward;
import org.apache.struts.action.ActionMapping;

import
    com.strutsrecipes.layers.actions.exceptions.ElementNotFoundException;
import com.strutsrecipes.layers.beans.Element;
import com.strutsrecipes.layers.business.BusinessFacade;
import com.strutsrecipes.layers.forms.SearchForm;

public class SearchAction extends Action {
    private static Log log = LogFactory.getLog(SearchAction.class);

    public ActionForward execute(
        ActionMapping mapping,
        ActionForm form,
        HttpServletRequest request,
        HttpServletResponse response)
```

```
        throws Exception {

        SearchForm searchForm = (SearchForm) form;
        Element element = null;
        List elements = null;

        BusinessFacade businessFacade = new BusinessFacade();
        element = businessFacade.getElement(searchForm.getSymbol());

        if (element == null) {
            throw new ElementNotFoundException();
        }

        request.setAttribute("element", element);
        return mapping.findForward("success");

    }

}
```

The important observation in listing 8.28 is not what you see, but what you don't! There is no JDBC or Hibernate logic. Nor is there any business validation. This Struts Action has no knowledge of business or persistence details. Its sole responsibility is to communicate with the business layer via the BusinessFacade and delegate a response. Complexities of the business layer are hidden from the Action. This design allows you to change the persistence or business layer with the confidence that the SearchAction will not also need changing. As long as the BusinessFacade maintains its API, there is no need to make a change to the Action.

You will notice that the SearchAction does not handle BusinessFacade exceptions. That's because we have delegated the management of exceptions to Struts' built-in declarative exception handling mechanism, as shown in recipe 5.4. Any new BusinessFacade exceptions can be maintained declaratively in the struts-config. xml file. Again, no code changes are required and promotion process is a snap.

That concludes our discussion of the Struts design portion of this recipe. Next, we delve into the business layer.

Business layer

Listing 8.29 presents the BusinessFacade. Our business layer is so small that the BusinessFacade is the business layer! The business layer consists of a single class—BusinessFacade. However, as the application grows, the business layer can grow in complexity without affecting the SearchAction because the BusinessFacade is the "face" to the business layer.

The responsibility of the business layer is to respond to requests for information or business processes. In this case, we are merely interested in business information. The business layer is responsible for interacting with the persistence layer. The golden rule of the Layers pattern is that a layer may only talk to its closest layer. It may never jump a layer. This makes sense because the business layer is responsible for business data and assumes the responsibility to ensure it is persisted. The responsibility to execute the mechanics of persistence lies with the persistence layer.

Listing 8.29   Business façade

```
package com.strutsrecipes.layers.business;

import org.apache.commons.logging.Log;
import org.apache.commons.logging.LogFactory;

import com.strutsrecipes.layers.beans.Element;
import com.strutsrecipes.layers.business.exceptions.*;
import com.strutsrecipes.layers.persistence.DAOFactory;
import com.strutsrecipes.layers.persistence.ElementDAO;
import
   com.strutsrecipes.layers.persistence.exceptions.PersistenceSystemExcepti
   on;
import
   com.strutsrecipes.layers.persistence.exceptions.UnableToReadException;

public class BusinessFacade {

    private static Log log = LogFactory.getLog(BusinessFacade.class);
    private static final String ELEMENT_DAO = "dao.element";

    public Element getElement(String symbol)
       throws UnableToGetElementException {

       Element element = null;
       ElementDAO elementDAO = null;

       try {
          elementDAO = (ElementDAO) DAOFactory.getDAO(ELEMENT_DAO);     ❶
          element = elementDAO.read(symbol);      ❷
       } catch (UnableToReadException e) {
          throw new UnableToGetElementException(e);
       } catch (PersistenceSystemException e) {
          throw new UnableToGetElementException(e);
       }

       return element;
    }
}
```

Taking a more detailed look at listing 8.29, at ❶ we use the DAOFactory to manufacture an ElementDAO. We employ the Factory pattern to hide the details of creating an ElementDAO. This allows us to easily change the implementation of the ElementDAO without disturbing the BusinessFacade. Next we use the ElementDAO created in ❶ to access the persistence layer ❷.

The important point to reflect upon is that the BusinessFacade has no knowledge of the persistence implementation. The data store could be a database, file, or in-memory cache. Notice the exceptions thrown by the ElementDAO also keep the DAO implementation secrets. In order to protect the SearchAction from the consequence of knowing about the persistence layer, we must intercept persistence exceptions and transform them into business exceptions. This allows us to change the persistence layer without impacting the SearchAction.

Persistence layer

Let's begin our exploration of the persistence layer by looking at the DAO interface, shown in listing 8.30.

Listing 8.30   DAO interface

```
package com.strutsrecipes.layers.persistence;

import com.strutsrecipes.layers.beans.Element;
import
  com.strutsrecipes.layers.persistence.exceptions.UnableToReadException;

public interface ElementDAO {
    Element read(String symbol) throws UnableToReadException;
}
```

The ElementDAO interface is very simple with just a single read method. Regardless of the ElementDAO implementation, the read method exception must be UnableToReadException.

Before delving into the DAOFactory, let's have a look at the implementation behind the ElementDAO interface. The ElementDAOImpl implements the ElementDAO interface, shown in listing 8.31.

Listing 8.31   ElementDAOImpl

```
package com.strutsrecipes.layers.persistence;

import java.util.List;
```

```
import org.apache.commons.logging.Log;
import org.apache.commons.logging.LogFactory;

import net.sf.hibernate.Hibernate;
import net.sf.hibernate.HibernateException;
import net.sf.hibernate.SessionFactory;
import net.sf.hibernate.Session;

import com.strutsrecipes.layers.beans.Element;
import com.strutsrecipes.layers.persistence.exceptions.*;

public class ElementDAOImpl implements ElementDAO {
    private static Log log = LogFactory.getLog(ElementDAOImpl.class);
    final private static String HQL_FIND_ELEMENT =
        "from com.strutsrecipes.layers.beans.Element as e where e.symbol = ?";
    private SessionFactory factory = null;
    private Session session = null;

    public Element read(String symbol) throws UnableToReadException {
        Element element = null;

        try {

            factory = PersistenceCache.getHibernateFactory();      ❶
            session = factory.openSession();                       ❷
            List elements =
                session.find(HQL_FIND_ELEMENT, symbol, Hibernate.STRING);   ❸

            if (!elements.isEmpty()) {                              ❹
                element = (Element) elements.get(0);
            }

        } catch (HibernateException e) {
            log.error("Hibernate error", e);
            throw new UnableToReadException(e);                     ❺
        } catch (UnableToCreateFactoryException e) {
            log.error("Hibernate error", e);
            throw new UnableToReadException(e);
        } finally {
            try {
                session.close();                                   ❻
            } catch (HibernateException e) {
                log.error("Hibernate session close", e);
                throw new UnableToReadException(e);
            }
        }

        return element;
    }
}
```

Let's have a look at the `ElementDAOImpl read` method. If you have read recipe 8.5 this code will look very familiar. The only difference is that the caching strategy employs the `PersistenceCache` class.

Let's step through the `read` method in listing 8.31.

First we obtain the Hibernate factory from the cache ❶. We'll have a look at the PersistenceCache later on. Then we use the Hibernate factory to obtain a session ❷ and use Hibernate SQL to retrieve the element matching the symbol ❸. Please refer to recipe 8.5 for more details. Next we obtain a reference to the `Element` object ❹. The Hibernate session `find` method returns a list, but as the table has a unique key constraint on the symbol column, we are certain the result will be at the first position. At ❺ we transform persistence implementation exceptions into generic persistence exceptions to hide persistence implementation details from the business layer. And finally, we preserve resources by closing the session ❻. We use the `finally` clause to guarantee the session will be closed even when exceptions are thrown.

Many applications use caching to help deliver fast response times. In listing 8.32, we present a Struts plug-in to cache Hibernate resources.

Listing 8.32 Persistence resource caching

```
package com.strutsrecipes.layers.persistence;

import java.io.IOException;
import java.io.InputStream;
import java.net.URL;
import java.util.Properties;

import org.apache.commons.logging.Log;
import org.apache.commons.logging.LogFactory;

import com.strutsrecipes.layers.persistence.exceptions.*;

import net.sf.hibernate.HibernateException;
import net.sf.hibernate.MappingException;
import net.sf.hibernate.SessionFactory;
import net.sf.hibernate.cfg.Configuration;

public class PersistenceCache {
    private static final String HIBERNATE_CONFIG_PROPERTY =
        "hibernate.cfg.path";
    private static final String FACTORY_PROPERTIES_FILE_NAME =
        "factory.properties";
    private static Configuration config;
    private static Class clazz = PersistenceCache.class;
    private static Log log = LogFactory.getLog(clazz);
```

```
private static Properties factoryProperties = createFactoryProperties();
private static SessionFactory factory = createHibernateFactory();

private static Properties createFactoryProperties() {
   InputStream is =
      clazz.getClassLoader().getResourceAsStream(
         FACTORY_PROPERTIES_FILE_NAME);
   Properties properties = null;
   try {
      properties = new Properties();
      properties.load(is);
   } catch (IOException e) {
      //swallow: factory will be null
      log.error("unable to get properties file", e);
   }

   return properties;
}

private static SessionFactory createHibernateFactory() {

   SessionFactory factory = null;

   try {

      URL url =
         PersistenceCache.class.getResource(
            getFactoryProperties().getProperty(
               HIBERNATE_CONFIG_PROPERTY));
      config = new Configuration().configure(url);
      factory = config.buildSessionFactory();

   } catch (MappingException e) {
      //swallow: factory will be null
      log.error("mapping error", e);
   } catch (HibernateException e) {
      //swallow: factory will be null
      log.error("hibernate error", e);
   } catch (UnableToCreatePropertiesException e) {
      //swallow: factory will be null
      log.error("hibernate error", e);
   }

   return factory;
}

public static SessionFactory getHibernateFactory()
   throws UnableToCreateFactoryException {
   //problem creating factory will result in a null factory
   if (factory == null) {
      throw new UnableToCreateFactoryException();
   }
```

```
        return factory;
    }

    public void closeHibernateFactory()
            throws UnableToCloseFactoryException,
                    UnableToCloseFactoryException {
        //problem creating factory will result in a null factory
        if (factory == null) {
            throw new UnableToCloseFactoryException();
        }

        try {
            factory.close();
        } catch (HibernateException e) {
            log.error("unable to close factory", e);
            throw new UnableToCloseFactoryException();
        }
    }

    public static Properties getFactoryProperties() throws
    UnableToCreatePropertiesException {
        //problem creating factory will result in a null factory
        if (factoryProperties == null) {
            log.error("factory properties file is null");
            throw new UnableToCreatePropertiesException();
        }

        return factoryProperties;
    }

}
```

In recipe 8.5 we use a Struts plug-in to create the Hibernate factory prior to storing it in the Servlet context. Because the business layer does not have access to the Servlet context we need another strategy. Moreover, using a Struts plug-in couples us to Struts and precludes opportunities to use other forms of presentation layers. In this recipe we have chosen to use a static factory [BLOCH] to create and cache persistence resource (listing 8.32). We use PersistenceCache as a static factory for the persistence properties file and Hibernate factory. Please see recipe 8.5 for details on creating the Hibernate factory. The properties file is created in the usual way and stored as a private static variable. Both the Hibernate factory and properties file are accessible using public getters.

In listing 8.33 we present a DAO factory to dynamically create a DAO. The properties file in listing 8.34 is used to configure the DAO factory to return a DAO implementation. The DAO pattern allows us to change the DAO implementation declaratively—no code changes required!

Listing 8.33 DAO factory

```
package com.strutsrecipes.layers.persistence;

import java.util.Properties;

import org.apache.commons.logging.Log;
import org.apache.commons.logging.LogFactory;

import
   com.strutsrecipes.layers.persistence.exceptions.PersistenceSystemExcepti
   on;
import
   com.strutsrecipes.layers.persistence.exceptions.UnableToCreateProperties
   Exception;

public class DAOFactory {

   private static Log log = LogFactory.getLog(DAOFactory.class);

   static public Object getDAO(String name)
      throws PersistenceSystemException {

      Properties factortyProperties = null;

      try {
         factortyProperties = PersistenceCache.getFactoryProperties();    ❶
      } catch (UnableToCreatePropertiesException e) {
         log.error("no factory properties file");
         throw new PersistenceSystemException();
      }

      String className = (String) factortyProperties.get(name);           ❷
      if (className == null) {
         log.error("no dao defined for class name " + name);
         throw new PersistenceSystemException();
      }

      Object object = null;
      try {
         Class classDefinition = Class.forName(className);                ❸
         object = classDefinition.newInstance();
      } catch (InstantiationException e) {
         log.error("InstantiationException");
         throw new PersistenceSystemException(e);
      } catch (IllegalAccessException e) {
         log.error("IllegalAccessException");
         throw new PersistenceSystemException(e);
      } catch (ClassNotFoundException e) {
         log.error("ClassNotFoundException " + className);
         throw new PersistenceSystemException(e);
      }
      return object;
   }
}
```

Listing 8.34 factory.properties

```
hibernate.cfg.path=/hibernate.cfg.xml
dao.element=com.strutsrecipes.layers.persistence.ElementDAOImpl
```

The `DAOFactory` is the last section of code to cover. Recall the `BusinessFacade` uses the `DAOFactory` to create the `ElementDAO`. We now know the `ElementDAO` interface is backed by `ElementDAOImpl` using Hibernate. Let's see how the `DAOFactory` works.

The `DAOFactory` uses the `name` argument passed in the `getDAO` method as a key to obtain the fully qualified class name from the factory.properties file. It uses reflection to instantiate an `ElementDAOImpl` object. Because the `ElementDAOImpl` class implements the `ElementDAO` interface, this factory satisfies its obligation. Changing the implementation from Hibernate to TopLink is as simple as creating a new implementing class and changing the factory.properties file `dao.element` key to reference the fully qualified name of the TopLink implementation class. There is no need to change the business or presentation layers.

Stepping through the code line by line, you see we use the `PersistenceCache` to obtain a reference to the factory `properties` object ❶. Next we use the `name` argument to obtain the fully qualified name from the factory properties file. Then at ❸ we use reflection to instantiate the object whose name was obtained at ❷. Because the method returns `Object`, the client class is responsible for casting the `Object` to the appropriate type. We could enhance robustness by applying type safety. This could be done by introducing a wrapper to return the `ElementDAO` interface [EJS], allowing the client to avoid casting and risking the chance of getting a `ClassCastException`.

◆ **Discussion**

Creating layered applications requires more thought and more work. You should consider using a layered design whenever the application is sufficiently complex or you expect it to become that way. Nonlayered applications can produce web pages very quickly, but perhaps at the expense of a longer-term view.

Layered applications have several benefits. They can:

- Allow you to develop layers concurrently, thereby getting to market faster.

- Facilitate communication by using a clear and common understanding of APIs.

- Allow you to identify and resolve problems quickly using the specialized nature of layers.

- Encourage the development of "layer experts," allowing you to create a wealth of expertise, which is more difficult to create among a team of generalists.

- Manage programming resource costs more efficiently (fewer skilled resources assigned to unskilled tasks). In addition, you can practice "just-in-time" acquisition of specialized resources and thereby reduce overall costs.

- Promote robust code, thus yielding a satisfied customer, which increases the probability of repeat sales.

- Promote code reuse and maintainability, leading to quicker enhancements and shorter time to market.

The application presented in this recipe is not perfect. There are always ways to make an application more robust and maintainable. You may decide to employ different design patterns or add another level of abstraction. For example, we could have used the Factory pattern to obtain the `BusinessFacade` as a means of hiding a POJO (Plain Old Java Object) or stateless session EJB implementation. Perhaps you may decide to externalize SQL and HSQL in a properties file to facilitate maintenance or performance tuning. There are lots of creative and interesting possibilities at your disposal. A word of caution: The art of creating robust and maintainable applications is to apply good judgment and pragmatism along the way. You must resist the temptation to overdesign, yet apply enough design to achieve long-term benefits.

◆ Related

- 8.5—Hibernate and Struts

◆ Reference

- [BLOCH] *Effective Java Programming Language Guide*, Item 1 and Item 2
- [CORE] *Core J2EE Patterns, Best Practices, and Design Strategies*; Integration Tier Patterns, Data Access Object
- [DEA] *Designing Enterprise Applications with the J2EETM Platform*, 2nd. ed.
- [EJS] *Elements of Java Style*, p. 73
- [UML] *Applying UML and Patterns: An Introduction to Object-Oriented Analysis and Design and the Unified Process*

8.7 *Enforce navigation*

◆ *Problem*

You want to make sure the user doesn't circumvent the application's intended navigation.

◆ *Background*

The HTTP protocol has proven to be an effective and efficient means of communication, but is has not been without challenges. The stateless nature of HTTP requires a little more elbow grease on the part of web developers. The classic shopping cart example is an excellent case in point. The user navigates from page to page entering information and choosing products to place in their shopping basket. Each request to the server has no knowledge of the previous one. It is up to the developer to record state information. An HTTP session object is a common means of recording state information, but a cookie, an EJB stateful session bean, and databases can also be considered.

Another implication of statelessness is "guaranteed navigation." There is no guarantee that the user has navigated through the application as intended. Although well-designed user interfaces control page flow, there is no guarantee that the user has not spoofed a request or used a bookmark. An application requiring a visit to the billing information input page, prior to the order page, may result in interesting and unintended results should the user circumvent the billing input page. A robust application enforces the intended page flow. In this recipe we show how to do exactly that.

This recipe is best illustrated in the context of a simple use case. Figure 8.2 describes a simple page flow. This recipe shows you how to enforce this flow.

In figure 8.2 we see page1 is the entry point. From there the user may navigate to page2 or page3. Once on page2, the user must have come from page1 or, in the case of a validation error, may have come from itself. The user may then navigate to page3. Page3 is assuming the user arrived by way of page2 or page1. Because page1 is an entry point, the user may navigate to page1 at any time.

The concept behind this solution is straightforward. Each page is associated with a unique token. Upon exiting a page, the application places the token associated with that page in the HTTP session under a known key. Upon entering a page, the application checks the token left by the previous page to see if it is a valid entry token. If the token is invalid, the user is sent an error page. With these concepts in mind, let's proceed to the recipe section for the implementation details.

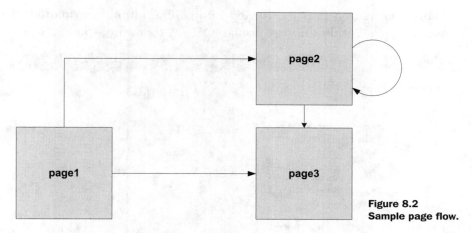

Figure 8.2
Sample page flow.

◆ *Recipe*

The recipe section is divided into two parts. The first part explains how to configure the code presented in this recipe to enforce navigation. The second part takes you through the implementation code. If you need to get started quickly, you can get by with part one and blindly type in the code in part two. Later, when you want to peek under the hood, you can delve into part two.

Let's get started by assigning unique tokens to each page, as shown in table 8.1.

Table 8.1 listed the tokens for each page. Next, we define valid entrance tokens for each page, as shown in table 8.2.

Table 8.2 lists the valid entrance tokens for each page. Recall, the user must visit page1 before page2. Because page1's token is "a," it has been added to the list of valid tokens for page2. Page2 may call itself to allow the user to fix validation errors. Therefore, page2's token "b" is added to page2's list of valid tokens. Similarly, the user must have visited page1 or page2 just prior to page3. Consequently, their tokens are listed as valid values for page3.

Table 8.1   Token assignments

Name	Value
Page1	a
Page2	b
Page3	c

Table 8.2   Valid entrance token assignments

Name	Value
Page2	a, b
Page3	a, b

This information must be turned into configuration information. We have chosen to represent this information as XML, as shown in listing 8.35.

Listing 8.35   XML configuration

```
<navigation>
   <tokens>
      <token>
         <name>/page1</name>
         <value>a</value>
      </token>
      <token>
         <name>/page2</name>
         <value>b</value>
      </token>
      <token>
         <name>/page3</name>
         <value>c</value>
      </token>
   </tokens>

   <validTokens>
      <validToken>
         <name>/page2</name>
         <value>a,b</value>
      </validToken>
      <validToken>
         <name>/page3</name>
         <value>a,b</value>
      </validToken>
   </validTokens>
</navigation>
```

Listing 8.35 is an XML representation of tables 1.1 and 1.2. The information nested under the <tokens> tag represents table 1.1. Similarly, <validTokens> represents table 1.2. Place this file as navigation.xml anywhere on your class path.

The only other thing you need to do is create the custom RequestProcessor (listing 8.37) and declare it using the <controller> tag in the struts-config.xml, as shown in listing 8.36. The custom RequestProcessor is responsible for enforcing navigation.

Listing 8.36   Struts-config.xml file

```xml
<?xml version="1.0" encoding="ISO-8859-1"?>
<!DOCTYPE struts-config PUBLIC "-//Apache Software Foundation//DTD Struts
    Configuration 1.1//EN"
             "http://jakarta.apache.org/struts/dtds/struts-config_1_1.dtd">

<struts-config>
  <global-forwards>
    <forward name="page1" path="/page1.do" />
      <forward name="page2" path="/page2.do" />
      <forward name="page3" path="/page3.do" />
  </global-forwards>

  <action-mappings>
    <action path="/page1" forward="/page1.jsp"/>
    <action path="/page2" forward="/page2.jsp"/>
    <action path="/page3" forward="/page3.jsp"/>
  </action-mappings>

  <controller nocache="true"

  processorClass="com.strutsrecipes.enforce.controller.EnforceNavigationRe
  questProcessor"/>

</struts-config>
```

Notice, the custom RequestProcessor is declared using the <controller> tag's processorClass attribute. We'll defer the importance of the nocache attribute to the discussion section. You are fully configured! After creating the custom Request-Processor in listing 8.37, you are ready to go. Read on if you want to see how the custom RequestProcessor gets the job done.

Now that we have configuration under our belt, let's have a peek under the hood to see how the EnforceNavigationRequestProcessor ticks.

We have chosen to implement this solution by extending RequestProcessor with the EnforceNavigationRequestProcessor class, and overriding specific methods. The RequestProcessor is an ideal place to trap requests because all requests are forced through it. The RequestProcessor's processPreprocess is the method that has been made available to provide developers with the ability to trap requests before they are processed. We use this method to check that an appropriate token was deposited by the previous page. The actual token validation logic has been relegated to the NavigationTokenUtils class. Upon detecting an invalid flow condition, the response is directed to an error page. Requests can exit the

RequestProcessor in three spots—processActionPerform as an Action, process-Forward as a forward, and processInclude as an include. We override these three methods to deposit the page's token in preparation for visiting the next page.

Let's have a look at the EnforceNavigationRequestProcessor, shown in listing 8.37.

Listing 8.37   EnforceNavigationRequestProcessor

```java
package com.strutsrecipes.enforce.controller;

import java.io.IOException;

import javax.servlet.ServletException;
import javax.servlet.http.HttpServletRequest;
import javax.servlet.http.HttpServletResponse;
import javax.servlet.http.HttpSession;

import org.apache.struts.action.Action;
import org.apache.struts.action.ActionForm;
import org.apache.struts.action.ActionForward;
import org.apache.struts.action.ActionMapping;
import org.apache.struts.action.RequestProcessor;

import com.strutsrecipes.enforce.actions.NavigationTokenUtils;

public class EnforceNavigationRequestProcessor extends RequestProcessor {
    private static final String TOKEN_KEY =
        "com.strutsrecipes.enforce.controller.token";          ❶

    protected boolean processPreprocess(
        HttpServletRequest request,
        HttpServletResponse response) {

        String path = null;
        String token = null;

        try {
            path = processPath(request, response);             ❷
        } catch (IOException e) {
            sendError(response, path);          ❸
            return false;
        }

        //the token is stored in the session
        HttpSession session = request.getSession();            ❹
        token = (String) session.getAttribute(TOKEN_KEY);

        if (!NavigationTokenUtils.isValidToken(token, path)) {
            sendError(response, path);                          ❺
            return false;
        }
```

```
        return true;      ❻

}

protected ActionForward processActionPerform(
    HttpServletRequest request,
    HttpServletResponse response,
    Action action,
    ActionForm form,
    ActionMapping mapping)
    throws IOException, ServletException {

    try {
        return super.processActionPerform(
            request,
            response,                              ❼
            action,
            form,
            mapping);
    } catch (IOException e) {
        throw e;
    } finally {
        try {
            setToken(request, response);       ❽
        } catch (IOException e) {
            throw e;
        }
    }

}

protected boolean processForward(
    HttpServletRequest request,
    HttpServletResponse response,
    ActionMapping mapping)
    throws IOException, ServletException {
                                                   ❾
    setToken(request, response);
    return super.processForward(request, response, mapping);
}

protected boolean processInclude(
    HttpServletRequest request,
    HttpServletResponse response,
    ActionMapping mapping)
    throws IOException, ServletException {
                                                   ❿
    setToken(request, response);
    return super.processInclude(request, response, mapping);
}
```

```
    private void sendError(HttpServletResponse response, String path) {

        try {
            response.sendError(
                HttpServletResponse.SC_BAD_REQUEST,
                "Invalid navigation " + path);
        } catch (IOException e) {
            log.error("unable to send error", e);
        }
    }

    private void setToken(
        HttpServletRequest request,
        HttpServletResponse response)
        throws IOException {

        String path = processPath(request, response);
        String token = NavigationTokenUtils.getToken(path);
        HttpSession session = request.getSession();
        session.setAttribute(TOKEN_KEY, token);
    }
}
```

⓫

⓬
⓭
⓮

Let's walk through the code in listing 8.37 to see how it's done.

First, we declare the known key used to track the value of the last token placed in session ❶. The processPreprocess method is used to intercept the request upon entry. In this method we need to make sure the token stored in session is valid for this page. We use the inherited processPath method to obtain the path ❷. The path is used to identify the page. Any problems obtaining the path results in an error response at ❸. Next we obtain the token stored in session ❹, and then at ❺ we use the NavigationTokenUtils to validate the token against the path. An invalid token causes an error page to be returned to the client. If the token is valid for the path, the processPreprocess returns a true value. A false value instructs the RequestProcessor to abandon the request, while a true value is the signal to continue as normal. If all went well, we return true at ❻.

Let's move on to the exit logic. The exit logic is responsible for setting the requested page's token on exit. Let's look at the first of three exit points. The processActionPerform method is invoked when the action-mapping is processing an Action. We use the inherited processActionPerform to process the Action in the usual way ❼. Regardless of what happened in the Action, we set the token at ❽. The second possible exit point is a forward. The processForward method is invoked when the action-mapping is processing a forward. We set the token

before processing the forward ❾. The third possible exit point is an include. The
processInclude method is invoked when the action-mapping is processing an
include. Similar to the processForward method, we set the token before processing the include in the usual way ❿.

Let's look at some of the convenience methods employed above. We send an
error using the response ⓫, and we log and swallow the IOException because
there is nothing much else the application can do in this situation.

Look at the setToken method. In order to obtain the token we need to get the
path, as shown at ⓬. We use the path to obtain the token from NavigationToken-
Utils ⓭, and then we set the token in the HTTP session ⓮.

The NavigationTokenUtils class is responsible for obtaining and validating
tokens based on the XML configuration file created earlier, as shown in listing 8.38.

Listing 8.38   NavigationTokenUtils

```
package com.strutsrecipes.enforce.actions;

import java.io.IOException;
import java.io.InputStream;
import java.util.ArrayList;
import java.util.HashMap;
import java.util.List;
import java.util.Map;
import java.util.StringTokenizer;

import org.apache.commons.digester.Digester;
import org.xml.sax.SAXException;

public class NavigationTokenUtils {

    private static NavigationTokenUtils INSTANCE          ❶
                   = new NavigationTokenUtils();
    private Map validTokenMap = new HashMap();            ❷
    private Map pathTokenMap = new HashMap();             ❸

    private NavigationTokenUtils() {                      ❹
       try {
          Digester digester = new Digester();
          digester.push(this);
          digester.addCallMethod("navigation/tokens/token", "addToken", 2);
          digester.addCallParam("navigation/tokens/token/name", 0);
          digester.addCallParam("navigation/tokens/token/value", 1);
          digester.addCallMethod(
                 "navigation/validTokens/validToken",
                 "addValidToken",
                 2);
          digester.addCallParam("navigation/validTokens/validToken/name",0);
```

```
        digester.addCallParam("navigation/validTokens/validToken/value",1);
         ClassLoader classLoader = this.getClass().getClassLoader();
         InputStream is = classLoader.getResourceAsStream("navigation.xml");
         digester.parse(is);

    } catch (IOException e) {
      System.out.println("error:"+e.toString());
    } catch (SAXException e) {
      System.out.println("error:"+e.toString());
    }
}


public void addToken(String name, String value) {             ❺
   pathTokenMap.put(name, value);
}

public void addValidToken(String name, String value) {
   StringTokenizer st = new StringTokenizer(value, ",");
   ArrayList al = new ArrayList();
                                                              ❻
   while (st.hasMoreTokens()) {
      al.add(st.nextToken());
   }

   validTokenMap.put(name, al);
}


private static NavigationTokenUtils getInstance() {          ❼
   return INSTANCE;
}

private Map getValidTokenMap() {              ❽
   return validTokenMap;
}

private Map getPathTokenMap() {              ❾
   return pathTokenMap;
}

public static String getToken(String key) {
   Map m = getInstance().getPathTokenMap();          ❿
   return (String) m.get(key);
}

public static boolean isValidToken(String token, String key) {    ⓫

   Map map = getInstance().getValidTokenMap();  ⓬
   List list = (List) map.get(key);
```

```
        //if starting point, then it shouldn't be in the map
        if (null == token && null == list) {
            return true;                          ⓭
        }


        //if not in map, then no restrictions
        if (null == list) {
            return true;             ⓮
        }

        return list.contains(token);      ⓯
    }


}
```

NavigationTokenUtils is a singleton which is automatically configured from the navigation.xml file when the instance is created. Jakarta Commons Digester is used to parse the XML file into two Maps analogous to the tables 1.1 and 1.2. The getToken(..) and isValidToken(..) use these Maps to do their jobs. To properly understand the self-configuring nature of NavigationTokenUitls, you need a good understanding of the Jakarta Commons Digester. We gloss over the Digester, but we encourage you to explore supplementary reading on this useful and versatile tool.

Let's step through listing 8.38.

NavigationTokenUtils is a singleton. The single instance is created when the class is loaded by the class loader. First, we create a static instance ❶. Then we create Maps analogous to the tables 1.1 ❷ and 1.2 ❸. We make the constructor private to ensure it is not externally instantiated ❹. The constructor creates an instance of the Digester, and pushes itself on to the Digester's stack. The Digester rules created in this method cause the addToken(..) and addValid-Token(..) methods to be called with the data in the XML file. The logging statements in this method use simple println statements, but it might be best to use your favorite logging package.

At ❺ the addToken(..) method is created. This method is invoked by the Digester to add an entry to the pathTokenMap. We create the addValidToken(..) method ❻, which is invoked by the Digester. This method receives a path name and a list of comma-delimited tokens. The list of tokens is created by using StringTokenizer and stored in an ArrayList. The path and the ArrayList are placed in the Map.

Next we provide a method to obtain an instance to the singleton ❼. The static methods in this class require access to the instance to obtain the Maps created at ❺ and ❻. At ❽ and ❾ we provide convenience methods to obtain the Maps created at ❺ and ❻. We then create a static method to obtain a token for a key ❾. We have chosen to use the path as the key.

The next step is to create a static method to determine if a token is in the list of valid tokens for a path ❿, ⓫. Let's look at this method in a little more detail. We obtain the list of valid tokens by looking them up in the validTokenMap ⓬. The first time the application is used in this session the token is null. The starting point must have no token preconditions. At ⓭ we assert this is true. A page without preconditions is not registered in the validTokenMap. At ⓮ we check for this condition. This means you need to be careful to make sure you have not forgotten to register a page in the XML file. If you feel unsure about this, you can enhance this recipe to recognize a special token, such as "*", to indicate no restrictions.

Finally, we check to see if the token is in the list of valid tokens registered for this page ⓯.

You don't really need to understand how the EnforceNavigationRequestProcessor and NavigationTokenUtils work, but the code is completely laid out in case you like to get down to the nitty-gritty details.

◆ *Discussion*

This recipe allows you to increase an application's robustness by ensuring the user has navigated through the application as intended. As developers, we sometimes forget that people push our applications to the limit. We need to account for applications being used to the edge—and beyond—of their capabilities.

We have chosen to store the token in the HTTP session. Alternatively, we could have chosen a client-based solution such as a hidden field or a cookie. Client-based solutions are inherently less robust. A clever user can craft a request to circumvent navigation. A more robust strategy is to store the token on the server side and out of the reach of users.

In addition, we chose to implement this solution in the RequestProcessor. Alternatively, we could have implemented this solution in the Action. Although an Action-based solution is viable, a RequestProcessor-based solution is more robust because all Struts requests must be directed through the RequestProcessor. In addition, it allows you to plug and unplug this functionality without affecting your application code. Moreover, you can reuse Actions in other applications without mandating the use of enforced navigation.

There is one "gotcha" to watch out for. This recipe requires that all pages are served by going to the server. The back button can cause havoc whenever pages are cached on the client. We recommend you set the `nocache` attribute to `true` on the struts-config.xml `<controller>` tag to defeat page caching and force a request to the server.

Robust and secure design is an important objective. This recipe gives you another tool to ensure you meet those objectives.

BEST   *Enforce navigation where required*—Applications dependent on naviga-
PRACTICE   tional flow should be responsible for validating the flow instead of rely-
ing on user-interface design.

◆ **Reference**

▪ [DIGEST] Apache Jakarta Commons Digester

8.8 *Use a database to store*
your message-resources properties

◆ **Problem**

You want `<message-resources/>` to access a database instead of a properties file.

◆ **Background**

Resource bundles are easily accessible within Struts applications. All you need to do is declare a `<message-resource/>` tag pointing to your resource bundle inside the struts-config.xml file, and all the properties within that resource bundle are made available to all of the standard Struts tags possessing `srcKey` and `bundle` attributes. The `<message-resource/>` tag eases the maintenance burden by decoupling the physical file name from the resource bundle.

As your application grows, you may find yourself handling monolithic flat property files. Understandably, maintenance may become difficult. One alternative may be to break down the properties files into smaller logical units by creating multiple message-resource bundles (see recipe 1.6, "Using multiple message-resource properties files in an application").

The dynamic nature of many large e-commerce sites demands constant change to both text and images. Business users may want to change text and images themselves without the complications of a deployment. Flat property files supply a less than ideal solution for this use case. A better alternative is to engineer

`<message-resources/>` to access a database. You could then build a user-friendly interface to allow business users to manage the content themselves.

The following recipe shows you how to back `<message-resources/>` with a database. To meet performance objectives, the solution minimizes database access by utilizing a simple caching technique.

◆ *Recipe*

The standard `<message-resources/>` implementation provides a default factory to obtain resource bundles from a properties file. In this recipe we override the default factory with our own JDBC factory. Our custom factory manufactures a JDBC implementation of `MessageResources`, whose express purpose is to serve database-stored key values. Let's see how it's done!

All `<message-resources/>` tags are declared in the struts-config-xml file. The usual way to declare a resource bundle as a `<message-resource/>` is shown in listing 8.39.

> **Listing 8.39   default struts-config.xml message-resources**

```
<message-resources parameter="resources.application"/>
```

The `parameter` attribute is the location of the properties file relative to the class path. Compare the above to listing 8.40, where the `factory` attribute is set to `com.strutsrecipes.JDBCMessageResourcesFactory`. In listing 8.40, the `parameter` attribute has a different job. Instead of specifying a properties file storing the message key-value pairs, the `parameter` attribute points to a JDBC properties file needed by the factory to access the database.

> **Listing 8.40   struts-config.xml message-resources using a custom factory**

```
<message-resources
    factory="com.strutsrecipes.JDBCMessageResources"
    parameter="jdbc.messageresources.properties" />
```

The next step is to create the jdbc.messageresources.properties file. Listing 8.41 reveals the contents of the file, showing the information needed to access the Postgre database used in this particular implementation. Although we have used Postgre, you are free to use your choice of database.

Listing 8.41   jdbc.messageresources.properties

```
jdbc.url = jdbc:postgresql://localhost:5432/cddev
jdbc.driver = org.postgresql.Driver
jdbc.username = myusername
jdbc.password = mypassword
jdbc.table = message_resource
jdbc.keyColumn = message_key
jdbc.valueColumn = message_value
jdbc.localeCountryColumn = locale_country
jdbc.localeLanguageColumn = locale_language
```

Listing 8.42 presents the SQL to create the message_resource database table. The table is populated using SQL commands or your favorite SQL client (not shown).

Listing 8.42   SQL to create message_resource database table

```
CREATE TABLE message_resource (
message_key text,
message_value text,
locale_country varchar(128),
locale_language varchar(128)
);
```

Finally, you need to create the JDBCMessageResourcesFactory, shown in listing 8.43.

Listing 8.43   JDBCMessageResourcesFactory

```
package com.strutsrecipes;

import org.apache.struts.util.MessageResources;
import org.apache.struts.util.MessageResourcesFactory;

public class JDBCMessageResourcesFactory extends MessageResourcesFactory {
    public MessageResources createResources(String propertiesFile) {
        return new JDBCMessageResources(this,propertiesFile);
    }
}
```

To use your own <message-resource/> factory, the factory attribute must point to a class extending MessageResourcesFactory. The new factory must override the createResources method and return a MessageResource implementation of your own choosing. Let have a look at the JDBCMessageResources implementation in listing 8.44.

Listing 8.44 JDBCMessageResources

```java
package com.strutsrecipes;

import java.util.HashMap;
import java.util.Properties;
import java.io.InputStream;
import java.io.IOException;
import java.sql.DriverManager;
import java.sql.Statement;
import java.sql.SQLException;
import java.sql.Connection;
import java.sql.ResultSet;
import java.util.Locale;
import org.apache.struts.util.MessageResources;
import org.apache.struts.util.MessageResourcesFactory;
import org.apache.commons.logging.Log;
import org.apache.commons.logging.LogFactory;

public class JDBCMessageResources extends MessageResources {
    private static String KEY_TABLE = "jdbc.table";
    private static String KEY_KEY_COLUMN = "jdbc.keyColumn";
    private static String KEY_VALUE_COLUMN = "jdbc.valueColumn";
    private static String KEY_LOCALE_COUNTRY_COLUMN =
                                     "jdbc.localeCountryColumn";
    private static String KEY_LOCALE_LANGUAGE_COLUMN =
                                     "jdbc.localeLanguageColumn";
    private static String KEY_DB_DRIVER = "jdbc.driver";
    private static String KEY_DB_URL = "jdbc.url";
    private static String KEY_DB_PASSWORD = "jdbc.password";
    private static String KEY_DB_USERNAME = "jdbc.username";

    private static Log m_Log = LogFactory.getLog(JDBCMessageResources.class);
    private HashMap m_Maps = null;

    public JDBCMessageResources(MessageResourcesFactory factory,
        String config, boolean returnNull) {
        super(factory,config,returnNull);
        init(config);
    }

    public JDBCMessageResources(MessageResourcesFactory factory,
        String config) {
        this(factory,config,true);
    }

    public String getMessage(Locale locale, String key) {
        String localeKey = locale.getCountry()+"_"+locale.getLanguage();
        HashMap map = (HashMap)m_Maps.get(localeKey);
        if (map==null) {
          return (getReturnNull()) ? null : "";
```

```
        }

        String mess = (String)map.get(key);
        if (mess==null) {
            return (getReturnNull()) ? null : "";
        }

        return mess;
    }

    private synchronized void init(String propertiesFile) {

        m_Log.info("Initializing JDBCMessageResources");

        InputStream ips = null;
        Properties props = new Properties();
        Connection con = null;
        ResultSet rs = null;
        Statement statement = null;
        InputStream is = null;
        String table = null;
        String keyColumn = null;
        String valueColumn = null;
        String localeCountryColumn = null;
        String localeLanguageColumn = null;
        String driver = null;

        m_Maps = new HashMap();

        try {
            ClassLoader classLoader =
                         Thread.currentThread().getContextClassLoader();
            if (classLoader == null) {
                classLoader = this.getClass().getClassLoader();
            }

            is = classLoader.getResourceAsStream(propertiesFile);

            props.load(is);

            table = props.getProperty(KEY_TABLE);
            keyColumn = props.getProperty(KEY_KEY_COLUMN);
            valueColumn = props.getProperty(KEY_VALUE_COLUMN);
            localeCountryColumn = props.getProperty(KEY_LOCALE_COUNTRY_COLUMN);
            localeLanguageColumn =
                         props.getProperty(KEY_LOCALE_LANGUAGE_COLUMN);
            driver = props.getProperty(KEY_DB_DRIVER);

            Class.forName(driver);

            con = DriverManager.getConnection(
```

```
            props.getProperty(KEY_DB_URL),
            props.getProperty(KEY_DB_PASSWORD),
            props.getProperty(KEY_DB_USERNAME)
        );

        statement = con.createStatement();

        rs = statement.executeQuery("SELECT * FROM "+table);

        while(rs.next()) {
            String locale_country = rs.getString(localeCountryColumn);
            String locale_language = rs.getString(localeLanguageColumn);
            String key = rs.getString(keyColumn);
            String value = rs.getString(valueColumn);
            String localeKey = locale_country+"_"+locale_language;

            if (m_Maps.get(localeKey)==null) {
                HashMap map = new HashMap();
                m_Maps.put(localeKey,map);
            }

            HashMap map = (HashMap)m_Maps.get(localeKey);
            map.put(key,value);
        }

        m_Log.info("Initializzation of JDBCMessageResources complete");

    } catch(ClassNotFoundException cnfe) {
        m_Log.fatal("Could not register driver: "+driver, cnfe);
        throw new RuntimeException(cnfe);

    } catch(IOException ioe) {
        m_Log.fatal("Could not load configuration information", ioe);
        throw new RuntimeException(ioe);

    } catch(SQLException se) {
        m_Log.fatal("Error loading messages from database", se);
        throw new RuntimeException(se);

    } finally {
        try {
            rs.close();
            statement.close();
            con.close();
        } catch(Throwable t) {
            m_Log.info("Error cleaning up JDBCMessageResources", t);
        }
    }
  }
}
```

You really don't need to understand the JDBCMessageResources implementation in listing 8.44. You can simply use it as is. However, if you decide to step through the code you will find that it creates a cache of messages by reading the database when the class is instantiated. The cache is accessed whenever the getMessage method is invoked. That's all there is to it!

◆ *Discussion*

In this recipe we show you how to access message-resources from a database instead of the usual properties file. The details on how to access the properties are hidden away in a factory and its supporting MessageResources class.

Depending on your own circumstances, you may choose to enhance the code presented above. For instance, you may decide to implement a lazy load to reduce the size of the cache. This might be suitable when you expect only a few of the properties to be requested. Otherwise, you may decide to load some properties up front, but lazy load the rest. You can achieve this by adding a "preload" column to the table to indicate which properties are preloaded on instantiation, and leave the rest for a lazy load.

Indeed, you are not limited to loading from a database. You may choose to store your properties in an XML file and read them in using the Apache Digester. The properties don't even have to be on the local machine. You can access them over a socket, via an EJB or as a Web service. The technique presented in this recipe arms you with a technique to extend the possibilities beyond a relational database.

◆ *Related*

■ 1.6—Multiple message-resource properties files in an application

Testing

You can only put as much intelligence into a system as was in the design engineer to begin with.

—Peter Orme,
British Aerospace test pilot

Testing is probably an application's greatest asset to long-term scalability and maintainability. Unless we have confidence our application works as intended, we may not be satisfying its business objectives. Testing can be a difficult endeavor, but the prospect of repeating tests at the push of a button may seem unrealistic. Fortunately, it's not. This chapter is devoted to helping you do just that. Although functional tests seem to garnish much of the limelight, we delve into other areas of testing that seem to get less publicity. Specifically, we explore performance testing, coverage testing, and testing with and without the container.

Testing seems to take on a special importance in larger teams. Team members are constantly checking code in and out of the repository. Without diligent testing it's impossible to achieve a stable code base. The ability to regression test your code before and after you make a change makes the development process go smoother. It's a good practice to make sure all unit tests are running before you check your code in. That way, the code base is as stable as possible for the next developer to begin work.

Testing is not only for the applications you are deploying today, but also for their future enhancements. Your investment in testing today will pay you back many times over in the future. A good test bed allows you to fearlessly deliver new features with the confidence that the entire application is still working as intended.

TESTING AIRCRAFT   Bill is a test pilot (he is a real person). He's in his fifties, which means he's a *very good* test pilot. He stays in great shape, has steely nerves, and a calmness about him that can't be forced, and it really takes a lot to get his feathers ruffled. He's the kind of guy that you could be in a car flipping through the air, and he'd look over at you and say, "I think we've rotated three times."

For Bill to get as old as he has and remain in this profession for more than 20 years, a great deal of planning needs to happen before he turns over the engines on the latest experimental plane trusted to his skill. A lot of this planning involves testing through engineering models, math, CAD/CAM systems, and other types of static testing. When he finally fires up the engines and takes off, he's pretty sure that everything's going to go well; and if something happens, he's will probably know what it is and it's probably going to be anticipated.

While Bill has been in some rather hairy situations, he's been able to come out of them, process the information, and save money and lives by applying what he's learned. Application testing often saves quite a bit of money and prevents crashes. Although these kinds of crashes don't break bones, they can break companies.

Many of today's leading programmers advocate writing out test cases even before the code. This type of development is known as Test Driven Development (TDD).

JUnit has been around long enough for most developers to create test cases for their domain models and other Java classes. What's been missing are plug-ins for Struts to make our lives easier when it comes to the many individual components of the Struts framework. `StrutsTestCase` and Cactus have begun to fill these gaps, and in this chapter we present recipes for them and other recipes to test various Struts extensions. The chapter contains:

- *Outside-the-container testing with `StrutsTestCase`*—Using `StrutsTestCase` to test an application without a container
- *Inside-the-container testing with `StrutsTestCase`*—Using `StrutsTestCase` and `Cactus` to test your application in an environment approximating your production environment
- *Testing `DynaActionForms`*—Using `StrutsTestCase` to test `DynaActionForms`
- *Module Testing*—Testing an application built with Struts modules
- *Performance Testing*—Testing the performance of your Struts application
- *Coverage*—Discovering which parts of your application are covered by your testing classes

  For more information on JUnit, you should consult http://www.junit.org. Everything is there to get the developer up and running, including excellent instructions and information for the beginner, intermediate, and advanced developer. The first recipe in this chapter, recipe 9.1, "Testing outside the container with StrutsTestCase," explains more about JUnit in its Background section.

9.1 *Testing outside the container with StrutsTestCase*

◆ *Problem*

You want to test your Struts application without using the container.

◆ *Background*

Testing is the cornerstone of a good development project, yet few teams do it well. On the surface, testing appears to have little appeal. It is a difficult, tedious, and time-consuming task which does not seem to offer high-profile check marks against the project plan. However, a good testing effort reduces the total effort because, despite our best efforts, we do make mistakes. Sooner or later we have to confront our bugs. Procrastinating to a later date puts us in a position of fixing things when the layout of the code is not in the forefront of our mind, causing us to compound our mistakes.

JUNIT   JUnit is an open source testing framework empowering Java developers with the tools required to write reusable unit tests quickly and easily. JUnit offers a simple API to invoke methods and check their results.

To build a JUnit test you create a plain old Java class extending `junit.framework.TestCase`. Each test class contains one or more public methods with method names starting with "test." Each of these methods represent a different unit test. In your unit test you set up your input, invoke the code to be tested, and verify the results. The `TestCase` parent class supplies several assertion methods to ease the burden of validating the results. You can place as many assertions in your test method as you like, but should any of them fail, the unit test fails. If any of the unit tests fails, the entire test case is flagged as a failure.

JUnit uses reflection to discover and invoke each method starting with "test." Frequently, unit tests in your test case share common activities to set up the unit test's precondition state. To makes things a bit easier, JUnit allows you to define a setup method in your test class. JUnit automatically runs the setup method prior to each and every test method. JUnit provides you with the opportunity to clean up your setup activities by automatically running the `teardown()` method after each `test()` method.

We encourage you to read the additional JUnit material listed in the reference section. *JUnit in Action* (Manning Publications) is a comprehensive source on testing with JUnit.

Most teams are testing at various levels. User acceptance, integration, regression, performance, and unit testing are only some of the various types of tests which can be performed. In this recipe we zero in on unit testing Struts applications. A unit test is a fine-grain test limited to a method of a class. Writing unit tests is hard work. You need to simulate input, execute the method, and verify the expected results. Fortunately, tools such as JUnit reduces that effort to a manageable level. JUnit [JUNIT] is a unit testing framework offering a simple API to verify that your code works as intended. JUnit is integrated with a number of front ends, often called runners, to make the job even easier. A number of popular IDEs support JUnit, but Apache Ant [ANT] is a common way of executing JUnit tests. Using Ant, you can run your unit tests whenever you run a build.

STRUTS
TEST
CASE   `StrutsTestCase` is a testing framework extension of JUnit designed to accommodate the special needs of Struts application testing. `Struts-TestCase` tests are created in much the same way as any JUnit tests,

except additional verify and assertion methods are available to verify Struts specific functionality.

`StrutsTestCase` enables you to declare the URL path and create request parameters. You simulate the invocation of the `ActionServlet` by invoking `actionPerform`. Among other things, the methods inherited from `MockStrutsTestCase` allow you to validate that the desired `Action-Forward` was returned, `ActionErrors` were created, and that JavaBeans were placed in context.

In addition, `StrutsTestCase` boasts several simulators to mock HTTP requests, responses, and sessions. For example, you can use `HttpSessionSimulator` to populate a session object to meet the preconditions of your unit test.

`StrutsTestCase` supports both mock object and in-container testing. Mock objects are objects masquerading as their real-life counterparts. They act as dumb servants to business objects. Mock objects can be other business objects, or they can be objects representing a container. Mock objects are useful when their fully functional counterparts are unavailable, or when you need your test to be independent of a container's implementation. The flip side of that argument is that Mock objects may not accurately reflect the real-life production experience of an in-container test. Fortunately, `StrutsTestCase` supports both Mock and in-container testing.

Mock object testing of Struts applications is supported by extending your test class with `MockStrutsTestCase`. You can change your test to use in-container testing by extending `CactusStrutsTestCase` instead of `MockStrutsTestCase`. Other than Cactus setup work, no other changes are required.

We encourage you to read the additional `StrutsTestCase` material listed in the reference section. The `StrutsTestCase` javadoc is an excellent source of material.

`StrutsTestCase` for JUnit [STRUTSTC] is an extension of JUnit intended to address the special needs of Struts applications. `StrutsTestCase` extends the JUnit API to provide you with tools to probe the workings of your Struts applications.

In this recipe we show you how to use `StrutsTestCase` to test a Struts application using the Mock Object approach. See recipe 9.2, "In-container testing with StrutsTestCase and Cactus," to see how you can implement in-container testing.

We start by creating a small application worthy of some testing. With our code base firmly in place, we write both positive and negative tests using the Mock Object approach. We conclude this recipe by presenting an Apache Ant script to automate the testing process. With `StrutsTestCase` under your belt, and the ability to run them with the push of a button, you will have gained new confidence in your code. More importantly, you will have the courage to refactor code without the worry of breaking your existing code base.

◆ *Recipe*

Let's start by creating something to test. In this recipe we revisit high school chemistry class by creating a small Struts application to access information from the periodic table. The user enters the 2-character element symbol on a search screen. After pressing the search button, the application returns the element's name, atomic number, and mass. If the user enters an invalid symbol, the application returns an error message.

Listing 9.1   index.html

```
<%@ page language="java" %>
<%@ taglib uri="/WEB-INF/struts-html.tld" prefix="html" %>
<%@ taglib uri="/WEB-INF/struts-logic.tld" prefix="logic" %>
<html:html locale="true">
    <head>
        <title>index</title>
        <html:base/>
    </head>
    <logic:redirect forward="search"/>      ❶
</html:html>
```

Let's inspect the code. The user accesses the application by entering http://localhost:8080/strutstestcase/index.jsp. Listing 9.1 presents index.jsp. Notice the user is automatically forwarded to "search" ❶.

Listing 9.2   Struts-config.xml file

```
<?xml version="1.0" encoding="ISO-8859-1" ?>
<!DOCTYPE struts-config PUBLIC
          "-//Apache Software Foundation//DTD Struts Configuration 1.1//EN"
          "http://jakarta.apache.org/struts/dtds/struts-config_1_1.dtd">
<struts-config>
  <form-beans>
     <form-bean name="searchForm"
                 type="com.strutsrecipes.strutstestcase.forms.SearchForm"/>
  </form-beans>
  <global-forwards>
     <forward   name="search" path="/search.jsp"/>      ❷
     <forward   name="searchsubmit" path="/searchsubmit.do"/>
  </global-forwards>
  <action-mappings>
    <action path="/searchsubmit"
```

```
            type="com.strutsrecipes.strutstestcase.actions.SearchAction"
            name="searchForm"
            scope="request"
            input="/search.jsp">
            <forward name="success" path="/element.jsp"/>
    </action>
  </action-mappings>
</struts-config>
```

Listing 9.3   search.jsp

```
<%@ page language="java" %>
<%@ taglib uri="/WEB-INF/struts-html.tld" prefix="html" %>
<html:html>
<body>
  <h1>Search for an Element</h1>

  <html:form action="/searchsubmit.do">
    symbol <form:text property="symbol"/>
  <html:submit value="Search"/>
  </html:form>
  <html:errors/>
</body>
</html:html>
```

Let's review the struts-config.xml file (listing 9.2) to see what happens next. A global forward ❷ directs the user to search.jsp (listing 9.3). The user enters a symbol on search.jsp (listing 9.3) and submits the form to searchsubmit.do. The struts-config.xml file instructs Struts to use SearchAction to process the request.

Let's continue exploring this application by reviewing the SearchAction in listing 9.4. If the search is successful, the Element bean is stored in the request context and the response is delegated to element.jsp. To add a little spice, we capture the user's IP address from the response and store it as a bean in the request context along with the Element bean. If unsuccessful, the input attribute is used to direct the response back to search.jsp. SearchAction creates an Action-Error to inform the user that an invalid request has been submitted. Search.jsp renders the error message using <html:errors/>. We haven't spent much time stepping through the code, but the application is trivial enough that you can understand it from the code listings. We invite you to review the code listings before progressing further.

Listing 9.4   SearchAction

```
package com.strutsrecipes.strutstestcase.actions;
import javax.servlet.http.HttpServletRequest;
```

```
import javax.servlet.http.HttpServletResponse;
import org.apache.struts.action.Action;
import org.apache.struts.action.ActionError;
import org.apache.struts.action.ActionErrors;
import org.apache.struts.action.ActionForm;
import org.apache.struts.action.ActionForward;
import org.apache.struts.action.ActionMapping;
import com.strutsrecipes.strutstestcase.beans.Element;
import com.strutsrecipes.strutstestcase.business.BusinessFacade;
import com.strutsrecipes.strutstestcase.forms.SearchForm;
public class SearchAction extends Action {
    public ActionForward execute(
        ActionMapping mapping,
        ActionForm form,
        HttpServletRequest request,
        HttpServletResponse response)
        throws Exception {
        SearchForm searchForm = (SearchForm) form;
        BusinessFacade businessFacade = new BusinessFacade();
        Element element = businessFacade.getElement(searchForm.getSymbol());
        if (element != null) {
            request.setAttribute("element", element);
            request.setAttribute("ip", request.getRemoteAddr());;
            return mapping.findForward("success");
        }
        ActionErrors errors = new ActionErrors();
        errors.add(ActionErrors.GLOBAL_ERROR,
            new ActionError("error.notfound"));
        this.saveErrors(request, errors);
        return mapping.findForward("failure");
    }
}
```

Before jumping into the test, we need to spend some time thinking about the scope of the test. The simple answer is to test everything, but that may not be reasonable, or appropriate. For instance, because the Struts framework is being tested with every build, there is no need to test Struts itself. However, we should certainly test the way we use Struts.

Let's enumerate the positive postconditions:

- Element and IP beans are created and stored in the request context.

- Uppercase and lowercase input can be handled successfully.

The negative postconditions are as follows:

- Element and IP beans do not exist.

- ActionError was created.

There are some gray areas. For example, should we verify that the path was set properly, or shall we limit the check to ensuring the correct `ActionForward` was returned? Shall we test whether the expected `ActionForm` class was passed to the `Action`? Each project and each developer will have their own opinion. We leave it to you to decide how much testing you want to do, but be aware the capability exists should you choose to be more thorough. For the purposes of this recipe we limit the scope of the test to the `searchsubmit.do` action mapping and the post-conditions outlined above.

Listing 9.5 Positive test

```
package com.strutsrecipes.strutstestcase.mocktest;
import com.strutsrecipes.strutstestcase.beans.Element;
import servletunit.HttpServletRequestSimulator;
import servletunit.struts.MockStrutsTestCase;
public class TestPositive extends MockStrutsTestCase {          ❶
   public void setUp() throws Exception {           ❷
      super.setUp();

      HttpServletRequestSimulator request =
          (HttpServletRequestSimulator) this.getRequest();
      request.setRemoteAddr("99.99.99.99");           ❸
   }
   public void tearDown() throws Exception {           ❹
      super.tearDown();
   }
   public TestPositive(String name) {
      super(name);
   }
   public void testLowerCase() {
         addRequestParameter("symbol", "au");           ❺
      postiveCase();           ❻
   }

   private void postiveCase() {
      setRequestPathInfo("/searchsubmit");           ❼
      actionPerform();           ❽
      verifyForward("success");           ❾
      verifyForwardPath("/element.jsp");           ❿
      assertNotNull(getRequest().getAttribute("ip"));           ⓫
      assertNotNull(getRequest().getAttribute("element"));           ⓬
     Element element = (Element) getRequest().getAttribute("element");           ⓭
      assertEquals(element.getSymbol(), "Au");           ⓮
      assertEquals(element.getName(), "Gold");           ⓯
      assertEquals(element.getMass(), "197");           ⓰
      assertEquals(element.getNumber(), "79");           ⓱
      assertEquals(getRequest().getAttribute("ip").
          toString(), "99.99.99.99");           ⓲
```

```
        verifyNoActionErrors();      ⑲
    }
    public void testUpperCase() {
        addRequestParameter("symbol", "AU");    ⑳
        postiveCase();
    }
}
```

Now it's time to test using mock objects! Let's step through listing 9.5 line by line.

We extend MockStrutsTestCase to indicate that we are performing a mock test ❶. Performing an in-container test is a simple matter of extending from Cactus-StrutsTestCase instead of MockStrutsTestCase. We then define logic that needs to run before each test ❷, and create an HttpServletRequestSimulator to simulate the client's IP address ❸. Note that super.setup() must be called.

Next we define logic that needs to run after each test ❹. Although we don't have logic to execute, we include the method as an example. Note that super.teardown() must be called. Now, we define our first test ❺ by creating a request parameter to simulate the users request for the "Au" symbol. As good students of reuse, at ❻ we call a private method to perform the rest of the test. At this point we set up the request path ❼ and simulate the submission of the request to the ActionServlet at ❽.

> **NOTE** StrutsTestCase searches your class path for struts-config.xml. If you need to store struts-confix.xml outside of the class path, you must use setConfigFile(java.lang.String pathname) to make your struts-config.xml file available to the test.

Now it's time to verify that your code performed as expected.

We expect the search to be successful, and so we verify that SearchAction returned the success ActionForward ❾. Next, we verify the struts-config.xml file was configured to return the "/element.jsp" path ❿. At ⑪ and ⑫ we verify that the IP and Element beans are not null. We do these checks to ensure we don't get a NullPointerException in any assert statements checking the content of these beans. Now, we access the Element bean for assertions in later steps ⑬.

At this point, we verify that the symbol is "Au" ⑭, verify that the name is "Gold" ⑮, verify that the Mass is "197" ⑯, verify that the Number is "79" ⑰, verify that the IP address is "99.99.99.99" ⑱ to match ❸, and finally at ⑲ we verify that no errors are created. And then we perform the same test to ensure the application handles uppercase input ⑳.

If any of the verifications fail, the entire test method is flagged as a failure.

Listing 9.6   Negative test

```
package com.strutsrecipes.strutstestcase.mocktest;
import servletunit.HttpServletRequestSimulator;
import servletunit.struts.MockStrutsTestCase;
public class TestNegative extends MockStrutsTestCase {        ❶
    public void setUp() throws Exception {        ❷
        super.setUp();
        HttpServletRequestSimulator request =
            (HttpServletRequestSimulator) this.getRequest();
        request.setRemoteAddr("99.99.99.99");        ❸
    }
    public void tearDown() throws Exception {        ❹
        super.tearDown();
    }
    public TestNegative(String name) {        ❺
        super(name);
    }
    public void testInvalidValue() {        ❻
        addRequestParameter("symbol", "xx");
        negativeCase();        ❼
    }
    private void negativeCase() {
        setRequestPathInfo("/searchsubmit");        ❽
        actionPerform();        ❾
        verifyInputForward();        ❿
        assertNull(getRequest().getAttribute("ip"));        ⓫
        assertNull(getRequest().getAttribute("element"));        ⓬
        String[] errors = { "error.notfound" };
        verifyActionErrors(errors);        ⓭
    }
    public void testEmpty() {
        addRequestParameter("symbol", "");        ⓮
        negativeCase();
    }
}
```

Let's test an unsuccessful search. Steps ❶ through ❾ are similar to the positive test, except we are testing invalid input. In this scenario, we expect the search to fail, so we verify that the Input was used instead of the "success" forward ❿. Next, we assert that the IP and Element beans do not exist ⓫⓬. At ⓭ we verify that an ActionError was created using the error.not.found key. If more than one Action-Error was created, we add additional elements to the errors array. Finally, we repeat the test to ensure the application responds as expected when the user fails to enter anything ⓮.

Listing 9.7 Automated build and test using Apache Ant

```xml
<project name="struts test case recipe" default="build-war">
    <property file="build.properties"/>

    <path id="classpath.base">          ❶
        <pathelement location="${servlet.dir}/${servlet.jar}"/>
        <pathelement location="${struts.dir}/${struts.jar}"/>
        <pathelement location="${log4j.dir}/{log4j.jar}"/>
        <pathelement location="${commons-logging.dir}/$
                                {commons-logging.jar}"/>
        <pathelement
           location="${commons-beanutils.dir}/${commons-beanutils.jar}"/>
        <pathelement
           location="${commons-digester.dir}/${commons-digester.jar}"/>
        <pathelement
          location="${commons-collections.dir}/${commons-collections.jar}"/>
    </path>

    <path id="classpath.test">          ❷
        <pathelement location="${webapp.dir}"/>
        <pathelement location="${webapp.dir}/WEB-INF/struts-config.xml"/>
        <pathelement location="${build.src.dir}"/>
        <pathelement location="${build.test.dir}"/>          ❸
        <pathelement location="${strutstest.dir}/${strutstest.jar}"/>     ❹
        <path refid="classpath.base" />
    </path>
    <target name="clean">          ❺
        <mkdir dir="${build.src.dir}"/>
        <mkdir dir="${build.test.dir}"/>
        <mkdir dir="${reports.dir}"/>
        <mkdir dir="${dist.dir}"/>
    </target>
    <target name="compile-domain"
            description="compile domain"
            depends="clean">          ❻
        <javac srcdir="${src.dir}"
            destdir="${build.src.dir}"
            debug="${javac.debug}"
            classpathref="classpath.base"/>
    </target>
    <target name="compile-test"
            description="compile test"
            depends="clean">
        <javac srcdir="${test.dir}"
            destdir="${build.test.dir}"
            debug="${javac.debug}"
            classpathref="classpath.test"/>
    </target>
    <target name="test-domain"
            description="run unit tests"
            depends="compile-domain,compile-test">          ❼
```

```
        <junit printsummary="yes"   ❽ haltonfailure="yes">
           <classpath refid="classpath.test"/>
           <formatter type="plain"/>   ❾
           <batchtest fork="yes" todir="${reports.dir}">   ❿
              <fileset dir="${test.dir}">
                 <include name="**/*Test*.java"/>   ⓫
              </fileset>
           </batchtest>
        </junit>
     </target>
     <target name="build-war" description="build war file" depends="test-
domain">   ⓬
        <war warfile="${dist.dir}/${warfile.war}"
             webxml="${webapp.dir}/WEB-INF/web.xml"
             manifest="${webapp.dir}/META-INF/MANIFEST.MF">
           <classes dir="${build.src.dir}"/>
           <fileset dir="${webapp.dir}">
              <exclude name="WEB-INF/web.xml"/>
           </fileset>
           <lib dir="${webapp.dir}/WEB-INF/lib"/>
        </war>
     </target>
  </project>
```

Finally, we present an Apache Ant script to build, test, and create the WAR file for this application. Note that a successful test is required for a successful build. If you have not already done so, you can download Apache Ant at http://ant.apache.org/. To run the Ant script in listing 9.7 you need to drop the JUnit JAR file into %ANT_HOME%/lib.

If you have previously used Apache Ant for automated builds, most of this script will seem familiar to you. Let's step through listing 9.7, drawing your attention to the portions relevant to testing.

We start by defining a base class path for the application code ❶, and then we define a test class path for compiling and running tests ❷. Notice we have included the struts-config.xml file in our class path. This allows StrutsTestCase to automatically find the struts-config.xml file. Now we include the compiled test class ❸ and the StrutsTestCase ❹.

We next prepare the build directories for application and test class files. We create directories for unit test reports and our WAR file ❺, compile our application code ❻, and then compile our StrutsTestCase unit test code ❼.

JUnit is capable of producing reports. The <junit> tag printsummary attribute ❽ triggers report generation. At ❾ we indicated the report should be formatted as plain text. Alternatively, you can choose xml. At this point, we identify the directory to hold the reports ❿. The include statement at ⓫ instructs JUnit to run only those tests in the ${test.dir} directory with names matching the "*Test*" pattern. Finally, we build the WAR file for the application ⓬.

◆ **Discussion**

There are few project activities more important than testing your code. It is equally true that a difficult and laborious testing effort can tip the scales of temptation, leading you down a path of unstable code and longer timelines. The upfront testing effort will pay you back many times.

Choosing the right tool for the job builds great inroads into easing the burden of testing. StrutsTestCase builds upon the JUnit testing framework to address the specific needs of Struts developers. The StrutsTestCase MockStruts-TestCase, and its in-container cousin CactusStrutsTestCase, offer many more methods than the ones touched upon here. Examining the JavaDoc reveals you have access to the request, response, and session objects, and even to the Action-Servlet. You can add a request parameter or you can clear them all at once. You can verify the existence of ActionErrors and ActionMessages, or the absence of them. You can verify the intended ActionForward was returned, or you can dig deeper to ensure the intended path was returned.

Robust code can be achieved with a rigorous and diligent testing effort. Using a tool such as StrutsTestCase can make the job all that much easier.

◆ **Related**

- 9.2—In-container testing with StrutsTestCase and Cactus

◆ **Reference**

- [ANT] Apache Ant
- [ANTMAN] Apache Ant Manual
- [JUNIT] JUnit
- [STRUTSTC] StrutsTestCase

9.2 In-container testing with StrutsTestCase and Cactus

◆ **Problem**

You want to test your Struts application using the in-container testing approach.

◆ *Background*

There are two fundamental approaches to unit testing; outside-the-container testing with Mock Objects and in-container testing using Cactus. In recipe 9.1, "Testing outside the container with StrutsTestCase," we explored StrutsTestCase using Mock Objects. In this recipe we will use StrutsTestCase to test our application using the Tomcat container instead of Mock Objects.

Each approach has merits and drawbacks. Indeed, each approach is appropriate depending on the testing objectives. Generally, Mock Objects execute faster and are container agnostic. The downside is that Mock Objects distance you from the actual production environment. Some containers have anomalies which need to be discovered and addressed prior to implementing your application. At some point, you need to test your application in an environment approximating production. In-container testing provides you with the opportunity to do just that. Cactus has become the de facto standard to run automated in-container unit tests using JUnit. Recognizing Cactus' popularity, Cactus has been integrated into StrutsTestCase.

In this recipe we show you how easy it is to leverage your existing StrutsTest-Case unit tests to test your application inside your container. We present an Apache Ant script to fully automate the process to compile your classes, start Tomcat, execute your unit tests, stop Tomcat, and generate unit test reports in HTML format. No manual intervention is required!

APACHE CACTUS TESTING FRAMEWORK
Apache Cactus is an open source JUnit-based framework employed to test server-side Java using containers such as Tomcat, Resin, JBoss, Orion, and BEA WebLogic. Cactus can be used to test servlets, servlet filters and JavaServer Pages. Cactus can run any JUnit-based tests including Struts-TestCase. Cactus works by coordinating unit tests between client-side and server-side processing.

Each and every test method inside a JUnit test class executes all six steps shown in figure 9.1. The test case class is instantiated on the client side and attempts to communicate with the server. The proxy redirector intercepts the request, instantiates the test case class on the server side, and runs the test. Two instances of the test are created: one on the client side and the other on the server side; the two work together to complete a single test. The job of the redirector is to handle the interaction between the client-side and server-side portions of the process and manage the life cycle of the server-side part of the test.

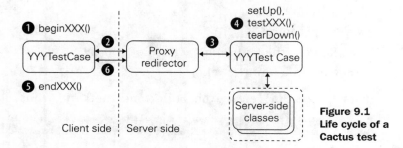

Figure 9.1
Life cycle of a
Cactus test

Referring to figure 9.1, the sequence of events are as follows. `beginXXX()` is used to set up the HTTP-related parameters to be passed to the redirector. `setup()`, `teardown()`, and `testXXX()` are used in much the same way as a JUnit test. `endXXX()` is used to assert additional results in the test.

Fortunately for `StrutsTestCase` users, the Cactus life cycle is hidden away and out of sight. Struts developers using `StrutsTestCase` can disregard the `beginXXX()` and `endXXX()` methods and continue to concentrate their efforts inside the JUnit test class. This enables `StrutsTestCase` tests to easily migrate to Cactus tests by simply extending `CactusStrutsTestCase` instead of `MockStrutsTestCase`. No mess, no fuss.

◆ *Recipe*

`StrutsTestCase` makes it very simple to leverage your exiting `MockObject` unit tests to perform Cactus tests. All you need to do is extend your unit test from `CactusStrutsTestCase` instead of `MockStrutsTestCase`. That's it! By using an Apache Ant [ANT] script specifically designed to run Cactus tests, you are ready to test your application inside the container.

Before diving into the Ant script, let's summarize everything it does:

- Define required class paths
- Declare Cactus-specific Ant tasks
- Compile application source code
- Compile unit test source code
- Create a deployable WAR file
- Create a WAR file engineered to run Cactus unit tests
- Build a temporary scaled-down version of Tomcat
- Start Tomcat

- Run unit tests
- Stop Tomcat
- Remove the temporary version of Tomcat
- Generate unit test reports

Before proceeding, ensure that both Tomcat and Ant are installed on your machine.

Listing 9.8 Apache Ant script to execute `StrutsTestCase` unit test using Cactus

```xml
<?xml version="1.0"?>
<project name="Cactus StrutsTestCase recipe" default="dist" basedir=".">
  <property file="build.properties" />               ❶
  <property file="${user.home}/build.properties" />        ❷

  <path id="project.classpath">          ❸
    <pathelement location="${servlet.jar}"/>
    <pathelement location="${struts.jar}"/>
  </path>
  <path id="cactus.classpath">          ❹
    <path refid="project.classpath"/>
    <pathelement location="${aspectjrt.jar}"/>
    <pathelement location="${cactus.jar}"/>
    <pathelement location="${cactus.ant.jar}"/>
    <pathelement location="${commons.httpclient.jar}"/>
    <pathelement location="${commons.logging.jar}"/>
    <pathelement location="${junit.jar}"/>
    <pathelement location="${strutstestcase.jar}"/>
  </path>
  <target name="init">        ❺
    <taskdef resource="cactus.tasks" classpathref="cactus.classpath"/>
  </target>
  <!-- compile application source -->
  <target name="compile.java" depends="init">
    <mkdir dir="${target.classes.java.dir}"/>
    <javac destdir="${target.classes.java.dir}"
           deprecation="${deprecation}"
           optimize="${optimize}">                     ❻
      <src path="${src.java.dir}"/>
      <classpath>
        <path refid="project.classpath"/>
      </classpath>
    </javac>
  </target>
  <!-- compile cactus unit tests -->
  <target name="compile.cactus" depends="compile.java">
    <mkdir dir="${target.classes.cactus.dir}"/>
    <javac destdir="${target.classes.cactus.dir}"
           deprecation="${deprecation}"
           optimize="${optimize}">                      ❼
```

```xml
      <src path="${src.cactus.dir}"/>
      <classpath>
        <path refid="cactus.classpath"/>
        <pathelement location="${target.classes.java.dir}"/>
      </classpath>
    </javac>
</target>
<!-- create the runtime war file -->
<target name="war"        ❽
        depends="compile.java"
        description="Generate the runtime war">
  <war warfile="${target.dir}/${project.name.file}.war"        ❾
      webxml="${src.webapp.dir}/WEB-INF/web.xml">
    <fileset dir="${src.webapp.dir}">
      <exclude name="cactus-report.Xsl"/>        ❿
      <exclude name="WEB-INF/cactus-web.xml"/>        ⓫
      <exclude name="WEB-INF/web.xml"/>
    </fileset>
    <classes dir="${target.classes.java.dir}"/>
  </war>
</target>
<!-- create distribution files -->
<target name="dist"        ⓬
        depends="clean, war, test"
        description="Generate the distributable files">
  <copy todir="${dist.dir}"
        file="${target.dir}/${project.name.file}.war"/>
</target>
<target name="clean" depends="init"
        description="Clean all generated files">        ⓭
  <delete dir="${target.dir}"/>
  <delete dir="${dist.dir}"/>
</target>
<target name="test.prepare" depends="war, compile.cactus">

  <!-- cactify the war -->
  <cactifywar srcfile="${target.dir}/${project.name.file}.war"        ⓮
      destfile="${target.dir}/test.war"        ⓯
      mergewebxml="${src.webapp.dir}/WEB-INF/cactus-web.xml">        ⓰
    <classes dir="${target.classes.cactus.dir}"/>        ⓱
  </cactifywar>
  <!-- Prepare the directories for the JUnit reports -->        ⓲
  <mkdir dir="${target.testreports.dir}/tomcat4x"/>
 </target>
<target name="test" depends="test.prepare"
    description="run tests">
  <!-- run tests -->
  <cactus warfile="${target.dir}/test.war" fork="yes"        ⓳
      failureproperty="tests.failed">

    <classpath>        ⓴
```

```
            <path refid="project.classpath"/>
            <pathelement location="${strutstestcase.jar}"/>
            <pathelement location="${target.classes.java.dir}"/>
            <pathelement location="${target.classes.cactus.dir}"/>
        </classpath>

        <containerset>           ㉑
          <tomcat4x if="cactus.home.tomcat4x"
              dir="${cactus.home.tomcat4x}" port="${cactus.port}"
              output="${target.testreports.dir}/tomcat4x.out"
              todir="${target.testreports.dir}/tomcat4x"/>
        </containerset>

        <formatter type="xml"/>      ㉒

        <batchtest>          ㉓
          <fileset dir="${src.cactus.dir}">
            <include name="**/Test*.java"/>
          </fileset>
        </batchtest>
      </cactus>
      <!-- JUnit reports -->
       <junitreport todir="${target.testreports.dir}/tomcat4x">      ㉔
          <fileset dir="${target.testreports.dir}/tomcat4x"
                   includes="TEST-*.xml"/>
          <report todir="${target.testreports.dir}/tomcat4x"
                  format="frames"/>
      </junitreport>
      <fail if="tests.failed">test failed!</fail>
    </target>
</project>
```

Let's step through the Ant script one target at a time.

We begin by declaring a properties file to define the location of the JAR files and the names of directories used throughout the Ant script ❶. Next we declare a user-specific properties file ❷ to override properties at ❶. It is a good practice to provide a means to customize property settings for a user's personal environment. We define the class path used to compile the application code ❸, and the class path used to compile StrutsTestCases unit tests using Cactus ❹.

Next we declare Cactus-specific Ant tasks ❺. Without this statement the Cactus Ant tasks at ⓮ and ⓴ cannot be recognized. The next step is to compile the application source code ❻ and the StrutsTestCases unit tests ❼. We then define a target to build an application WAR file ❽ and use the <war> task to build the application WAR file ❾. This WAR file can be used to deploy your application. Next, we exclude the cactus-report.xsl file from the WAR file ❿; this file is used to generate unit test reports. And now we exclude the cactus-web.xml file ⑪. This file is used at ⑯ to prepare a "cactified" WAR file.

We copy over the WAR file to the distribution directory ⑫, which is used to hold deployable artifacts, and then we wrap things up by creating a housekeeping target to clean up directories ⑬.

In order to execute Cactus unit tests, we need a WAR file containing the Cactus JARs required to execute Cactus unit tests on the server side. The WAR file must also contain a web.xml file tailored for Cactus-specific needs. The `<cactifywar>` task cracks open the application WAR file, injects the required JARs, massages the web.xml file, and saves the new WAR file under a different name. The `<cactify-war>` task is said to "cactify" a WAR file. Walking through the steps, we specify the application WAR file to be cactified ⑭, and then we specify the name of the cactified WAR file ⑮. The web.xml file of the cactified WAR file needs to be tailored to accommodate the needs of Cactus. The contents of the XML file specified with the `mergewebxml` attribute ⑯ are blended with the application WAR web.xml file. The cactified WAR file is used exclusively for unit-testing purposes.

At this point we specify Cactus unit test classes ⑰. We then prepare the directory to hold JUnit reports ⑱, and execute the `StrutsTestCase` Cactus unit tests ⑲. At ⑳ we specify the class path required to run the `StrutsTestCase` Cactus unit tests.

The `<cactus>` tag ⑲ is where all the excitement happens. Digging a bit deeper, you see that we create a temporary version of Tomcat for the exclusive purpose of running Cactus unit tests. The `<cactus>` tag `dir` attribute is used to locate the installed version Tomcat. The minimum Tomcat files required to run Tomcat are copied over to a temporary directory.

The temporary version of Tomcat is started. The `output` attribute is used to define the file used for the Tomcat console output.

`<batchtest>` is used to execute the unit tests at ㉓. Cactus uses the `<cactus>` tag `port` attribute to connect to Tomcat. This should be the same port number specified in your Tomcat configuration. The location of the unit test reports is specified with the `todir` attribute. The formatter tag at ㉒ is used to define XML as the report format. After the unit tests have completed running, Tomcat is stopped, and the temporary version of Tomcat is removed

Although we have chosen to run our unit test inside the Tomcat 4.x container, we could have chosen JBoss, Resin, Orion, or Weblogic. In fact, we could have run our tests against all of them! To keep things simple, we specify just one container in the `<containerset>` at ㉑. Adding additional containers is a simple matter of adding additional containers to the `<containerset>`. The Servlet example in the Cactus [CACTUS] distribution acts as an excellent reference on how to do this.

Finally, we generate unit test reports in HTML **24**.

This Ant script is generic enough to accommodate any `StrutsTestCase` unit test suite. After tailoring the build.properties file to suit your needs, you can reuse this script for all your Struts application testing.

◆ Discussion

In-container testing is an important step in the testing effort. You need to test your application in an environment closely resembling your production environment. Mock Object testing is useful when your container is unavailable, or you have a tight window in which to run your test. You may decide to use the Mock Object approach on a day-to-day basis, but run the Cactus test on a weekly basis. The needs of your project should drive out your testing strategy.

Fortunately for `StrutsTestCase` users, in-container testing using Cactus is quite straightforward once you have a fully automated process in place. Using the Ant script presented in this recipe, you can run your test case in an environment approximating your production scenario. Because `StrutsTestCase` allows you to easily migrate Mock Object tests to Cactus, the additional effort to run in-container tests is minimal.

◆ Related

- 9.1—Testing outside the container with StrutsTestCase

◆ Related

- [ANT] Apache Ant
- [ANTMAN] Apache Ant Manual
- [CACTUS] Apache Cactus
- [JUNIT] JUnit
- [STRUTSTC] StrutsTestCase

9.3 *Testing DynaActionForm with StrutsTestCase*

◆ Problem

You want to use `StrutsTestCase` to test `DynaActionForms`.

◆ Background

`DynaActionForms` are an excellent way to reduce trivial coding by defining your forms declaratively in the struts-config.xml file. Although `DynaActionForms` are easy to use, there is still the opportunity to make mistakes.

To refresh your memory on DynaActionForms we suggest you read recipe 1.11, "Implementing DynaActionForms". To jog your memory on StrutsTestCase we suggest you read recipe 9.1, if you haven't already.

In this recipe we will show you how to use StrutsTestCase to test DynaAction-Forms. We will peek inside the DynaActionForm to ensure it was created as intended. Inside we will find the form bean definition we created in the struts-config.xml file. Probing the DynaActionForm is easy once we realize that all DynaActionForms implement the DynaBean interface.

The DynaBean interface defines accessors and mutators to manage DynaBean property values. In addition to bean properties, the DynaBean interface defines a getDynaClass method to obtain a reference to the DynaBean's DynaClass interface. In turn, the DynaClass interface has accessors to allow us to obtain a list of Dyna-Properties. Each DynaProperty encapsulates a property name and type pairing. In this recipe we will make good use of these interfaces to ensure the DynaForm was created as intended.

◆ *Recipe*

Let's create a DynaActionForm.

> **Listing 9.9** **DynaForm created in struts-config.xml**

```
<form-bean name="shoutForm"
           type="org.apache.struts.action.DynaActionForm">
    <form-property name="name" type="java.lang.String"/>
    <form-property name="address" type="java.lang.String"/>
    <form-property name="phone" type="java.lang.String"/>
</form-bean>
```

In listing 9.9 we create the shoutForm DynaForm with three properties. Each property is of type java.lang.String.

Let's use StrutsTestCase to validate the form bean created as defined in listing 9.9.

Looking over listing 9.9 reveals several testable assertions:

- The form must be a DynaActionForm.
- The form must have exactly three properties.
- The property name and type must match those defined in listing 9.9.
- The properties must be populated as expected.

Listing 9.10 `TestDynaActionForm` **unit test**

```
package com.strutsrecipes.testdynaactionform.mocktest;
import org.apache.commons.beanutils.DynaProperty;
import org.apache.struts.action.DynaActionForm;
import servletunit.struts.MockStrutsTestCase;
public class TestDynaActionForm extends MockStrutsTestCase {
    public void setUp() throws Exception {
        super.setUp();
        setConfigFile("/struts-config.xml");               ❶
    }
    public TestDynaActionForm(String name) {
        super(name);
    }
    public void testShoutForm() {
        this.setRequestPathInfo("/echo.do");
        addRequestParameter("name","Mark");                ❷
        addRequestParameter("address","123 main street");
        addRequestParameter("phone","905-555-1212");
        actionPerform();
        verifyForward("success");
        //assert type dynaform
        Object form = getActionForm();                     ❸
        assertEquals(form.getClass(), DynaActionForm.class);
        DynaActionForm dynaForm = (DynaActionForm) form;   ❹
        DynaProperty[]actualDynaProperties =
            dynaForm.getDynaClass().getDynaProperties();   ❺
        DynaProperty [] expectedtargetDynaProperties = {   ❻
            new DynaProperty("phone",    String.class),
            new DynaProperty("name",     String.class),
            new DynaProperty("address",  String.class),
        };
        assertTrue(DynaPropertiesHelper.isDynaPropertiesMatch(  ❼
            actualDynaProperties,
            expectedtargetDynaProperties)) ;

        assertEquals("Mark", dynaForm.get("name"));
        assertEquals("123 main street", dynaForm.get("address"));
        assertEquals("905-555-1212", dynaForm.get("phone"));
    }
}
```

Let's carefully step through listing 9.10 to see how we verify each assertion.

We begin by defining the location of the struts-config.xml file ❶. Alternatively, we could have omitted this statement by placing the struts-config.xml file in the class path. Next, we set up the request by setting the request path and parameter couplets before invoking the ActionServlet ❷. At this point we obtain the form and verify that the class type is DynaActionForm ❸.

Now, we peek inside the DynaActionForm to make sure the properties are defined and populated as expected. We can confidently cast the form because the assertion at ❸ ensures the class type is DynaActionForm ❹. We next obtain an array of DynaPropertys by accessing the DynaBean interface getDynaClass method ❺. We use the DynaClass to obtain the list of DynaPropertys.

In the next step we need to do a little fancy footwork to make sure that there are just three properties of the names and types we expect—no more, no less. We have created DynaPropertiesHelper helper class to take responsibility for this job. Let's continue with the test, then backtrack to look over DynaPropertiesHelper. First, we create an array of DynaPropertys to represent the expected values ❻, and then we use the DynaPropertiesHelper to verify that the expected DynaPropertys match the actual result ❼.

If all the assertions are true, the DynaActionForm matches the definition created in listing 9.9.

Listing 9.11 `DynaPropertiesHelper` class

```
package com.strutsrecipes.testdynaactionform.mocktest;
import java.util.Arrays;
import org.apache.commons.beanutils.DynaProperty;
public class DynaPropertiesHelper {
    static public boolean isDynaPropertiesMatch(
        DynaProperty[] sourceDynaProperties,
        DynaProperty[] targetDynaProperties) {
        int length = sourceDynaProperties.length;
        if (length != targetDynaProperties.length) {          ❶
            return false;
        }
    DynaPropertyComparator comparator = new DynaPropertyComparator();   ❷
    Arrays.sort(targetDynaProperties, comparator);
    Arrays.sort(sourceDynaProperties, comparator);
                                                               ❸
    for (int i = 0; i < length; i++) {
        if (!sourceDynaProperties[i]
            .toString()
            .equals(targetDynaProperties[i].toString())) {     ❹
            return false;
        }
    }
    return true;
    }
}
```

Let's return to the DynaPropertiesHelper to see how we compared the two Dyna-Property arrays. Java provides an equals method in the java.util.Arrays utility class to verify that two arrays are equal to each other. To use the methods in this class, the objects in your array must implement `Comparable`. Unfortunately, `DynaProperty` does not do this. As a workaround, we sort the arrays, then compare the `toString()` values of the sequential array pairing. Let's review listing 9.11 to see how this is done.

First, we verify that the length of the two arrays match ❶, and then we create a `Comparator` to compare our `DynaProperty` array elements ❷. This is necessary because `DynaProperty` does not implement `Comparable`. Next, we use the comparator we created at ❷ to sort the arrays using the `Arrays` sort method ❸. Finally, we use the `toString` values to compare each set of array elements ❹.

Listing 9.12 `DynaPropertyComparator` implements `Comparator`

```
package com.strutsrecipes.testdynaactionform.mocktest;
import java.util.Comparator;
import org.apache.commons.beanutils.DynaProperty;
public class DynaPropertyComparator implements Comparator {
    public int compare(Object object1, Object object2) {
        if (!(object1 instanceof DynaProperty)) {
            throw new ClassCastException();
        }
        if (!(object2 instanceof DynaProperty)) {
            throw new ClassCastException();
        }
        DynaProperty dynaProperty1 = (DynaProperty) object1;
        DynaProperty dynaProperty2 = (DynaProperty) object2;
        int value =
                dynaProperty1.getName().compareTo(dynaProperty2.getName());
        if (value != 0) {
         return value;
        }
        return  dynaProperty1.getType().getName().
                compareTo(dynaProperty2.getType().getName());
    }
}
```

Listing 9.12 presents the implementation of the `Comparator` we used in listing 9.11 ❷. `DynaPropertyComparator` compares the two `String` values of the name and `type` properties.

Note that the recommended implementation of `Comparator` calls for stringent rules to ensure that utilities depending on the comparable interface perform as expected. Notably, the `compareTo` method must obey the reflexive, symmetric, and transitive rules imposed by the `equals` method [BLOCH]. Because we don't have access to the `DynaProperty` equals method, we have chosen to stretch the rules to make sorting easier.

◆ Discussion

`DynaActionForms` are easy to use and reduce maintenance efforts, but our butter-fingers slip on occasion. We need to persevere with a diligent testing effort to ensure our applications remain rock solid. In this recipe we look under the hood of the `DynaActionForm` to verify it was created as intended. We leverage the fact that `DynaActionForms` implement the `DynaBean` interface to poke and prod `DynaActionForms`. After a small learning curve with the `DynaProperty` class and `DynaBean` and `DynaClass` interfaces, we are able to ascertain the correctness of the `DynaActionForm` declared in the struts-config.xml file.

◆ Related

- 1.11—Implementing `DynaActionForms`
- 9.1—Testing outside the container with StrutsTestCase

◆ Reference

- [BEANUTILS] BeanUtils package
- [BLOCH] *Effective Java Programming Guide*, Item 11, Consider Implementing `Comparable`
- [JDOC] Comparable Interface JavaDoc

9.4 Testing modules

◆ Problem

You want to test an application built using Struts modules.

◆ Background

Getting control of the struts-config.xml file on a large project can be a frustrating experience. Fortunately, Struts 1.1 introduced modules to allow you to divide a larger application into several smaller functional applications. A module-based application may consist of one or more modules and a "default" application. Although transparent to the user, the application transfers control between modules and between the default application and a module.

In practice, module development is farmed out to one or more autonomous teams, enabling application development and testing to proceed in several parallel streams. The degree of interconnectivity between modules precipitates interdependencies between teams. One team cannot test until the other team is done. This condition is at odds with the principal objective which modules were designed to address—that is, providing an environment which permits autonomous teams to develop in parallel.

The solution to this sticky problem is to apply the principles of Design by Contract [DBC] to module testing. Each module has a job to do and depends on a set of preconditions. Moreover, a module's postconditions are another module's preconditions. If we build autonomously, then we must test in the same fashion. Stated another way, modules have contracts with one another. The contracts depend on the validity of the precondition state and are responsible for delivering the postcondition state [UML]. Holding modules accountable to their contractual obligations allows us to test modules in parallel. An integration test validates that contracts work together.

Defining relationships between modules is not only a good testing practice, but it is also an excellent design practice as well. Defining and understanding the responsibilities of each module yields a better design and a smoother development effort.

The following guidelines will serve you well in module testing:

- Enumerate contracts by identifying points of contact between modules and the default application.
- Define contracts by defining both preconditions and postconditions.
- Create unit tests to verify contracts have been satisfied.

Once you have tested each module on its own, the next step is to "integration" test the interaction between all the modules.

◆ *Recipe*

Now that we have our test strategy in place, let's take it for a spin! In this recipe we use StrutsTestCase [STRUTSTC] to test a simple module application by following the guidelines stated in the background section. In practice, StrutsTestCase may not be sufficient to test some of the View portions of the postconditions. For those tests you need to seek out tools to test the View part of the equation.

To illustrate this recipe we consider a retail application. In our fictitious application, each module represents a product line, such as garden supplies or toys. The user enters the default application by pointing the browser at http://127.0.0.1:8080/estore/index.jsp. The user is presented with a welcome page of links. Each link transfers the user to the module representing a product line. Each product line page presents a list of products pertinent to the product line and a single link back to the welcome page. As there are no relationships between product lines, the user's navigation is restricted to the area between the default application and the module. The user must return to the default application to choose another product line. There is no direct interaction between modules.

For brevity's sake, we define only some of the application contracts in table 9.1.

Table 9.1   Contractual agreements inherent to the application.

Application contracts			
ID	**Operation**	**Precondition**	**Postcondition**
A	Enter application	■ Path is welcome.do	■ `Forward` is welcome.jsp ■ No error
B	Transfer control from default application to garden module	■ Path is index.do ■ `type` request parameter is set to `garden`	■ The `Forward` is `success` ■ The path is /garden/index.jsp ■ `products` attribute exists ■ `products` are returned ■ No errors
C	Transfer control from garden module to default application	■ `prefix` request parameter is empty ■ `page` request parameter is set to index.jsp ■ Path is /switch.do	■ The path is index.jsp ■ No errors

Let's create test cases for each contract.

Listing 9.13   struts-config.xml file

```
<?xml version="1.0" encoding="ISO-8859-1" ?>
<!DOCTYPE struts-config PUBLIC
        "-//Apache Software Foundation//DTD Struts Configuration 1.1//EN"
        "http://jakarta.apache.org/struts/dtds/struts-config_1_1.dtd">
<struts-config>
  <form-beans></form-beans>

  <global-forwards>
    <forward    name="books"
                contextRelative="true"
                path="/books/index.do?type=books"/>
    <forward    name="garden"
                contextRelative="true"
                path="/garden/index.do?type=garden"/>
    <forward    name="toys"
                contextRelative="true"
```

```
                          path="/toys/index.do?type=toys"/>
        <forward   name="welcome"
                          path="/welcome.do"/>
    </global-forwards>
    <action-mappings>

     <action     path="/welcome"
                  type="org.apache.struts.actions.ForwardAction"
                  parameter="/welcome.jsp"/>
    </action-mappings>
</struts-config>
```

Listing 9.14   struts-config-garden.xml file

```
<?xml version="1.0" encoding="ISO-8859-1" ?>
<!DOCTYPE struts-config PUBLIC
        "-//Apache Software Foundation//DTD Struts Configuration 1.1//EN"
        "http://jakarta.apache.org/struts/dtds/struts-config_1_1.dtd">
<struts-config>
  <form-beans>
    <form-bean name="productForm"
               type="com.strutsrecipes.testmodules.forms.ProductForm"/>
  </form-beans>

  <global-forwards>
    <forward    name="welcome"
                path="/switch.do?prefix=&amp;page=/welcome.do"/>
  </global-forwards>
  <action-mappings>
      <action    path="/index"
                 type="com.strutsrecipes.testmodules.actions.ProductsAction"
                 name="productForm">
                 <forward name="success" path="/index.jsp"/>
      </action>

      <action    path="/switch"
                 type="org.apache.struts.actions.SwitchAction"/>
  </action-mappings>
</struts-config>
```

Before getting started you should inspect the default application (listing 9.13) and the garden module (listing 9.14) struts-config.xml files to get a feel for the application.

Listing 9.15   The user enters the application at the default application using the welcome.do Action

```
    public void testDefault() {
      setRequestPathInfo("/welcome.do");
```

```
        actionPerform();
        verifyForwardPath("/welcome.jsp");
        verifyNoActionErrors();
    }
```

Listing 9.15 presents the initial access by the user (contract A). This test is the same as a nonmodule test.

Listing 9.16 The user transfers control from the default application to the garden module

```
    public void testDefaultToGardenModule() {
        setConfigFile("garden","/WEB-INF/struts-config-garden.xml");      ❶
        setRequestPathInfo("/garden","/index.do");      ❷
        addRequestParameter("type", "garden");

        actionPerform();
        verifyForward("success");
        verifyForwardPath("/garden/index.jsp");
        assertNotNull(getRequest().getAttribute("products"));

        List products = (List) getRequest().getAttribute("products");

        assertEquals(products.size(), 3);

        verifyNoActionErrors();
    }
```

Listing 9.16 presents our test for contract B. There are only two small changes required to module-enable this test for StrutsTestCase. First, we add a leading argument indicating the module name for the struts-config.xml file ❶, and then we add a leading argument to represent the module used for the request ❷.

Listing 9.17 The user transfers control back from the garden module to the welcome.do

```
    public void testGardenModuleToDefault() {
        setConfigFile("garden","/WEB-INF/struts-config-garden.xml");      ❶
        addRequestParameter("prefix", "");      ❷
        addRequestParameter("page", "index.jsp");      ❸
        setRequestPathInfo("/garden","/switch.do");      ❹

        actionPerform();
        verifyForwardPath("index.jsp");

        verifyNoActionErrors();
    }
```

Listing 9.17 presents our test for contract C. Listing 9.17 is very similar to listing 9.16, except we show you how to use a `SwitchAction`. We begin by adding a leading argument indicating the module name for the struts-config.xml file ❶. Next, we add the `prefix` request parameter ❷. Note that an empty `prefix` parameter signals a transfer of control to the default application. At ❸ we add the second mandatory parameter required to switch, and then we set up the path to the `Switch Action` ❹.

◆ *Discussion*

Once you have the hang of `StrutsTestCase`, module testing is straightforward. The tricky part is to be able to test modules independently of one another. A good approach is to define contracts within your application to frame your tests. Once all the interfaces are tested, you can move forward with an integration test. With a little extra effort you can test your modules in parallel and reduce inter-team dependencies.

> **BEST PRACTICE** *Use Design by Contract to design module tests*—Without proper planning, module testing can produce project bottlenecks as teams stagger the module completion dates. To alleviate this condition, design your unit tests to meet the contractual obligation of your modules. Schedule an integration test when all modules are complete.

◆ *Related*

- 9.1—Testing outside the container with StrutsTestCase

◆ *Reference*

- [DBC] Applying Design by Contract, in Computer (IEEE), vol. 25
- [JUNIT] JUnit
- [STRUTSTC] StrutsTestCase
- [UML] Applying UML and Patterns: An introduction to Object-Oriented Analysis and Design and the Unified Process, Use Case Model; Adding Detail with Operation Contracts

9.5 *Performance testing Struts applications*

◆ *Problem*

You want to test the performance of your Struts application.

◆ *Background*

Virtually every application considers performance a critical success factor. Your application may meet all business requirements and be an architectural master-piece, but failing to meet acceptable user-response times will relegate it to the digital junkyard. Performance expectations are wide ranging. Everyone has a different perception of "fast." Seasoned mainframe "green screen" users have been spoiled with excellent application responsiveness; whereas Internet users have learned to be very patient. Regardless of expectations and past experiences, a well-performing application engages the user and promotes acceptance of your application. The best way to mitigate the risk of implementing a poorly performing application is to conduct performance testing.

When one considers the complexity of modern-day applications, the job of performance testing can seem daunting. Applications have become a tightly woven fabric of technologies yielding an interesting tapestry of interconnected software. The shear complexity of some architectures can make testing a formidable challenge.

Fixing performance problems can become increasingly expensive as the project lifecycle marches on. Skilled and expensive development resources should be called upon to address performance problems in a timely manner. Although performance problems can be expensive to correct, the job to test for performance is not cheap either. Usually, a dedicated environment is created to host performance testing. This means additional hardware, software, licenses, physical space, and people need to be allocated. It can be an expensive endeavor!

The best way to manage the complexity and expense of performance testing is to create a performance test plan. A plan helps you define your performance requirements by settling on an approach and managing costs. A performance plan can be as comprehensive or as rough as your project dictates. Having a plan is the best way to meet your performance requirements.

Many projects delay performance testing until late in the project life cycle when timelines are tight and fixes are expensive. A more effective approach is to treat performance as any other user requirement by stating the performance requirement up front and testing to see if it has been met. *Continuous performance testing* describes the process of conducting performance tests on a continual basis, ideally as part of the regular build process. This strategy allows performance problems to be discovered early when the cost is low and the opportunity to repeat them can be avoided.

Let's spend some time identifying the kinds of tests we are going to run.

- *Timed test*—Ensures that a single test run by a single user executes within a time limit.
- *Load test*—Measures the application responsiveness by repeatedly executing tests with a predetermined number of concurrent users. The test may ramp up the users gradually or increase their number all at once. There are various types of load tests, but the most popular are a throughput test and response-time-under-load test.
  - *Throughput test*—Measures the number of requests executed within a given time period
  - *Response-time-under-load test*—Ensures each unit test meets a performance expectation while under load
  - *Burst test*—A variation of a load test that spikes the load between two periods of normal load. Similar to the load test, a burst test can be measured as a throughput or response-time-under-load test during or following the burst of activity. The purpose of the burst test is to observe the impact of a burst of activity on the application once the burst is over. For instance, the burst may force the application into heavy garbage collection, thereby impacting the application in the postburst period. If bursts are rare, then this test is not useful. However, if the application has regular bursts, then this test may be more significant.

In this recipe we will show you how to use `JUnitPerf` [JPERF] to create performance tests by leveraging your existing `StrutsTestCase` unit tests. `JUnitPerf` is an open source JUnit-based framework that decorates existing JUnit tests to ensure your code performs within expected time constraints.

◆ *Recipe*

In this recipe we demonstrate four types of performances tests: timed, throughput, response-time-under-load, and burst. Because `StrutsTestCase` is nothing more than a wrapper to a JUnit test, we can use the existing `StrutsTestCase` as a test bed to test the application's performance by using `JUnitPerf`.

Before getting started you need to download `JUnitPerf` [JUNITPERF], JUnit [JUNIT], and `StrutsTestCase` [STRUTSTC].

We start off this recipe with a timed test to verify that a single unit test can be executed by a single user in under a second.

Listing 9.18 `JUnitPerf` **timed test**

```
package com.strutsrecipes.performancetesting.mocktest;
import com.clarkware.junitperf.TimedTest;
import com.clarkware.junitperf.TestMethodFactory;
import junit.framework.Test;
import junit.framework.TestSuite;
public class StrutsAppTimedTest {
    public static Test suite() {            ❶
        long maxElapsedTime = 1000;          ❷
        Test test = new TestMethodFactory(TestPositive.class,
                          "testUpperCase");   ❸
        Test timedTest = new TimedTest(test, maxElapsedTime);    ❹
        TestSuite suite = new TestSuite();   ❺
        suite.addTest(timedTest);        ❻

        return suite;        ❼
    }
}
```

Let's step through the timed test in listing 9.18

We begin by creating the `suite()` method returning `Test` ❶. This method is automatically called by the JUnit runner. We set our time limit to be 1000 milliseconds ❷, and then we create a test for the `testUpperCase StrutsTestCase` unit test ❸. We use the `TestMethodFactory` to ensure that the test fixture isn't shared between multiple threads. Next we create a `TimedTest` for the test case at ❸ with a 1-second limit ❹, followed by the creation of a `TestSuite` object to hold the performance tests ❺. We then add the `TimedTest` to the `TestSuite` ❻ and return the `TestSuite` containing our `TimedTest` ❼.

In listing 9.18 we leverage our existing `StrutsTestCase` unit test to validate that the `testUpperCase` unit test in `TestPositive` runs in less than a second. The test is passed as long as the test does not exceed one second and the underlying unit test passes.

Next, we run a throughput test to assert that the cumulative amount of time for 100 users to complete a test is less than ten seconds.

Listing 9.19 `JUnitPerf` **throughput test**

```
package com.strutsrecipes.performancetesting.mocktest;
import com.clarkware.junitperf.LoadTest;
import com.clarkware.junitperf.LoadTest;
import com.clarkware.junitperf.TimedTest;
import com.clarkware.junitperf.TestMethodFactory;
import junit.framework.Test;
import junit.framework.TestSuite;
```

```
public class StrutsAppThroughputTest {
    public static Test suite() {

        int maxUsers = 100;          ❶
        long maxElapsedTime = 10000;          ❷

        Test test = new TestMethodFactory(TestPositive.class,          ❸
                        "testUpperCase");
        Test loadTest = new LoadTest(test, maxUsers);          ❹
        Test timedTest = new TimedTest(loadTest, maxElapsedTime);          ❺
        TestSuite suite = new TestSuite();
        suite.addTest(timedTest);

        return suite;

    }
}
```

Looking over the throughput test in listing 9.18, you see that we set the number
of users to 100 ❶ and set the time limit to 10 seconds ❷. Next, we create a test
for the testUpperCase StrutsTestCase unit test ❸. We then wrap the test with a
LoadTest, passing in the number of concurrent users ❹, and finally we wrap the
LoadTest with a TimedTest ❺. The TimedTest asserts that the LoadTest must complete in less than 10 seconds.

A throughput test ensures all tests fits in a time window, but it does not place
a limitation on any individual test. A response-time-under-load test validates
that each individual test under the load test does not exceed a time limit.

Listing 9.20 JUnitPerf response-time-under-load test

```
package com.strutsrecipes.performancetesting.mocktest;
import com.clarkware.junitperf.LoadTest;
import com.clarkware.junitperf.LoadTest;
import com.clarkware.junitperf.TimedTest;
import com.clarkware.junitperf.TestMethodFactory;
import junit.framework.Test;
import junit.framework.TestSuite;
public class StrutsAppResponseUnderLoad {
    public static Test suite() {

        int maxUsers = 100;          ❶
        long maxElapsedTime = 100;          ❷

        Test test = new TestMethodFactory(TestPositive.class,          ❸
                        "testUpperCase");
        Test timedTest = new TimedTest(test, maxElapsedTime);          ❹
        Test loadTest = new LoadTest(timedTest, maxUsers);          ❺
        TestSuite suite = new TestSuite();
```

```
        suite.addTest(timedTest);

        return suite;
    }
}
```

In listing 9.20, we set the number of users to 100 ❶ and set the time limit for each individual test to 100 milliseconds ❷. We then create a Test for the testUpperCase StrutsTestCase unit test ❸. Now we create a TimedTest for each test ❹. For the test to pass, each and every test must not exceed 100 milliseconds and its underlying unit test must pass. At ❺ we place the TimedTest under a load of 100 concurrent users.

A burst test verifies the application can handle a sudden burst of activity between two normal periods of activity. To simulate a burst of activity we simulate a small load test followed by a heavy load. The heavy load can be tested for throughput or response-time-under-load.

Listing 9.21 JUnitPerf burst test

```
package com.strutsrecipes.performancetesting.mocktest;
import com.clarkware.junitperf.LoadTest;
import com.clarkware.junitperf.LoadTest;
import com.clarkware.junitperf.TimedTest;
import com.clarkware.junitperf.TestMethodFactory;
import junit.framework.Test;
import junit.framework.TestSuite;
public class StrutsAppBurstTest {
    public static Test suite() {
        Test test;
        Test loadTest;
        Test timedTest;
        TestSuite suite = new TestSuite();

        test = new TestMethodFactory(TestPositive.class, "testUpperCase");
        loadTest = new LoadTest(test, 50);                                    ❶
        suite.addTest(loadTest);

        test = new TestMethodFactory(TestPositive.class, "testUpperCase");
        loadTest = new LoadTest(test, 200);                                   ❷
        timedTest = new TimedTest(loadTest, 9000);
        suite.addTest(timedTest);

        return suite;
    }
}
```

In creating the burst test in listing 9.21, we first create a small load test for 50 users ❶, and then we create throughput test for a heavy load of 200 users in nine seconds ❷.

In this test we limit the test to measuring the burst, but we could have created a small-load throughput test for the period following the burst. This guarantees the burst does not adversely impact the application during the period after the burst.

◆ *Discussion*

In this recipe we presented four popular performance tests using StrutsTestCase and JUnitPerf. Although these tests will serve you well, a thorough performance testing effort has greater depth. You should consider creating a performance test plan to help you drive out performance testing goals, performance expectations, resource requirements, and other facets of your testing effort. Once your plan is in place you need to define your performance tests. You need to have a clear understanding of both the performance expectations and the application usage to design your performance tests. For example, if you expect a large number of users to access the applications at peak times, then you need to create burst tests. If you expect some pages to be used more heavily than others, then you should target load testing in those areas. A good understanding of application usage is critical to a successful performance test.

There is one "gotcha" to keep in mind. Because JUnitPerf decorates Struts-TestCase, you may need to adjust the time limits upward to correct for the setup() and teardown() methods of the underlying StrutsTestCase test.

Performance testing can help make sure your application is scalable. Increasing the load in your tests should result in a linear increase in performance times. If performance times increase exponentially, your application is not scalable. A scalable application allows you to solve your performance problems by throwing hardware, memory, and CPU at the problem. A nonscalable application usually mandates application changes.

Integrating performance testing into the build process is a good practice. Simply add your JUnitPerf tests to your Apache Ant build script, as you would any other StrutsTestCase test, and you are away to the races. Delaying performance testing until the end of the project positions you to repeat your mistakes, and derails you from discovering good performance development practices earlier in the project life cycle. Discovering and tackling performance problems early can save you time and money and minimize frustration.

Although we have concentrated on performance testing application code, performance testing extends to all the points between the application and the user. The database, application server, JVM, network routers, your ISP, and the client machine are only a few of the contributing pieces to the overall performance experience. In addition, you need to account for "edge cases," such as the first time the application is accessed. Startup tests can be used to probe performance during an initial burst of activity, such as class loading, obtaining and caching database connections, EJB home interface lookups in JNDI, and so on.

Once you have discovered a performance problem you may need tools to help you dig deeper. Sitraka PerformaSure [PERFORMASURE] and Borland OptimizeIt ServerTrace [OPTIMIZEIT] are only two of the many products on the market that help detect and isolate problem areas.

Conducting performance testing is a worthwhile effort. It helps you identify problems early, minimizes the costs of addressing them, and leads to a robust application. `JUnitPerf` is a great tool to get you started as it allows you to leverage your existing `StrutsTestCase` tests for performance tests.

BEST PRACTICE *Create a performance test plan*—A performance plan can play a key role in achieving your performance goals. The exercise of creating the plan forces you to consider the scope of your test effort. It provides you with a means to communicate goals, deliverables, approach, resourcing, scheduling, and a bug-fixing strategy. After each project, you should review your plan to evaluate what worked and what didn't. You can use your experience to fine-tune your effort for the next round.

◆ *Related*

- 9.1—Testing outside the container with StrutsTestCase

◆ *Reference*

- [CONTPERF] Continuous Performance Testing
- [JUNIT] JUnit
- [JUNITPERF] JUnitPerf
- [OPTIMIZEIT] Borland OptimizeIt ServerTrace
- [PERFORMASURE] Sitraka PerformaSure
- [STRUTSTC] StrutsTestCase

9.6 *Testing coverage*

◆ *Problem*

You want to know which parts of your application are untested.

◆ *Background*

There is little argument that an excellent testing effort yields a robust application. However, the testing effort you place up front will continue to bear fruit in the maintenance cycle. Approximately 80% of the application's cost is found in application maintenance. The cost to build the application is pale by comparison. Creating a good test bed takes you a long way to reducing maintenance costs. With a good test bed under your belt, you can blaze forward with new features. With regression tests in your back pocket, you are confident your application still hangs together when all is said and done. It is far more expensive to fix regression defects when you trip over them by accident.

Software applications naturally evolve over time. Failing to refactor the design eventually precipitates a maintenance nightmare. A commitment to design refactoring keeps your application humming along well into the future. Despite the long-term benefit of refactoring, there continues to be resistance to it. An automated set of regression tests eases the burden to refactor your code.

The terms "good test bed" and "complete set of tests" have been thrown around rather loosely. What is a decent set of tests? How do you know when you have it? Working with business users to make sure you have tests for all relevant business scenarios is probably the best place to start. Once you have normal scenarios firmly in place you can start to drive out "edge cases." Your test cases should cover as many branches in the code as pragmatically possible. At a minimum you should have metrics indicating which lines of code have been missed entirely. No matter how hard you try, it is difficult to blanket your code with tests. A coverage testing tool can be an important asset to strengthen your level of confidence and point out areas of weakness.

In this recipe we use jCoverage [JCOVERAGE] to root out untested code. jCoverage can be downloaded free of charge under the GNU General Public License (GPL). jCoverage works by *instrumenting* application class files. Instrumentation of class files refers to the act of instating a mechanism to monitor class behavior. jCoverage instruments class files by weaving jCoverage byte code into your application class file. The jCoverage byte code injected into your application class files tracks and records which lines and code branches have been executed during unit testing. The results are written to the jcoverage.ser file.

Using Apache Ant we show you how you can add jCoverage coverage testing to your current build process. Using jCoverage you can measure the degree of unit test coverage of any JUnit test, including StrutsTestCase.

◆ **Recipe**

Listing 9.22 shows you everything you need to employ jCoverage. Before getting started, you need to download jCoverage from http://jcoverage.com/. We encourage you to review the documentation and examples bundled in the download.

Let's get at it!

Listing 9.22   Ant script using jCoverage

```xml
<?xml version="1.0" encoding="UTF-8"?>
<project name="struts cookbook coverage recipe using jcoverage"
         default="main"
         basedir=".">
  <property file="build.properties"/>          ❶
  <path id="classpath.log4j">                  ❷
    <pathelement location="${log4j.jar}"/>
  </path>
  <path id="classpath.jcoverage">              ❸
    <pathelement location="${jcoverage.jar}"/>
  </path>

  <path id="classpath.struts">                 ❹
    <pathelement location="${servlet.jar}"/>
    <pathelement location="${struts.jar}"/>
    <pathelement location="${commons-logging.jar}"/>
    <pathelement location="${commons-beanutils.jar}"/>
    <pathelement location="${commons-digester.jar}"/>
    <pathelement location="${commons-collections.jar}"/>
    <pathelement location="${strutstestcase.jar}"/>
    <path refid="classpath.log4j"/>
  </path>

  <path id="classpath.strutsconfig">           ❺
    <pathelement location="${strutsconfig.xml}"/>
  </path>

  <path id="classpath.webapp">                 ❻
    <pathelement location="${webapp.dir}"/>
  </path>
  <taskdef classpathref="classpath.jcoverage" resource="tasks.properties"/>   ❼
  <target name="main"           ❽
          depends="clean,init,compile,instrument,test,coverage"
          description="clean build, instrument and unit test"/>
  <target name="clean" description="clean">      ❾
```

```
    <delete>
      <fileset dir="${build.dir}"/>
      <fileset dir="${basedir}">
        <include name="jcoverage.ser"/>
        <include name="jcoverage.log"/>
      </fileset>
    </delete>
  </target>
  <target name="init" description="create build directories">     ⓾
    <mkdir dir="${build.dir}"/>
    <mkdir dir="${build.classes.dir}"/>
    <mkdir dir="${build.coverage.dir}"/>
    <mkdir dir="${build.instrumented.dir}"/>
    <mkdir dir="${build.reports.dir}"/>
  </target>
  <target name="compile" description="compile classes">     ⓫
    <javac srcdir="${src.dir}"
           destdir="${build.classes.dir}"
           failonerror="yes" debug="yes">
      <classpath location="${junit.jar}"/>
      <classpath refid="classpath.log4j"/>
      <classpath refid="classpath.struts"/>
    </javac>
  </target>
  <target name="instrument" description="jcoverage instrumentation">     ⓬
    <instrument todir="${build.instrumented.dir}">
      <ignore regex="org.apache.log4j.*"/>
      <fileset dir="${build.classes.dir}">
        <include name="**/*.class"/>
        <exclude name="**/*Test.class"/>
      </fileset>
    </instrument>
  </target>
  <target name="test" description="run unit tests">     ⓭
    <junit fork="yes" dir="${basedir}"
           errorProperty="test.failed" failureProperty="test.failed">
      <classpath location="${build.instrumented.dir}"/>     ⓮
      <classpath location="${build.classes.dir}"/>
      <classpath refid="classpath.jcoverage"/>     ⓯
      <classpath refid="classpath.struts"/>
      <classpath refid="classpath.strutsconfig"/>
      <classpath refid="classpath.webapp"/>

      <formatter type="xml"/>     ⓰
      <batchtest todir="${build.reports.dir}">     ⓱
        <fileset dir="${src.dir}">
          <include name="**/Test*.java"/>
        </fileset>
      </batchtest>
    </junit>
  </target>
```

```
   <target name="coverage" description="reports">      ⓲
     <report srcdir="${src.dir}" destdir="${build.coverage.dir}"/>
    <report srcdir="${src.dir}" destdir="${build.coverage.dir}" format="xml"/
   >
   </target>
 </project>
```

Let's walk through the steps of listing 9.22. We begin by declaring the properties file used to define the parameters peppered throughout the script ❶. We then define a path to Log4J ❷ and a path to jCoverage ❸. Now we create a path for Struts dependencies ❹, and we create a path to the struts-config.xml file to accommodate the StrutsTestCase tests ❺.

At ❻ we create a path to web application. StrutsTestCase ActionServlet uses this path to find application resources. Next, we define the jCoverage Ant tasks ❼. The tasks are defined using the tasks.properties file in the jcoverage.jar file. We then find the default project target ❽. The "main" target controls the target execution sequence using the depends attribute.

The clean task ❾ is our first working target. Its job is to delete the compiled classes created by a prior run and remove the jcoverage.ser and jcoverage.log files. It is important to purge these files to ensure you don't cross-pollinate your results. A new set of files at the start of each run guarantees your results are germane to the current run.

The init target ❿ creates all the directories we need:

- *build.dir*—Holds build artifacts
- *build.classes.dir*—Holds noninstrumented application class files
- *build.coverage.dir*—Holds coverage reports
- *build.instrumented.dir*—Holds instrumented application class files
- *build.reports.dir*—Holds JUnit reports

We now compile our application and unit test Java files in the usual manner ⓫. Notice that debug is turned on. jCoverage instrumentation requires that compile jobs are performed with debug on. At ⓬ we instrument the classes we created at ⓫. In the context of software, "instrumentation" refers to the act of employing a mechanism to monitor the behavior of software. In particular, jCoverage instruments the class files created at ⓫ by interlacing jCoverage byte code with application code. Notice all the class files are instrumented except the unit test. Our interest is limited to the application code, not unit tests.

Next, we run the unit tests ⓭. As the unit tests execute, the jCoverage byte code injected at ⓬ is tracking how many times each line of code is executed. Notice the instrumented class files are placed ahead of the uninstrumented class files ⓮. Placing the instrumented class file higher in the class path ensures the instrumented class files are loaded by the classloader instead of the noninstrumented ones. If the order were reversed, jCoverage would report your application as untested.

The byte code injected at ⓬ requires the help of classes found in the jcoverage. jar file ⓯.To generate an XML report we set the formatter type at ⓰ to be xml. Next we execute StrutsTestCase tests in the usual way ⓱. We have chosen to execute StrutsTestCase unit tests, but you are free to use any JUnit test. And finally, we generated both HTML and XML reports ⓲.

Let's have a look at coverage reporting.

The jCoverage HTML reports present an application-wide code coverage view of your unit tests (figure 9.2). You can easily drill down to obtain both package-level (not shown) and class-level details (not shown). The class-level report highlights portions of the code which remain untested. The application and package summary reports present line and branch coverage results in both numeric and

jcoverage | summary

Coverage Report

Overall	files	lines	%line	indicator	%branch	indicator
Overall coverage figures	6	199	94%		100%	

Set view:

By Name
By Coverage (Most covered first)
By Coverage (Least covered first)

Packages

packagename	files	lines	%line	indicator	%branch	indicator
com.strutsrecipes.strutstestcase.actions	1	12	100%		100%	
com.strutsrecipes.strutstestcase.beans	1	20	50%		100%	
com.strutsrecipes.strutstestcase.business	1	113	100%		100%	
com.strutsrecipes.strutstestcase.forms	1	4	100%		100%	
com.strutsrecipes.strutstestcase.mocktest	2	50	100%		100%	

All Java™ files

file	lines	%line	indicator	%branch	indicator
com.strutsrecipes.strutstestcase.actions.SearchAction	12	100%		100%	
com.strutsrecipes.strutstestcase.beans.Element	20	50%		100%	
com.strutsrecipes.strutstestcase.business.BusinessFacade	113	100%		100%	
com.strutsrecipes.strutstestcase.forms.SearchForm	4	100%		100%	
com.strutsrecipes.strutstestcase.mocktest.TestNegative	22	100%		100%	
com.strutsrecipes.strutstestcase.mocktest.TestPositive	28	100%		100%	

Figure 9.2 jCoverage Report: provides summary and detail information indicating how much of the code base has been tested.

graphical representations. The widely accepted JUnit-style red and green success-failure graphical bars make you feel right at home.

◆ *Discussion*

You have now stepped through an Apache Ant script line by line to see what you need to do to get coverage testing off the ground. Let's take a step back to review what went on. jCoverage works by instrumenting your application byte code. When the unit test runs, the jCoverage byte code injected into your class file kicks in. As your unit tests put your code through its paces, jCoverage is watching. As each line is executing, jCoverage is recording the number of times each line is executed into the jcoverage.ser file. As the suffix implies, jcoverage.ser is a serialized statistical object used to record execution behavior of your code under the influence of your unit tests. The report task uses the jcoverage.ser file to generate handsome looking reports.

The generation of jcoverage.ser is a 2-stage process. At stage 1 the instrumentation task is employed to map line numbers to byte code in the jcoverage.ser file. Stage 2 fires up when unit tests are executed. As your application code is exercised by the unit tests, jCoverage is busily squirreling away statistical information into the jcoverage.ser file. At the end of stage 2 the jcoverage.ser file knows which lines and branches of code were executed. If your organization orchestrates multiple builds to generate a single deployment artifact, you can use the merge task to blend multiple jcoverage.ser files.

If your organization is trying to bring some visibility to unit testing, you may want to take advantage of the check task. The check task can be used to fail the build unless a minimum line and branch coverage level has been met.

There are a couple of "gotcha"s worth noting. First, the jcoverage.ser file must pass through both stage 1 and stage 2. A common mistake is to use a stale jcoverage.ser file or perhaps forget to include the class path to the instrumented classes. Remember, stage 2 is executed by the instrumented class files. Second, the jCoverage uses its manifest file to enforce the physical placement of dependent third-party JAR files. We recommend you inspect the jCoverage sample application or the manifest file to make sure everything is placed where it needs to be.

Some testing is out of `StrutsTestCase`'s reach. For example, figure 9.1 reports only 50% coverage on the Element bean. Drilling down to the class level report reveals that the no-argument constructor is never called, nor are some of the bean properties. This situation exists because an argument constructor is used in the business layer, but the no-argument constructor must exist to satisfy the JavaBean specification [JAVABEAN]. In addition, because the bean properties are accessed in the JSP, `StrutsTestCase` does not exercise a unit test to invoke them. In this case, you may want to consider an `Element` bean unit test to complete your coverage.

Remember that a sea of "green bars" on your jCoverage reports does not necessarily mean you have completely blanketed your application code with unit tests. The multitude of business scenarios can result in unforeseen code permutations. The more you understand your business, the better the chances of dropping a unit test net over your application.

Unit testing yields benefits in both the development and maintenance cycles. Everyone wants to do a good job, but it's difficult to know when you have reached that point. A good automated coverage tool, such as jCoverage, can help you reach that goal.

> **BEST PRACTICE** *Employ continuous coverage testing*—Coverage testing should be automated and incorporated into the normal build process. You may want to test your coverage level on a daily basis, or you may decide to test at predefined project milestones. Either way, automating coverage testing allows you to monitor and increase testing visibility.

◆ *Related*

- 9.1—Testing outside the container with StrutsTestCase

◆ *Reference*

- [JAVABEAN] JavaBean Specification
- [JCOVERAGE] jCoverage
- [JUNIT] JUnit
- [STRUTSTC] StrutsTestCase

references

[ADOBE] Adobe http://www.adobe.com

[ANT] Apache Ant http://ant.apache.org/

[ANTMAN] Apache Ant Manual http://ant.apache.org/manual/

[BEANUTILS] BeanUtils package http://jakarta.apache.org/commons/beanutils/apidocs/
org/apache/commons/beanutils/package-summary.html

[BLOCH] Bloch, Joshua. *Effective Java Programming Language Guide*. (Boston, MA: 2001;
ISBN 201310058).

[CACTUS] Apache Cactus http://jakarta.apache.org/cactus/index.html

[CASTOR] Castor http://castor.exolab.org/

[CFJD] ChoiceFormat Javadoc http://java.sun.com/j2se/1.4.2/docs/api/java/text/Choice-
Format.html

[CONTINT] Fowler, Martin. Continuous Integration. http://www.martinfowler.com/articles/
continuousIntegration.html

[CONTPERF] Continuous Performance Testing http://www.theserverside.com/resources/
article.jsp?l=ContinuousPerformance

[CORE] Alur, Deepak, Dan Malks, and John Crupi. *Core J2EE Patterns, Best Practices, and
Design Strategies*. (Indianapolis, IN: 2003; ISBN 131422464).

[CTRYCODES] ISO 3166 Codes (Countries) http://userpage.chemie.fu-berlin.de/diverse/
doc/ISO_3166.html

[DBC] Applying Design by Contract, in Computer (IEEE), vol. 25

[DEA] *Designing Enterprise Applications with the J2EETM Platform*, 2nd ed. Stearns, Beth, Greg Murray, Inderjeet Singh, et al. http://java.sun.com/blueprints/guidelines/designing_enterprise_applications_2e/web-tier/web-tier5.html

[DIGEST] Apache Jakarta Commons Digesterhttp://jakarta.apache.org/commons/digester/index.html

[DISPACT] Struts DispatchAction Javadoc http://jakarta.apache.org/struts/api/org/apache/struts/actions/DispatchAction.html

[EJS] Vermeulen, Ambler, Bumgardner, Metz, Misfeldt, Shur, & Thompson, *Elements of Java Style*. (Cambridge, UK: 2002; ISBN 521777682).

[HIA] King, Gavin, and Christian Bauer. *Hibernate In Action*. (Greenwich, CT: 2002;ISBN 193239415X).

[HIB] Hibernate home page http://www.hibernate.org/

[HTML401] HTML 4.0.1 Specification http://www.w3.org/TR/html401/

[HTTP] HTTP Protocol Specification, redirect http://www.w3.org/Protocols/rfc2616/rfc2616-sec10.html

[I18NBASICS] Shirah, Joe Sam, *Java Internationalization Basics*. http://www-106.ibm.com/developerworks/java/edu/j-dw-javai18n-i.html

[ITEXT] iText http://www.lowagie.com/iText

[ITEXTJ] iText Java documentation http://itext.sourceforge.net/docs/

[JAKARTA] Jakarta http://jakarta.apache.org

[JAVABEAN] JavaBean Specification http://java.sun.com/products/javabeans/docs/spec.html

[JAXB] JAXB http://java.sun.com/xml/downloads/jaxb.html

[JCL] Jakarta Commons Lang component http://jakarta.apache.org/commons/lang.html

[JCOVERAGE] jCoverage http://jcoverage.com

[JDANT] Hatcher, Eric, and Steven Loughran. *Java Development with Ant*, (Greenwich, CT: 1999; ISBN 1930110588). http://www.manning.com/hatcher/

[JDOC] Comparable Interface JavaDoc http://java.sun.com/products/jdk/1.2/docs/api/java/lang/Comparable.html

[JGURU] jGuru http://www.jguru.com/

[JMS] Sun's Java Message Service Tutorial http://java.sun.com/products/jms/tutorial/

[JSBE] Williamson, Alan R. *Java Servlets by Example*. (Greenwich, CT: 1999; ISBN 188477766X). http://www.manning.com/Williamson/

[JSR000154] JSR-000154 Java Servlet 2.4 Specification http://jcp.org/aboutJava/communityprocess/first/jsr154/index3.html

[JUNIT] JUnit http://www.junit.org

[JUNITPERF] JUnitPerf http://www.clarkware.com/software/JUnitPerf.html

[LAYOUT] Struts Layout http://struts.application-servers.com/

[MFJD] MessageFormat Javadoc http://java.sun.com/j2se/1.4.2/docs/api/java/text/Message-Format.html

[MFORMAT] Message Format Java API http://java.sun.com/j2se/1.4.1/docs/api/java/text/MessageFormat.html

[MVC] Model-View-Controller http://java.sun.com/blueprints/guidelines/designing_enterprise_applications_2e/web-tier/web-tier5.html

[OPTIMIZEIT] Borland OptimizeIt ServerTrace http://www.borland.com/opt_server-trace/index.html

[PDFRM] Portable Document Format Reference Manual http://partners.adobe.com/asn/developer/acrosdk/docs/pdfspec.pdf

[PEAA] Fowler, Martin. *Patterns of Enterprise Application Architecture*. (Boston, MA: 2002; ISBN 321127420).

[PERFORMASURE] Sitraka PerformaSure http://www.sitraka.com/performasure/perfor-masure.shtml

[PL] Ambler, Scott W. "The Design of a Robust Persistence Layer for Relational Data-bases" http://www.ambysoft.com/persistenceLayer.pdf

[RB] ResourceBundle API http://java.sun.com/j2se/1.4.2/docs/api/java/util/ResourceBun-dle.html

[REFPERF] Sosnoski, Dennis. "Java Programming Dynamics, Part 2: Introducing reflec-tion." IBM DeveloperWorks http://www-106.ibm.com/developerworks/java/library/j-dyn0603/?Open&ca=daw-ja-news

[RFC1738] RFC 1738 http://www.ietf.org/rfc/rfc1738.txt

[SAC] Struts Action Class http://jakarta.apache.org/struts/api/org/apache/struts/action/Action.html

[SERVSPEC] Java Servlet Specification http://java.sun.com/products/servlet/

[SIA] Husted, Ted, Cedric Dumoulin, George Franciscus, and David Winterfeldt, *Struts In Action*. (Greenwich, CT: 2002; ISBN 1930110502).

[SOS] Andrews, Mark. Story of a Servlet: An Instant Tutorial http://java.sun.com/products/servlet/articles/tutorial/

[SSLDOC] SSL Overview http://wp.netscape.com/security/techbriefs/ssl.html

[SSLEXT] SSL Extension for Struts HTTP/HTTPS Switching http://struts.ditlinger.com/

[SSLSPEC] SSL Specification http://wp.netscape.com/eng/ssl3/

[SSLTOM] SSL Tomcat Configuration http://jakarta.apache.org/tomcat/tomcat-4.0-doc/ssl-howto.html

[STRUTSTC] StrutsTestCase http://strutstestcase.sourceforge.net/

[TILECEDRIC] Cedric Dumoulin's Tiles Library documentation http://www.lifl.fr/~dumoulin/tiles/

[UML] Larman, Craig. *Applying UML and Patterns: An Introduction to Object-Oriented Analysis and Design and the Unified Process*, 2nd ed. (Indianapolis, IN: 2001; ISBN 130925691).

[URI] W3 URI Specification http://www.w3.org/Addressing/URL/uri-spec.html

[WAR] Web archive file http://access1.sun.com/techarticles/simple.WAR.html

[WBP] Gunther, Harvey W. "WebSphere Application Server Development Best Practices for Performance and Scalability" http://www-3.ibm.com/software/webservers/appserv/ws_bestpractices.pdf

[XALAN] Xalan http://xml.apache.org/xalan-j/

[XMLPERF] XML Performance Benchmarks http://www.sosnoski.com/opensrc/xmlbench/

[XMLSPEC] XML Specification http://www.w3.org/XML/

[XSLFO] XSL-FO Specification http://www.w3.org/TR/xsl/slice6.html

[XSLTSPEC] XSLT Specification http://www.w3.org/TR/xslt

index

Symbols\Numerics

< character 68
character 67
{0} 63
{0}/{1}
  default message for layout
    pager 239
401 unauthorized 320

A

Abstract Action 155–156
Abstract Base Action 154
Abstract Struts Action 154, 157
abstraction 405
acceptance 62
acquire resources 353
Action
  guarding 319
  protext 319
Action authorization
  override 342
action mapping
  input attribute 247
  parameter attribute 270
  protect 336
  validate attribute 246
ActionErrors 45–46, 48, 51, 58,
    63, 65, 245–246, 256, 261,
    263, 273, 341, 387–388,
    390, 430–431, 434
  format 247
ActionErrors.
    GLOBAL_ERROR 45

ActionForm
  responsibility 268
  validate 244
  validation 336
ActionForward
  and jsessionid 18
  default application 14
  default application from
    URL 14
  discussed 15
  not used in web.xml 15
  redirected 18
  transfer from index.jsp 15
  using constants 33
  using DynaActionForms 40
ActionMapping
  extend 306
  type attribute 308
249
ActionMessage 47–48, 51, 54,
    60–61, 63–66, 68–69
actions
  exposing to page 140
  keep short – best practice 236
ActionServlet 22, 336, 339,
    353–357, 384–385,
    446, 465
  responsibilities 339
adapter 364
Adobe 371
  download 372
advisory title 303
aggregate, errors 44
AggregateException 266
AggregateExceptionHandler 267

airline reservation 62
Alert Window 322
alternate row colors 80
alternate text 303
altKey 303
analyze 345
anomalies 438
anonymous 318
Ant 3, 13, 250
  acronym explained 7
  best practice 13
  build.log output 12
  build.properties 11
    substitution parameters 12
  build.properties code
    listing 11
  build.properties file 9
  build.xml file 9
  Cactus 439
  command 9
  compile-domain target 10
  create build.xml 7
  create script 7
  defacto build tool 3
  default project attribute 9
  directory naming 28
  DynaActionForm 40
  embedding version
    numbers 12
  explained 3
  first steps 7
  <javac> tag 10
  jCoverage 463
  JSP, declaring location 10
  JUnit 427

Ant *(continued)*
mail tag 10
parameters 13
powerful tool 13
recipe 6
recipe description 6
reusable scripts
best practice 13
running 9
separate deployment and
development 4
standard project properties 9
tag 10
testing 436
used daily 13
WAR file, declaring location
and name 10
Apache Digester 423
Applets, option for Struts 2
application
intuitive 62
quality 50
application context 354
Application Server
JBoss 3
Weblogic 3
Websphere 3
application usability 53
application.proprties 268
architecture 318
args, with layout pager 239
arguments
for layout pagerStatus
tag 240
array 63
ASCII 89
ASCII codes 89
ASP 158
associate 52
attributes
for layout tab tag 231
of skinResources 201
of tab and tabs tags 230
audience 62
audit 329
authenticate 327, 336, 347
authentication 318
base64 320
basic 320
container-based 319
domain-level 320

HTTP digest 321
HTTP form 321
HTTPS Client 321
mechanisms 320
realm 324
SSL 330
strategy 319
authorization 318, 320
automated 436, 438, 468
Ant best practice 13
ant build 6
build process 13
functional testing 13
testing 444
automated build 462
autonomous teams 449

B

B2C 351
back button 417
and crumbs 223
backwards compatibility 364
backwards navigation 218
batch program 391
<batchtest> 443
Bayern, Shawn 140
BEA WebLogic 438
<bean:message> 46, 299
format 65
bean:write 114
<bean:write> 47
beginXXX() 439
BodyTagSupport 82
bookmark 406
Boolean, logic present tag 128
browser support 371
buffer 73, 94
flush 369
build.properties 7
build.xml
adding resource bundles 28
bundle, attribute and tabbed
panes 226
Burst Test 456
business errors 256
business exceptions 398
business façade 367, 373, 394
business layer 70, 73, 79, 256,
306, 329, 372, 393, 396
responsibilities 393

business logic 58, 377
and tag libraries 100
sensitive 320
Business Objects
and Action class 97
deciding how MVC works
with, 103
business rules 58
BusinessException 258
Business-to-Consumer 349
byte code injection 466
ByteArrayOutputStream 369
bytecode 378

C

cache 72, 78–79, 423
Struts 79
caching 273, 352–353, 357,
400, 417–418, 461
strategy 400
cactify 443
Cactus 426, 428, 437–440,
442–444
Ant tasks 442
build.properties 444
connect to Tomcat 443
lifecycle 439
mergewebxml attribute 443
port attribute 443
proxy redirector 438
report format 443
report location 443
report.xsl 442
servlet example 443
StrutsTestCase 444
Tomcat 443
Tomcat shutdown 443
Tomcat startup 443
war file 443
web.xml 443
Cactus lifecycle 439
<cactus> 443
CactusStrutsTestCase 428, 433,
437, 439
cactus-web.xml 441
Castor 368
certificate keystore, create 331
CGI vs. tag libraries 100
challenge 336
change, constant 417

changeRowColor, JavaScript and selected row 205
Choice format 67
cipher 329, 335
circumvent navigation 406
class loader 72, 369, 385, 415
ClassCastException 404
  problem with integers 119
classpath 299, 383, 418
clean up session objects 153
client side tabs recipe 232
coarse-grain 338
Cocoon, option for Struts 2
code branches 462
code changes, not required 72
coffee 318
cognitive 50
collate 57
collection 81
  errors 50
  messages 47
collections and bean define tag 121
color code 80
colors, sets 80
colspan, attribute used in tabbed panes 228
column sort with Struts-Layout tags 173
comma delimited 336
Comparable 448
comparator 448
complex applications
  and logic present tag 137
  in team environments 148
complex conditional logic 306
complex views with logic present tag 128
complexity 395–396, 455
ComponentContext 360
composition 378
confidentiality 329
configuration parameters runtime 70
configure, tasks for Struts-Layout use 175
confirmation 62
<constant> 278
<constant-name> 278
<constant-value> 278

Constants
  java code 32
  java file 32
  recipe 32
constructor 45
container managed security 327
<containerset> 443
Content-Disposition 90
ContentLength 369
ContentType 369
Continuous Performance Testing 455
contracts 450
control
  and actions 98
  message queue 55
controller 339
controller tag 95, 296, 340
Controller, action class, keep short 236
<controller/> 249
<controller> 94, 408
controllerClass 359, 362
ControllerSupport 360
controllerUrl 362
controls, types 328
cookie 321, 416
country code 300
coupling 376, 393
  Struts 402
coverage testing. See testing
coverage testing tool 462
createResources 419
critical decisions and tag library use 99
critical success factor 455
CRUD 270, 378, 391
crumbs
  browser view 221
  controlling boundaries 223
  customizing 223
  listing for dynamic 221
  method to limit crumb size 223
  navigation best practices 224
  separator attribute 223
  setting 223
  tag listing 221
crumb-trails, dynamic and static 218

cryptographic algorithm 329
CSS 321
  and accessing bean resource 145
  and logic present tag 130
  and MVC 99
  contextual elements with layout panel 190
  default directory with Struts-Layout tags 194
  extra CSS files with Struts-Layout tags 201
  image references with Struts-Layout tags 194
  in JSPs 38
  interation with layout panel tag 190
  linking stylesheets recipe 37
  listing for layout panel tag 188
  listing with layout panel 191
  location of 176
  placement 37
  relative paths 37
  skins with Struts-Layout tags 193
  solid references 6
  Struts-Layout simple table 180
  style block for complex table 186
  style blocks and Struts-Layout tags 193
  styleClass attribute layout panel tag 190
  with custom skin 195
  with layout panel tag 188
  with selectable rows 202
  with Struts-Layout tags 174, 177, 180, 186–187, 189, 191, 193–194, 196, 199–200, 205, 214, 216, 219, 223, 228–229, 232, 238
    "onglet" prefix 230
    attributes for tab(s) tags listed 231
    attributes in tab(s) tags 230
    browser view 230
    custom skins 196

CSS *(continued)*
  details for tabs 226
  French namespaces 229
  layout pager tag listing 237
  listing for tree
    navigation 214
  listing for use with tabbed
    panes 229
  pager tag 233
  special tabbed pane
    classes 228
  styleClass declaration with
    layout pager tag 238
  tab(s) attributes listed 231
  tabbed panes 226
    classes explained 230
  table listing for tabs
    classes 232
  tree navigation 208,
    214, 216
    eccentricities 216
  tree navigation debugging
    with 216
  wire diagram
    reference 229
  with layout pager tag 237
  with layout pagerStatus
    tag 240
CSS Style Sheets linked with
  html rewrite tag 150
cultural differences 309
culturally friendly 309
custom JSP tag 80
custom message queue 53
custom queue 55
custom skins
  and layout skin tag 195
  creating 201
custom validator 312

D

DAO 392
  create dynamically 402
  declarative 402
  factory 402, 404
Data Access Object Pattern 392
data input 75
Data Mapper pattern 378
data source layer, persistence
  layer 393

data store 398
data transfer object 256, 268
data validation 268
data, insert 62
database 73, 256, 321, 329,
    378, 406, 417
  access 418
  dialect 383
  driver 383
  minimize access 418
  type 378
database connections 357,
    364, 461
database server, start 379
DB2 379
debugging 379
declarative exception handling
    243, 256, 342, 390–391, 396
  employ 342
  exceptions aggregate 261
  how works 256
  use case 257
declaratively 316, 330
decorates 460
decouple 417
decrypt 329, 335
dedicated environment 455
default Action classes
  for Struts-Layout 177
default.css and layout skin
    tag 194
defensive copy 357
define contracts 450
definitions and Tile
    mappings 162
delegate 339, 367
delineate 90
denial-of-service attack 94
deployable artifacts 443
  build process 6
deployment 417
design by contract 450
design patterns 55
  vs. reality 171
design practice, contracts 450
design refactoring 462
destroy() 353–355, 357, 385
dialog box 320
Digester 415, 423
  rules 415
  stack 415

directory for layout tags 199
disaster recovery 352
DispatchAction 268
  reflection 270
  use 270
doAfterBody 84
document management
  and logic equal tag 135
doGet 353
domain authentication 319
domain layer, business
    layer 393
domain model 378
doPost 353
doStart 84
doStartTag 84
drawbacks 44
DTO 256, 268
DynaActionForms 41,
    444–445
  and logic equal tag 135
  getting variables from form
    bean 40
  pitfalls 41
  recipe 38
  recipe description 6
  recipe explained 38
  StrutsTestCase 444
  testing. *See* testing
  useful 444
DynaBean interface 445
DynaBean property values 445
DynaClass 445, 447
DynaForm testing
  assertions 445
dynamic 62
dynamic content 125
dynamic messages 44
dynamic tables with paging 233
DynaProperties 445
DynaPropertiesHelper 447
DynaPropertyComparator 448

E

easy to use 62, 71
Einstein 369
EJB 357, 405–406, 423, 461
elements
  hiding with logic present
    tags 127

email 249
encapsulate 45
encapsulate business logic 367
encapsulation 392
encode 89
    automatic 89
    scheme 89
encrypt 329–330, 335
encryption 321
endXXX() 439
<engine> 324
Enumerate contracts 450
environment 444
ergonomic 79
error handling mechanisms 256
error messages
    list 57
    placement 50
    purpose 44
error page 322
error queue 50
error scenarios 256
errors
    and logic present tag 127
    categorize 57
    generalized 49
    list 62
errors.footer 46, 246
errors.header 46, 246
exception handler 341–342
    default 261, 266
exception strategy benefits 261
ExceptionHandler 256,
        261, 263
    extend 267
exceptions 41, 65, 258, 262,
        264, 267–268, 390, 398
    aggregate 243
    bulking 262
    business layer 267
    class hierarchy 257
    classification 257
    collection 262
    global 257, 260
    handle 260
    local 257, 260
    local vs. global 257
    logging 260
    register 340
    runtime with layout skin
        tag 195

strategy 257
swallow 273
expensive 455
expose 73
externalize SQL 405

F

Façade Pattern 392
factory
    DAO 402
    Hibernate 384
    JDBC 418
    <message-resource> 419
    resource bundle 418
    static 402
    XSLT transformer 369
Factory Pattern 392
<field> 283
file
    transfer 89
    upload 90
File Upload 89
    limiting file sizes 95
    tag attributes 94
FileInputStream 72
filter
    and bean write tag 114–115
    bean write tag – false 115
    bean write tag – HTML/
        XML 115
    bean write tag – true 114
    best practices 115
finally 400
findForward 306
fine-grained 364, 378
fine-grained protection 346
flat-file authentication 323
flexibility 394
form beans
    exposed with bean resource
        tag 146
    exposing to page 140
format
    custom 63
    dates 63
    numbers 63
    time 63
formatter tag 443
FormFile 91
formset inheritance 315

<formset> 313
forward
    attribute in layout tab
        tag 232
    locale 305
frames and MVC 98
frameworks
    hallmark 339
    persistence 391
FrontBase 379
functionality
    and logic present tag 127

G

garbage collection 456
garbage collector 357
generic error page 258
getContextPath and html
        rewrite tag 148
getDynaClass 445
getResource 71
getVariableInfo 85
global 328
global exception 268
global forwards
    and html rewrite tag 151
    exposed by bean resource
        tag 146
    exposing to page 140
global queue 45
globalize 298
Globals.ERROR 62
Globals.ERROR_KEY 45,
        47, 62
Globals.LOCALE_KEY
        296–297, 303, 305,
        311, 315
Globals.MESSAGE_KEY 62
good practice 52
gotcha 56, 69, 79, 94, 301,
        316, 342, 345, 353, 357,
        417, 460
    JavaScript and selected
        row 205
Graphic User Interfaces
    no equivalent Struts tags and
        HTML 151
GRASP principles 276
green screen 455
group security 343

guaranteed navigation 406
GUI
    altering look with logic
        present tag 127
    and logic equal tag 136
    and panels 187
    and Struts-Layout tags 175
    crumbs, best practices 224
    debugging with logic present
        tag 130
    exposing WEB-INF elemnts
        in 147
    finding variables in
        development 130
    migrating to tiles 163
    simple table with
        Struts-Layout 178
    tools for Struts-Layout 182
    using logic equal tag 136
    using logic present tag 133
guideline 49
    message tags 49

H

hard-coding 303
hardwired 47
harvest 79
HashMap, used to pass
    parameters 151
hbg.xml file 382
header 47, 57
heavy load 459
hexadecimal 89
Hibernate 378
    alias 389
    artifacts 379
    close session 384
    commit 391
    definition 378
    environmental
        information 383
    example 379
    exceptions 390
    factory 379, 385, 400
    factory cache 384
    factory close 385
    features 391
    <generator> 382
    hidden 394
    <id> 382

implementation specific
    features 383
job 382
key generation 382
map columns 382
performance 384
primary key 389
replacement parameter 389
search 389
selecting objects 389
transform 391
update 391
ways to search 389
Hibernate Query
    Language 378
Hibernate SQL 389
hibernate.cfg.xml
    classpath 383
hidden field 416
high cohesion 276
high-traffic sites and
    images 112
high-volume sites 243
hijack, Action 342
hot spots 341–342
    controller 339
    definition 339
HQL 389
href, attribute in layout tab
    tag 232
HSQL 405
HTML 46
    and layout panel tag 191
    and skins 194
    and tabbed panes 229
    filtering in bean write
        tag 114
    functionality with logic
        present tag 128
    in beans 115
    limitations 371
    listing of rendered tabbed
        panes 227
    validating complicated
        strings 115
    view of complex table 186
    with Struts tags instead of
        Struts-Layout 182
HTML table 80
    alternate row colors 80
<html:errors/> 247, 261, 342

<html:errors> 44, 269
<html:image> 302
<html:img> 302
<html:javascript> 255
<html:messages> 44
HTTP
    challenges 406
    mechanism 16
    stateless 406
    unsecured protocol 330
HTTP 1.0 320
HTTP protocol 406
Http Request
    get handle to session 154
HTTP session 378
    volume 378
HTTP Status 400 337
HTTPS 321
https 334
HttpServletRequestSimulator
    433
HttpSession 136, 153–154, 156
    scope with bean define
        tag 119
    serialized in appservers 153
HttpSessionSimulator 428
httpsPort property 332
Hypersonic 379
    command 379
    dialect 383
HypersonicSQL 379

I

IDE 379, 427
images 302, 417
    and directory structure 111
    limitations with Struts
        tags 112
    size attributes and 113
IMAP 329
immutable 297, 356–357
include directive 123–125
    compared with action 123
includes, different types
    discussed 125
in-container testing 428,
    437–438, 444
    popularity 438
increase 354, 373, 460, 468
increase load 460

increase performance 354
increased flexibility 54
incremental compile 379
information management 243
Informix 379
Ingres 379
inheritance 378
in-memory cache 398
input, clear 75
instrumenting 467
   definition 462
integration 69
Interbase 379
interface, user 50
internationalization 44, 67
  bulit-in support 301
  maintenance 301
internationalize
  steps 298
  text 47
  tiles 309
Internet Explorer 321
Internet Media Type 89
IOException, swallow 413
isRoles() 337
isUserInRole 341
iterate 46, 55
iterate tag, extend 80
IterateRowTei 85
iteration index number 84
iText 372, 376
  download 372

J

Jakarta Project, an open source
  movement 2
JAR files for Struts-Layout
  tags 175
Java IO package 94
Java programmers
  experienced 62
Java Server Pages, Cactus 438
Java Swing
  compared with layout panel
    tag 188
  similarities to tree in
    Struts-Layout 209
JavaBeans 64, 68, 368, 428
javadoc 69
java.lang.Exception 261

JavaScript 100, 105, 108, 122,
  149–150, 177, 187,
  193–195, 198–200,202,
  204, 206–207, 210, 216, 252
  alert 253
  and html rewrite tag 149–150
  and tabbed panes 229
  and tree navigation 207
  attributes in tree action 212
  attributes used with tree
    navigation 215
  in tree action 211
  locating files with skins
    problems 199
  required files for
    Struts-Layout 177
  selectable rows 202
  tabbed pane reference 227
  tabbed panes 225
  validation, reuse 255
java.text.ChoiceFormat 67
java.text.MessageFormat 63
java.util.ArrayList and
  Struts-Layout 178
java.util.Collection
  and dynamic crumbs 221
  and Struts-Layout tags.
    See Struts-Layout tags
  with layout pager tag 236
  with Struts-Layout tags 173
java.util.Collections 120
  and bean define tag 120
java.util.HashMap
  with Struts Layout 183
JAXB 368, 371
jCoverage
  common mistake 467
  download 463
  graphical representations 467
  reports 466
  stage-1 467
  stage-2 467
  statistical information 467
jcoverage.ser 467
JDBC 394, 396
  properties 418
JDBCMessageResourcesFactory
  418
JDK v 1.4 330
JMS 70, 72, 357
  queue 70

JNDI 461
jsessionid 5, 16
  and bookmarking 18
  background 17
  recipeJSESSIONID 16
JSP 32, 46–48, 52, 55, 59–61, 65,
  68, 80, 88, 90, 98, 185, 188,
  221, 239, 245–246, 299,
  301, 304, 325, 334, 356, 361,
  363, 366, 371–372,
  375–376, 389, 394, 468
???error??? –
  message-resources 29
accessing
  message-resources 31
ActionForward 14
adding a skin tag 198
as framework 2
base tag placement 36
bean define code listing 120
bean define tag 116
bean resource tag 139
bean write tag nested in logic
  present tag 129
before tags 99
bundle attribute in tags
  30–31
client-side validation 252
code using bean resource 145
constant variable on page 34
constants and MVC
  boundaries 34
CSS 38
different directories from
  CSS 37
DynaActionForms 41
dynamic tabs 232
errors with Struts-Layout
  tags 201
exposing struts-config to
  View 140
images 111
in team environments 148
include action 124
include compile time
  issues 123
include, difference
  between 123
includes compared 123
JavaScript and selected
  row 205

JSP *(continued)*
  layout collectionItem tag 180
  layout panel tag 188–189
  linking stylesheets 37
  linking stylesheets recipe
      explained 37
  listing with layout panel
      tag 189
  listing with tabbed panes 227
  logic present tag 127
  logic present tag listing 130
  migrating to XML
      definitions 167
  MVC1 97
  page portability and tiles 162
  pager tag implemented 236
  parameters as constants 33
  precompiled with Ant 7
  public static final Strings
      tree navigation 213
  session attributes 154
  skinned 174
  static tree methods 208
  Struts 2
  tabbed panes 225
  tag libraries 99
  the View layer 97
  Tiles 164
  tiles definitions 164
  tiles definitions, differences
      with XML 167
  tree navigation 213
  tree navigation listing 214
  tricks using html rewrite
      tag 149
  URL rewriting 18
  usage of different 125
  use in 15
  using base tag 36
  using constants in 35
  using message tag 27–28
  violating MVC in 103
  without includes, simple 122
  without Struts 2
  xtags 140
JSP tag libraries
  and business logic 100
  by shawn bayern 101
JSP tags
  server-side 100
  works well with Struts 101

<jsp:useBean/>
  and Struts-Layout tags 179
  with Struts-Layout 185
JSSE download, install 330
JSTL 87, 115, 139–140, 296
  and tag attributes 104
  future vs Struts tags 104
  in Struts-EL 104
  option for Struts 2
  overlap with Struts' tag
      library 104
  Shawn Bayern 103
JTree, similarities with Struts
    Layout tree 215
judgment 405
JUnit
  Ant 427
  assertions 427
  automated build 427
  automatically run 427
  build tests 427
  description 427
  execute 427
  fail 427
  install 436
  reports 436
  runners 427
JUnitPerf 461
  definition 456

K

key
  attribute and tabbed
      panes 226
  attribute for layout
      pagerStatus tag 240
knowledge 65
known key 406

L

language code 300
language variances 301
lastSelRow, JavaScript attribute
    and selected row 205
layered application 391
layers 393
  benefits 393, 404
  exceptions 398
  golden rule 397

Hibernate 393
  illustrate 393
  Struts 393
  use 404
Layers pattern 392
layout.pager.next.img
  skin with pager 233
layout.pager.next.label
  skin with pager 233
layout.pager.previous.img
  skin with pager 233
layout.pager.previous.label
  skin with pager 233
lazy load 423
  hybrid 423
LDAP 321, 329
Lego 394
LGPL 372
licenses 455
lightweight 319
limit 67
limitation 345, 347
line of defense 243
links 106, 110, 112, 124, 130,
      148, 151–152
  and migration to Struts 152
  for js and CSS 149
Load Test 456
locale
  forward 305
  set 298
locale sensitive 67, 72
localize
  country code 305
  forward alternatives 309
  images 302
locate information 80
lock 329
log out 326
<logger> 324
<logic:messagesPresent>
    47, 55
look and feel tabbed panes 229
low coupling 271

M

maintainability 49, 392
  vs development 171
maintainable 276, 305,
    345, 405

maintenance 53, 275, 286, 330, 335, 343, 417, 449
and weak design 99
maintenance cycle 462
maintenance nightmare 462
malicious 320
manage complexity 455
manage content, business users 418
mask 73
maxPageItems, attribute for layout pager tag 236
Mckoi SQL 379
memory 301
MenuComponent and visitor pattern 216
MenuComponent.addComponent method in creating trees 213
menu.jar 175, 208
and tree navigation 208
MenuRepository and tree navigation 213
mergewebxml 441, 443
message queue 51, 53, 55–56, 70
global 65
MessageFormat 376
message-formatting 62
MessageResource 72, 93
MessageResourceFactory 419
message-resources 26–28, 30, 70, 72, 74
alternate 301
changes in Struts 1.1 25
default code listing 25
in struts-config file 26
listing in struts-config file 31
location in struts-config 27
modify for multiple resources 27
placement in struts-config file 28
249, 417
<message-resources> 299
messages
classification 62
formatting 63
groups 57
organize 62
property 53

render 48
method, HTTP request parameter 270
metrics 462
Microsoft SQL Server 379
migration 252
mismatch paradigm 378
mission statement 302
mock
HTTP request 428
HTTP response 428
HTTP session 428
Mock Object
useful 444
Mock Objects 426, 428, 433, 438
useful 428
MockStrutsTestCase 428, 432–434, 437, 439, 446
Model-View-Controller 393
with JSP 97, 102
modify output 67
modularity 345
module testing 454
ModuleConfig 355, 384–385
modules 355, 426, 449–451, 454
available documentation 24
caveats 26
changing names 23
creating 21
creating separate 20–21
deciding to merge 20
default application 452
interconnectivity 450
invoking actions in other modules 23
messages and struts-config 31
multiple resource bundles 21
number of resources allowed 26
principal objective 450
problems connecting resource bundles 28
recipe explained 19
reference 28, 31
referring outside of context 23
resource bundles 25
separate directories 21
sharing resources 21
testing. See testing

various Jakarta modules 2
with multiple resources 27
monolithic 417
MPL 372
multi-language 298
multipart/form-data 89
multiple facades 394
MVC 46, 49, 171, 393
ActionForward with 14
and Smalltalk-80 97
and Struts 97
and Struts logic tags 99
in Struts context 2
loose definitions 99
Struts separation 3
violations 98
MySQL 379

N

name, attribute in layout collection tag 185
namespace 80
navigation 406
and 218
strategies, best practices 207
tabbed panes 225
trees 206
using tabs, best practices 225
when to use trees 206
NavigationTokenUtils 413
navigation.xml 408
nocache attribute 409
noncache attribute 417
non-scalable 460
non-SSL links 330
null values
best practice 138
empty tag 128
present tag 128
number of last displayed item arg for layout pager 239
NumberUtils 286

O

Object
in session or parameter 132
typing with bean define tag 119
object model 378

Object-Oriented Design 392
Object-Relational Mappers 378, 391
Objects, relationships in tree navigation 213
onclick, JavaScript attribute in tree navigation 215
onglet, prefix and tabbed panes 230
ongletMiddle, attribute and tabbed panes 229
ongletSpace, attribute and tabbed panes 228
ongletTextDis, attribute and tabbed panes 228
ongletTextEna, attribute and tabbed panes 228
onRowClick
  and Struts-Layout 187
  JavaScript and selected row 206
onRowDoubleClick, and Struts-Layout 187
onRowSelect, JavaScript and selected row 206
onSubmit 253
OOD 392
OptimizeIt 461
Oracle 379
ordinality 63
organize 80
Orion 438, 443
outside-the-container testing 438
over design 405
override, locale 305

P

page, attribute in layout tab tag 232
pageContext 107–108, 117, 124, 130, 149
pageKey 303
  attribute 111
pager
  tag implemented inside JSP 233
  tag. See Struts-Layout tags
pageScheme 335
panels and tabbed panes 226

parameter attribute
  and logic present tag 131
parameter markers, ways to replace 63
parameter replacement 63
parent-child relationships in tree navigation 215
password 320
pattern
  Data Access Object 392
  Façade 392
  Factory 392
  Layers 392
  Separation of Concerns 393
pattern-mappings 326
PDF 371
  attachment 376
  browser 372
  ContentLength 376
  ContentType 376
  create 372
  flush 376
  Headers 376
  pops up 376
  programmatic functionality 377
PdfWriter 375
performance 72, 335, 352, 378
  fixing problems 455
  Hibernate 384
  objectives 418
  reflection 273
  testing. See testing
  Tiles controller 364
  vs MVC 171
performance development practices 460
performance expectations 460
performance experience 461
performance plan 461
  scope 455
performance problem detection 461
performance requirements 455
performance test plan 460
  benefits 455
  definition 455
performance testing
  build process 460
  define 460
  delay 455

effective approach 455
  goals 460
  popular 460
  types 455
  See also testing
performance tuning 405
PerformaSure 461
persist 73
  file 91
persistence
  time 378
persistence exceptions
  generic 400
persistence layer 393
  change 398
  responsibilities 393, 397
persistence services 378
PHP 158
physical space 455
picture 302
planning 62
plug-in 30, 195–196, 281, 332, 352, 356–357, 386, 389, 426
  cache Hibernate resouces 400
  clobbering 357
  configuration 243
  create Hibernate 385
  custom skin 196
  example 354
  Hibernate 378–379, 384
  implementation steps 354
  implementing 353
  in Struts modules 24
  interface 353
  life-cycle 353
  message-resources placed after 27
  message-resources plug-in 25
  register 356
  SSL 332
  validator 312
<plug-in> 385
plurals 69
  gender specific 69
Pointbase 379
POJO 405
policy 319
polymorphism 378
pool 357

port 331
portability 377
Portable Document Format.
    See PDF
portals and panels 187
postal codes 313
post-conditions 450
Postgre 418
PostgreSQL 379
Pot-au-feu, recipe 171
pragmatism 405
pre-conditions 450
prefix 272
presentation
    reason for using
        Struts-Layout 173
    with logic equal tag 135
presentation layer 393
    coupling 391
    responsibilities 393
preserve resources 400
private fields 346
problems with crumbs 223
processActionForward 341
processException 340–341
processing events 82
processorClass 342, 409
    placed before
        message-resources 27
processRoles 339, 341
production scenario 444
productivity 275–276
    user 62
productivity tool 256
progress 379
project lifecycle 455
project plan 426
proof of concept 49
Property Files
    See Resource Bundles
property files 299
    and tabbed panes 226
    attribute in layout
        collectionItem tag 186
    internationalization 300
    of layout skins 200
    tree navigation settings 215
    See also Resource Bundles
protect 95, 357, 393, 398
    areas 343
    fields 346

protect fields
    techniques 347
protocol 334
prototypes 391
proxy redirector, cactus 438
purge 73

Q

quality 49
queue name
    choose 56
    prefix 56
queue, delete 55

R

random number 90
read-only objects 357
realm 324
reduce complexity 395
reduce effort 426
refactor 280, 377, 429, 462
refactoring
    and migrating to Struts 148
reflection 273, 356, 378, 404
    DispatchAction 270
    JUnit 427
regression tests 462
regular expressions 247,
    252, 312
relational paradigm 378
relationship, queue name and
    field 52
release resources 353
rench 69
repetitive 44
replacement marker 63
repopulate the cache 357
request parameter and tree
    navigation 209
RequestProcessor 246,
    336–339, 342, 408–410,
    412, 416
    create 341
    default 336
    extend 339
    locale 296
    processActionPerform 412
    processForward 412
    processInclude 413

processPath 412
processPreprocess 412
reset 75
reset method 298
Resin 438, 443
resource bundles 44, 46, 51
    and tabbed panes 226
    declare 418
    internationalize 298
resources
    cache 353
    load 353–354
response.EncodeURL
    and html rewrite tag 148
Response-Time-Under-Load
    456
responsiveness 455
reuse 345, 367
    deny 391
risk 56
road signs 302
roadmap 75
robust 323, 327, 345, 405
roles 325–326, 328, 337
    add 342–343, 346
    list 336
    omission 336
    register 336, 340
    validate 337
runtime 69

S

sanity checks 269
SAP DB 379
saveErrors 47, 51
saveMessages 48, 54
scalable 460
scale 343
    scope request 47
scope attribute, best practices in
    tags 119
scripting variable 55, 59, 81
    from context attribute 118
    using bean define
        (simple) 118
scriptlets 44
search
    automatic 46
    terminates 302
search sequence 301–302

secure 349
Secure Socket Layer 321, 329
security 319
  browser 320
  business logic 320
  databases 320
  enterprise 320
  flat file 320
  group 343
  hole 326
  limitations 337
  policy 319
  role 320
  Struts limitations 338
  toolbox 347
security access,
    fine-grained 347
security mechanism
    336–338, 347
  proprietary 342
security model 319
  custom 328
security risk 286
security role 343
security strategies 319
security violations 337
  detection 338, 342
SecurityRequestProcessor
  register 340
SecurityViolationException
  339–341
selectedTabKeyName attribute
  in layout tabs tag 232
separate directories, tiles and
    definitions 162
Separation of Concerns 393
serializable 292
Server Error 500 261
servlet 353
  destroy state 353
  initialization state 353
  remove 353
  service state 353
  specification 353
Servlet Container 296, 321
  and tiles 168
  loading skin resources 196
  Orion 3
  Resin 3
  Tomcat 3
servlet context 402

Servlet Filters 438
Servlet Lifecycle 353
Servlet specification 320
Servlet specification 2.3 338
session and crumbs 221
session attributes
    method to remove all 155
    remove attributes 154
session object 406
setAltImage, tree navigation
    attribute 216
setImage, tree navigation
    attribute 216
setLocation, tree navigation
    attribute 216
setOnClick, tree navigation
    attribute 216
setTitle, tree navigation
    attribute 216
setup() 433, 439, 460
shopping basket 406
shopping carts 349, 406
  and logic equal tag 135
simple 44
single point of entry
    and MVC 99
size 93
skinResources
  attributes 200
  property in plug-in 196
skins
  and crumbs 223
  and tree navigation 209
  applications with
      Struts-Layout 194
  browser view of skin in
      tree 215
  introduced as concept 174
socket 423
solve performance
    problems 460
sort 57
/sort.do
  action with layout pager
      tag 238
  default mapping needed for
      layout pager 238
  invoked with pager tag 239
sort.token.required and
    sorting 201
spoof 336–337, 406

SQL 419
  client 419
srcKey 303, 417
SSL 321, 329, 335
  Action 329, 333
  basics 329
  convert 329
  definition 329
  enable 330
  secure page 332
  submit 334
  Tomcat 330
SSL HTTP request 330
SSL HTTP/1.1 Connector 331
SSL links 330
  format 330
  switch 330
ssl-ext 329
  install 331
sslext
  namespace 335
  taglib 334
sslext.jar 332
stack trace, eliminating with
    tags 130
startup 44, 64
stateful session bean 406
static crumbs, limited
    appeal 218
static factory 402
storage medium 378
strategies 336
  navigation best
      practices 207
strength 63
StringTokenizer 84, 415
Struts
  associating CSS to JSPs
      Associate Style Sheets 37
  directory structure 165
  DynaActionForms 38
  managing constants 32
  migrating from legacy
      JSP 148
  multiple
      message-resources 27
  multiple modules 19
  safe integration 3
  specify a resource file 25
  tags using "title" element 29
  what it doesn't do 3

Struts 1.1 49, 51, 248, 256,
    261, 339
Struts Action and
    HttpServletRequest 153
Struts Forms
    associate errors to fields 50
    display errors, messages 44
    message groups, creating 57
    message queues, custom 53
    message replacement
        parameters 62
    message resources from
        action 69
    wizard, create 73
Struts HTML tag library
    ability to resolve and encode
        paths 109
Struts in Action 2
Struts messaging, ways to use 44
Struts tag library
    and rtexprvalue 104
    bean, define 113, 116
        best practices 121
        coding practices 121
        from field 118
        java.util.Collection 120
        name attribute 117
        setting type and scope
            attributes 119
        usage 116
        value attribute 117
        with pager tag 236
    bean, include 102
        different from action or
            directive 122
        setting forward
            attribute 124
    bean, message 4, 26
    bean, resource 102
        attributes 138
        code listing 145
        usefulness of 146
    bean, write 114
        filter false 115
    bundle attribute, using 28
    define, attributes 116
    html
        base 36
        baseStrutsHtmlRewrite 35
        define 102
        img 102

img limitations 112
img, example 111
link 102, 106
link, Related tags 108
link, URL string
    without 106
rewrite 102, 108,
    148–149, 152
rewrite, first tag to use 148
rewrite, use when
    migrating 151
rewrite, uses 149
rewrite, various ways of
    using 151
write 102
logic
    empty with logic present
        tag 133
    equal 102
    equal settings 137
    iterate 120
    iterate, substitution for
        Struts layout 182
    notEqual 135
    notEqual settings 137
    notPresent 132
    notPresent, code listing 131
    present 102
    present functionality
        explained 128
    present uses 127
    present, code listing 131
    present, developing
        with, 133
    present, test for null 138
    redirect 18
logic, iterate similarities to
    layout pager tag 233
MVC Separation 97
not try/catch/finally best
    practice 129
peudo try/catch block in
    JSP 134
Struts with AntStrutsAndAnt 6
struts-bean tags and tabbed
    panes 225
<struts-config> 299
struts-config.xml 25, 27, 29, 70,
    73–74, 94–95
    and Struts-Layout default
        actions 177

and tile mappings 159
application.properties file 25
breaking into modules 20
calling an XML tile definition
    from Action 167
configure for tree
    navigation 208
DynaActionForms 39
linking CSS 37
locating message-resources 27
maintenance with
    ActionForward 16
master vs module files 21
message-resources
    mapping 25
modify for multiple
    resources 27
module restrictions 24
multiple configurations 5
multiple
    message-resources 29
param value 22
placement of message-
    resources node 28
simple XML Form Beans 38
synchronicity 19
tiles plug-in 159, 165
unlimited resource files 26
using ActionForward 14
welcome page and
    jsessionid 17
with bean resource tags 138
with simple includes 126
without modules 19
Struts-EL 103–104
    and scripting variables 104
    explained 104
Struts-Layout tag library 170
Struts-Layout tags
    completing installation 177
    create a dynamic table
        (complex table) with
        selectable rows 202
    create a dynamic table
        (complex table), pager
        reference 236
    Creating a navigation
        tree 206
    Creating bread crumb
        trails 217
    Creating tabbed panes 224

Struts-Layout tags *(continued)*
    extendable 187
    layout
        collection 173, 179, 181,
            203–204, 237
            attributes populated 185
            JavaScript and selected
                row 206
            selectable rows 202
            with paging 233
        collectionItem 173, 179,
            181, 185, 203–204, 237
            selectable rows 202
            with paging 233
        crumbs 218, 220
        html 195, 226
            drawbacks 195
        pager 173, 237
            position with layout
                pagerStatus tag 240
        pagerStatus 239
            where to position 240
        panel 189, 226
            and tiles 192
            listing 188
            title 190
        skin 194, 214
            and layout html tag 195
            tree navigation 213
        tabs 225–226, 230
            attributes 230–231
            listing 226
        treeview 198, 208
    Pager tag use 233
    project explained 175
    running 199
    Selectable Rows in table 201
    tree navigation 213
    under continuous
        development 173
    with 203
struts-logic tags
    and tabbed panes 225
    relativity to tabs 232
StrutsTestCase 426–428,
    436–440, 443–445,
    449–450, 454, 456–461,
    463, 465–468
    ActionErrors 437

ActionMessages 437
actionPerform 428
ActionServlet 428, 437
automation 428
classpath 443
definition 427
how to use 428
JUnit 428
migration 439
outside the container 426
simulators 428
struts-config.xml
    inside classpath 433
    outside classpath 433
style sheet 193–194, 227,
    365, 370
    and layout panel tag 190
    linked with 38
    using tabbed panes with 226
styleClass
    attribute for layout pager
        tag 236
    attribute for layout panel
        tag 190
    attribute in layout collection
        tag 185
    attribute with skins 199
    JavaScript and selected
        row 205
stylesheet 193–194, 370
successful 80
SwitchAction 23
    code 23
    listing 23
Sybase 379
synchronize 357
synchronized collection 357
system errors 256
SystemException 257

T

tabbed panes
    and Struts-Layout 225
    creating 225
    simple implementation of 226
    source from browser 228
<table/>
    and layout panel tag 191
tabs
    browser view 230

creating 225
listing in Struts-Layout 226
navigation, best parctices 225
rendered source listing 227
wire diagram showing
    relationships 229
tabular data 80
tag 302
Tag Libraries
    as 100
    life cycle of 100
TagExtraInfo 82
taglib 81, 332
taglib uri, sample for layout
    tags 176
tamper 329
TCP/IP 329
<td/> and layout panel tag 191
teardown() 433, 439, 460
test bed 462
test strategy 450
testing 352
    acceptance 427
    ActionServlet simulation 433
    challenge 455
    coverage 426
    determine cases 431
    DynaActionForms 426
    gray area conditions 432
    importance 437
    in-container vs outside-the-
        container 438
    integration 427, 450
    interfaces 454
    modules 426, 449
        guidelines 450
        interfaces 454
    negative 428
    performance 426–427
    positive 428
    regression 427
    test performance 438
    unit 427
    unit test scope 431
    unsuccessful 434
    view 450
TestMethodFactory 457
testXXX() 439
text messages, informational 44
text rearrange 63
text/html 368–369

text-less images 302
<th/> and layout panel tag 191
third-party JAR 87
throughput test 456
tiles 297, 309–312, 328,
    343–345, 358–360,
    362–364
  and directory structure 162
  and encapsulation 161
  and MVC 99
  and Struts actions 166
  and tabbed panes 225
  battle with logic tags 103
  best practices 163
  definition 310
  extending 312
  feature 311
  internationalize 309
  JSP to XML definitions 164
  more uses 164
  snippets of code 161
  template 159
  when to use 163
  XML vs. JSP definitions 167
Tiles controller
  Action 362
  best use 364
  Class 359
  create 358
  declare 362
  performance 364
  pros and cons 358
  register 359
  rule of thumb 364
  type decision 364
  types 358
  types contrast 363
Tiles XML definitions
  capabilites 168
tiles-defs.xml 164, 167, 358
  plug-in to
    struts-config.xml 142
Timed Test 456
title
  attribute and layout panel
    tag 188
  attribute in layout
    collectionItem tag 203
titleKey 303
TLD 86
  Struts-Layout tags 176

to 417
token, store 416
Tomcat 322, 324, 329, 335–336,
    338, 342–343, 345, 347,
    365, 438–440
  authentication 320
  in-container testing 438
  related to jsessionid 19
  set up SSL 330
  SSL 330
  SSL test 331
  temporary version 443
TopLink 394, 404
total number of pages
  arg for layout pager 239
transaction 73, 384
transform XML 365
transform XML to HTML 365
transparent 89
tree
  browser view of 215
  configuring layout tags
    for 208
  Java listing to create 209
  navigarion with 206
Trees
  and Struts-Layout tags 177
treeview
  action and Struts-Layout 208
  opening and closing tree 209
TreeviewAction
  default method for
    Struts-Layout 208
tried-and-true 44
type attribute, best practices in
  tags 119
typesafe enumeration 55

U

unauthorized access 319
  action mapping 336
unescaped contents 46
unique key constraint 400
unique token 406
unit test
  definition 427
  reduce effort 427
universal 321
unordered list 47
unpredictable results 69

unSelect, JavaScript and
  selected row 205
uploading 90
  files with Struts 89
  size 93
URI scheme 333
URL
  adding JavaScript with html
    rewrite tags 149
  and html rewrite tag 151
  and images 112
  QueryString with crumbs 223
  rewriting with html rewrite
    tags 148
URL request string using
  HashMap to pass
  parameters 150
URL rewriting inside
  jsessionid 17
URL scheme definition 330
<url-pattern> 326
user friendly 80
user interface 329
utility class 72

V

valid token 407
validate method 298
  override 271, 316
validate() 243
validateEmail 250
validating tokens 413
validation 57, 243–245,
    249–253, 256, 262, 269,
    271, 273, 275, 277,
    282–283, 289, 292, 295,
    312–316, 393, 396,
    406–407, 409
  arguments 251
  basic 243
  bypass 286
  client-side 247, 252
  cross-form validation 287
  custom 252, 255
  depends 250
  dispatch 271, 273
  driver license number 287
  duplicate 280
  DynaForms 251
  error message 289

validation *(continued)*
  form 298
  form bean 246
    alternatives 247
    use 247
  internationalize 251
  lightweight 244
  locale 313
  localize 313
  mask 312
  minimum 250
  msg 250
  object oriented 248
  range 312
  required 249
  reuse 244
  rules 282
  scenarios 315
  server-side 247
  services 289
  simple 251
  simple server-side 243
  Struts 244
  turn off wizard validation 283
  wizard 244, 282
  wizard alternatives 286
validation rules 313
  find 313
  library 292
  maintainable 276
validation-rules.xml 243, 247
  sample 249
validation.xml 243, 247, 312
  purpose 249
Validator 243, 247, 252,
    277, 282, 287, 297, 313,
    316, 358
  benefits 251
  concatenate constants 279
  constants 244, 276
    how to use 278
    replacements 276
  custom 287, 292
  formset constants 276
  global constants 276
  internationalize 312
  locale sensitivity 315
  logical name 288
  multiple constants 279
  pluggable 287
    configure 288

validation-rules 288
  wizard support 282
Validator constants
  override 276
ValidatorActionForm 243, 284,
    290, 312
ValidatorForm 243, 283,
    290, 312
  subclass 284
validator-rules.xml
  JavaScript 252
validators
  basic 312
  gotcha 316
  plug-in 312
variant not supported 306
Vector 182, 234, 357
  of Maps, for selectable
    rows 202
  with Struts-Layout 183
Velocity 366, 372, 377
VeriSign 321
View
  and bean resource tag 145
  and logic equal tag 136
  and MVC (Tiles) 158
  beware of sending unfiltered
    information 115
  capturing errors with logic
    tags 129
  include components 122
  role of logic in 97
visit()
  method 216
Visitor Pattern, in tree
  navigation 216
visual 80
visual cues 80, 87

W

WAR file
  Ant target 10
  attaching to email with
    Ant 12
  built w/Ant script 7
  changing name with Ant 12
  create automatically 7
  create manually 6
  default application.properties
    file 25

  explained 6
  in build.xml 7
  location after Ant build 12
  manual creation 6
  purging during Ant build 10
  source files 6
  to target location 7
  with Ant recipe 6
wart 49
weakness 63
Web Services 365, 423
WEB-INF
  adding struts-tiles.tld 159
  directory, additions for
    Struts-Layout 176
  tiles-definitions.xml 164
  xtags tld file 139
326
web.xml 87, 175, 436, 441, 443
  altering for modules 21
  code listing for modules 22
  defining 16
  excluding in Ant build 10
  listing with ActionForward 14
  modified tag 15
  modifying for Struts-Layout
    tags 175
  module parameters 23
  no direct use of
    ActionForward 15
  registered modules 23
  registering multiple
    struts-config modules 21
  resource bundle pointer 25
  welcome-file-list 15
width attribute
  and layout collectionItem
    tag 180
  and layout tabs tag 226
  for layout pagerStatus tag 240
  in tab(s) tags 230
Winterfeldt, David 248
wire diagram of tabbed
  panes 229
Wizard 73
  multi-form 293
wizards 57, 78
  and crumbs 218
  multi-form 73
  single-form 73
  understand 74